SLAVERY IN FLORIDA

Florida A&M University, Tallahassee
Florida Atlantic University, Boca Raton
Florida Gulf Coast University, Ft. Myers
Florida International University, Miami
Florida State University, Tallahassee
University of Central Florida, Orlando
University of Florida, Gainesville
University of North Florida, Jacksonville
University of South Florida, Tampa
University of West Florida, Pensacola

LARRY EUGENE RIVERS

SLAVERY

AM I NOT A MAN AND A BROTHER?

UNIVERSITY PRESS OF FLO

IN FLORIDA

TERRITORIAL DAYS TO EMANCIPATION

GAINESVILLE   TALLAHASSEE   TAMPA   BOCA RATON   PENSACOLA

ORLANDO   MIAMI   JACKSONVILLE   FT. MYERS   SARASOTA

Copyright 2000 by Larry Eugene Rivers
Printed in the United States of America on acid-free paper
All rights reserved

14 13 12 11 10 09   6 5 4 3 2 1

First cloth printing, 2000
First paperback printing, 2009

LIBRARY OF CONGRESS CATALOGING-IN-PUBLICATION DATA

Rivers, Larry E., 1950-
Slavery in Florida: territorial days to emancipation/Larry Eugene
Rivers.
p. cm.
Includes bibliographical references (p.) and index.
ISBN 978-0-8130-1813-3 (cloth: acid-free paper)
ISBN 978-0-8130-3381-5 (paper)
1. Slavery—Florida—History. 2. Plantation life—Florida—History.
3. Slaves—Florida—Social conditions. 4. Florida—Race relations.
I. Title.
E445.F6 R58 2000
975.9004'96—dc21 00-034415

The University Press of Florida is the scholarly publishing
agency for the State University System of Florida, comprising
Florida A&M University, Florida Atlantic University, Florida Gulf
Coast University, Florida International University, Florida State
University, New College of Florida, University of Central Florida,
University of Florida, University of North Florida, University of
South Florida, and University of West Florida.

University Press of Florida
15 Northwest 15th Street
Gainesville, FL 32611
http://www.upf.com

With love and gratitude
to my wife and sons
Betty Jean, Larry Omar, and Linje Rivers

CONTENTS

FIGURES

MAPS

PREFACE

The nature and dynamics of slavery have intrigued and puzzled historians throughout the twentieth century, although our understanding of the institution took revolutionary turns beginning with revisionist works written in the 1960s and 1970s. Subsequently, the levels of interest and controversy remained high through the 1980s and 1990s, and they show no signs of diminishing as scholars continue to debate into the new century. Areas of specific focus for these studies have ranged widely, with topics including slave personality; slave women; slave resistance; slave profitability; the slave family; slave religion, music, education, and folklore; slave culture; the role of the overseer and driver; slave trading; and patterns of slaveholding. Additionally, scholars have viewed the peculiar institution from the perspective of the slaveholder, as well as from the point of view of the bond servant.[1]

Although many works on slavery have thus delved into the particular, other studies have examined the subject from a general or regional context or other broad perspective. For example, Peter Kolchin's *American Slavery* focused broadly on colonial and antebellum slavery, as well as on slave life and the end of servitude in the white South. Deborah Gray White's *Ar'n't I a Woman?*, John Blassingame's *The Slave Community*, Kenneth M. Stampp's *The Peculiar Institution*, Richard Wade's *Slavery in the Cities,* and Eugene D. Genovese's *Roll, Jordan, Roll* offered additional significant contributions to our general understanding of the subject.

In recent years students of southern history have begun to complement these works by exploring the diversity of the southern slave experience and by focusing on individual states and counties. For instance, Charles Joyner's *Down by the Riverside,* Randolph B. Campbell's *An Empire for Slavery,* Brenda E. Stevenson's *Life in Black and White,* Clarence L. Mohr's *On the Threshold of Freedom,* and Barbara Jeanne Fields's *Slavery and Freedom on the Middle Ground* contrasted race relations patterns in the South and southwest areas and the black belt cotton-, tobacco-, and rice-producing regions during slavery and the Civil War. These county- or state-based studies provide significant insights into the lives of bond servants.

Florida offers an excellent laboratory, in the tradition of county- and state-based studies, for a close examination of the variations of slave experience and race relations patterns. First, Florida's population remained small during the antebellum period, permitting a comprehensive review of all available source material. Second, Florida affords the opportunity for insight through internal contrast. The territory and state were divided regionally and culturally. The parts included Middle Florida (the area framed by the Apalachicola River on the west and the Suwannee River on the east); East Florida (eastward of the Suwannee River and including the peninsula); and West Florida (the area in the far western panhandle that lies between the Perdido River on the west and the Apalachicola on the east). Middle Florida represented a more traditional Old South, slave-worked, cotton-producing economy and society. On the other hand, East and West Florida maintained some attitudes, experiences, and traditions of the former Spanish colony. The experience of one region offers a fresh viewpoint for examination of the other areas. Further, the presence of armed blacks among the Seminole, Creek, and Mikasuki (Miccosukee) Indians in the peninsula created tensions that led to what may have been the largest slave rebellion in United States history (the Second Seminole War, 1835–1842). The events leading up to the conflict and the war itself permit us an unparalleled opportunity to gain insight into the development of slave codes, political context, and race relations patterns.

Although a helpful study of antebellum slavery in Florida is available, a comprehensive and up-to-date revisit is overdue.[2] Julia Floyd Smith's *Slavery and Plantation Growth in Antebellum Florida* was published a generation ago. The study's findings were welcomed by scholars, although they were limited in their focus. Particularly, Smith directed her attention primarily to large slaveholders and the phenomenal growth of the peculiar institution in Middle Florida. She touched on slave labor, slavery and the law, and slave trading only to a lesser extent.[3] Smith's work offered little systematic examination of slavery or of regional diversity. Additionally, much of the research was limited to the perspectives of the slaveholding class. It did not analyze systematically slave life on the large and small units of Middle Florida, slave life in East or West Florida, the slave family, slave religion, slave resistance, social interactions between whites and blacks, social interaction among blacks, social interaction between blacks and Indians, or master-slave relationships from the point of view of both the slaveholder and the slave. Further, the study did not examine the role of blacks as overseers or slave drivers or the roles of slaves during the Civil War. These omissions call for a treatment of the black experience in Florida in a larger, more comprehensive context and over a relatively longer period of time.

Researching Florida's nineteenth-century history, including its experience with slavery, presents a challenge to historians. Fires, floods, rot, neglect, and other maladies have taken substantial tolls on the types of source materials taken for granted in many other states. Nonetheless, when utilized together, a variety of resources permit a deep and rich look at slavery and the slave experience. These resources include plantation records, travelers' accounts, newspapers, slave narratives and ex-slave interviews, slave owners' letters and diaries, and census and other government-generated data. I profited from the Work Projects Administration's interviews with ex-slaves. Understanding the pitfalls in using slave testimonies, I believed, as Paul D. Escott has stated, that "the presence of a number of black interviewers added greatly to the value of the slave narratives."[4] In Florida ten of the eleven compilers could be identified as black. Presumably, black interviewers obtained information that former slaves were reluctant to tell whites.[5] Although a relatively small number of such interviews were undertaken, the Florida narratives afford more information than do many other collections on such topics as the slaves' participation and interest in the Civil War, their desire for liberation, slave breeding, miscegenation, and day-to-day work routines.

An additional facet of this work requires mention. I have endeavored to examine slavery in Florida without adhering to any particular theoretical model. I have not intended to use this study simply to test a specific idea, concept, or interpretation. Although I do focus somewhat on slaveholders, the core of this study does not specifically concentrate, as Jeffrey Young has put it, on "slaveowners' paternalism and their participation in a capitalistic economy." Rather, my goals, similar to those urged by Young, are to explain and offer a comprehensive and well-documented portrait of how enslaved blacks fared under the peculiar institution in antebellum Florida.[6]

My thinking on the subject has been driven by these aims. Slavery existed as a complicated affair that evolved and varied from time to time and from place to place. Accordingly, information gleaned from Florida's experience could be utilized to support and challenge the theoretical models current among historians. Instead of doing so, I have chosen to utilize models, where appropriate, to assist in providing context and explanation rather than as flat statements of historical truth. In the process I have tried to seek answers from available sources. Among many others, the questions include the following: Was slavery different on the small and large units of Middle Florida? Was slavery different in East and West Florida when compared with Middle Florida? What role did family and religion play in the lives of bond servants? What were the physical and psychological conditions of servitude for Florida bondsmen and -women? How were enslaved blacks generally treated? What social interaction occurred between slaves, whites, and Indians in antebellum Florida? How did the Civil War affect slavery in Florida? And, what role did bond servants play in destroying the peculiar institution by May 1865?

This project took me nearly two decades to complete. I am indebted to many individuals and institutions for their support and encouragement over the many years that I researched this topic and prepared this manuscript for publication. For reviewing the manuscript and providing insightful suggestions for its improvement I offer thanks to

Donnie D. Bellamy, regents professor of history at Fort Valley State University; William W. Rogers Sr., professor emeritus of history at Florida State University; Maxine Jones, professor of history at Florida State University; Bob Hall, associate professor of history and director of the African American Studies program at Northeastern University; Jerrell H. Shofner, professor emeritus of history at the University of Central Florida; Jane Landers, assistant professor of history at Vanderbilt University; Daniel L. Schafer, professor of history and chair of the Department of History at the University of North Florida; and, especially, nineteenth-century-Florida scholar Canter Brown Jr.

Numerous others also deserve mention. I thank the following individuals for their generous research assistance and financial support, as well as encouragement over the years: Aubrey M. Perry, professor of psychology, Florida A&M University; Charles U. Smith, professor of sociology, Florida A&M University; Frances J. Stafford, history professor emeritus, Florida A&M University; Keith Simmonds, professor of public administration, Florida A&M University; David Jackson Jr., assistant professor of history, Florida A&M University; Roland M. Smith, Vice President for Student Life, University of Delaware; David Coles, assistant professor of history at Longwood College; Joan Morris and Jody Norman, Florida Photographic Collection, Florida State Archives; Mary Ann Cleveland, Cynthia C. Wise, Dorothy Williams, and Randi Bailey, Florida Collection, State Library of Florida, Tallahassee; Joe Knetsch, Bureau of Survey and Mapping, Division of State Lands, Florida Department of Environmental Protection, Tallahassee; Peter A. Krafft, director of Cartography for the Florida Resources and Environmental Analysis Center at Florida State University; Nathan Woolsey, Milton; Elizabeth Alexander and Bruce Chappell, P. K. Yonge Library of Florida History, University of Florida; Mark I. Greenberg, Museum of the Southern Jewish Experience; David Nolan, St. Augustine; Taryn Rodriguez-Boette and Charles A. Tingley, St. Augustine Historical Society Research Library; Ann Murphey, Tampa; Fay Farmer and Bonney A. McClellan, Keystone Genealogical Library, Monticello; Charles Carroll Fishburne Jr., Quincy; Miles Womack, Quincy; Willie Speed, Apalachicola; George Chapel, Apalachicola; Tom Hambright, May Hill Russell Monroe County Public Library, Key West; Vernon Peeples, Punta Gorda; William G. Dayton, Dade City; Hal Hubener, Lakeland Public Library; Julius J. Gordon, Tampa; Tom Muir and Marshall L. Emerson, Historic Pensacola Preservation Board; Darcie MacMahon, Florida Museum of Natural History; and Michael Woodward, Rosemonde R. Wade, Kenneth Harris, Lyle Britt, Therese Lewis, James James, Sonya Pridgen, Lambide Moore, Kasinda R. Swain, Niera Marshall, Dariyall D. Brown, and Lisa Smith, my students at Florida A&M University. Let me offer a special word of thanks to my late friend John W. Blassingame, whom I met in 1970 at our undergraduate alma mater, Fort Valley State University. I thank Ken Scott, Meredith Morris-Babb, Gillian Hillis, and the rest of the staff at the University Press of Florida for guiding this work to publication. I also offer a word of gratitude to Joe Abbott for his meticulous copyediting of this manuscript.

I owe my deepest debt to my family. I would like to thank my ancestors. Those who have gone on to glory—such as my mother Lavonia Williams Rivers, my father Phelix Rivers Jr., and my grandfather Phelix Rivers Sr.—deserve gratitude beyond measure for their untiring support while living and their continued inspiration now. I sincerely appreciate my mother-in-law, Mrs. Annie M. Hubbard, who allowed me to take over every available table with all my papers during the past several Thanksgiving and Christmas holidays to work on my manuscript. My sons Larry Omar and Linje Eugene have been quite understanding through this ordeal, even excusing me from playing sports with them on some Saturdays while I tried to work on the manuscript. My wife, Betty Jean, whom I met at the Fort Valley State University many years ago, has kept me focused with her unconditional support through thick and thin. I dedicate this book to her and our sons.

Of course, any errors of fact are mine alone.

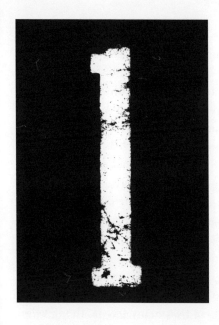

RACIAL CONTACT AND THE AFRICAN PRESENCE, 1500–1845

The United States did not acquire Florida until 1821, and echoes of the territory's colonial past served as the backdrop for the evolution of slavery within its limits. By the time the Stars and Stripes first flew over the capitals at St. Augustine and Pensacola, Spain had ruled the land for almost three hundred years. Even before Florida came under the Spanish banner, blacks had already been instrumental in that nation's empire building in the Americas. What had been true of the empire generally became true in Florida. African Americans arrived with Spaniards well before the colony had been organized, and they remained significant players after the Spanish flag ceased to fly over it. In the process traditions were developed and folded into the social fabric that affected the nature of race relations and slavery well into the nineteenth century.[1]

As Spain, much like other European powers, expanded its empire around the world in the fifteenth and sixteen centuries, distinct race relations patterns evolved. Free and enslaved Africans played prominent roles in the quest for overseas possessions, assuming the mantle of the empire's principal labor force. Disease, war, and mistreatment eventually decimated indigenous New World Indian populations. Not surprisingly, then, a reduced Indian population in "La Florida," coupled with a chronic shortage of Europeans, produced a demand for African laborers. The demand increased after the mid–sixteenth century. "Florida's first slaves came from southern Spain," one historian noted, "where a significant African population filled a variety of important functions—laboring in mines and agriculture and in less onerous tasks as artisans, petty merchants, and domestics."[2]

Well in advance of the time when permanent black settlers arrived in Florida, other persons of African origin had passed through the sometimes-punishing land. Significantly, not all of them were slaves. Free Africans Juan Garrido and Juan Gonzalez [Ponce] de León accompanied Juan Ponce de León in 1513 on his voyages of discovery to the American Southeast. By 1526 the first known enslaved Africans arrived among the six hundred Spanish settlers brought to North American shores by the Lucas Vazquez de Ayllon expedition. The word *slave* could easily mislead in the case of these individuals. In addition to performing the hard labor commonly associated with slavery, these Africans were also considered by Spanish officals as "skilled artisans" and domestics from Spain.[3]

Questions about the treatment of free and enslaved Africans within the Spanish Empire stir great debates among historians. Although racial prejudice existed in Spain and its New World colonies, evidence suggests that Spanish law and custom afforded slaves rights not systematically found in the Old South or in other slave systems with European origins. Michael Mullin, for instance, delved into the nature of slavery in the Caribbean, comparing British ways with those of the Spanish during this early period. He concluded that, particularly with respect to Florida, Spain's shortage of soldiers and laborers gave free and enslaved Africans some leverage, a subject that I will discuss at greater length. Mullin argued that because Florida's early population of blacks remained relatively small, conditions did not necessitate harsh slave codes. In these circumstances Spanish authorities generally allowed a paternalistic system that permitted slaves to work under the task system, as opposed to the gang system later commonly used in the Old South. The task system encouraged initiative and the enhancement of individual skills, while relying to some extent on self discipline. It permitted slaves ample time to engage in their own social and economic activities. Yet the reality of day-to-day enforcement of these laws remains open to dispute. Spanish authorities certainly desired to profit from Florida, and more-rigid treatment may often have proved the accepted route to riches.[4]

Given the benefit of these historical lessons, it may be seen that Spain organized Florida for reasons both internal to the empire and personal to the colony's founders. It probably came as a big surprise that when Pedro Menéndez de Avilés established St. Augustine in 1565, he found persons of African descent remaining in the peninsula from prior European expeditions. Further, although Menéndez brought with him the institution of Spanish slavery, he found it difficult to maintain. What with the allure of escape into the peninsula's vast wilderness and slaves' desire for freedom over any form of harsh or mild servitude, Menéndez suffered the untimely departure of some of the fifty Africans living among the settlers. Thereafter, Spain faced chronic labor shortages during the formative years of St. Augustine's development. The only available solution required importation of more enslaved Africans. Over time, bond servants who declined flight or else fled unsuccessfully would become an indispensable part of Spain's quest to maintain, build, and expand its empire in the American Southeast. All the while, the reputation of Florida's interior peninsula as a refuge for runaways began to spread far and wide.[5]

Once settled within Florida's Spanish community, blacks naturally sought to improve their circumstances. During the late seventeenth and eighteenth centuries, especially, free blacks of African descent agreed to help defend St. Augustine against hostile European powers in exchange for certain liberties. Black inhabitants had formed themselves into a militia unit at least by 1683. Many of those who served could trace their family lineage to Spain through several generations. The free black militia served several functions: to reinforce blacks' commitment to the St. Augustine community; to advance blacks within the society; and to permit the maintenance of social relationships between persons of African descent and other Spaniards. Students of the subject have found that miscegenation became common. Generally, black women intermarried with Spanish men in St. Augustine. Many blacks eventually gained a degree of social status in the community.[6]

During the later years of Florida's first Spanish period (1565–1763), some blacks found the more relaxed racial climate to their liking. St. Augustine's vulnerability to attack—combined with its isolated position, need for a dependable work force, and reliance on armed black defenders—indeed had produced patterns of day-to-day living and working that varied even from the empire's standards. They were far different from the harsh conditions associated with the Old South. Jane Landers notes that, as in other Spanish colonies, "slavery [in Spanish Florida] was not exclusively based on race. A slave's humanity and rights and liberal manumission policy eased the transition from slave to citizen."[7] As a result, the upward mobility of slaves in Spanish colonial Florida did not appear to be as difficult as in other major colonial centers of the American South. When Spain later fought English settlers in the American Southeast, slaves from the British colonies to the north took advantage of the tensions and sought refuge in Florida. As of 1683 the Spanish government granted freedom to runaways from the English colonies, regardless of race, based on conversion to Roman Catholicism.[8]

By the 1730s Spanish Florida existed as a haven for runaway slaves from Georgia and the Carolinas. The case of Francisco Menéndez provides an illustration. A runaway enslaved West African from the Carolinas, Menéndez and his followers agreed to help defend Florida from primarily British attacks in exchange for their liberty and the establishment of their own community. The arrangement gave birth to the town of Gracia Real de Santa Teresa de Mose (Fort Mose), established in 1738 as the first free black settlement in North America. Located two miles north of St. Augustine, it welcomed fugitive slaves and Native Americans alike. The refuge did not come without cost. Two years after its founding, the English led by James Oglethorpe captured Fort Mose and other small Spanish outposts in a series of hard-fought battles. Determined blacks and Spaniards recaptured the fort by June 1740. Its former occupants rebuilt Fort Mose. At least fifteen women, seven boys, eight girls, and thirty-seven men were living there by 1759. Four years afterward its inhabitants were evacuated to Cuba with Spain's temporary loss of Florida to the British in the wake of the Seven Years' War.[9]

During the twenty years of British rule that began in 1763, the quality of black life in Florida balanced precariously on the dictates of new colonial policies. White settlers from colonies to the north quickly established large-scale plantations. Virtually all of them were located in the new colony of East Florida, which included the peninsula and northeast Florida westward to the Apalachicola River. Wealthy investors established cotton, indigo, rice, and sugar plantations much like those found in Georgia and South Carolina. Although earlier British colonies in North America had witnessed an initial pattern of using family members and indentured servants for labor, many of the whites who now settled in the peninsula depended on slaves to farm the new lands. In fact, James Grant, first governor of British East Florida, encouraged Carolina migrants John and James Moultrie, Richard Oswald, William Drayton, Duke Beel, and Francis Kinlock to bring their large numbers of slaves to cultivate the region's huge agricultural enterprises.[10]

Instead of bringing their families from the older colonies, most of these men looked initially at Florida as a temporary home and a place to earn high profits from slave labor. Grant had committed himself to the proposition that East Florida, which boasted fewer than two hundred whites when he arrived in 1764, could become a prosperous place with implementation of a slave labor–based economy. He encouraged fellow planters to bring or import "seasoned" enslaved Africans who were familiar with the staple crops to be grown and with the area's language. The governor sought to profit from slave labor himself when he purchased slaves within the St. Augustine community for his indigo and rice plantation. By the 1780s East Florida had become a part of the rice coast that stretched from Cape Fear in North Carolina to the St. Johns River. Grant used his plantation to school slaveholders and overseers to control and direct enslaved Africans, the colony's most important investment and source of labor. Over time, some of the river plantations prospered through the use of such labor, managed sometimes by black slave drivers trained at the governor's direction.[11]

Eventually, though, international events negatively impacted East Florida's success and expansion. The slave-based economy was disrupted when war erupted in the mid-1770s between Britain and thir-

teen of its North American colonies. Although existing as the fourteenth and fifteenth British American colonies, East and West Florida
remained loyal to the empire during the American Revolution. The
devotion carried its own price. Georgia patriots seized the opportunity
to cross the border and raid loyalist plantations in northeastern Florida.[12]

Much as had occurred during times of crisis in the previous Spanish
era, Florida slaveholders looked to the black population for assistance.
East Florida's governor, Patrick Tonyn, created four black militia companies to join in the provincial defense. Here again blacks played a
significant role in maintaining Florida's colonial integrity, with potential freedom as an incentive for their services. Disappointment resulted. Despite blacks' voluntary service and an absence of slave conspiracy or rebellion, white leaders—fearful of the perceived threat of
runaway blacks and their Indian allies—began to adopt harsh slave
codes similar to those found in South Carolina. The promise of freedom evaporated for most, with the possible exception of a few blacks
who engaged in the revolutionary fighting. Instead, owners relocated
slaves to more stable places, such as Savannah, Georgia, and the Ba-
hama Islands before Florida fell into the hands of the Spanish for the
second time as a result of the 1783 peace treaty.[13]

In the midst of the revolutionary tumult and harsh slaveholder reactions, some slaves helped themselves to freedom. In the now-tradi-
tional fashion, many of them escaped from large plantations along the
St. Johns River to join potential Indian allies in the interior. Based on
the 1683 sanctuary policy, others sought refuge among the returning
Spanish in 1783 on grounds of religious conversion. Facing pressure
from the United States government, as well as from slaveholders in
South Carolina and Georgia, the colonial government officially re-
scinded the sanctuary policy by the 1790s. The black percentage of
Florida's population grew from 27 percent in 1786 to 57 percent by 1814,
when most blacks were classified as slaves. Still, the remaining free
blacks continued to live, work, and defend their liberty in the relatively
more hospitable climate of Spanish Florida.[14]

The advent of the Second Spanish Period in 1783 heralded no
peaceful interlude as continuing conflicts between the United States,
Britain, and other colonial empires repeatedly threatened renewed

warfare. By the nineteenth century's second decade, the tensions had erupted in the War of 1812, among numerous other fights of greater and lesser magnitude. One of them, the Patriot War of 1812 to 1814, grew out of expansionist desires of both the United States and Britain in the Florida peninsula. Yet again black militiamen backed Florida's colonial government, while black warriors in the interior assisted in the fighting. Subsequently, many of the black warriors responded to calls from English recruiters for War of 1812 service along the Gulf coast and in the ill-fated effort to capture New Orleans.[15]

With the British defeat at New Orleans in January 1815 and the war's end, the British introduced a new element into Florida's racial equation by leaving black warriors in control of a powerful fortress on a bend in the Apalachicola River. The outpost came to be known as the "Negro Fort." The idea of a group of free blacks maintaining such a settlement did not sit well with white planters just beginning to exploit newly opened cotton lands a few miles to the north in southwestern Georgia and southeastern Mississippi territory, the future Alabama. Many of them viewed control of the fort by its garrison of about 350 free blacks as a direct threat to slavery. By late 1816 whites had pressured the United States Army to act. In an illegal invasion of the Spanish colony, troops destroyed the Negro Fort on the pretext that blacks had impeded the free movement of whites up and down the Apalachicola River. In the attack a hot cannon ball fired by one of Andrew Jackson's subordinates struck an open powder magazine, killing 270 of the fort's inhabitants.[16]

Fortunately for Florida's free black population, other refuges existed at the time of the Negro Fort's destruction. One of them had grown out of the Patriot War's early fighting. As patriot invaders from Georgia raided and destroyed along the St. Johns River in 1812, Seminole and black warriors responded with counterraids. As time passed, the Georgians determined to attack their foe's homelands in and around today's Alachua County. A pitched battle on September 27 turned back the Americans but sent black warriors fleeing into the peninsula for protection against reprisal. As historian Canter Brown discovered, they rested only after reaching the Manatee River. There the warriors and their families established a settlement within today's Bradenton.[17]

The Manatee refuge—apparently called Angola—grew in population and importance in the years that followed its founding. Reportedly, English officials transported eighty black War of 1812 veterans there in 1815. When United States troops again invaded Florida during the First Seminole War, once more they targeted black warriors for capture or destruction. After a hard-fought encounter on the west bank of the Suwannee River in April 1818, the Negro Fort's survivors and some of their peers eluded Andrew Jackson's soldiers and hastened toward the Manatee River. It appears possible that, by the following year, Angola's population had reached six or seven hundred.[18]

The First Seminole War convinced Spanish authorities to cede Florida to the United States, but the assault on the liberty of blacks persisted and grew with final approval of the resulting Adams-Onís Treaty by the United States Senate in early 1821. Immediate evidence of that reality surfaced with sudden violence. While Andrew Jackson was preparing to accept the colony on behalf of its new owners, Lower Creek Indians closely associated with him and his planter supporters launched a fierce slave raid into southern Florida. In May and June they ravaged interior villages. At Angola, according to a contemporary account, "[they] surprised and captured about 300" settlers, returning them to slavery. Perhaps 250 persons escaped down to the Florida Keys, to be taken to the Bahamas by coastal fishermen. The remainder of the survivors slipped into the interior, to the protection of villages in the upper Peace River area of today's Polk County.[19]

With the destructive Manatee slave raid as prelude, the American occupation of the peninsula ushered in another era in Florida race relations as slavery became a major focal point of black, white, and red conflict during much of the subsequent territorial and statehood period up to the Civil War. New rulers replaced the relatively mild Spanish slave codes with harsher ones echoing those of the American Deep South.

Why harsher codes so quickly? Under American control in 1821, Florida possessed a total population of twelve thousand, the majority consisting of free blacks, fugitive slaves, or Seminole, Creek, or Mikasuki Indians. The threat posed by these experienced warriors appeared to multiply as word spread of the suitability of mostly uninhabited Middle Florida (the land stretching from the Apalachicola River to the

Suwannee) for cotton culture. Nervous planters hesitated to invest in lands and slaves in so unprotected a situation. The destruction of the Negro Fort and of Angola had served a purpose, but too many potential hostiles remained at large for comfort.[20]

This situation left eager planters with two immediate demands: either deport the Indians and blacks or temporarily restrict them to a peninsular reservation; and establish laws and practices contrary to Spanish customs that would insure against slave flight or slave rebellion. Florida's experience thus runs contradictory to arguments made by some historians that harsh slave codes resulted from future needs anticipated by far-sighted planners. Rather, the real and immediate potential for slave insurrection and race war drove demands for quick action.[21]

Before we examine the results of the Middle Florida planter demands, a word concerning West Florida's experience is in order, since the isolated area often is omitted from general discussions of the Florida saga. Although much of America's frontier area—including Alabama, Mississippi, and other nearby regions in the West—experienced rather rapid growth in the 1820s and 1830s, the population in the West Florida region around Pensacola, the territory's only other town, increased slowly. Such had been the case during the Second Spanish era, and it continued well into the territorial period. Black free and slave labor formed an indispensable part of Pensacola society, but numbers were few and West Florida did not advance toward economic profitability until the 1840s.[22]

Consequently, racial patterns and thus stringent control over the free and black enslaved population evolved much more slowly during the early years in territorial West Florida than they did in Middle Florida, where the black population grew much larger and more quickly. Florida's population within control of governmental authority consisted of fewer than forty-five hundred people in 1821, with eight hundred residing in West Florida and the remainder in the eastern region below the St. Mary's River on the north and running to St. Augustine on the south. That distribution changed rapidly as slaveholders learned of fertile Middle Florida soil and began moving into the territory in increasing numbers by 1825. Of the 34,730 Floridians listed in the 1830 census, only two thousand—including six hundred enslaved Africans and one hundred free blacks—lived in West Florida around Pensacola. The majority already called Middle Florida home.[23]

The developing Middle Florida plantation belt existed in stark contrast to the evolving situation in East and West Florida, where Spanish traditions persisted. In East Florida, by way of illustration, free black holdovers from the Spanish era who lived in settled communities continued to benefit from liberties not afforded elsewhere. Race relations patterns afforded tolerance for infractions of social strictures common in other places. Indeed, East Florida slaveholders such as George J. F. Clarke and Carlos Clarke had black wives and openly raised their families. Franciso X. Sanchez raised two mulatto children with black women. It appears that the care of his "black families" came first, followed by his white family. In Zephaniah Kingsley's case, his African wife, Anna Madgigaine Jai, lived as an intimate part of his nuclear family. With the Spanish legacy still so prevalent in the early territorial Florida period, many East Florida circles thus accepted miscegenation and interracial families as a part of everyday life in the region.[24]

Middle Florida's experience differed markedly. For one thing, whereas most East and West Floridians were poor and transient by experience, the heart of Middle Florida's new population hailed from the cream of southern planter society. Into the region came wealthy emigrants from Kentucky, Maryland, Virginia, North Carolina, South Carolina, and Georgia. Not content with the concept of subsistence living, they intended to exploit the area's rich new lands to build a world that in only a few decades would echo the wealthiest precincts of the Old South cotton kingdom.[25]

In constructing Middle Florida's plantation society, the new arrivals approached their investment in the region in a manner radically different from their predecessors during the British occupation of 1763 to 1783. In that former time individual slaveholders left their families in the older states. Now, immediate families and other relations accompanied the pioneer entrepreneurs. They took care, though, not to sever kinship ties with friends and relations left behind, many of whom possessed enormous social and political influence in their home states. One student of the subject, Edward E. Baptist, has pointed out that this dynamic was not generally the case for many pioneers who settled in parts of the southwestern cotton frontier. The benefit for Middle Floridians included helpful associations when the question of statehood was aired during 1839 to 1845. They also helped to encourage subsequent waves of immigration, as bright economic prospects and encouragement from relatives on the scene prompted other family members to relocate. The experience of the prominent Branch-Bradford-Whitaker families of North Carolina, whose members settled in Leon County during and after the 1820s, offers one of many examples.[26]

As groups of families pushed into the region, the Middle Florida cotton belt expanded. By the 1830s it included Jackson, Gadsden, Leon, Jefferson, Madison, and Hamilton Counties. It was a virtual barony that centered on the territory's newly minted capital city of Tallahassee. In this area over 70 percent of all slaves who lived in Florida from the beginning of the territorial period to the Civil War's end worked small and medium-sized farms or else labored on large plantations. From that core the cotton belt reached out in the late 1840s and 1850s until it extended on the west from Jackson County across the Suwannee River on the east down to the upper peninsula's Alachua and Marion Counties.[27]

Because the growth and prosperity of this new cotton kingdom depended on pushing armed blacks and Indians away from the plantation lands and into remote areas of the peninsula, the ultimate likelihood of a violent clash appears in hindsight to have been inevitable. Although history has focused on Indians' attitudes and actions in events leading up to the eventual war, the influence and impact of black warriors and their families should be considered as well. They, especially, resisted the persistent attempts by newly arrived whites from the older southern states to hinder their freedom and restrict their movement. Their tempers flared when territorial officials representing the planters aided the cruel work of slave catchers, who routinely penetrated supposedly reserved lands to capture unwary men, women, and children. Unquestionably, their adamant stance found its roots in the semiautonomous lifestyle free blacks had enjoyed under Spanish rule. It was buttressed, though, by the letter of the Adams-

Onís Treaty. That document had guaranteed them the rights of United States citizens, although government representatives beginning with Andrew Jackson chose, for the most part, to ignore the promise.[28]

The actual steps toward war occurred in fairly rapid succession over thirteen years. The episodes, in turn, spurred Middle Florida planter demands for harsher slave code laws to preserve order while turmoil beset the peninsula. With Governor William P. DuVal's participation and the blessings of planters already arrived in the panhandle, the United States government concluded a treaty with Indian leaders in 1823. This treaty, the Treaty of Moultrie Creek, created an interior reservation that limited Indians and associated blacks to lands reaching from about present-day Ocala on the north to southern Polk County on the south. The removal of families and clans from the panhandle and upper peninsula resulted in severe privation, a condition compounded by the peculations of government contractors, many of them planters. War almost erupted in 1826 and 1827 as a consequence. In the latter year the territorial council launched a small flood of repressive legislation.[29]

National events then set the stage for an escalation of the stakes. In March 1829 Andrew Jackson assumed the presidency. In an early initiative he won passage of the Indian Removal Act to relocate the nation's eastern tribes to west of the Mississippi. In Florida agents concluded treaties under questionable circumstances in 1832 and 1833 as black warriors and Upper Creek leaders planned resistance from a base in the remote southern end of the reservation. In the intervening years increasingly apprehensive council members continued to heap new laws on the slave code. As of 1832 the lawmakers had gone far beyond the normal strictures applicable to slave management and slave insurrection by attempting to ban manumission and white sexual relations with blacks, prohibitions that flew in the face of East and West Florida conventions.[30]

By 1835 the policies designed to make Florida and the United States safe for white settlers had reduced the territorial society, particularly that of East Florida, to the point of panic. Throughout the intervening period black counselors and Indian warriors had involved themselves in every detail of planning for resistance to forced migration. Dating back centuries before the American attacks on the Negro Fort in 1818 and on the Manatee River settlement in 1821, blacks had stood fast in trying to hold on to their Florida homes against what they viewed as a systematic pattern of American aggression aimed at returning them to the bonds of slavery. Now they prepared to contest the matter to the death.[31]

The First Seminole War had focused its violence on black Floridians, and so, too, did the Second Seminole War. At the time, an estimated sixteen hundred blacks lived within the reserved lands, with 1,110 or more slaves settled on plantations to the immediate north and east. When hostilities flared into open warfare in December 1835, the patient efforts of free black agents paid off when slaves revolted throughout the region. Their actions probably amounted to the largest slave rebellion in United States history. One historian insisted that "hundreds—if not over 1,000 or more—bondsmen" left the plantations. The large number of black combatants led General Thomas S. Jesup to declare that it was not an Indian war but a "Negro war," and the fighting skills of blacks led some whites to acknowledge that the black warriors often fought better than did their Indian counterparts.[32]

The names of many of the freedom fighters call out to posterity. Leaders and advisers such as Abraham, Harry, and Ben Bruno actively participated in the seven-year war, not only influencing black followers but also providing encouragement and direction for Seminole and Creek participants. Young men tested by battle, especially Gopher John or John Horse, later would negotiate successfully the removal of blacks to the west instead of their enslavement. Their hard-won skills eventually served Florida's black warriors well as they continued to fight to preserve their freedom during the next three decades in Oklahoma, Arkansas, Texas, and Mexico.[33]

Overwhelming resources at the command of United States troops ultimately spelled doom for the black fighters' struggle to remain in Florida. The American victory, in turn, left the Middle Florida planter aristocracy firmly in control of territorial government. By then the foundation of Middle Florida society was based firmly on slavery. With the peace the white Floridians in Middle Florida, and increasingly in East Florida, could concentrate on expanding their land and slave-holdings without the threat of another large-scale slave insurrection by blacks and their Indian allies.

Just one more plank needed to be added to the societal and govern mental platform before complete control would lie in Middle Florida planters' hands. The great planter leader Richard Keith Call, a Virginian and protege of Andrew Jackson, saw that future before many others. Realizing that only statehood would eliminate potential meddling by national authorities and the possibility that East Florida might sever itself from the remainder of the territory, he took the lead as territorial governor to galvanize Middle Florida hegemony. The Middle Florida elite saw cheap land worked by enslaved Africans and federal land transfers in aid of internal improvements and an expanded slave-based economy as additional benefits of statehood. East Floridians, mostly impoverished from the war and clinging to their own traditions, vehemently opposed such efforts. West Floridians, remote from the centers of debate, remained somewhat lukewarm to the issue.[34]

In the end the planters won, thanks in good part to an East Florida Democrat, David Levy Yulee, who backed statehood to obtain needed support for railroad construction. Call and his Whig planter allies pushed a draft constitution through a convention held in late 1838 and early 1839. Even so, territory wide the voters approved it by only a narrow margin. Then, as congressional delegate, Levy took up the statehood fight. He enlisted southern allies based on ties of kinship and friendship with Florida planters and called for a new slave state to match growing free state power. Ultimately, the timing of Floridians' request for statehood made Yulee's task easier because the residents of Iowa were petitioning for admittance as a free state. Many southern congressmen saw Levy's logic and supported his proposal, permitting a narrow win. By March 1, 1845, both houses of Congress had approved the measure pairing Florida with Iowa as new states. President John Tyler signed the law on his last full day in office, March 3. Thus, Florida entered the nation as its twenty-seventh state and fourteenth slave state.[35]

Call's vision proved accurate. With statehood, Floridians moved ever closer to acceptance of Old South ideas and ideals. By the 1850s the political and economic power of Middle Florida planters in politics would grow in proportion to their land holdings and acquisition of enslaved Africans. After 1852, sectional tensions created a political vacuum and only the Democratic party mattered. Meanwhile, the whispers of three and one-half centuries of Spanish experience and tradition echoed ever more softly. Only in a few places in the peninsula and the far western panhandle did the old ways persist, but they had survived long enough to impress their image deeply on the institution of slavery in Florida.[36]

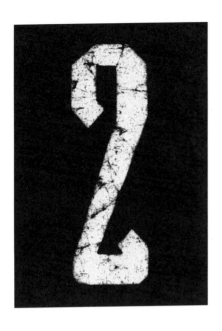

ON MIDDLE
FLORIDA'S
LARGE
PLANTATIONS

Within the Middle Florida cotton kingdom that sat astride the center of Florida's panhandle, slavery flourished in a manner not too dissimilar from other affluent segments of the Old South's cotton empire. The institution never remained in stasis, though, and changes over time altered its nature, especially as threats of peninsular violence and slave insurrection prompted legislators and owners to enforce standards far more rigid than in East and West Florida.

Within that broad framework, complexities abounded. According to former Jackson County slave Margrett Nickerson: "dey useter jest take uncle George Bull and beat him for nothing; dey would beat him and take him to de lak and put him on a log and shev him in de lak, but he always swimmed out. [He would] git his hoe and go on back to work. Dey beat him lak dat and he didn' do a thin' to git dat sor uf treatment." By contrast, Louis Napoleon claimed that "his master and mistress were very kind to the slaves and would never whip them." Regarding the rhythms of daily life, he recalled an unvaried routine. "Just before the dawn of day, the slaves were aroused from their slumber by a loud blast from a cow-horn that was blown by the 'driver' as a signal to prepare themselves for the fields," an interviewer recounted. "At the setting of the sun, with their day's work done," the account continued, "they returned to their cabins and prepared their evening's meal."[1]

As other scholars of the peculiar institution have noted, descriptions of servitude such as those given by Margrett Nickerson and Louis Napoleon likely represented extremes of the circumstances and physical conditions of servitude. Probably, the experiences of most enslaved blacks in Middle Florida fell somewhere in the middle ground. Indeed, many factors—including a slave owner's personality and character, the jobs bond persons had to perform, and the number of slaves on a plantation—helped to determine the nature of day-to-day life.[2]

Early historians often insisted on a brighter picture of slavery, adopting the relatively rosy views recorded by many owners and their family members. Ellen Wirt McCormick, to cite one example, assumed that the physical and material conditions on the large Wirt plantation in Jefferson County were so good that she effectively could threaten to sell Eliza to "Cherokee Planters without one feeling of regret" if she continued to do her assignments poorly. Laura Randall, reflecting the sentiment of many large slaveholders, insisted on slavery's desirability, since slaves on her father's Leon County plantation "worked moderately and loved their work."[3]

Many elements affected an individual slave's circumstances. A student of Texas history observed, "No set of physical circumstances could make slavery right; nevertheless, work loads, material conditions, and punishments determined the day-to-day existence of a slave."[4] These circumstances also applied to Florida, which paralleled Texas in growth and expansion from the 1830s to 1860. As this chapter and two following ones will explore in detail, though, a full picture requires a depth of understanding and an even broader appreciation of the myriad forces at play.

As was mentioned in the introduction, Middle Florida had emerged as the territory's "black belt" by 1830. Within three decades its soil was producing 85 percent of all cotton grown in the state. The vast majority of Florida's slaves lived in this region, consisting of Jackson, Gadsden, Leon, Jefferson, and Madison Counties. Hamilton County also is often included as a Middle Florida county because it lies west of the Suwannee River, but its plantation culture did not equal that in the rest of the region. Sixty percent of all slaves lived in the basic five-county area by 1830; approximately 70 percent lived and worked there in 1860. About 98 percent of these bond servants belonged to slave-holders who reported agricultural occupations on the 1840, 1850, and 1860 censuses. The remaining 2 percent resided in the few small towns that dotted the landscape.[5]

Planters, that is to say owners who held at least 20 bond persons and possessed more than five hundred acres, remained relatively few but dominated the slaveholder class. They and their families constituted only 13.8 percent of the population by 1830. Some thirty years later their numbers had increased to 21 percent, with 397 persons owning over five hundred acres and more than twenty bond servants. On the Civil War's eve, the large majority of Middle Florida planters (73 percent) owned between twenty and forty-nine slaves. Reflective of other slaveholding patterns in the South, the small-planter class owned the bulk of slaves in Middle Florida throughout the antebellum period.[6]

Although cotton would come to rule Middle Florida and its agriculture, owners involved many slaves in experiments and continuing efforts with other crops. Significantly, in the territory's formative years some slaveholders tried their hand at cultivating sugarcane, an effort often associated with the harshest slave-labor conditions. These attempts occurred most often in Leon, Madison, and Jefferson Counties. John and Robert Gamble, William Bailey, William B. Nuttall, and William F. Braden, among others, produced large cane crops. But a short growing season and frost often damaged the crops. As a result, after the mid-1830s sugarcane was never a significant money crop for Middle Floridians. Yet John and Robert Gamble, as well as some Braden family members, became so convinced that sugarcane could make slaveholders rich that they relocated to the Manatee River country during the 1840s to produce cane and molasses on a large scale.[7]

Generally, slaveholders owning large areas grew sugarcane only for their own consumption, especially after about 1835. Nancy DeLaughter, for example, harvested small quantities of sugarcane for her own use in Madison County, and overseer Amon DeLaughter often recorded the work of bond servants in his mother's cane fields. Ex-slave Acie Thomas recalled the cultivation of sugarcane on a Jefferson County plantation where he resided as a youngster. He noted that the "cane was ground on the plantation and converted into barrels of syrup and brown sugar." Thomas added: "The cane grinding season was always a gala one. There was always plenty of juice, with the skimmings from the syrup for all."[8]

Gadsden County provided an additional alternative crop to cotton. There, perhaps as many as one-third of the bond servants engaged in cultivating tobacco. During the 1840s and 1850s the slaves labored at a variety of related tasks for growers such as the company of Forman and Muse, Gadsden tobacco planters and merchants. The bond servants prepared the tobacco for shipment to Tallahassee or else to Bainbridge or Thomasville, Georgia, as well as to foreign markets. Unfortunately, few bond servant reminiscences exist to amplify the realities of Gadsden tobacco culture. On the other hand, Acie Thomas and Bolden Hall recalled the cultivation of tobacco on their masters' Jefferson County plantations. Gadsden nonetheless reigned supreme over Florida tobacco production, claiming 68 percent of all leaf grown in the state by 1860.[9]

Planters often cultivated a variety of crops other than their staple. They grew corn along with the cotton, for instance. On many large and small plantations, sweet potatoes, greens, squash, okra, and other garden vegetables were nurtured. Also requiring slave attention, livestock roamed many parts of the Middle Florida countryside. Closer care was given to domestic animals in the farmyards. Former slave Margrett Nickerson's words may represent the experiences of many: "Dere wuz . . . cotton, co'n, tate fields to be tended . . . and cowhides to be tanned, thread to be spun."[10]

These exceptions aside, cotton became the staple crop of choice in Middle Florida, just as it did in much of the Lower South. The growing cycle for the fiber started around March or April. Slaves planted seeds and covered them by hand with a harrow. During May through August bond servants cultivated the young plants with shallow plows or sweeps. Louis Napoleon remembered May especially as a time when bond persons were "busily engaged in their usual activities" tending the fields. From August to January, he continued, "cotton was picked, ginned, pressed, and shipped to market."[11] Then the annual cycle started over again for the bond servants.

Whatever the crop, tending to it and performing the host of other chores required on the farm or plantation occupied most of the slave's daylight hours. As Margrett Nickerson's comments suggested, required labor seemed always at hand. Overseer Amon DeLaughter had little trouble making sure that his mother's forty-two slaves stayed busy year-round. Records of George Noble Jones's plantations reveal bond persons routinely working on projects ranging from clearing land to harvesting crops while completing a multiplicity of other assignments.[12]

The slave's day began early. On Kidder Meade Moore's Jefferson County plantation, Bob, the wagoner, stood outside his cabin "every morning at daybreak" and blew his bugle to wake the bond persons. Achille Murat required his Jefferson County slaves to be in the fields at "sunrise" most mornings. At the DeLaughter plantation bond servants had to be prepared to begin work at sunrise from May to October. Thus, as Charles Joyner fittingly asserted, "Slave workdays began before dawn. The sound of a bell, horn, or conch summoned the slaves to the fields." They often remained for the day. Louis Napoleon reminisced that "slaves would bring their breakfast and lunch with them to the fields, returning at the end of the day to have evening meals in their cabins."[13]

Farming on the large units required the labor of male and female slaves. Although not always the case, men usually handled the heaviest work, such as digging ditches, plowing, and removing trees. As Deborah Gray White has noted, though, slaveholders "often treated black women like men." She further concluded, "There is no question that slave women worked as hard as their male counterparts." This situation applied to black women in Middle Florida. They performed the work usually assigned to men—plowing, cutting trees, and ditching. The majority also sowed corn and cottonseed, drove horses pulling harrows to cover the seed, and worked as hoe hands.[14] Although women on the DeLaughter plantation usually worked in the hoe gang, Caroline, Marenda, and Fannie formed a part of the plow gang. The owner of El Destino in Jefferson County listed Kate as a plow hand, but most of the other women—including Betsy, Mary, Maria, Penny, and Harriet—labored on the hoe gang. On the William Wirt estate some of the men and young boys plowed the field, whereas the women

hoed weeds and grass from around the cotton.[15] Owners thus habitually called on women to complete the same types of arduous tasks as
their male counterparts.

On the larger units consisting of fifty slaves or more the routine was
different. There slaveholders sought to develop a division of labor, with
men and women assigned certain tasks. Job descriptions often were
broken down into the two broad categories of field hands and house
servants. To organize the fieldwork, the planters utilized two systems.
One kept the slaves in gangs, and the other addressed completion of
specific tasks. The majority of Middle Florida planters normally opted
for the gang system, a practice that generally occurred in the Old
South cotton lands.[16]

The courses followed by George Noble Jones and Nancy DeLaughter provide illustrations. Both planters depended on hoe gangs, plow
gangs, and trash gangs. The hoe gang generally consisted of women,
the plow gang included men, and the trash gang comprised younger
and older bond servants. All the DeLaughter slaves, regardless of age,
apparently worked in the fields during peak times. Men and women
planted crops of cotton or corn. According to Margrett Nickerson, "de
plowers . . . [then came] 'long and put dirt to 'em." On the Jones plantations the same kinds of arrangements prevailed.[17]

Sometimes slaveholders employed both systems. Such was the case
with William Wirt of Jefferson County and Achille Murat of Leon
County. Wirt compromised by allowing most of his slaves to use the
task system during the height of the cotton-picking season. Enslaved
blacks essentially pressured Murat to permit them to modify work routines to their advantage. Although the planter initially stuck with the
gang system only, he later allowed some of his slaves to work by task.
Obviously, some of the French immigrant's bond servants performed
well under the new arrangement. Murat ultimately decided that they
worked more efficiently than before, usually finishing with their assignments around three or four o'clock each afternoon.[18]

Questions of work requirements for children pose problems for the
Middle Florida historian because it is difficult to determine from available evidence when children engaged in regular work routines. It is
certain that they became an integral part of the labor system. Children

worked at early ages, and, as Wilma King has noted, "many chores were not gender-specific."[19] Records note that planters assigned young children to the tasks of knocking down old cotton stalks, gathering firewood, running errands, carrying water, and taking care of the livestock. Laura Randall of Jefferson used a male child to carry mail to town once a week. At Wirtland in the same county, "Caroline, a little negro" girl waited tables. She also served as a chambermaid, scouring "out the houses, etc."[20]

The chores for children ran the gamut of possibilities from house to field. Acie Thomas and Louis Napoleon recalled taking care of chickens and other fowl as youngsters. Amon DeLaughter required young Joe and Jane to gather firewood and to cut down cotton stalks on the plantation. Ex-slave Amanda McCray claimed youngsters carried "water and food" to the slaves in the fields, along with "picking seed from cotton lint . . . and minding the smaller children." Margrett Nickerson asserted that she had to "tote meat an' stuff frum de smokehouse to de kitchen and to tote water in and git wood for granny to cook de dinner and fur de sucklers who nu'sed de babies, an' I carried dinners back to de hands." Clarifying the age at which young children began work on the medium-sized and larger units of Middle Florida, Shack Thomas vividly recollected laboring in the fields "as soon as he was large enough to help his parents raise corn, peanuts, a little bit of cotton and potatoes."[21]

Children typically were trained for tasks—whether farmyard, field, or domestic—at an early age. Slaveholder wills abound in instructions to executors to train young slave boys and girls. Margaret Cotton of Leon County, for example, bequeathed her son "one slave by age six" to be trained as a valet. Amanda McCray remembered being trained as a youngster to be a house servant, cook, and seamstress. Young Randall Jr. of the Pine Hill Plantation in Leon County was trained, as his father had been, to be a wagoner who took products to and from Tallahassee for his master. Shack Thomas "learned several trades in addition to farming; one of them was carpentry."[22]

Most of the large Middle Florida planters preferred not to manage their slaves directly, usually opting instead to seek out white overseers and sometimes white slave drivers to perform this duty. Overseers and drivers could make or break plantations, and slaveholders hired and fired them in a seemingly never-ending effort to find the most capable men to manage their holdings.[23] Overseers lived an uncomfortable and often precarious existence because they served as a buffer between the estate owner and the laborers they were employed to supervise. Many of the men were disliked by the planter class and regarded with disdain by the slaves.[24]

Often bond servants would seek to undermine the overseer's or driver's authority by going directly to the owner with complaints. Louis Napoleon, who labored under a white driver, explained his experience. "[If the driver] whipped any of them," an interviewer recorded, "all that was necessary for the slave who had been whipped was to report it to the master and the 'driver' was dismissed, as he was a salaried man."[25] In 1856 George Noble Jones's Jefferson County plantation hands complained of cruel treatment. Overseer John Evans responded to Jones's intervention: "Your negroes behave badly behind my back and then run to you and you appear to beleave what they say." As Julia Floyd Smith has observed, "The overseer was responsible for working the slaves and for disciplining and punishing them, so the resentment [from bond servants] was natural."[26]

An exception, or at least the possibility of exceptions, should be mentioned. Available documentation offers only sketchy detail on the actual number of Middle Florida overseers, and the figures that exist seem extremely low. For the period from 1821 through the 1840s little is known. Census records for 1850 do list 430 white Florida overseers, and the 1860 survey discovered 468 men managing plantations.[27] The numbers seem low because they fail to indicate that blacks served as overseers but were not counted as managers by census takers.

Understandably, it remains difficult to determine the exact number of planters who used black overseers or the number of overseers themselves. Yet public records reveal slaveholders who openly circumvented the law requiring a white to be present to supervise slaves. Jefferson County sheriff John S. Taylor, for one, directed a black man to work as his plantation overseer for years. Absentee owner William Wirt also arranged for a black overseer to manage his bond servants. Under pressure from authorities Thomas Randall, Wirt's son-in-law, resorted to trickery to accomplish the same end. He employed William West to supervise slaves at one plantation but assigned him no actual duties, thereby satisfying the letter of the law.[28] Many more bondsmen probably served as overseers. The fact that Jefferson County citizens grew alarmed in 1851 when numerous plantations were left completely to the management of blacks buttresses the argument.[29]

Along with the presence of some black overseers, the work of black drivers or foremen who exercised responsibility for directing the daily activities of slaves was important. They were important cogs in the plantation machinery although they were beneath the overseer in the estate hierarchy. Many times they, too, found themselves walking a tightrope. They tried to please the owner and the overseer while attempting to persuade the workers to produce. At the same time they had to avoid alienating themselves from the slaves with unreasonable work demands. "The slave driver occupied a position which was prestigious," Peter Parish has asserted, "but precarious."[30] Louis Napoleon recalled that a slave driver named Peter Parker replaced a white slave driver who had joined the Confederate army. Fortune, a five-foot, dark-complexioned man, managed to exist in both the owner's and the slave's world. On the Bryan Croom plantation consisting of sixty-five slaves and three thousand acres, Fortune supervised fifteen or sixteen hands. Overseer R. Saunders considered him "a good driver" who practiced "a trade which a very few Negroes have talent or judgment to acquire."[31]

From his small world on the Croom plantation, Saunders failed to grasp that many Middle Florida owners similarly were relying on black men. They included talented individuals such as "Old Ben" and "Driver Billy" on the Chemonie plantation and "intelligent and trustworthy" slave foremen Alfred, Ned, Henry and Randall on Edward Bradford's huge Pine Hill plantation. Jefferson County's John C. Neal described the characteristics of one of his runaway slaves, who likely was a driver. "[George has] always had charge of his masters [sic] affairs," he declared. He "is rather an intelligent fellow, can read well and most probably write." George N. Jones owned Prince, who served as a driver for more than ten years, and Ephraim, foreman of the plow gang on his El Destino plantation for the same length of time.[32] Such examples suggest the presence of far more black slave drivers in Middle Florida than the record has indicated heretofore.

Some blacks not considered slave drivers nonetheless assumed roles of responsibility on occasion. Bondsmen served as wagoners, for example, delivering goods, taking cotton to shipping points, or transporting guests to town. Bob performed those functions on the Kidder Meade Moore plantation. Louis Napoleon recalled his father's assuming the same role. "His duties were to haul the commodities raised on the plantation and other things that required a wagon," an account related. On the Bradford plantation wagoners Randall Jr. and Laurence carried food to town for their master. Randall Sr. hauled cotton twenty miles from the Pine Hill plantation in Leon County to the railroad terminus at St. Marks.[33]

Some slaves traveled hundreds of miles for their masters on their own responsibility and without supervision of any kind. Shepherd Mitchell's experience permits a glimpse at such a situation. According to his daughter, Charlotte Martin, Mitchell was "a wagoner who hauled whiskey from Newport News, Virginia," to Madison County, Florida. Another example arises in the case of James Page. A Baptist minister of widespread repute, Page served his Leon County owner as a coachman and wagoner from a base at Bel Air plantation. In carrying out his duties and religious vocation, the bondsman traveled as far north as Thomasville, Georgia, as far south as Key West, and, presumably, many places in between.[34]

If the actions of Leon County's John Gamble and Madison County's Nancy DeLaughter typify the policies of other slaveholders in the region, many owners relied on bond servants to transport their personal belongings, along with cotton and other crops and products, to the port towns of Newport, Magnolia, and Port Leon for transshipment by sea. So many male slaves apparently were allowed to haul cotton and other products without the presence or assistance of whites that the practice became a matter of public concern. Jefferson County's grand jury, at least, indicated as much in 1851.[35]

Even though they might be restricted to plantation grounds, some males on larger units spent much of their time performing jobs that entailed duties other than fieldwork. These specially trained bond servants worked as brick masons, coopers, cobblers, tanners, carpenters, blacksmiths, wheelwrights, and general mechanics. As on most larger southern plantations, no precise number or percentage can be given to those workers among Florida's bondsmen who engaged largely in nonfield labor.[36]

As a rule of thumb, a few skilled bondsmen generally could be found on plantations with fifteen or more slaves. On his eighty-five-slave Leon County establishment, Edward Bradford oversaw a blacksmith, several carpenters and coopers, a brick mason, and several wheelwrights. Between his two estates, one in Madison and the other in Gadsden County, Augustus H. Lanier benefited from the services of carpenters, brick masons, and wheelwrights. Among the 160 bond servants on William Kilcrease's Gadsden County operation, carpenters, brick masons, mechanics, blacksmiths, tanners, and coopers labored at their special skills.[37]

Owners took great pride in the results of the work of slave artisans, a fact reflected in the artisans' value upon sale. Thomas Randall, for one, exulted in the fact that his skilled bondsmen made beautiful and durable bricks for his houses and chimneys. When H. C. Withers of Gadsden County advertised slaves for sale in 1840, he singled out a capable blacksmith for attention. Similarly, the slave trading firm of William Garrett and Thomas R. McLintock advertised the availability of one hundred individuals in 1835, carefully highlighting the fact that "several [are] good mechanics of different professions."[38]

Slave women also performed nonagricultural duties. Laundresses and ironers, seamstresses, cooks, spinners, and weavers all contributed to plantation operations. Louis Napoleon could remember his mother's accomplishments as a spinner, since she "loom[ed] cloth for the Randolph family and slaves." In the same vein Laura Randall noted in her 1827 journal that Betty served as a tailor and "spinner when we can get any thing for her to spin." Many slave women possessed or learned a variety of skills. Randall mentioned, for instance, that Betty also could "cook for the People I suppose and the Over Seer." An owner's insistence on a slave's performing a variety of functions sometimes could cause problems. Eliza, a bond servant on the Wirtland plantation in Jefferson County, felt that her status as a house servant meant that she was to cook only. When her duties were expanded to include nursing one of the Randall babies, she resented and resisted the change.[39]

Special domestic skills elevated women within the plantation hierarchy, enhanced their value and appeal to potential buyers, and served as a source of family pride within the slave quarters. Even within the household a pecking order could be uncovered, with seamstresses, midwives, and herb doctors held in higher esteem by their peers than house servants. Advertisements often singled out women with such special talents, as seen on the large H. C. Withers plantation. As for family pride, Amanda McCray provided insight. An interviewer preserved her memory of having been "trained to be a house servant, learning to cook and knit," from her blind mother. McCray, having learned such skills, came to love "making beautiful hooped dresses that required eight to ten yards of cloth."[40]

Slaves who worked primarily as skilled laborers and house servants had, in many respects, an easier daily routine than field-workers. They did not work outdoors under the summer sun and in the winter cold, and their jobs generally involved less physical effort. It was no surprise that skilled workers and house servants resisted transfer to the fields. When Ellen Wirt McCormick tried to sell Charles, an experienced sawmill hand, to a man who wanted a general laborer, the slave "took it upon himself to tell [the prospective buyer] that he had never been in the field and done any hard work." McCormick recorded, "Of course, Mr. Crong decline[d] closing the bargain."[41] Some years later McCormick endeavored to get a house servant to work in the fields. He finally reached the conclusion that Lucy was "unfit for the field, yet, she makes no objection to cooking." Henry Minor, one of William Wirt's skilled carpenters, asked to be sold when he was instructed to do fieldwork.[42]

The wide range of duties, responsibilities, and forced labor occupied much of each slave's time, but custom required owners and overseers to grant some breathing spells. After having worked through the week, bond servants looked forward to having at least an occasional half day off on Saturdays. Depending on the time of year, Nancy DeLaughter, in the manner of many other planters, allowed her bond servants to stop fieldwork at noon. On one August Saturday, though, her overseer recorded that he gave "negroes some time in eve[ning]" off.

Whether Pine Hill plantation's owner granted all slaves half a day off on Saturdays remains open to question, but his daughter Susan B. Eppes claimed that "Saturday afternoon was a holiday for every mother of a family." Kilcrease family estate records reflect that their Gadsden County slaves also occasionally received half a day off on Saturdays, depending on the workload.[43] In any event most bond persons on Middle Florida's large plantations could look forward to having Saturday afternoons off to attend to their own concerns during at least some seasons of the year.

Although some slaves enjoyed a Saturday break, most enslaved persons looked forward as a matter of course to Sundays as a day of relief from regular duties. Many planters, on the other hand, regarded the day as the time for slaves to worship. Bolden Hall of Jefferson County acknowledged as much when he recalled Sunday as a day when the slaves were "permitted to attend church with their masters to hear the white preacher." Susan Eppes claimed that "Blacks were preached to every other Sunday." Whatever the frequency, resentments often flowed from the mandated practice. Margrett Nickerson remembered her master's meanness of spirit but noted that he would afford the slaves time off on Sundays. With an edge of bitterness, she added, "De overseer would com an' wake you up an' make you go to church." For some persons Sundays offered change from daily regimentation. Louis Napoleon recollected the day as one of worship but also as one when bond servants enjoyed permission to "visit other plantations where religious services were being held."[44]

The work routines of most bond persons halted during holidays and special occasions. Acie Thomas's memories of such events came as happy ones. "[The slaves had] time off for frolics (dances), (quilting-weddings)," he reminisced. "These gatherings were attended by old and young from neighboring plantations," Thomas continued. "There was always plenty of food, masters vying with another for the honor of giving his slaves the finest parties." Many times, the ex-slave added, the master would supply the music and participate in many of the activities of the slaves, especially wedding ceremonies. As exemplified by the practices on the plantations of John and Robert Gamble, Achille

Murat, William D. Moseley, and others, holidays and special occasions typically included the Fourth of July, a Thanksgiving day, and a few days at Christmas.[45]

In a sentiment shared by bond servants throughout the South, Middle Florida slaves considered Christmas holidays an especially important time and tradition. On medium-sized and larger plantations bond persons came to expect small gifts and extra rations of food, as well as time off from work. "At Christmas time the slave children all trouped to 'de big house' and stood outside crying 'Christmas gifts' to their master and mistress," Amanda McCray recorded. "They were never disappointed," she continued. "Gifts consisted mostly of candies, nuts, and fruits, but there was always some useful article of clothing included." Governor Richard K. Call's daughter, Ellen Call Long, a romanticist at heart, wrote that Christmas was "the negro's carnival; they were permitted a week of idleness in holiday; those of the plantations visit town in the best article, hence, general greeting, feasting, and dancing among them." That Long's memory did not describe the experience of all Middle Florida slaves seems clear, but many likely enjoyed the kind of interlude that she recalled. Buttressing McCray's account, Long also confirmed that bond servants expected a "conventional 'Christmas gift'" from their masters.[46]

Providing themselves some degree of personal independence, blacks on Middle Florida's plantations developed an internal economy much as their ancestors had done in some of the more established northern states during the seventeenth and eighteenth centuries. As a part of their daily routine and responsibilities, some slaves worked their own garden plots. Others kept hogs and chickens. With permission from their owners, slaves sold their crops, meat, and eggs at the local marketplace or else arranged for their masters to handle the transactions. Accounts of numerous examples survive. Ellen Call Long recorded that bond servants on Richard K. Call's plantation earned money from the "extra crops, or chickens" that they raised "independent" of the master. Achille Murat permitted his slaves to till garden plots and to sell any excess at the Monticello market. Murat sometimes would buy the crops himself and then sell them to his own advantage. Robert Gamble paid Wally, Jake, and John Cox $17.95 for 1,180 pounds of cotton and ten bushels of corn they had grown collectively in their large garden patch. The slaveholder generally compensated bond servants with money for the extra staple crops they grew in their gardens, as well as for the livestock they raised.[47]

Others sometimes received money as inducement or else as reward for assignments well done. Robert Gamble gave "Wally, the head man at Wirtland during the 1840s," $5 annually for good service. He also provided Brass with $4 for taking good care of the hogs. Amon Delaughter, overseer for his mother Nancy Delaughter, allotted bond servant Frank $8, Edmon $10, Mike $4, Marenda $9, Birl $8.25, and seven others from $1.90 to $6 for work well done during the start of the planting season in April 1858. Other owners, including John Gamble and William Wirt, acted similarly.[48]

Although the large majority of bond servants worked, lived, rested, and occasionally profited to a small degree on their masters' lands, significant exceptions created different circumstances for numerous individuals. Although the Florida legislature passed laws against hiring out slaves in 1822, 1824, 1831, 1855, and 1856, the efforts proved largely unsuccessful in curtailing the practice. In fact, the hiring out of slaves became, as Julia Floyd Smith observed, a common practice in Middle Florida as early as the mid-1820s and continued to be so for the remainder of the antebellum period. Amanda McCray's owner carried the practice into the Civil War era by hiring her out to cook for Union soldiers.[49]

Options for lease arrangements and the labor they provided proved plentiful. Researcher Donnie D. Bellamy has explained that the sources usually are "silent regarding what services the hired slaves performed for their employers." Yet, logically, it must be assumed that they worked at the same variety of tasks as other bond servants. In doing so they filled vital needs of numerous categories of persons and businesses. To cite one example, Thomas Randall, one of Middle Florida's earliest settlers, used rented slaves to begin developing a plantation after his 1828 arrival in Leon County. Then and afterwards, bond servants might be had for just about any period of time. One Leon County planter advertised that he would "hire out the slaves on his plantation . . . by the month, or for the remainder of the year." They might also be obtained by the day or week or for multiple years.[50]

Costs for slave leasing naturally varied with the period of the lease, the skills of the worker, and the availability of labor generally, but some examples permit a feel for amounts involved. As late as 1845 Ellen McCormick and her husband received $25 per month, a figure ranging toward the high end of the spectrum, for leasing Henry. In 1845 Andrew Young's estate hired out twenty-one slaves at prices ranging from a low of $5 to a high of $72 per bond servant for the year. On January 2, 1850, James Mosely contracted for a bondsman with a Major Ward "for $90 till Jany 1851." Other available records suggest that Middle Florida bond servants typically merited a lease payment of at least $100 per year during most of the antebellum period.[51]

Although laws sternly prohibited the practice, some bond persons accepted or seized responsibility for hiring themselves to others. This allowed the affected slaves to exercise some control over their time and conditions of their employment. In a number of instances considerate owners anticipating their own demise paved the way for slaves to act in the owner's future absence. Gadsden County's Jonathan Robinson stipulated in his will that "Boy George the carpenter shall be allowed to choose his own employer annually during his life time," with the profits of his hire going to his estate. Robert Edmunds of the same county, also by will, allowed his slaves to select persons for whom they would work, provided that the lessees gave "satisfactory security to my executors."[52]

Just as a sale might carry a slave beyond Middle Florida's bounds, so too might a lease. Railroad companies and the military figured heavily in such contracts. During the financial crisis that followed the Panic of 1837, Louis Goldsborough, the Wirtland plantation manager from 1834 to 1839, hired out bondsmen to the railroad in Pensacola, since the company would "pay $200.00 a year for every man, and . . . feed, clothe, and pay doctor's bills besides." He also hired out bondsmen to United States Navy contractors in West Florida. Prominent owners such as Thomas Randall, John and Robert Gamble, Benjamin Chaires, and William Wirt frequently leased bond servants in a similar manner to railroad companies, construction companies, the military, or small entrepreneurs in places as far away as Escambia and Duval Counties.[53]

The role of railroads as lessees of slaves offers insight into a separate dynamic of Middle Florida slavery that appeared in the 1850s. Many well-established planters by then found less need for the work of some of their highly skilled craftsmen. This came at the same time that the planters placed greater emphasis on cotton production. When the owners transferred the artisans to the fields, as Christopher Linsin concluded, "[they] saw their skills squandered." To avoid the problem, many masters rented out their bond servants. Sometimes these slave owners merely carried on a long-standing tradition, and at other times they initiated a new practice. Whichever case, leading men such as Richard K. Call, Benjamin Chaires, John Shepard, John Parkhill and others rented slaves to the railroad companies in West, Middle, and East Florida from 1832 to 1858 and made between $120 and $190 a year for each male. The demand for railroad laborers grew with enhanced construction in the late 1850s, with companies advertising that they would pay $180 per year for each leased worker. A review of five hundred Middle Florida probate records and appraisals revealed that over 70 percent of the planters or their executors hired out at least one or two skilled bondsmen during the 1850s and 1860s to the railroads or to other contractors.[54]

Manufacturing establishments and small businesses also served as a market for leased bond servants. Eugene Genovese has pointed out that "manufacturers found it . . . easier to induce [planters] to lease slaves to them" than to invest cash in their industrial enterprises. From 1830 to 1860, though, none of Middle Florida's counties hosted more than thirty small business establishments of varying sizes, and few of them qualified as manufacturers. Planters nonetheless seemed more than willing to fill whatever small-labor requirements the enterprises created. For example, in the twenty-four business establishments in Leon County in 1840, ninety-four workers were slaves. Joseph Braden, who listed himself as owning only two slaves in 1850, employed over fifty bondsmen to work in his sawmill.[55]

A small number of bond persons lived in Middle Florida's few villages and towns. All told, less than 3 percent of the region's total slave population could claim such a nonrural home. Many of them were house servants for wealthy planters with town houses. They might be owned or leased. Banks Meacham lent Robert Meacham, a future state senator, to his Tallahassee relations. Numerous skilled slaves lived in the villages and, especially, at Tallahassee, the only town of real consequence. In 1840, for instance, the capital's population balanced between 815 whites and 786 black slaves, with 15 free blacks in addition. There black carpenter and contractor George Proctor hired slaves such as Pompey to assist in his highly regarded building projects. Other slaves labored in stores, lumberyards and mills, and small manufacturing establishments.[56]

In summary, the largest segment of Middle Florida's slave population labored as agricultural workers on middle-sized or large plantations. Men, women, and children generally tended the cotton, sugarcane, and tobacco fields during much of the antebellum period, although they performed a wide range of other chores, many requiring sophisticated or domestic skills. At least 15 percent of all slaves served at one time or another as skilled laborers or as house servants. Children also worked at odd jobs, with some being trained for particular tasks well before the age of twelve. Blacks served additionally as overseers and drivers on the plantations of Middle Florida, sometimes with or without the title.

Work for the master constituted a great part of each slave's life, but not every day was consumed in such endeavors. A sizable number of planters in the region gave slaves a half day off on Saturdays, and most gave them all day off on Sundays. Bond persons assumed roles of responsibility and degrees of independence from their owners, as well; some managed garden plots for their own subsistence, and, with their masters' permission, sold any excess for money to buy personal items.

A significant portion of the slave population, to the contrary, worked away from the master's plantation at least some portion of their lives. Although demand ran high for field-workers during the 1850s and 1860s, at least 20 percent of the skilled males were hired out or in some other fashion continued to work exclusively in their trades. Many of them lent their efforts to railroad and related transportation companies, the military, or small industries and businesses.

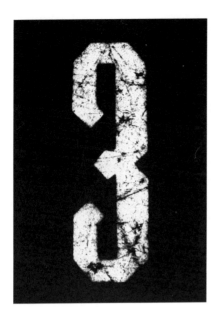

ON MIDDLE FLORIDA'S SMALL PLANTATIONS

Middle Florida's slave majority sustained the substantial plantations of the region's cotton kingdom, but the larger segment of the land-owning grower population operated smaller establishments. These less-than-grand plantations and farms nonetheless constituted an essential element in the area's slave economy. Although the same dynamic applied through much of the cotton South, scholars have neglected the physical conditions of enslaved blacks held by small and medium-sized farming concerns. To assist in filling that gap, this chapter explores the lives and work routines of the bond servants who inhabited a neglected rural world.

Statistics assist in setting the scene. In 1830, out of a total of 954 slaveholders in Middle Florida, 823 or 86.2 percent owned fewer than twenty slaves and five hundred acres. Some thirty years later, 79.1 percent of 1,888 slaveholders held the same type of estates. During the 1850s, 72 percent of all slaveholders in the rural areas held nine slaves or less. The number of slave owners with nine slaves or less increased from 685 in 1830 to 1,150 by 1860. These individuals constituted 60 percent of the small slaveholding families by the Civil War's eve. Thus, from 1830 to 1860 the majority of slaveholders in Middle Florida owned nine or fewer slaves.[1]

Questions of class difference between large planters and lesser operators can easily be exaggerated. The cultivation of cotton by small and medium-sized farmers and the ginning of it by larger planters bonded small and large slaveholders to Middle Florida's largely cotton-based economy. The buying of extra foodstuffs from small farmers by larger planters further created a spirit of cooperation between the two classes. With an abundance of cheap fertile land on the Florida frontier, small and large planters all sought to prosper as they increased their land holdings over time. Much like their more affluent counterparts, small farmers engaged in continuing efforts to compel their bond servants to work in a fashion that the owners believed to be consistent and productive.[2]

In such circumstances small planters often found common ground with and sought to emulate the success and lifestyles of their wealthier and influential neighbors. Particularly, the dream of larger slaveholdings and the subsequent need for an overseer were benchmarks for many men that they had arrived "in society." James M. Denham and Canter Brown have recently published the reminiscences of one old Florida hand, George Gillett Keen. Keen's use of the characterizations and racial epithets popular among poorer whites at the century's turn are offensive, but his words sum up sentiments shared by many Middle Florida farmers of the antebellum period. The recollection involves Keen's hunting in the 1840s with planter friends from Hamilton County:

> We would go for three or four days on a camp hunt, having a nigger to drive the wagon, carry the grub and haul in the meat. When the day's hunt was over, supper eaten and all seated around the fire, the subject of farming was introduced. One would say, I've got the best overseer I ever had; another would say, my overseer is a worthless fellow, a third would say I am pretty well satisfied with my overseer, and so on.
>
> I would sit there like a bump on a log. You bet I never wanted anything worse in my life than I wanted a plantation of niggers so I could talk about my overseer. I had some niggers, but not enough to have an overseer; that's what worried me. When hunting time come round I was in but when overseer talk was the topic of the day I was ten feet above high water mark on dry land.
>
> I wanted niggers. How to get them was the question.[3]

For slaves on the smaller estates life could both mimic and differ markedly from the large plantation experience. Similar to their counterparts on larger plantations, the majority of bond persons spent most of their time preparing land for cotton, tobacco, some sugarcane, and other crops for human and livestock consumption. They removed trees, plowed, planted, cultivated, and harvested. The same planting routine that endured on large plantations existed on smaller farms, with plowing beginning in January and the preparation of fields for planting cotton, tobacco, and other crops from February through March, followed by a five- to six-month growing season. Plowing and hoeing of crops continued until June. A month or so later, slaves would begin the arduous task of picking cotton until December, at which time, the whole monotonous routine would start over again.[4]

On many of the smaller farms, though, cotton production was less important than on larger places. A substantial percentage of land owners grew subsistence crops for human consumption. Although bond servants cultivated many acres of cotton and tobacco, their daily agricultural duties differed accordingly. Crops such as watermelons, sweet potatoes, corn, black-eyed peas, squash, and other garden vegetables were grown. Patience Campbell of Jackson County remembered eating greens and corn grown on her master's small farm.[5] Judge David L. White of Gadsden County recorded in a diary covering 1839 to 1842 that his eight hands were clearing land for the planting of potatoes, corn, and other crops. Willis Williams of Leon County recalled that his master planted many acres of corn for human and animal consumption.[6] During 1861 and 1862 Rabun Scarborough's nineteen bond servants planted plenty of "potatoes and corn" on his 550-acre Gadsden County farm. Such planting of garden crops was the norm for small and middle-sized operations.[7]

As with the larger concerns in Gadsden County, small plantations and farms there typically favored tobacco rather than cotton. Given the commitment to the crop by smaller growers, by 1860 the county produced almost twice as many pounds of leaf as all other Florida counties combined.[8] Willis Williams remembered that his master grew a "bountiful supply" of leaf, as would have been true of many of his peers. Much of the county's tobacco probably grew on units cultivated by one to fifteen hands. For John Smith and his handful of bond servants tobacco was the primary crop from 1829 until the 1850s. David D. Smith, a Virginia transplant, also came to Gadsden County around 1829. By 1845 he listed fifteen bondsmen and 440 acres of land. With his labor force, Smith became one of many small slaveholders who led Gadsden and the state in tobacco cultivation by the 1850s.[9]

Small slaveholders in Middle Florida nurtured crops besides cotton, tobacco, and garden vegetables. Although there were more sugarcane farms and plantations in East Florida by the Civil War's end, a few small slaveholders, especially in Gadsden County, tried their hand at cultivating it as a staple crop. Slaves planted seed cane in the early spring after readying the fields. From October until March bond servants cut, stripped, and hauled the cane to the sugar mill. There, as Julia Floyd Smith described, "it was fed through rollers which pressed out the juice into barrels." The juice then had to be emptied from the barrels into large iron or copper kettles to be boiled down to crystal sugar. All told, in 1860 Gadsden growers produced 123 barrels of sugar, each of one thousand pounds. The amount represented one-fourth of the state's output, with East Florida's Marion and Manatee Counties leading in production.[10]

The dynamics of cane culture typically involved work conditions considered among the harshest faced by slaves in the Old South. Some owners evidenced little concern for the toll exacted from their workers. Rabun Scarborough was such a man. On one occasion he decided that his wife had started the process of making sugar before the proper cool weather had arrived. His concern, however, was not about the heat's effects on his slaves. "Is it not too early to make sugar?" he inquired of his wife. "The weather is too warm and I think the cane (must) mature a good deal yet." Scarborough added, "I do not want the gin to run when the weather is so warm it will be too hard on the mules."[11]

Although small slaveholders adopted a more diversified approach to growing than the large planters, cotton remained the major staple crop of most small farmers in the Middle Florida region from 1821 to 1860. According to the 1850 and 1860 agricultural returns for the area, approximately 70 percent of all small slaveholders grew cotton.[12] Willis Williams's reminiscences afford some insight into the matter. His master, Thomas Heyward, operated both a small farm in the country and a general store in Tallahassee. Still, Williams asserted that Heyward, much as other farmers, knew that "cotton was the main product of most southern plantations and the owner usually depended upon the income from the sale of his yearly crop to maintain his home and upkeep of his slaves and cattle." The Williams account continued: "It was necessary for every farm to yield as much as possible and much energy was directed toward growing and picking large crops." Although Heyward enjoyed success as a merchant, he always remembered that his country property could yield "a bountiful supply of cotton."[13]

In the absence of overseers and drivers, bond servants experienced a far closer working relationship with owners on the smaller Middle Florida cotton farms than occurred on the larger spreads. Conversely, owners paid more immediate attention to the slaves and the results of their efforts. For example, Gadsden County farmer Scarborough directly or through his wife carefully supervised the work of his bond servants in clearing acreage for cotton cultivation. When absent temporarily, he still directed each step of the process, insisting on one occasion that his wife have the slaves gather the "cotton . . . as soon as possible." David L. White carefully followed the daily cotton picking achievements of his slaves and boasted that his eight slaves collectively had picked 292, 278, and 248 pounds in one three-day period during late December 1835.[14]

The often-sophisticated divisions of labor frequently seen on the larger plantations were rarely duplicated on smaller estates. As aptly noted by Drew G. Faust, "[work] routines differed according to the size of a particular slaveholding."[15] Men, women, and children labored together to farm crops and to perform day-to-day chores. Women joined men in handling heavy assignments such as plowing, felling trees, ditching, and attending to livestock.[16] With some exceptions (discussed below) gender distinctions were seldom recognized in most other types of work assignments. The number of slaves available for assignment simply did not permit other practices.

One Gadsden County grower's diary covering the late 1830s and the early 1840s affords a glimpse at daily routine. Confirming historian Julia Floyd Smith's findings, Judge David L. White specified that his slaves' work began at dawn. The slaves then performed a variety of chores with few distinctions drawn between domestic and fieldwork.

Still, it was necessary to accomplish particular tasks in a specified time frame. White recorded in 1839, not surprisingly, that Julia and Bob plowed while Nanny hoed. He often noted that all hands, including the young children, kept themselves busy with the never-ceasing requirements of the farm. Time and again he mentioned two major chores joined in by all: clearing land and picking cotton.[17]

Similarly, most of White's neighbors of the same circumstances and status used slaves for a variety of chores. They included the clearing of new land and the planting and picking of cotton. George Bullock, one of 175 small farmers listing less than nineteen slaves in Jackson County during the 1850s, owned six bondsmen during the general period. Patience Campbell grew up on the two-hundred-acre farm and recalled well her mother's having to toil in the cotton field for their owner. Greens, corn, and other crops on the farm demanded attention. The number of laborers on the Bullock farm never exceeded thirteen. Accordingly, Patience Campbell's memories also included times when everyone helped with the picking and weighing of the cotton.[18]

Slave women living on the smaller places shouldered many responsibilities beyond fieldwork. They labored as spinners, weavers, seamstresses, and cooks, as well as serving in a range of other capacities. Much like the men, women often were expected to perform skilled duties while completing a variety of other chores. Many black women cooked not only for the master's family but also for their own loved ones and other bond servants. Willis Williams recollected such a state of affairs in the case of his mother, who cooked for everyone on the farm, including the slave owner's family. When they were done with their chores, Williams recalled, he and the other children "were fed right from the master's table." David White's slave, Nanny, cooked for all the bond persons when she was not otherwise occupied hoeing.[19]

As White's example illustrates, owners expected children to contribute from their tender years. "A child's entry into the labor force made an impact upon the wider community," Wilma King has explained, "since it meant an additional hand despite the size, performing jobs." As a general matter, the farm or plantation's size, the number of slaves present, and the whims of the owner helped to determine the age at which young children began work. As also was true on the larger units, many chores assigned to children were gender specific, although the young people routinely helped out whenever and wherever their size and strength permitted.[20]

If ex-slaves Patience Campbell, Douglas Parish, and Willis Williams are representative of what children did on the smaller units in Middle Florida, their perceptions and reminiscences offer a glimpse at what small slave owners generally expected from the young children. Children received training at relatively young ages for performing numerous tasks. Many helped, for example, with separating the cottonseed from the fiber. At about age seven or eight Patience Campbell was already assisting "other children about her age and older in picking out cotton seeds from the picked cotton." She also recalled being taught "spinning and weaving" at the tender age of ten. Douglas Parish thought his "first job was picking cotton seed from the cotton." When about twelve years of age, he became a stable boy and soon learned about the care and grooming of horses from an old slave who had charge of the Parish stables. As a youngster Parish "[kept] the buggies, surreys, and spring wagons clean." At nine, Williams took care of his younger siblings while his mother worked.[21]

Sometimes owners used children to perform for the slaveholder's amusement, a potentially profitable enterprise. As a young boy Douglas Parish evidenced talent for being a "very good runner." An interviewer explained what occurred as a result. "It was a custom in those days for one plantation owner to match his 'nigger' against that of his neighbor," the man recorded. "[Parish] was a favorite with [his owner] because he seldom failed to win the race." The owner trained his young boys by running them to the boundary of his plantation and back again. The ex–bond servant commented that, as a young boy, he could win a bag of silver for his master at an event like the "Fourth of July races." But if he lost the race his owner could be "hard to get along with for several days." This particular youngster looked at these events as fun, with the lure of a "jack-knife or a bag of marbles" if he were triumphant in his races. His owner probably viewed the matter quite differently, as regular work routine that he wanted the young bond servant to master.[22]

Large planters might own numerous bond persons who performed little or no fieldwork because they possessed highly prized specialized skills such as carpentry or brick masonry. Most small planters could not afford such an extravagant approach to slaveholding. If probate records, diaries, and sales advertisements are any indication, the majority of small farmers owned few highly skilled workers. If they did, the owners required such laborers to undertake all manner of farm chores, including fieldwork. Thus, David L. White might direct his slave George, a skilled craftsman, to build him a chimney but only after the bondsman had attended to necessary plowing. Typically, small slaveholders like George Bullock, James Parish, and others worked their bond servants at any task, regardless of skilled occupation, gender, or age.[23]

Seen from another perspective, the majority of skilled workers on the smaller units engaged in daily routines hardly less taxing than those followed by field hands. Patience Campbell informed one interviewer that her "father was not only a capable field worker but also a finished shoemaker." Her account continued: "After tanning and curing his hides placing them in water with oak bark for several days and then exposing them to the sun to dry, he would cut out the uppers and the soles after measuring the foot to be shod." Afterwards, he could be found plowing the field for the planting of cotton. Other slave testimonies indicate similar assortments of work obligations expected of skilled bondsmen. Douglas Parish remembered his father, Charles Parish, labored in the cotton fields, where the chief product of the Parish plantation was grown. Yet his "father was [also] a skilled bricklayer and carpenter," who taught him the trade. On Thomas Heyward's small Leon County farm, Willis Williams's father "did carpentry and other light work around the place."[24]

Although exact figures are not available, a few slaves on smaller estates appear to have benefited from better work conditions than those endured day to day by field hands, particularly if they managed to transfer from the farm to a town. Willis Williams recounted that Thomas Heyward held a plantation out in the country from Tallahassee and kept slaves there. Heyward also owned a fine home in the town, as well as a large grocery store and a produce house where he kept additional slaves. Williams's mother became the cook at the town house, which permitted his father to begin apprenticing under a white carpenter while doing light work around the place. The former bondsman claimed that other slaves in town did little work, although they "tended the garden and the many chickens, ducks and geese on the place." The only bond servant of the Reverend Francis H. Rutledge had easier duties then field slaves. Although Rutledge traveled in rural areas and had accumulated sizable holdings in real estate and personal property, he engaged in no farming. His slave conceivably served him simply as a house and body servant.[25]

Although most small slave owners directly supervised their bond servants, some slaves carried a great deal of responsibility for their own daily routines. A situation could occur in which an owner found his time divided between a farm and a related business. Cyrus Dearborn, a merchant, probably assigned certain responsibilities to his six bondsmen, since they all worked at his store during the 1820s and 1830s. Their work continued when the owner was absent. Handling tobacco took skill. Accordingly, the nine slaves belonging to John W. Malone, who worked for the tobacco growing and exporting company of Forman and Muse from 1845 to 1851, likely learned to rely on their own initiative in carrying out delicate tasks.[26]

Another, although related, situation in which slaves of small owners exercised personal responsibility arose from necessity in the absence of overseers and drivers. Throughout the South and the southwest generally, little specific evidence concerning slave managers and drivers on Middle Florida's small units remains for examination. A majority of these slaveholding families, though, employed no overseers because their operations were too small to warrant or afford the expense. With few white managers on their farms, slaveholders often worked alongside their bond persons. Frequently, blacks—who may not have been considered drivers, foremen, or overseers—emerged as leaders without the title.[27] In the circumstances, blacks helped to manage the farms of their masters at various times, including during the owner's absence. Robert Meacham's experience offers an illustration. A slave and the natural son of Gadsden County's prominent planter-politician Banks Meacham, the bondsman served as an "unofficial leader" and recalled superintending for "my old boss." By 1853, when Robert turned eighteen, his master claimed thirteen laborers, and Robert already considered himself a supervisor among them. His fellow slaves likely looked up to the literate bondsman. He not only oversaw some of their work routines, but, by candlelight, he apparently also taught at least a few of them to read and write.[28]

Owner Rabun Scarborough probably used Prince as the "unofficial manager" of his small farm when he went off to serve in the Civil War. In letters to his wife the slaveholder often referred to responsibilities given to Prince, directing the bond servant on one occasion to put "up the seed cane [and] to take down the shortest & put it up wet & put plenty of dirt on it." In another letter Scarborough instructed his wife to direct Prince to work with other slaves and "clear cut the fence corners all round the plantation." He continued: "I want Prince to begin to clear as soon as possible. I want the piece cleared next to McMillan's field between our field & the road through the old briar field." Within one week the slave owner inquired of his wife, "Does Prince understand where I want him to clear?" He added, "Tell Prince to be sure to have the fodder well taken care of for I know there is plenty of that if it is not wasted." The owner further informed his wife that he thought Mr. Whittle, an overseer, "will take charge of our place" at a future date. Like the bond servants of Banks Meacham and Rabun Scarborough, many more bond servants effectively served as slave drivers and overseers than the record otherwise would suggest.[29]

Middle Florida's small and medium-sized slaveholders, like their southern counterparts, believed that shoring up "absolute power" over their bond servants would ensure efficient planting and harvesting. Reflecting large-area plantations in the region and across the cotton South, their treatment of enslaved blacks depended on several factors. Among them were the whims of the individual owner, how well slaves performed their assignments, and how closely they adhered to work rules established on the farm or plantation. Patience Campbell lived on the eight-slave farm of George Bullock from the mid-1850s to the mid-1860s. She recalled her owner as being "very kind" as long as her mother "toiled in the fields." As a child, Patience was permitted by her owner to spend "most of her time playing in the sand."[30] On the same theme, when Robert Meacham was a child, his master required him to perform "some" work on the farm staffed by thirteen slaves, but he remembered mostly riding around with his master in his carriage.[31]

Willis Williams's experience echoed that of Campbell and Meacham. He recalled that he "fared well during the first nine years of his life under slavery." After that he was free.[32]

The flip side of the owner's whim could involve brutality and physical pain. Although David L. White's slaves performed their work and responsibilities without testing the owner's temper, White's neighbor Joseph Wade obviously had a hard time with his slaves during the cotton picking in August 1838. White recorded that Wade flogged Robert and Jinny. A month later Bob absented himself from the farm, only to return two days later. On the day of his return Bob and Henry absconded together. The record fails to indicate whether the bondsmen returned on their own or were captured or what further punishments they suffered.[33]

The typical experience lay somewhere between superficial generosity and cruelty. The work routines of laborers on James Parish's eleven-slave farm in 1840 probably reflect the general situation. Often, in attempting to establish good work habits, masters such as Parish sought to walk the middle ground between threatening punishment and carrying it out. According to Douglas Parish, Parish personally punished his slaves, never permitting an overseer to do so. Even that event rarely occurred. "If the slave[s] failed to do their work," the ex-slave observed, "they were reported to [the master]." Then, the master "would warn them and show his black whip which was usually sufficient."[34]

The hiring out of bond servants by the smaller owners filled an economic need for them just as it did for the larger planters. Labor remained scarce at times in Middle Florida, and, as Eugene Genovese has argued, yeoman farmers with few bond persons contributed to the labor supply by hiring out the few slaves they owned. The record clearly demonstrates that large planters rented out enslaved Africans to individuals, to industries, and to construction and railroad companies. Even so, the record fails to indicate exactly what work the leased slaves were expected to perform for the lessees. The record suggests that females and males were hired during different times of the year and for different periods of time. Many of them, Christopher E. Linsin has noted, were likely rented out as house servants, butlers, valets, coachmen, nannies, and common field hands.[35]

The records offer a few hints that provide greater specificity. William P. Barnes, Elizabeth Henry, and John Pratt, all small farmers in Jackson County, rented out skilled female domestic servants to neighbors. The women performed duties as seamstresses, cooks, and house servants. Gadsden and Leon County small farmers followed the same pattern as their neighbors on larger regional units. They hired out female bond servants from one day to one year. The wife of Cyrus Dearborn, who had trained six bond servants to work in her husband's store, leased them out for a year after her husband died.[36]

Other examples help to clarify terms and conditions. David White rented out two of his eight bond servants, Jack and Amelia, to a Mr. Hodges from December 18, 1838, to December 25, 1839. The lease fee remains unknown. John Evans, a small slaveholder who served as an overseer on George Noble Jones's large plantation in Jefferson County, rented out his two slaves. Evans noted that he had "come to the Conclusion to heir out my Negroes another year and go to overseeing again." Sarah H. Pope was the administratrix of Sampson Pope's Jackson County estate. From the estate's twelve bond servants, she hired out Morris to John Bird for $140 in 1839 and seven slaves in 1840 for an eleven-month period. The prices ranged from $45 for Nancy to $133 for Morris. In the same county John Rix's administrator hired out Evaline and her two children, along with Jane, for a total of $175.25 in 1837. Of 250 probate records surveyed, over 75 percent of all administrators of small slaveholders' estates in Middle Florida hired out bond servants at one time or another.[37]

Regardless of whether bond servants worked in the fields, in stores or shops, or were hired out to perform various other tasks, they looked to the time when they could rest from their labors. Yet few records indicate whether slaves on the smaller units enjoyed the same half day off on Saturdays and all day off on Sundays for religious worship and personal activities given to slaves on the large estates. Seemingly, though, the slaves generally got at least Sundays off. Julia Floyd Smith concluded that regardless of the size of a Middle Florida farm or plantation, "slaves were never worked on Sundays and on many plantations were given a half day off on Saturday." She also declared, "Christmas Day was always a holiday and this celebration was sometimes extended for several days or more through New Year's Day."[38] William Williams's recollections confirm her assessments. He remembered slaves having Sundays off to attend church. Where one was available, blacks invariably sat in the balcony.[39]

How farm property for slave gardens on the smaller holdings was allocated remains unclear. Most units likely were so small that slaves grew vegetables for themselves and their masters in one large garden patch. That was the case on Thomas Heyward's farm in Leon County. Doubtlessly, exceptions abounded, again at the whims of individual owners. No available records shed light on the similar question of whether slaves earned small sums of money from activities such as selling chickens or livestock. That probably occurred on many of the smaller units.[40]

It is clear that the majority of bond servants on the small units of Middle Florida performed a variety of tasks. Most worked primarily in the cotton and tobacco fields during a good part of each year. Generally speaking, men, women, and children on the smaller units performed such duties as tending livestock, cultivating field crops and gardens, clearing land, and rendering other tasks necessary for the farm or small plantation's survival. Even the few skilled workers on the small units worked in the fields as a part of their general labor. Some slaves served as house servants and worked the fields as well. A few bond servants held unofficial positions of responsibility. Slaves presumably earned some money through their own efforts. All told, a slave in a small holding was more closely tied to the owner's whims than was his equal on larger plantations. Owners worked directly with the slaves, and the nature of personal rapport could create factors—good or bad—that directly influenced the quality of life.

Map 1. West, Middle, and East Florida during slavery days.

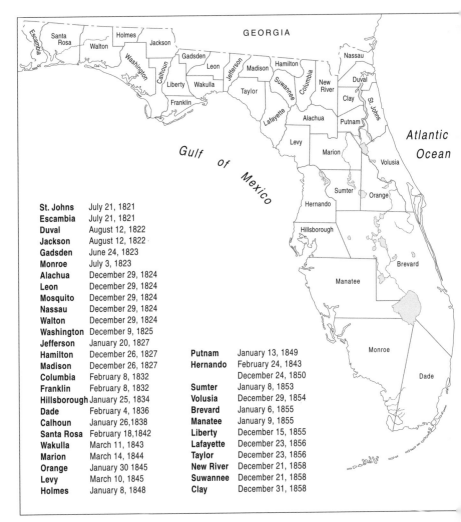

St. Johns	July 21, 1821		
Escambia	July 21, 1821		
Duval	August 12, 1822		
Jackson	August 12, 1822		
Gadsden	June 24, 1823		
Monroe	July 3, 1823		
Alachua	December 29, 1824		
Leon	December 29, 1824		
Mosquito	December 29, 1824		
Nassau	December 29, 1824		
Walton	December 29, 1824		
Washington	December 9, 1825		
Jefferson	January 20, 1827		
Hamilton	December 26, 1827	Putnam	January 13, 1849
Madison	December 26, 1827	Hernando	February 24, 1843
Columbia	February 8, 1832		December 24, 1850
Franklin	February 8, 1832	Sumter	January 8, 1853
Hillsborough	January 25, 1834	Volusia	December 29, 1854
Dade	February 4, 1836	Brevard	January 6, 1855
Calhoun	January 26,1838	Manatee	January 9, 1855
Santa Rosa	February 18,1842	Liberty	December 15, 1855
Wakulla	March 11, 1843	Lafayette	December 23, 1856
Marion	March 14, 1844	Taylor	December 23, 1856
Orange	January 30 1845	New River	December 21, 1858
Levy	March 10, 1845	Suwannee	December 21, 1858
Holmes	January 8, 1848	Clay	December 31, 1858

Map 2. Florida counties and their dates of formation, 1821–58.

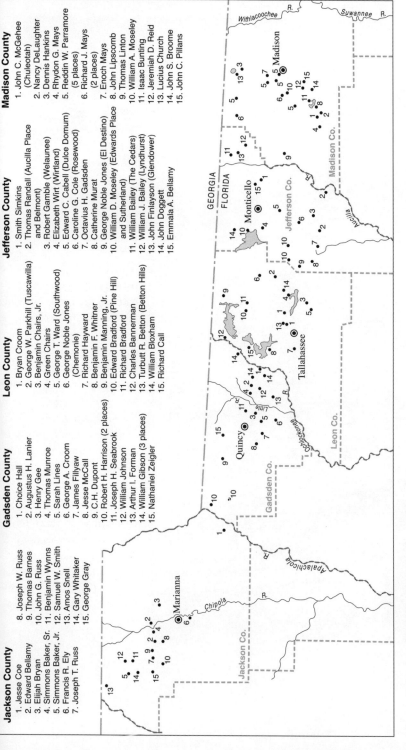

Jackson County

1. Jesse Coe
2. Edward Bellamy
3. Elijah Bryan
4. Simmons Baker, Sr.
5. Simmons Baker, Jr.
6. Francis R. Ely
7. Joseph T. Russ
8. Joseph W. Russ
9. Thomas Barnes
10. John G. Russ
11. Benjamin Wynns
12. Samuel W. Smith
13. Amos Snell
14. Gary Whitaker
15. George Gray

Gadsden County

1. Choice Hall
2. Augustus H. Lanier
3. Henry Gee
4. Thomas Munroe
5. Sarah Lines
6. George A. Croom
7. James Fillyaw
8. Jesse McCall
9. C.H. Dupont
10. Robert H. Harrison (2 places)
11. Joseph H. Seabrook
12. William Johnson
13. Arthur I. Forman
14. William Gibson (3 places)
15. Nathaniel Zeigler

Leon County

1. Bryan Croom
2. George W. Parkhill (Tuscawilla)
3. Benjamin Chairs, Jr.
4. Green Chairs
5. George T. Ward (Southwood)
6. George Noble Jones (Chemonie)
7. Richard Hayward
8. Benjamin F. Whitner
9. Benjamin Manning, Jr.
10. Edward Bradford (Pine Hill)
11. Richard Bradford
12. Charles Bannerman
13. Turbutt R. Betton (Betton Hills)
14. William Bloxham
15. Richard Call

Jefferson County

1. Smith Simkins
2. Thomas Randall (Aucilla Place and Belmont)
3. Robert Gamble (Welaunee)
4. Elizabeth Wirt (Wirtland)
5. Edward C. Cabell (Dulce Domum)
6. Caroline G. Cole (Rosewood)
7. Octavius H. Gadsden
8. Catherine Murat
9. George Noble Jones (El Destino)
10. William D. Moseley (Edwards Place and Sutherland)
11. William Bailey (The Cedars)
12. William J. Bailey (Lyndhurst)
13. John Finlayson (Glendower)
14. John Doggett
15. Emmala A. Bellamy

Madison County

1. John C. McGehee (Chuleotah)
2. Nancy DeLaughter
3. Dennis Hankins
4. Rhydon G. Mays
5. Reddin W. Parramore (5 places)
6. Richard J. Mays (2 places)
7. Enoch Mays
8. John Lipscomb
9. Thomas Linton
10. William A. Moseley
11. Isaac Bunting
12. Jeremiah D. Reid
13. Lucius Church
14. John S. Broome
15. John C. Pillans

Map 3. Substantial Middle Florida plantations, 1850.

Above, 1. Juan Garrido, a free African-born explorer, partici pated in the Indian wars in Hispaniola and accompanied Juan Ponce de Leon in the "d covery" of Florida. This illustra tion portrays Garrido accompa nying Hernando Cortes on h Mexican campaign. From Fr Diego Duran, *Historia de las Indias de Nueva Espana v Isla de Tierra Firme* (Mexico: Edi tors Nacional, 1951, original 1581).

Left, 2. The free black village Gracia Real de Santa Teresa Mose sat two miles north of Augustine as late as 1763. Co tesy Florida Museum of Nat History, Fort Mose Exhibitio

1 cm

3. Archaeologists discovered this handmade eighteenth-century St. Christopher's medal at the site of the Gracia Real de Santa Teresa de Mose near St. Augustine. St. Christopher is the patron saint of travelers and of Havana, Cuba. The medal also reflects the beliefs of many eighteenth-century Africans in transmigration to Africa after death. Courtesy Florida Museum of Natural History, Cat. No. 89-2-0.

An antebellum Tallahassee street scene during the 1830s showing slaves in Middle ·ida's plantation belt. Some bond servants worked in the town of Tallahassee. Drawn by 1cis Comte de Castelnau. Courtesy Photographic Collection, Florida State Archives.

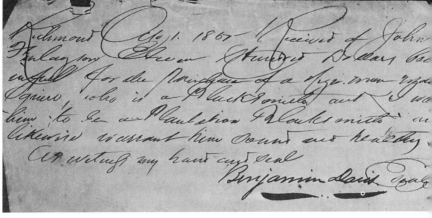

5. John Finlayson became one of the largest slaveholders in Middle Florida, holding 18
more slaves by the early 1860s. Here is a receipt for a blacksmith named Edward Sq*
Finlayson purchased the slave from Benjamin Davis of Richmond, Virginia, for $1,100. C
tesy Photographic Collection, Florida State Archives.

6. In Florida, especial
what became known a
Middle Florida, cotto.
emerged as the cash c
of choice during the a
bellum era. Its cultiva
and harvesting depen
as shown here, on the
bor of enslaved blacks
Courtesy Photographi
Collection, Florida St
Archives.

7. The process of cotton culture depended on slaves performing numerous chores, including gathering, ginning, packing, and shipping the crops. Although this illustration represents the many steps of cotton culture on coastal South Carolina plantations, enslaved blacks carried out many of the same processes in Middle Florida and, increasingly as time passed, in adjacent areas of West and East Florida. Courtesy Photographic Collection, Florida State Archives.

8. Slave women often performed the same fieldwork as men, as evidenced by this photograph of a Leon County woman plowing with an ox during the early 1910s. Courtesy Photographic Collection, Florida State Archives.

9. Sometimes horse mules, or oxen were available for plowin In such cases, as su gested by this photo graph taken after en cipation, slaves were compelled to under such exhausting wo Courtesy Photograp Collection, Florida State Archives.

Left, 10. Onetime slave Creasy Lloyd of Narcoossee in Osceola County reportedly lived almost to one hundred years of age. Courtesy Photographic Collection, Florida State Archives.

Below, 11. Lewis Hicks, a slave of the Robert Hendry family, helped to pioneer today's Hardee County. Courtesy Canter Brown Jr.

12. These four Hillsborough County pioneers had survived slavery and attained at least ninety years of age when this photograph was taken in 1923. *Left to right:* Aaron Bryant, Isaac Berry, Stephen Harvell, and Nathan Tucker. Stephen Harvell worked as a cowhunter for owner James Lanier, and Bryant lived at Tampa and later served as a soldier in the Union army. Courtesy Tampa Bay History Center.

Above, 13. As was true of a number of the Tampa Bay area African American pioneers shown in this 1923 photograph, ties of family and place held many freedmen to the areas of Florida in which they endured bondage. *Left to right:* Peter Nelson, Isaac Smith, Monroe Messer, Samuel Bryant, Manuel Stillings, and Andrew Johnson. The name of the seventh man is unknown. Courtesy Tampa Bay History Center.

Left, 14. Dorcas Bryant arrived in the Tampa Bay area during the mid-1850s from the vicinity of Albany, Georgia. With her came sons Aaron, Berry, Peter, and Samuel. Dorcas's husband, Moses, apparently was compelled to remain behind. Courtesy Canter Brown Jr.

15. A former slave family outside their cabin during the 1870s in Florida. Courtesy Ph
graphic Collection, Florida State Archives

16. Robert Meacham, the mulatto son of Dr. Banks Meacham of Gadsden County, later distinguished himself as a public official and African Methodist Episcopal minister. Courtesy Canter Brown Jr.

17. Stella Meacham, wife of Robert Meacham. Courtesy Canter Brown Jr.

Lake City, Fla. The Arch in The Boneyard.

18. Some slaves in all areas of Florida either received encouragement or otherwise were permitted to tend their own gardens. "Aunt Aggie" Jones of Lake City utilized skills developed in slavery times to maintain a "Boneyard," where she grew vegetables and flowers as late as 1918. Her garden became a tourist attraction of sorts, as suggested by this illustration of Aunt Aggie and "The Arch in the Boneyard." Courtesy Photographic Collection, Florida State Archives.

Tallahassee Sept 17th 1862
Received from Alexander Gallie twenty
three hundred Dollars in full payment
for three slaves (named Langford, Kitty,
and Maria sold him by me and whom
I hereby warrant sound in every respect
$2300 00/100

Hannah S Craig

Tallahassee Sept 17th 1862
Received from Mrs Permilia H Gallie six
hundred Dollars in full payment for
one slave (named Adaline sold Her
by me and whom I hereby warrant sound
in every respect
$600 00/100   Hannah S Craig

19. A slave sales receipt from Tallahassee, dated September 17, 1862. Tallahassee, located in Leon County and founded in the 1820s as Florida's capital city, became the hub for slave-trading activities during the antebellum period. Sometimes sales of enslaved blacks resulted in the breakup of slave families. Courtesy Photographic Collection, Florida State Archives.

20. Abraham (or Abram) Grant, who later served as a bishop of the African Methodist Episcopal Church, lived his childhood as a Columbia County slave. Courtesy Photographic Collection, Florida State Archives.

21. The Reverend James Page became the first black ordained minister of Florida and the first pastor of the Bethel Missionary Baptist Church in Tallahassee. Preaching duties carried him from Thomasville, Georgia, to Key West during the slavery era. Courtesy Photographic Collection, Florida State Archives.

22. Thomas Warren Long escaped from Duval County to fight for freedom during the Civil War, preaching the gospel to fellow soldiers when he could. Afterward, Long joined the African Methodist Episcopal clergy and represented Marion County as a state senator. Courtesy Florida Photographic Collection, Florida State Archives.

23. One of the most common forms of punishment for slaves in Florida was whipping. Here an overseer is attacking a woman with a paddle. Enslaved blacks usually were whipped with a leather strap, although paddles such as the one shown often were used. Courtesy Photographic Collection, Florida State Archives.

24. Material conditions for slaves varied from region to region in Florida and over time. Enslaved blacks on Zephaniah Kingsley's Duval County estate lived in fairly well-constructed one- or two-room tabby houses with brick fireplaces, as shown here in a photograph taken in the 1870s or 1880s. Courtesy Photographic Collection, Florida State Archives.

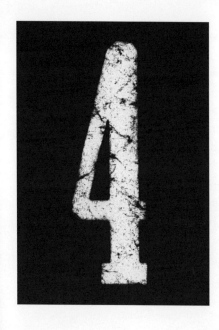

IN EAST
AND WEST
FLORIDA

During the antebellum era Middle Florida offered the picture of a thriving and integral component of the cotton South. In contrast, the larger territory embraced within East and West Florida evolved subject to different traditions and influences. The regions contained different demographic characteristics, depended on economic foundations that varied significantly from the state's more affluent plantation belt, and tended to organize slave labor by use of alternative techniques. Although a substantial majority of Florida's slaves did not live in East and West Florida, it was there—especially in the peninsula—that population grew quickest in the immediate pre–Civil War era and where the future of Florida agriculture would have to be decided. An examination of the slave experience in these districts not only offers a window on the physical condition, or work and responsibilities, of enslaved blacks but also affords a mirror to permit a better understanding of Middle Florida's slave experience.

One note of qualification should be sounded before discussing East and West Florida's distinctive experiences. During the 1820s and 1830s, speculators and planters snapped up most of the prime cotton land available in the Middle Florida region that stretched from the Apalachicola River to the Suwannee River. During the same period, the presence first of armed black and Indian warriors followed by the Second Seminole War of 1835 to 1842 limited the southern reaches of the peninsula's frontier settlement roughly to present-day Alachua County. Subsequently, poorer frontier families, devastated by the war, moved southward toward old Marion, Hernando, and Hillsborough Counties to take advantage of a federal free-land program. Into the vacuum moved more and more cotton planters, some from Middle Florida, others from southern cotton states. Marion County and, to a lesser extent, Hernando County came to be dominated, for example, by South Carolinians in the 1850s. These planters brought with them a culture that varied significantly from that traditionally associated with East Florida. Effectively, they extended the Middle Florida culture by 1860 from Suwannee and Columbia Counties on the north to Marion and Hernando on the south.[1]

Heritage counted for much in East and West Florida during the four decades prior to the Civil War. As discussed in chapter 1, the traditions behind it in good part were Spanish. To recap briefly, two principal settlements, one in East Florida and the other in West Florida, were established by the Spanish during the mid-sixteenth century. St. Augustine in East Florida came first, founded in 1565. During the ensuing two centuries of Spanish rule, race relations in the colony, as Jane Landers has shown, evolved in a form milder and more flexible than they did later in the cotton South.[2]

The Spanish regulated slavery in East Florida by a complex set of codes that largely protected the rights of the unfree persons living in and near St. Augustine. Many enslaved persons could own property and sue in the courts against owners and others. During the first Spanish period, which ended in 1763, enslaved Africans could win or earn their freedom with relative ease, a condition necessitated by the relative ease of escape. With the fortified settlement at Fort Mose shining like a beacon of freedom for most of the period from 1738 to 1763, many blacks—including runaways from the English colonies to the north— found freedom in Florida. Other blacks won their freedom by serving in the militia and protecting St. Augustine against intruders.[3]

Then, for the twenty-year span that commenced in 1763, a far different system prevailed under British rule. As scholars have noted, a three-caste racial system of whites, free blacks, and slaves that had existed prior to 1763 became a two-caste society consisting basically of free whites and black slaves. The new planter colonists held racial attitudes reflective of whites in other established slave colonies to the north. With a gradually increasing enslaved African population in East Florida, British rulers replaced Spanish laws that largely lacked harsh racial dimensions with slave codes that were restrictive and race based.[4]

Through this early period a somewhat different set of circumstances characterized West Florida and its capital of Pensacola. The town, founded first in 1559 but then abandoned in 1561 until 1698, developed its race relations traditions over 130 years later than did St. Augustine. Although the same set of laws that governed race policies in the east applied at Pensacola, the western black population grew much more slowly than in East Florida. Several factors explained the difference. First, from 1693 to 1763 Spain fought battle after battle with the French, English, and Indians over the broad region. With only a small military force to protect settlers, with reinforcements and supplies hard to obtain, with much less desirable land than either East or Middle Florida, West Florida attracted fewer immigrants. Accordingly, few enslaved Africans were compelled to make the area home.[5]

From 1763 to 1783 the Anglo population of West Florida—then a separate colony under British rule—and particularly of Pensacola grew. Yet the area failed to experience the rapid increase in the number of Africans that occurred in East Florida. Still, to the extent that race relations attitudes became a matter of concern, the attitudes of West Florida were copied from the East Florida pattern. Americans with rigid attitudes toward slavery brought their bond servants with them from South Carolina and Georgia. Accordingly, rigid race-related policies gradually crystallized in the region. Even so, the importance of the point easily could be exaggerated given the small numbers of slaves introduced. As historian William Coker has shown, West Florida did not develop economically during the British period because of competition from Mexico in producing staple crops and the lack of available labor.[6]

With the return of the Spanish to control in 1783, the east and the west quickly reverted to prior laws and customs, although the passing years brought a new influx of settlers with Anglo ideas. Especially in East Florida, emigrants from the United States took advantage of policies designed to lure needed new blood and financial support into the colony. In 1790, the year the policies came into force, three hundred whites brought one thousand black slaves into the Spanish territory. Over the next fourteen years, 750 heads of white immigrant families took loyalty oaths. More than five thousand slaves accompanied them to new Florida homes. The new arrivals found themselves greeted by fifty or so other families, revolutionary Tories who had chosen to remain in East Florida after Spain reassumed control.[7]

Interestingly, Spain remained in power in Florida long enough after the arrival of the Americans to change the newcomers' attitudes about race and slavery rather than to be changed by the newcomers. The presence of the Tories, who already had adjusted, was a factor. Beyond that, the Spanish law and its administration deprived advocates of southern ways of the official buttressing needed to maintain a harsher scheme. Finally, just as the Spanish had already discovered, the ease of slave escape in East Florida discouraged maintaining a system that kept slaves disgruntled and resentful. Blacks did not reconstruct Fort Mose during the Second Spanish period, but refuges on the Apalachicola and Manatee Rivers kept its symbolism of freedom alive. Meanwhile, slaves from Georgia and South Carolina proved to slaveholders in Florida the futility of copying old ways from those states. Hundreds of the new nation's bond servants slipped away to the protection of peninsular Indian and black communities.[8]

One important legacy of the Spanish traditions traceable into East Florida after its acquisition by the United States was the organization of slave labor by the task system. As noted, the gang system would be used more commonly in Middle Florida. To some extent owners from coastal areas of South Carolina and Georgia already were accustomed to the practice, but in 1821 its Florida origins lay hundreds of years in the past. "There is a rule on Sea Island plantations [regarding] finishing [of] tasks require[d] each day to be done," explained planter Kingsley B. Gibbs in 1841. "It occurs during the long days of summer," he continued, "that the hands is generally done his task by 2 P.M., often sooner, so they have abundance of time to work their own crop fish, etc."[9]

East Florida's slave experience would involve great diversity and complexity. Yet the task system came to epitomize labor organization in most developed coastal areas, along the St. Marys and St. Johns Rivers, and in other places. It was especially the case where sea island cotton, sugar, indigo, rice, and some other staple crops were grown. Work schedules established for bond persons by Winston Stephens and Zephaniah Kingsley reflected the experiences of the region's many small and large farming operations. Slaves on these farms and plantations generally started work at 5:30 A.M. and completed assignments by 5:00 P.M., if not earlier. In places such as Stephens's small Rose Cottage, where few slaves were kept, routines varied more from day to day and throughout the year than on Kingsley's larger plantation. According to surviving accounts, slaves generally were pleased with the task system. They worked more efficiently and tended to be less troublesome for owners when allowed to complete their assignments well before day's end.[10]

The task system also prevailed in West Florida. The Bagdad Lumber Mill, for example, required slaves to cut a minimum of ten trees per day. The daily task could be accomplished with relative ease because some bondsmen received money for exceeding quotas. Examples of similar situations may be found where enslaved blacks were used as teamsters and loggers by the region's two largest lumber companies. Likewise, slaves who worked in constructing the military installations around the area often approached their jobs by task.[11]

After the United States took control of Florida in 1821, the task system and other Spanish colonial ways persisted in the old inhabited places. Unlike the experience of 1763, when virtually all Spanish Floridians departed the colony, many residents remained behind in 1821. Their numbers included the onetime Americans and their slaves who had accustomed themselves to more relaxed racial attitudes. Having become accustomed to the more lenient system, these individuals and families often prospered. Isaiah Hart, for instance, moved from small-scale farming, cattle grazing, and occasional slave stealing to founding Jacksonville, occupying numerous federal and territorial offices, and developing a two-thousand-acre plantation. On a smaller scale Hart's success was repeated in the experiences of numerous of his fellow holdovers.[12]

Onetime Spanish Florida residents such as Isaiah Hart remained influential in great part because East and West Florida grew so slowly, particularly when compared to Middle Florida, an area that in 1821 was virtually unpopulated. With slow growth the slave population remained small as well. In 1830 the territory had 34,730 residents, 47.1 percent of whom were blacks (mostly slaves). East Florida—comprising Nassau, Duval, St. Johns, Alachua, Mosquito (Orange), and Monroe Counties—contained 4,095 or 26.4 percent of all slaves, many of whom were holdovers. Ten years later the number of slaves had increased modestly, but the region still held only slightly more than 17 percent of the territory's bond servants. By 1860 growth in East Florida had boosted its slave population but only to 20 percent of the state's holdings.

West Florida's story unfolded with an even more discouraging picture of settlement and development. The region never possessed a large percentage of slaves during the antebellum period. Exclusive of Middle Florida–oriented Jackson County, the region consisted of Escambia, Walton, and Washington Counties in 1830. They listed 1,899 or 12.2 percent of all slaves in the territory that year. Census takers in 1840 found that the area's percentage of Florida's slaves had declined radically, to 6 percent. The figure rebounded to only 7 percent by 1860.[13]

Small populations with small numbers of slaves dictated generally small slaveholdings, at least smaller than what was typical of Middle Florida. Only about twenty-five East Florida planters possessed twenty or more slaves and five hundred or more acres of land in 1840. By the Civil War's eve, approximately 87 percent of East Florida masters owned fewer than twenty slaves. Most of the owners claimed only a small slave family or, perhaps, two families. Since the vast majority of East Florida slaves lived on farms and plantations, it becomes clear that the large majority of East Florida slaves resided in rural areas. They worked at some form of agriculture and lived and worked in close proximity to the owner's family although not to large numbers of other slaves.[14]

West Florida's large slaveholdings could be counted on the fingers of two hands. As Brian Rucker has noted, "West Florida was never an

agriculturally oriented region like the 'black belt' of Middle Florida."
Most slaveholders listed themselves in occupations other than farming
and planting in the 1850 and 1860 censuses. Only a few owners involved bond persons in agriculture. The majority of owners held between one and five bondsmen each. In the area Joseph Forsyth, E. E.
Simpson, William A. Jones, Henry Hyer, Henry Ahrens, and George
Willis collectively listed the majority of slaves in 1860. State senator
Jackson Morton of Escambia County emerged as West Florida's single
largest slaveholder prior to the Civil War.[15]

Conditions in East and West Florida generally afforded the typical
slave fewer restraints and somewhat greater control over daily living
conditions than those of Middle Florida. Still, the temperament and
whims of owners could result in agonizing pain or relative ease. Because a larger percentage of area owners were small slaveholders and
worked directly with slaves, the owners' personal attitudes toward
bond servants loomed larger than in Middle Florida.

Owners always could display a meanness of spirit regarding slave
control or evidence downright cruelty in the wink of an eye. Suwannee
County's Douglas Dorsey recalled the potential for arbitrary treatment and violence while recounting an incident that happened to his
mother, Anna. The owner's wife, whom Dorsey described as brutal,
called to Anna while she was working at house chores. When Anna did
not respond because she could not hear the command, the mistress
"seized a large butcher knife and struck at Anna." Attempting to ward
off the blow, Anna received a gash on the arm that took a long time to
heal. Douglas wanted to kill the mistress for the cruel treatment his
mother endured. Squire Jackson grew up on a Duval County plantation and vividly remembered that his mother "picked or hoed cotton,
urged by the thrashing of the overseer's lash." Anna and Sarah Murray
experienced the same kind of treatment, recording that the lash was
used to "keep them in line."[16]

On the other hand, many area bond servants remembered better
experiences. As an aged former Columbia County slave, Mary Minus
Biddle recalled that her "master Lancaster Jamison was a very kind
man and never mistreated his slaves." Mary's mother cooked on the
place, her father "tended" the farm, and she and her brother and sister

performed various chores. Jamison, Mary added, also gave slaves from other estates permission to visit his plantation when there were parties.[17]

The work demanded of slaves depended on the size of the plantation, the type of work performed, and the character of the owner. Because many eastern district farms were modest operations, slaves found themselves required to engage in many types of work, including a variety of miscellaneous chores. George Edwards remembered life on such places. Born in St. Augustine, the onetime slave recalled doing a variety of jobs on Niles Lopez's small farm. The jobs at hand depended mostly on the time of the year. Lopez, Edwards noted, grew a little sugarcane but mainly raised greens, potatoes, corn, and other crops for human and animal consumption. Former slave Uncle Jack worked on the Buckingham Smith farm and also handled a variety of odd jobs for his master. Mary Ann Murray recollected a variety of jobs, as well, especially her mother's duties in the master's garden.[18]

Other small operations, such as Major Starke's Orange County farm and Winston Stephens's place in Putnam County, required bond servants to perform a multiplicity of chores. Sugarcane, cotton, and numerous fruits and vegetables received attention. Starke bragged that his twelve acres of sugarcane, planted in 1846 by his four slaves and subsequently tended by them, yielded an average of twenty-five hundred pounds to the acre. Stephens not only tried his hand at sugarcane but also grew cotton, peas, corn, and potatoes. He raised cattle, as well. Slaves cared for almost everything, although Stephens seemed particularly pleased with the amount of cotton picked by one of his slaves. He noted in 1861 that "Jane is the proudest negroe on the River as she has picked over 30 lbs. of cotton per day."[19]

Whether Jane and other women on the Stephens farm felt as their master is questionable. But, just as was true of their male counterparts, they certainly performed many duties. In addition to whatever else they were ordered to do, at Stephens's Rose Cottage they planted, plowed, hoed, dug ditches, picked cotton, cooked, and took care of children. On one occasion Stephens informed his wife, "Jane and the two small boys have dug about one third of the ditch." He added, "They will have to pick cotton next week but will perhaps get over to work one or more days on the ditch." Later he recorded that "Burrel and Jane are ploughing, began Monday." Mary Biddle's example makes the point that sometimes women worked just like men. "Mary was very active with the plow, she could handle it with the agility of a man," her sister recalled. "This prowess gained her the title of 'plow girl.'"[20]

Sometimes the many burdens placed on slave women overwhelmed them. By 1862, for example, the work at Rose Cottage had become so intolerable that Jane insisted that she would "rather be whipped to death than worked to death." She may have been an exception because East Florida's reputation leaned toward little painful slave punishment. In Winston Stephens's case no available information suggests that he ever whipped his bond servants despite what he saw as their constant grumbling about their tasks. The owner believed that he treated his slaves well and, on at least one occasion, gave one of them permission to carry a gun for hunting purposes.[21]

Despite whatever protests his bond people might mount, Stephens, along with other masters in the area, held nearly absolute power over his bond servants. Like most of his peers he viewed them as inferior beings. Stephens's wife, Octavia, suggested such attitudes in a letter she wrote her husband in 1863. Believing that the South had lost the war, she despaired, "I think if we fight much longer we will come down as low as slaves, and I think we had better give up." At Tampa, New Jersey–born Catharine Hart adopted a patronizing tone. "Negroes are very good to perform hard labor," she informed a relative in 1860, "but they have no management about them." Judge Leslie Thompson reflected the sentiment of many whites and slaveholders when he declared, "The superiority of the white race over the African negro should be ever demonstrated and preserved [and] the degraded caste should be continually reminded of their inferior position."[22]

Small and diversified farming might have been East Florida's norm, but the area contained a number of large plantations. There, as in Middle Florida, sizable crews of bond servants grew large amounts of cotton and sugarcane for planters such as Zephaniah Kingsley. As mentioned above, the number of such establishments grew in the 1850s, as the Middle Florida plantation belt spread eastward and southward to Columbia, Alachua, and Marion Counties. Claude Augusta Wilson, born and raised on a large East Florida plantation, recorded that "about 100 slaves, including children" picked cotton there.

After the fiber "was picked from the fields the seeds were picked out by hand," he explained; "the cotton was then carded for further use" (AS-FN, 358).

Available public records and several slave reminiscences corroborate Wilson's claims about the large size of some East Florida plantations. Sarah Murray lived with her parents, Freeman and Nellie Brown, on a substantial estate owned by a Mr. Signlaw near Ocala. Sarah remembered her mother cooking in the master's house while her father and brother, Prince, worked in the sugarcane fields. Typical of the region, her father and brother carried out other duties including, but not limited to, growing cotton, rice, peas, cabbage, and several kinds of other vegetables. When the cotton was picked or the sugarcane harvested, Prince and his father also lent their hands at their owner's cotton gin and sugar houses.[23]

Cotton and cane production ranked high in importance on many of the large plantations. Even so, some diversity of agriculture remained a constant. According to former slave Adam Sanks, who was born on the Venancio Sanchez plantation near St. Augustine, he and his fellow youngsters helped others with "all kind of house work, including hoeing in each cotton row." Sanks recalled his youth as a time when he worked on the Sanchez plantation doing odd jobs.[24] Stephen Harvell, who was raised in the Hillsborough County area, said that just about everybody in the region "raised a heap of [sugar]cane and boiled it in vats and kettles at different places."[25] John H. McIntosh, who owned two plantations, put his 180 bond servants to work cultivating cotton and sugarcane during the 1850s, and A. B. Nance grew the same crops on his thousand-acre plantation worked by over one hundred slaves.[26]

Newspaper slave advertisements reflected important points concerning such agricultural endeavors. The ads not only recognized the importance to the peninsular economy of farms and plantations that grew both cotton and cane; they also expressed the difficulty of obtaining slaves skilled at working both crops, as well as the many other chores demanded on East Florida operations. Sellers routinely searched for such bond servants, so routinely, in fact, that supply appears never to have met demand. Fortunate were sellers such as the man who advertised in the St. Augustine Florida Herald in 1834 that he held "30 Negroes accustomed to the culture of Sugar and Cotton." Far more common was a claim such as John Platt's administrator made in Hernando County in 1856: he simply placed before the public "two likely young men, one girl, and two children."[27]

Still, cotton and cane never predominated in East Florida as cotton did in Middle Florida. Other crops offered the potential for cash-crop status. Indigo, for instance, emerged as a crop of choice for many farmers and planters in Duval, St. Johns, and Putnam Counties. Its production in Florida dated back to the British period and continued through the antebellum era. The skills of Africans and their descendants had proved crucial to the crop's successful cultivation. As one historian has noted, "Black slaves had become the laborers of choice in the . . . indigo fields of British America." On Winston Stephens's farm Burrel and other slaves cultivated the crop. Slaveholders such as John H. McIntosh, A. B. Nance, and others directed their bond servants to plant and tend hundreds if not thousands of additional acres.[28]

Usually, slaves on indigo plantations worked by the task method but not always when cotton and cane production was involved. Douglas Dorsey recollected working subject to an organizational plan closer to the gang system on a Suwannee County plantation, where "cotton, corn, cane, and peas . . . was [sic] raised in abundance." He mentioned, for instance, that slaves would "leave for the fields at 'sun up' and remain until 'sun-down.'" Claude A. Wilson echoed Dorsey's experience by recalling conditions on the plantation where he once lived and worked. He asserted that early every morning the bond persons were awakened by "a 'driver' who was a white man, and by 'sun-up' would be . . . in the fields." Wilson added: "All day they work[ed], stopping at noon to get a bit to eat, which they carried on the fields from their cabins. At 'sun-down' they would quit work and return to their cabins."[29]

The large East Florida sugar and cotton plantations paralleled their Middle Florida counterparts by relying on some highly skilled slaves who labored mostly at jobs other than fieldwork. Slaveholders who owned substantial numbers of bond servants needed and easily justified keeping individuals specially trained as carpenters, brick masons, coopers, cobblers, tanners, blacksmiths, and mechanics. A. B. Nance's blacksmith, two coopers, carpenter, and brick mason numbered among his ninety slaves. Francis Richard's will mentioned a carpenter valued in 1837 at the substantial amount of $1000. The slaves of Duval County's Isaiah D. Hart included a brick mason, a cobbler, and additional slaves who spent time building chimneys. Although the percentage of skilled workers among slaves in East Florida is difficult to determine, it may reasonably be said that owners with over fifteen slaves usually kept one or two skilled bond servants.[30]

Also reflecting a similarity to the Middle Florida experience, a few East Florida slaves at times exercised responsibility for managing farms and plantations. Given East Florida's somewhat more tolerant atmosphere, they did so more openly than was the case in the state's plantation belt. Anna Kingsley, for example, managed Zephaniah Kingsley's Laurel Grove plantation on numerous occasions. Abraham Hannahan Kingsley, according to historian Daniel Schafer, "was the general manager of all [of Zephaniah's] planting activities," and an "African named Peter was in charge at Springfield." Winston Stephens's slave Burrel cared for his master's farm during the early 1860s while Stephens commanded a Confederate regiment. Winston's wife, Octavia, notified her husband on one occasion, "Burrel burned off the new ground a week ago after rolling my logs, he is now hauling rails himself and put Tom to cutting logs with the others until he gets some rails hauled[;] then they are to 'follow behind him with the fence.'" She continued: "He says he thinks he will be ready to start ploughs in three weeks." Stephens made no attempt to mask his dependence on Burrel in writing back to his wife. "Tell Burrel to continue his duty as a good servant and make a good crop," he declared, "and I will make him a nice present at the end of the year."[31]

Opportunities for black drivers accompanied those for managers and, as in Burrel's case, sometimes overlapped. Douglas Dorsey of Suwannee County remembered a driver named January on the plantation where he was held. January's duties "were to get the slaves together in the morning and see that they went to the fields and [he also] assigned them to their tasks." Dorsey's account added: "He worked as the other slaves, though, he had more privileges. He would stop work at any time he pleased and go around to inspect the work of the others, and thus rest himself. Most of the orders from the master were issued to him." On Buckingham Smith's St. Johns County farm, Uncle Jack led his fellow bond servants, becoming a trusted servant of his master.[32]

The labor of many older children on farms large and small recalled the duties required of adults, but younger children toiled as well. Generally, the young people took care of a variety of chores until they reached the age of twelve, when they began to work in the fields or to be trained for a specific skilled job. Few, if any, sources recount the lives and daily work routines of specific children in West Florida, but a number of former slaves who lived in the state's northeastern corner and further down the peninsula recorded their experiences as youths. As a lad Squire Jackson assisted his mother with the picking and handling of cotton on the small Duval County farm where they lived. Between the ages of ten and thirteen, Douglas Dorsey built fires and helped with the meals and other chores on his master's Suwannee County plantation.[33]

The girls worked as well as the boys. When Sarah Brown Bryant was brought as a child from South Carolina to Hillsborough County in 1856 at about the age of nine, she first milked cows and churned butter. Shortly after, she worked at the Tampa Hotel before serving as nurse for children in the Charles Brown family. During the Civil War Sarah carried water and tended a saltworks on the Alafia River. Born and raised on a small farm in Columbia County, the young Mary Biddle was given the responsibility, along with her brother and sister, of washing the dishes after every meal.[34]

Much more so than in Middle Florida, East Florida slaves might work in places other than on a farm or plantation. A number of bondsmen perfected skills in the cattle business, especially in Alachua, Hillsborough, Manatee, and Polk Counties. The role of Florida's black cowhunters has received far less attention than has that of their peers in Texas. How many slaves worked as cowhunters remains hard to determine with any accuracy, although the nature of their lives is somewhat clearer. Stephen Harvell's experience permits a glimpse at their work. Born on February 2, 1840, in Alachua County, he was taken at age sixteen to eastern Hillsborough County by his owner James Lanier. Harvell reminisced late in life that he "used to be in the woods horseback two or three weeks at a time for [Lanier] raised stock." He continued: "I kept his stock mostly. All over the country there was cattle. Lanier had 500 or 600 [head of cattle] in the woods." The cowhunters drove many cattle from south Florida to Georgia during the antebellum period. Harvell remembered helping to round up and keep the cattle out of "the woods until the men bought them and shipped them to Savannah."[35]

Other blacks followed a similar path. Tom Moore and Prince A. Johnson, to name two, worked as slave cowhunters in the same region as did Harvell. Joseph and Richmond Crews, slaves of cattleman Dempsey Crews of today's Hardee County, tended their masters' beeves. Among others, cattlemen Stephen Hollingsworth; George and James Hamilton; Francis A. Hendry; John I. Hooker; Louis, James, and John Lanier; Streaty Parker; and Levi Pearce also owned slaves who likely tended their herds in the "pineywoods" and "prairies" of southwest Florida.[36]

For a minority of East and West Florida slaves, towns such as Fernandina, Jacksonville, St. Augustine, Tampa, and Apalachicola afforded conditions of work and life that were better than those commonly endured by farm or plantation workers. "The urban environment moderated slavery's harshness and provided opportunities to broaden the sterile world of the bondsman," according to St. Augustine historian Thomas Graham. "In town there were even free Negroes with whom the slaves could associate," he explained, adding, "The labor of the slaves was seldom arduous." The use of a task system in Jacksonville and other places allowed bond servants a degree of freedom on completion of their daily tasks. "Slavery here is a very mild form," future Union general and Freedmen's Bureau head Oliver O. Howard commented from Tampa in 1857. "You wouldn't know the negroes were slaves unless you were told." Howard noted further, "White men work with the negroes particularly at any trade." At Apalachicola, according to historian William W. Rogers, "Blacks were fairly unrestricted, some living apart from their masters in rented houses."[37]

The trades and vocations of slaves in the East Florida towns varied greatly. At St. Augustine "they were often employed as general handymen, common workers, fishermen, farmers, draymen, and semi-skilled laborers," according to Graham. "Women worked as cooks, housekeepers, and domestic servants," he added, noting that "some trusted, responsible slaves managed stores, oversaw farms, or cared for their masters' homes." To permit slaves to help manage stores and other businesses, some masters taught them to read and write and the basics of mathematics. James McKay apparently did so for Isaac Howard at Tampa in the late 1840s and 1850s, and Stepney Dixon likely used the same skills to assist the Blount family with their Bartow store.[38]

Although Florida's towns were small, slaves nonetheless formed a large and important segment of their population. In 1850 Jacksonville boasted 1,045 residents, 440 of whom were slaves (plus 73 free blacks). At Ocala 59 slaves joined 184 whites, and at St. Augustine about one-third of the locals were bond servants. Ten years later slaves made up 35 percent of the total at St. Augustine, 39 percent at Fernandina, 42 percent at Jacksonville, 49 percent at Lake City, and 52 percent at Palatka. Given all the services performed by slaves in the town-building process, it is little wonder that in the post–Civil War years skilled ex-slaves serving as artisans, contractors, builders, and public officials helped to propel Florida toward becoming the South's most urban state.[39]

The circumstances at Pensacola and Key West deserve special mention. By 1850 Pensacola led all of Florida's towns in population with a total of 2,164. Slaves made up 34 percent of the inhabitants. Ten years later Key West vied with Pensacola for the honor. The former contained 2,832 persons. Of them 435 were slaves, and 156 were free blacks. Pensacola had 2,876 people, with 957 (33 percent) listed as slaves and 130 (5 percent) as free blacks. Surviving accounts suggest that the racial climate in both the cosmopolitan port towns tended toward unusual toleration. Federal Writers' Project field-worker Martin Richardson attributed conditions still prevailing at Pensacola in 1936 to "a thoughtful and considerate amity between races" and "a fortunate absence of the bitter exploitation of slave by master so commonly found in regions purely agricultural during the early days of Florida." A correspondent summed up the situation at Key West in 1853: "The negroes, in a very large proportion, [seemingly] outnumber the whites, and are possessed of such freedom as renders their living in juxta position a matter of almost impossibility."[40]

The relative benefits of town over rural life for slaves reversed dramatically when plague beset the communities, posing immediate, life-threatening challenges. Diseases such as measles or the dreaded yellow fever struck coastal ports repeatedly in the territorial and early statehood years. At least 150 civilians (whites and blacks), many of them probably slaves, perished from the fever at St. Augustine in 1821. "This vile Black vomit" was no respecter of skin color. New to semi-tropical perils, the territorial secretary informed national officials that "the sickness rages beyond any thing I ever saw or heard of." As late as 1857 Jacksonville lost 127 persons to the "yellow jack." In 1858 dozens more followed at Tampa. Illustrating the terror that beset stricken towns, a resident reported, "Our city is about depopulated, and presents more the appearance of a church yard than a thriving business place." Another Tampan claimed that "the mortality is greatest with the children and fearfully preponderates with the white over the black." Yet a Key West correspondent had insisted during an outbreak the previous year that "the negroes have all been attacked." As late as 1864 slaves at Key West faced death from the fever. "As if a panic had seized the residents . . .," commented one onlooker, "everyone who can get out of it is striving to do so." Unfortunately, others made that decision for those held in bondage.[41]

Hiring out or renting slaves constituted a practice even more common in East and West Florida than in Middle Florida. Although available evidence does not permit determination of exact numbers or percentages, the vast majority of East Florida slaveholders rented out some or all of their slaves at one time or another. Given the relative complexity of the area's economic underpinnings, the arrangement suited the needs of many businessmen far better than investing large capital sums in purchases. It suited, as well, the moral objections that some East Floridians held privately against the purchase of other human beings. Maria Louisa Daegenhardt of Tampa remembered, "My father did not believe in slavery, but always kept a negro hired by the year."[42]

The situation at Jacksonville provides insight on the extent of hiring out policies. There, 8 percent of the region's slaves lived and worked. Probate records, estate sales records, advertisements, and runaway notices suggest that many, if not most, of them commonly worked under hire. In doing so they labored as carpenters, longshoremen, and mechanics; they also staffed timber mills and cotton warehouses. With several railroad construction projects underway in the mid-to-late 1850s, the town served as a center for worker recruitment. This opportunity offered lucrative possibilities for owners, appealing especially to guardians and administrators of estates under probate. Typically, the *Jacksonville News* called for one hundred to two hundred blacks to work on the Florida railroad in 1855. Four years later the *Jacksonville Standard* ran notices for thirty blacks. The *Florida Republican* advertised the rates of railroad hire. Slaves commanded $.75 a day and board or else $1 without board. Skilled workers could reap for their owners amounts that ranged up to $2 per day.[43]

Just how tolerable labor by hire proved to be naturally varied with employers and types of job. Sometimes the practice applied during only a part of each day. This could occur because the prevalent task system permitted slaves time off after completion of assigned chores and allowed them thereafter to earn money using the skills that they had acquired, thus making hiring out quite attractive for some bond servants. Other times, owners simply permitted slaves to take care of their own time, so long as steady income resulted. As late as 1862 a visitor at Key West surprised himself by discovering that masters permitted bond servants to "hire their own time and make what they could, paying to [their] master[s] a portion of their earnings."[44]

Allowing for the often brutal work associated with railroad construction, turpentine distilling, and sawmilling, most laborers at least accepted hiring out because the practice proved so enduringly popular. When coupled with the looser reins typical for East and West Florida, some slaves found the dynamics of hiring out—particularly in towns— enhanced the possibilities for freer lives. Circumstances often left bondsmen without immediate supervision or control. At Apalachicola, according to one historian, "they hired themselves out, paid their masters money, but otherwise were uncircumscribed in their conduct." Another described conditions at St. Augustine: "Many lived in their own homes, away from their master's residence, almost as if they were free men."[45]

Southerners with more traditional perspectives feared the loose bonds that East and West Florida permitted for these slaves and cried out for action by authorities. St. Augustine's George R. Fairbanks, who later wrote one of the state's best early histories, pleaded with his town council to enforce "severe policing." One Key West resident grew so alarmed that he forecast, "The day does not beam far distant in the horizon when the African sceptre will sway supreme." In 1842 the St.

Johns County grand jury weighed in on the issue, bewailing "the almost universal usage among Slave owners in making the slaves in substance *free dealers* by allowing them to go forth and hire themselves by the day or otherwise to who ever may incline to employ them." Its presentment continued: "[This practice] is of necessity followed by a relaxation of discipline and in them a forgetfulness of duty, gives them the possession of money and affords them the means of debauchery and cannot but lead to the ultimate ruin of the slave." Jacksonville attempted to regulate the practice by requiring bond persons to acquire work badges before they could be employed or else to pay fees, but this and other measures achieved little success.[46]

Although many individuals benefited from hiring-out policies, the record reveals numerous exceptions. Tim apparently had piloted boats on the St. Johns River for about fifteen years before he escaped in 1860. Jupiter took leave, as well, absconding from Henry D. Holland's Duval County turpentine distillery in 1851. At the thirty-five sawmills along the St. Johns River, conditions often rated poor. A. W. Walker's Bakers Island establishment numbered among them, as illustrated by the 1840 flight of Abraham Brown, George Isaac, and William Isaac.[47]

Corporal punishment could figure prominently in a slave's resentment of hiring out. The Winston Stephens plantation Rose Cottage witnessed an example. Two young boys, Tom and Mose, were hired out to a Mr. Vann. According to Mose as expressed by Octavia Stephens, Vann whipped the slave "for nothing." In doing so Vann told Mose that "he had hired them cheap but they should work double to pay him, and he was going to take the bark off their back etc and so on" if they did not work to his satisfaction. Vann's conduct stemmed, it seems, from second thoughts about hiring the boys, whom he called "Guinea niggers." Reportedly, he preferred "Carolina niggers," who, he believed, worked harder.[48]

The West Florida experience with hiring out deserves a few more comments. The majority of slaves there were hired out a good part of the time. As Brian Rucker correctly noted, "West Florida's slaves were not agricultural workers toiling on cotton, rice, sugar, or tobacco plantations." Accordingly, owners often had no personal use for their bond servants. "Slave owners did not want their slaves back," Earnest Dibble explained, because "they had no other use for them than to rent them." Lessees especially included the military facilities at and near Pensacola, lumber companies, and textile mills.[49]

Because agriculture figured only to a minor extent in West Florida, the hiring-out experience of slaves there often involved heavy construction or industrial work that required special training and skills. Obviously, textiles, lumbering, brick making, and labor on federal construction projects figured prominently. That such skilled work could be expected from blacks flew in the face of the racist perceptions of some residents. One newspaper lambasted desires of entrepreneurs to make West Florida the state's industrial center because the inferiority of black slave laborers would not permit success. The passage of time proved the argument incorrect.[50]

The conditions to which these industrial workers were subjected remains uncertain. Several accounts suggest that both men and women were whipped for work-related and other infractions. On the other hand, a contemporary observer described the young black women working at the Arcadia textile mill as "well clad, well fed, moderately worked, and in every way humanely treated, they are very happy and contented." If so, quite a few individuals were affected. The number of black women working at the plant increased from forty during the 1840s to more than one hundred by the 1850s. Whether the account accurately assesses conditions can be questioned, though, and no slave testimonies are available for West Florida.[51]

Whenever and under whatever arrangements slaves worked in East and West Florida, they nonetheless eagerly awaited time off. Some bond persons apparently even insisted on contract stipulations guaranteeing certain free days. As a general matter most slaves received Saturday afternoons and Sundays as free time to spend with family members, worship, hunt, fish, work in their gardens, or hire out their time. Winston Stephens typified farmers who followed this practice, although the demands of the farm sometimes justified exceptions in his mind. Claude A. Wilson, however, recalled Sunday as "the only day of the week in which they were not forced to work." Squire Jackson may have enjoyed Saturday afternoons off, but he recollected Sundays when "the boys on the plantation would play home ball and shoot marbles until church time." He added, "After church a hearty meal consisting of rice and salt picked [pickeled] pork was the usual Sunday fare cooked in large iron pots."[52]

As in Middle Florida, certain holidays also offered slaves times when they could expect not to work. According to Kingsley Gibbs, slaves usually received a day off for the Fourth of July, two days for Thanksgiving, and four days (sometimes more) for Christmas. During at least one Christmas in the 1840s, his overseer gave bond servants on the plantation extra rations and four days off during the Christmas holidays. "[I] got the Beef for the people on yesterday, and gave out double allowances of corn and salt also," he recorded on one occasion, "so that the Negroes could feed their holliday visitors—of course, no work for anybody."[53]

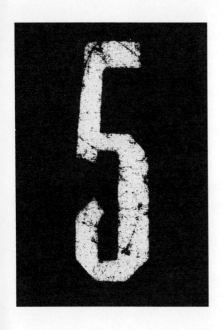

THE FAMILY

From 1821 to 1865 most Florida slaveholders made sure "their people" never forgot the fact of their bondage, yet those whom they enslaved sought to cushion the harsh edges of their captivity by striving to create and maintain families.[1] Bond servants in large numbers believed in their marriages, endeavored to have them solemnized, and committed themselves to their unions. Because slave owners and public officials declined to compile records that recognized these slave unions, incorrect perceptions of slave attitudes toward marriage and family life have persisted. Zephaniah Kingsley, a large northeast Florida planter, understood, though. He saw that his slaves had a "strong attachment to their homes, to their wives and children, and to domestic life." Fortunately, runaway slave notices, estate appraisers' accounts, probate records, reminiscences, sale notices, and plantation diaries and journals help illustrate the strength of kinship ties. In some cases they reflect slave unions that produced stable families over as many as four generations.[2]

One stumbling block that inhibits our understanding of slave family life is our inability to agree on a standard concept or definition of just what constituted a slave family in nineteenth-century Florida. Surviving records list many women with children and without husbands, even though most or all had husbands who lived on other farms or plantations. Records portray some slave couples as husband and wife, denoting the master's acceptance of a marriage, but identify other women as single who had been married but then lost a spouse. To bridge this crevasse of understanding, some historians have argued for the use of "coresidential" or "coresidential consensual" union among slaves instead of using the phrase "married couple."[3]

The status of a slave marriage can be considered in several different ways. In one sense it existed extralegally, statutory law having failed to sanction slave unions. Authority rested solely with the owner. He or she possessed the technical right to break up a marriage for a variety of reasons or on whim. Slaves, to the contrary, believed in their own hearts and minds that they were married, especially when some event such as jumping over a broom signified the solemnization of a union. In at least one case two slaveholders even permitted their slaves to be "legally" married. No record mentions whether the ceremony ever came under challenge, but in St. Johns County, where ameliorated race relations dated back to the Spanish era, owner Catherine Solana allowed John Solana, a house servant, to wed Harriet Alvarez, a slave belonging to Geronimo Alvarez. The ceremony occurred on June 15, 1839, and was presided over by Father Cladius Rampon.[4] This case is atypical, but it points to the seriousness with which slaves regarded nuptials. As will be seen, such serious commitment could serve in practice to restrict an owner's prerogatives in the interest of saving a family.

Coresidential consensual unions and nonconsensual unions existed in Florida. Certainly, some social arrangements between enslaved Africans were not of their own choosing. Masters with an interest in increasing their "stock" forced slaves to live together, regarding females simply as breeders. Charlotte Martin recalled how her master profited when he selected the "strongest and best male and female slaves and mated them exclusively for breeding." She commented, "The huskiest babies were given the best of attention in order that they might grow into sturdy youths, for it was those who brought the highest prices at the slave markets."[5] Some women, according to Douglas Parish, "fared better than the majority of female slaves." He remembered that his mother, Fannie, lived with his father, Charles, and that she was regarded as a "breeder" who only had to bear and care for children on the plantation.[6]

Masters' motivations for encouraging or compelling slave unions involved numerous elements, but the most compelling reason was that owners benefited financially when children were born to their bond servants. George Noble Jones, by way of illustration, quickly shared news of his good fortune when his gang of 120 slaves showed a natural increase of "over ten percent" in one year, with fourteen births, three deaths, and no miscarriages. Many planters concerned themselves regularly about such "natural increase." Owners thus perceived the slave family, in good part, as a means of increasing and perpetuating their properties.[7]

For slaves, though, a totally different meaning of family prevailed. That meaning emerges from a careful examination of the various structures of the slave family, such as the nuclear, the single or simple, and the extended family. The slave's efforts to create, establish, and overcome obstacles in maintaining a viable family life are evident and important. When assessing slave accomplishments, one must remember that factors beyond slaves' control always imperiled family life. Living in the world that the slaveholder controlled, bond servants could not always succeed in their efforts to live as husband and wife or to raise their children according to their own standards. Yet against great odds slaves succeeded to an impressive degree in forging, beyond the master's view, a family life for themselves and their kinfolk.

The start of the process in Florida did not bode well for family life, particularly for newly relocated slaves. The 1820s and 1830s brought thousands of them to the territory, but many arrived as the product of broken unions or families. David, a slave of William and Elizabeth Wirt, knew the pain involved in such a family split. After making the long journey to Florida in 1828, he informed plantation manager Thomas Randall that he was not pleased with being separated from his wife and children in Maryland. The bondsman asked to be sold if he could not be reunited with his wife. Randall, fearing that David "would infect the whole body of the black community with his despondence," agreed to act. Within an eleven-month period, David's wife and several of their younger children had joined him. They were purchased by the overseer. Randall recognized the powerful emotions at play. "I regret I was not at home to witness the reunion of David and his wife," he informed owner Wirt, then the attorney general of the United States. Such unfortunate separations of husbands and wives, children, and other kinfolk frequently happened during the early territorial years of the 1820s and 1830s. That was the period when planters from the more established slave states moved long distances in search of fertile land for the production of staple crops.[8]

These disruptions tended to reinforce, rather than frustrate, slave desires to organize and maintain themselves in family units. The demographics of the time and place helped. Parity existed, for instance, between male and female slaves in Middle Florida during the early 1830s. Males (those age ten to fifty-five) constituted 52.4 percent of the region's slave population, whereas females totalled 47.6 percent. A decade later the male-female ratio balanced more evenly, with males adding up to 50.7 percent and females to 49.3. Of 103 sets of examined will and estate slaves records dated from 1821 to 1830, only fifty-six listed slaves. Excluding seven owners with one slave, only eight, or 16 percent, of forty-nine listed bond servants in family units consisting of couples, couples with children, or single mothers. This statistic suggests the disruptions of family life in those early years.[9]

Census data and other listings from will and estate sales records shed further light on the demographic potential for slave unions and the actual results. During the 1850s and 1860s, the male-female ratio (those age ten to sixty) remained constant in Middle Florida, with each gender approximating 50 percent. Thus, Middle Florida differed from some Caribbean colonies because its ratio of enslaved male and female Africans in Middle Florida remained rather balanced.[10]

As slavery grew in Middle Florida from 1830 to 1860, the number of slave family units generally increased. Of 301 surveyed will and estate records for this period, only 179 slaveholders listed two or more slaves. Of that number only 52 (29 percent) listed or recognized slaves either as husbands and wives, as parents with children, or as single or simple families.[11] Even that increase over the thirty-year period may understate the case. As slavery became a more permanent institution in the region, slave families gained a degree of stability. "[Bond persons] often found partners from neighboring farms or plantations," Peter Parish has noted, "and this often restricted married life to weekend conjugal visits."[12] Thus, it is probable that a larger percentage of slaves found mates or had families than the record suggests, since many had kinship ties on other farms and plantations in the region.[13]

Much like Middle Florida, East Florida—particularly Duval, St. Johns, Alachua, and Nassau Counties—witnessed a uniform ratio of males and females between the ages of ten and fifty-five, with males and females totaling 51 percent and 49 percent, respectively, in 1830. A decade later the male-female ratio in the same age categories remained largely constant. Of the twenty-five probate records surveyed, only five slaveholders listed slaves in their wills from 1821 to 1830. Two listed their slaves in family units of husband, wife, and children.[14] Males (51 percent) and females (49 percent) between the ages of ten and sixty remained generally even during the 1840s through 1860. The result was an equitable distribution of male and female slaves. Of 201 available wills, ninety-one slaveholders listed their slaves. Excluding the slave owners who had only one bond servant, forty-three out of eighty-one, or 53 percent, listed their bond people in either two-parent, two-parent-with-children, or matrifocal family units from 1831 to 1865. Generally, the effort of many East Florida slaveholders to maintain the two-parent or single-parent family unit affected the nature of race relations in the region. Although East Florida held only 26 percent of all Florida slaves in 1830, and between 10 and 13 percent from 1840 to 1860, slave family units consisting of two parents or single mothers remained the highest of the three regions.[15]

In West Florida males outnumbered females between the ages of ten and fifty-five by a factor of 61 to 39 percent in 1830. The percentage of females increased to 46 percent a decade later before dropping to around 41 percent during the 1850s. Of the available twenty-four wills, inventories, appraisements, and estate sales from 1821 to 1830, fifteen slaveholders listed slaves. Of that number, six (40 percent) of the slaveholders recognized slaves in family groups, most single mothers with children. From 1831 to 1865, 36 out of 111 probate records, inventories, appraisements, and estate sales listed or mentioned slaves. Of the thirty-six, twelve (33.3 percent) listed bond servants in either two-parent, two-parent-with-children, or matrifocal family units. Although the actual numbers increased, the percent of bond servants listed in some type of family unit, as reflected in the data, declined slightly during the thirty years prior to the Civil War.[16] As was true in Middle and East Florida, though, bond servants either had marriages abroad or had extended kinship ties into surrounding plantations and even counties.

During the first decade that followed Florida's 1821 acquisition by the United States, less than 25 percent of all slaves in the available 146 surveyed will and estate records were grouped in either two-parent, single-mother, or extended-family units. For 1831 to 1860 the figure jumped to about one-half of all slaves inventoried from 532 such documents. Still, single-parent and extended households, along with solitaires, continued to be the norm in Florida up to the Civil War, with two-parent households seen less often.

Kinship connections expanded in Middle and East Florida from 1840 to 1860, according to the available inventories. Of the slaves in the two regions, 60 percent held clear kinship connections by 1860. A higher percentage of slaves were listed in single-family groups in West Florida. Kinship connections beyond two generations proved much more difficult to trace there, especially in the 1850s. Despite a migration of some East Florida planters to new homes in the central and southern peninsula during the 1850s and early 1860s, the records in East Florida still grouped most slaves in family units.[17]

Family life became less tenuous in Middle Florida during the period 1840 to 1860, when the plantation economy had begun to mature. The creation of two-parent, single-parent, and extended-family households became a reality for more slaves because of demographic changes that took place during the 1850s and early 1860s. The slave population in the basic five-county region (Jackson, Gadsden, Leon, Jefferson, and Madison Counties) increased to 60 percent in 1850 and remained at that level ten years later.[18] With larger plantations, slaves had better opportunities of finding mates and maintaining kinship ties.[19]

Slaves had more of an opportunity to create and maintain familial relationships on large plantations than on smaller estates. Still, slaves on smaller plantations and farms were not entirely blocked. Records of smaller estates (those with fewer than twenty slaves) listed more slaves as single parents. This resulted from a lack of available partners on the smaller units. The situation likely caused many bondsmen to seek "abroad wives" on other farms and plantations, thereby restricting married life to weekend conjugal visits. Whether farming operations were on small or large units, surveyed records showed the majority of East Florida slaves in family groups of two parents with children or a mother with offspring.[20]

Slaveholders appreciated the fact that gender imbalance on plantations might create behavioral problems. The result could be slaves not working or else absconding. Young males outnumbered females on the El Destino plantation in Leon County, for instance. The bondsmen made it known that they disapproved of one overseer's involvement with a slave woman, which further exacerbated the imbalance. The slaves made their point by a work slowdown that rendered them unproductive enough to cause a second overseer, John Evans, to seek the first man's dismissal. Evans informed the owner that if his workers saw the first overseer's "negroes around them Ideling, why they want to doe so two."[21] The Bradford plantation in Leon County also suffered from a lack of marriageable women. When Jordan, the carriage driver, lost his wife, "the master arranged to buy a mixed Indian/Black woman." The purchase reportedly delighted Jordan.[22] East Florida's Zephaniah Kingsley reflected concerns of his neighbors by attempting to balance his holdings so that slaves could live in their own "cabins as married couples."[23]

Thus, although bondsmen and -women may have lacked control over their own lives from 1821 to 1865, they sought to establish familial relationships against severe odds. Some slaveholders, weighing control issues against potential asset accretion, even acted to hinder the development of black family life. They did so often by refusing permission for cross-plantation marriages. Amon DeLaughter, overseer on his mother's Madison County plantation, did not allow slaves to marry off the plantation or to enjoy any slave visitations. Whether he successfully stopped marriages off the plantation is uncertain. It is known that several of his neighbor's bondsmen would visit the DeLaughter lands without permission from their owners. Douglas Dorsey recalled bond servants suffering from restrictions on the Suwannee County plantation where he lived. Dorsey's master could not fully command the deference of his bond servants, although many were "lashed on the bare back" for venturing off the plantation grounds.[24]

More masters may have succumbed to the divided-residence idea

than opposed it, and those who did knew that the arrangement pro-
moted peace and order in the slave quarters and that it served to restrain violence and escape. John Evans, the overseer at Chemonie
plantation, at first refused to allow slaves such marriages or visits off
the plantation. After experiencing problems with the workforce because of the rule, he relented, at least to a degree. In 1851 he allowed
Peggy to marry Ansler. The groom lived on the El Destino plantation,
also owned by George Noble Jones. The following year the overseer
authorized James and Martha, as well as Lafayette and Lear, to marry
between the two plantations. Tom, a slave hireling in Tallahassee, had
been married to Delia at Chemonie for over twenty years. They had
two children. Eventually, so many bond servants from El Destino married slaves at Chemonie that the owner, in order to keep track, requested a list of "all the names of Negroes on Chemonie in Famleys."[25]

Other planters compromised with their bond persons over marriage
off the plantation, although again with limitations. John and Robert
Gamble, Thomas Randall, and William Wirt owned plantations in Jefferson and Leon Counties and were interrelated by blood or marriage.
They allowed their slaves to marry spouses from any one of their plantations. Oftentimes, members of the planter families would take careful note of any such unions, writing back to relatives in Virginia and
Maryland about them. Laura Wirt Randall illustrated that interest
when she informed relations that several of the slave women at Wirtland were engaged to bondsmen owned by her uncle John Gamble.
Randall had given each of the women dresses to wear when they married.[26]

Even in the more tolerant East Florida climate, slave families existed only with the master's approval, and marriage required permission. St. Augustine authorities at times required slaves to obtain express leave even to visit their spouses. In 1858 Daniel not only sought
permission from his wife's master but also from the city of St. Augustine to sleep with his wife at her owner's house. Adam Sanks remembered that his parents, Eve and Isaac, needed permission to marry, as
well as to visit each other on separate plantations.[27]

Sometimes slaveholders used divided-residence marriages to control or discipline bond servants. D. N. Moxley, an overseer at El Destino, wanted George N. Jones to forbid Tom, who lived in Tallahassee,

from visiting his wife Delia because of the husband's intransigence toward the overseer. The owner agreed, temporarily suspending the slave's visitation rights. The divided residence of Sarah, owned by Winston Stephens, and her husband Jacob, held by John Hopkins, did not seem to cause either owner any problems. On the other hand, the parents had an older child who was owned by another planter, and that allowed Stephens leverage with them. He hired the child and permitted her to stay with Sarah on an annual basis. In doing so he eased tensions on three plantations and created a hedge against future problems.[28]

Family life for Middle Florida slaves improved greatly on the larger units as bond servants established extended kinship ties. In Leon, Gadsden, and Madison Counties, for example, the presence of grandparents came to be a fact of life. Such family continuity is illustrated by surviving wills and estate sales records.[29] In 1856 Madison County's Jeremiah Reid listed forty- seven-year-old matriarch Violet, her seven children, and her sixteen grandchildren as a part of his estate. Violet had become pregnant at age thirteen, giving birth to her first daughter Amy at fourteen. Fortune, the slave driver on Bryan Croom's Goodwood plantation in Leon County, and his wife enjoyed a "stable marriage," which lasted over thirty years, from the 1840s until well after the Civil War. The couple gave life to six children and lived to see at least two grandchildren.[30]

As Violet's story suggests, slave women often gave birth to their first children at young ages, a phenomenon not all that unusual for contemporary poor white or black women. The contents of thirty relevant Middle Florida wills help to illustrate the point. Of women listed in family units with their ages and the ages of their children specified, 70 percent had their first child between the ages of fifteen and sixteen. Presumably, marriages had come at an even earlier age, at least in many cases.[31]

The fact that so many slaves belonged to two-, three-, and even four-generational families declares with a voice heard clearly over the distance of time their deeply held desire for family continuity. In Middle Florida, three-generational families could be found with ease. Acie Thomas treasured memories of her parents, Thomas and Mary, as well as of her grandparents, who once lived on Jefferson County's Folsom plantation. Margrett Nickerson recounted tales of her parents, Edmund and Rachel Jackson, her stepfather, her grandmother Phoebie Austin, and her uncles Robert and Joe. Willis Williams well remembered his grandmother Rachel Fitzgiles, not to mention his parents, Wilhemina and William. George fled his owner's Jefferson County plantation but not without his three-generational family. It included his wife, Lettus; their children Liz, Beny, Adam, and Susan; and Susan's one-year-old son.[32]

Little evidence survives to help describe the slave family in West Florida, but available sources clearly portray two-, three-, and four-generational families in northeast Florida. Frank Berry, too young when a slave to remember the experience, still distinctly recalled his kinship ties on a St. Augustine plantation. His grandmother, mother, stepfather, and siblings, plus the children he and his wife had after the war, all figured prominently in his memory. Jimmy, Louisa, and their children—as well as Henry, his wife, children, and grandmother— lived on Francis Richard's St. Augustine estate. Even the owner joined in recognition of multigenerational families, providing in his will that, if his only "legitimate" son died, the above-mentioned slaves were to go to Richard's "second family of colored children." Squire Jackson moved to Jacksonville from a Madison County plantation at age three, yet he considered himself a slave of "the fourth generation," with solid recollections of his great-grandparents, grandparents, and parents.[33]

Similar families abounded in most of East Florida, as illustrated by several Putnam County examples. By the early 1860s one three-generational grouping consisting of Big Minerva, her daughter Minerva, and the younger Minerva's children all stayed together at William Moseley's plantation. Banger and his wife, Dicey, lived on the Clark Stephens place, and Banger's son and daughter-in-law, Burrel, and Big Jane, along with their children Mose, Joe, Jane, and Jess, resided at Winston Stephens's Rose Cottage. The three-generational family managed to remain together through the end of slavery and for many years thereafter. Burrel and Big Jane kept their marriage in a solid and thriving condition until her death in 1871.[34]

The record of so many successful and lasting slave families cannot change the fact that the will of a master could destroy any slave union. As historian Philip Morgan noted of eighteenth-century Chesapeake and Lowcountry slaves, "Constancy of slave families must be understood within a context that recognizes the essential insecurity of all slave marriages."[35] That caveat explains Adam Sanks's memories of the dissolution of his parents' marriage. The event occurred, he recorded, when Colonel Marvin moved out of St. Augustine with Adam's father.[36]

The breaking up of a slave family could eventuate from a variety of causes, but complications arising from a master's death offered one common reason. If a master passed away, slaves might be sold to raise cash to pay off debts or might be dispersed among family members and other legatees. Probate and slave sales records clearly picture easy recourse to the disruption of slave families for the convenience of the owner and his heirs, as shown from a survey of four hundred Middle Florida will and probate files, slave ads, and personal correspondence. Gadsden County's Jesse Potts, to name just one such owner, made it plain in his will that his nine slaves, consisting of one family and two solitaires, could be sold in whatever manner suited his widow. The five children of Prince and Tammy on John Whitehead's Leon County plantation were split among four family members in 1847. Ten years later Edward Tabb of Madison County bequeathed siblings Sarah (aged five) and Jim (aged two) to his daughter Amanda. He made no mention of the disposition of the mother or father.[37]

Masters facing bankruptcy, whatever their personal feelings may have been, enjoyed little choice but to separate families by selling them to different buyers. Elizabeth Delaney's five family groups, totaling twenty-seven slaves, were disconnected and sold at auction to satisfy her husband's creditors. Thirteen-year-old Adeline endured the same experience when officials separated her from her family to be sold at the Tampa courthouse door to satisfy a judgment against the girl's owners. A mother and her child were separated and sold in Duval County to satisfy debts acquired by Andrew Branning. Sarah Ann Brown Bryant was detached from her family in South Carolina and sold to a Hillsborough County planter because of debts incurred by her previous owner. Sarah remembered her mother begging the owner to keep the family together, to no avail. Only freedom at the Civil War's end allowed some balm for the pain, permitting Sarah to visit her mother in Charleston.[38]

The passage of time after settlement, the building up of multigenerational slave families, and the tender age of slave children did not affect the willingness of some Middle Florida masters to separate slave families. Owners' families in Florida grew larger and multigenerational as the decades passed. The enhanced number of heirs, in turn, seriously compromised the integrity of slave families. The terms of three hundred relevant area wills examined for this study provided, on the average, for four heirs to inherit five bond servants each. Such divisions could not help but necessitate splits of numerous slave families.[39] As for younger children, an eight-month-old baby was taken from the mother on the Louis Mattair plantation and, according to Douglas Dorsey, "sold to the highest bidder." James H. McArvers allowed his mother to take two minor children, Green and Rose, to her Floyd County, Georgia, home in 1842.[40]

Some slave children were predestined to be separated from their parents or mothers. Daniel Campbell of Gadsden County specified in his will that his son Archibald receive Isabel but not her future increase. Campbell desired that two of his daughters receive one child "each and no further." Eliza James, also of Gadsden County, stipulated that Lucy, a child of thirteen, would go to James's daughter Elizabeth, but Lucy's future "increase [was] to be equally divided" between James's four grandchildren. Following the same pattern, a Jackson County master gave Eliza to his son but assigned Eliza's future children to his other son. In Leon County John Moore directed that his young son was to receive the future "increase of his Rachel and Sally up to six," after which their slave offspring were to be divided among the rest of Moore's children.[41]

Exceptions to the general rule existed even in Middle Florida. In isolated cases slaveholders proved adamant in their unwillingness to separate families. When owner William Croom left Gadsden County for Mississippi in 1856, one slave family's members insisted that they did not want to leave the state. So Croom sold Manuel, his wife, and their children as a group for $3,800, and they remained in Florida. Thomas Triplett took a path far different from many of his Gadsden County peers in his estate planning. He directed that his executors were to "keep my slaves . . . together and . . . on my place."[42]

The experiences of West and East Florida differed to some extent from that of Middle Florida. In the west the importance of slave-holding had declined by 1860. There the majority of masters typically sold bond persons individually, according to need or desire.[43] In the east many masters pursued their financial self-interest by separating families; on the other hand, numerous owners made an effort to keep at least the single or simple family units together. In St. Johns County, for instance, James R. Anderson sold Davy and his wife, Betsey, and Bob, his wife, Peggy, and their children in family groups. Zephaniah Kingsley's will stated, "I do hereby authorize my executors not to sepa-rate the [slave] families." Isaiah D. Hart, John Price, Francis Richard, David Turner, A. B. Nance, J. H. McIntosh, and others kept slaves together and sold them in single family units. Similarly, William R. Ashley's will directed that his slaves "not be separated but sold in one body at Public Auction." The majority of area probates, when a rel-evant provision appeared, requested that "children" be sold, at least, with their mothers.[44]

Presumably as a means of keeping slave families together, some masters allowed slaves the opportunity of selecting their new masters or heirs. In the northeast Mary Hobkirk willed that her slave Charlotte be "sold to a master of her choice."[45] Although Middle Florida planters usually expressed no preference about the division of their slaves, Nancy DeLaughter of Madison County allowed one slave family's mem-bers to select their next master from among DeLaughter's children. John Whitehead permitted the seamstress Matilda the option of se-lecting either of his sons as her master. Abraham Dupont wanted his slaves divided evenly among his heirs, but he also stipulated that slave "families shall not be separated but if this can not be avoided then it is my request that their wishes be consulted in the adjustment of differ-ences."[46]

In all Florida regions the common practice of hiring out slaves af-fected the stability of slave families because it placed family members at a distance from each other. That process often explains the absence of husbands and fathers in family lists maintained by or for slaveholders. At least when Tom Blackledge, one of the El Destino slaves of George N. Jones, was hired out to W. G. M. Davis in Tallahassee, he was permitted to return on weekends to visit his family. The fifteen-year-old twins of Burrel and Big Jane at Rose Cottage in Putnam County, although rented out to another plantation, received the same kind of permission to visit their parents.[47]

Migration within Florida added to the factors that could rend a slave family. Many wealthy persons suffered from the Second Seminole War, the economic depression known as the Panic of 1837, and the subsequent collapse of Middle Florida's preeminent financial institution, the Union Bank. Even so, the Indian war's end in 1842 opened up new opportunities in the peninsula. Accordingly, numerous prominent names relocated to the onetime war zone. Robert Gamble was one such man. He established a sugar plantation on the Manatee River, bringing with him one hundred bond servants to work his crops. Friends and relations joined him there. During the decade beginning in 1845 about one-tenth of Jefferson County's slaveholders followed their example, leaving for Central or South Florida. Other counties experienced similar migrations. The costs of such widespread relocations, coupled with decisions about whom to take and whom to leave behind, compelled the split of many slave families. During the Civil War, a similar phenomenon would strike northeast Florida slave families, when Unionist and Confederate owners moved themselves and their bond persons out of reach of the other side.[48]

The forced relocation of a slave away from his or her family members did not mean that the slave quietly acquiesced in the owner's plans. Many slaves sought to maintain their ties at all costs. Advertisements often illustrated that point, as in the case of Sandy, who was believed to be "near Gov. Call's plantation where he has a wife." Fearing that their family would be separated, Nelson, his wife Judy, and their son and daughter disappeared from Cornelius Beasley's plantation. July fled from the Jacksonville wharves seeking his wife at Palatka. One incident emphasizes the lengths to which a slave might go to return to his family. Twenty-two-year-old Lewis stole a horse at Fort Brooke (Tampa) during the height of the Second Seminole War and galloped through one hundred or more miles of hostile Indian territory on his way back to South Carolina.[49]

A few statistics indicate the frequency of these kinds of escapes. Advertisements suggest that owners believed 50 percent of the runaways in northeast Florida were attempting to reunite with a husband or wife. In Middle Florida 60 percent were believed to be gone in search of spouses. A clear majority of runaways in both districts had absconded in search of relatives. In a few instances children disappeared from plantations in search of a parent, usually a mother. Runaways tended to be male because responsibilities for children hindered the ability of women to depart. The margin stood at five to one in northeast Florida, expanded to six to one in Middle Florida, and contracted to three to one in West Florida. Typically, runaways varied in age from their twenties to their early forties.[50]

The specifics of runaway advertisements made clear the motivations of many runaways. "Harrison . . . a bright mulatto . . . 25 years old" was thought to be traveling to South Carolina from St. Augustine "in pursuit of his wife." Andrew pursued his old kinship ties when he took a "gray mare" and left Covington County, Alabama, for Gadsden County, where he had formerly lived as the slave of Jesse Yon. Abram disappeared from Leon County in search of his wife. Bill escaped from Putnam County and was said to be in search of his "wife in Nassau County." George and John fled a St. Johns plantation and were "probably lurking in the neighborhood of Whitesville on Black Creek, Duval County, East Florida, where they have their wives."[51]

As the statistics indicated, some women, with or without children, took flight as well. After being sold in Pensacola to a cruel Jackson County planter, Kathy soon ran away with her children. Levenia absented herself from the Tallahassee plantation of John R. Rhodes for over five months and was thought to be with her husband who lived "in the neighborhood of Quincy." During the four years that Venis and her children stayed away from their owner, she was alleged to have had "two or three" more children.[52]

Sometimes children and teenagers escaped in search of parents. One owner offered a $200 reward for two children who had departed Duval County in search of their "freed mother." Joseph absented himself from Black Creek and was thought to be going to St. Augustine where his "mother lives." In Jefferson County William D. Moseley caught a "small negro girl" escapee belonging to Robert Hayward and sent her home. A seventeen-year-old boy, who had been working in Jacksonville, made his escape and was probably heading to South Carolina, where he had been purchased. A fifteen- or sixteen-year-old boy jailed at Thomasville, Georgia, had absented himself from the James Lewis plantation near Tallahassee.[53]

Attempts to maintain family ties, whether by runaways or by married partners, parents, or children living elsewhere, were assisted greatly by day-to-day realities that permitted bond servants more freedom of movement than the wording of laws and ordinances might suggest. As a practical matter enslaved blacks, especially males, routinely received permission to visit spouses who lived elsewhere. Visits might come on weekends, at night, or even during the workday when the bondsman was on the way to the marketplace or running other errands. Saturday-night and Sunday visits were most common, but slaves took every opportunity they could find. When Thomas Randall sent supplies from his Belmont plantation to his father-in-law's Wirtland plantation, Jacob willingly seized on the opportunity to go so that he might visit "his wife and family."[54]

Nighttime seems to have been the right time for many slaves to move about from one plantation to the next. The nocturnal excursions provoked the ire and fears of numerous owners. Nancy DeLaughter, to name one such planter, felt herself beset with night-walking slaves leaving her lands and also visiting her plantation from her neighbors' property. Nancy's son Amon, on one occasion, whipped Prince for constantly riding a horse at night. Jane Murray spoke in 1835 as though it was a common occurrence for slaves to roam from one plantation to another looking for a dance to attend. Slaves became accustomed to strolling and roving in St. Augustine at all times of the night. During the Second Seminole War, white citizens wanted them off the streets before 9:00 P.M. The town fathers on that occasion met with little more success than various planters in the countryside at other times.[55]

A willingness to face punishment in order to see loved ones argues persuasively for the great importance that slaves attached to kinship ties. It was no wonder that slaves desired to formalize their relationships with ceremonious marriages. Such marriages formed an important part of the familial experience. Florida slaveholders often assisted by allowing their slaves to marry whom they chose. In much of the South the custom of jumping together over a broomstick marked slave marriages, but, more than has previously been recognized, religious ceremonies of various kinds occurred in Florida. Louisa Wirt Anderson described a Jefferson County slave wedding at which her brother Dabney presided but that lacked the sophistication of planter nuptials. Anderson noted, "The evening before last we attended Betsey's wedding—Dabney officiated as minister—it was a laughable scene." Whites often performed such services, but many Middle Florida owners allowed black preachers, men such as John Parkhill's Baptist slave James Page, to perform marriages. In a similar manner Burrel, a preacher at Winston Stephens's Rose Cottage in Putnam County, probably conducted wedding ceremonies throughout northeast Florida during the 1850s and early 1860s.[56]

Louisa Anderson might find a simple slave wedding amusing, but the typical slave's views of marriage and family were much more serious. The anger involved when a couple was split apart was palpable. Hattie Reed, daughter of planter A. M. Reed, learned the lesson in East Florida during 1862. On that occasion she found herself dealing alone with Jake, a fugitive who had returned to seek revenge on Hattie's father for selling Jake's wife to buyers in Georgia. As Hattie put it, Jake wanted "to meet Pa face to face to teach him what it is to part man and wife."[57]

The sincerity of commitments was shown by the endurance of so many slave marriages. A quick look at post–Civil War county marriage records supports the point, with thousands of Florida slaves remarrying each other legally after the conflict's end. For example, Robert Meacham met his future bride in the early 1850s, and by 1858 they had their first child. Others followed as the happy couple maintained their relationship through the Civil War and emancipation. On July 23, 1866, in Tallahassee Robert and Stella were married for the "second" time, as provided for in the new era by Florida law. They stayed together until Robert's death at Tampa in 1902. Ike Berry remembered being married and fathering seven children before the Civil War, and he also opted to stay with his first bride until her death. In many instances onetime slaves requested that official marriage records note the longevity of relationships. Thus, in Hillsborough County Andrew Isaac Varnes and Molly Williams Varnes proudly proclaimed on September 15, 1866, that they "had lived together for 15 years." Earlier the same year in Polk County, Jacob and Lucinda Williamson observed that they "have lived together as man and wife for some time."[58]

To the extent that a cruel system permitted, parents nurtured their children and protected their families. They did so despite all the other demands placed on adult slaves. Mama Duck recalled that slave mothers who had babies were usually back in the fields a couple of days after giving birth. Willis Williams could not recall his father but affirmed that his mother, the cook on the Thomas Heyward place in Leon County, "saw to it that her children were well fed." Although they did not sit with the master's family to eat, Williams claimed that his mother made sure their family was served the same food "from the master's table." When Burrel was away from the Stephens plantation, his wife, Big Jane, and daughter Sarah cooked, plowed, hoed, dug ditches, and performed other chores around the place, while also caring for the children.[59]

Slave women enjoyed one advantage that southern white women did not, especially on the large plantations. Although the white women largely lived miles apart, black women could interact with each other on a daily basis. The situation, as Deborah Gray White has explained, "allowed black women to develop a cooperative mentality." Black women assisted each other in childbirth, child care, and the health care of children. Obviously, women bond servants who worked in the fields alongside men or in the master's house could not always take care of their children's every need. Many times older slave women would assume the mothers' duties. Some slave women cooked for the entire slave community, freeing up mothers and fathers to perform tasks for themselves and their young when at their cabins.[60]

Despite all the difficulties of life, black men also maintained a presence and carved out a recognizable role in the household. Mary Minus Biddle's memory on that point remained very clear. She fondly recalled that her "pappy" would oftentimes "sit in front of the fireplace until a late hour in the night and on arising in the morning the children would find in a corner a number of roasted potatoes which their father had thoughtfully roasted and which the children readily consumed." Mary's father did more than roast potatoes. He also grew healthy food for the family. Occupied by labor during the day, he tended his garden by night. He accomplished the task, Biddle claimed, by "setting up huge scaffolds in the field which burned and from the flames that this fire emitted he could see well enough to do what was necessary." Shack

Thomas's father undertook to instill in his children a sense of heritage and family history. Thomas reminisced that his father would "spend hours after the candles were out telling him and his brothers about his capture and subsequent slavery."[61]

Naming practices reflect the important and influential role of fathers and husbands. Enslaved blacks maintained some elements of their grammar, phonology, and lexicon in their names and the naming of their descendants. On plantations throughout Florida sons received the names of their fathers. At the Bryan Crooms place in Leon County, Fortune called one of his sons Little Fortune. Little Randall of the Pine Hill Plantation in the same county was named after his father. On the John Finlayson plantation where over 180 bond servants grouped in at least ten family units, fathers were mirrored in sons named Little Edmond, Little Stephen, Little Henry, Little Joe, and Little Isaac.[62]

Because more men than women possessed special skills, fathers occupied a better position to provide extra support for the family and to obtain small gifts for spouses and children. Several carpenters, bricklayers, and coopers worked on Achille Murat's plantation. They were able to furnish their families with additional food and clothing because they could sell their services and products at the "market" in town. James Page—a coach driver, preacher, and house servant of John Parkhill—made money when tipped by visitors for his services. Besides providing for his own family, Page even purchased a pair of shoes for the plantation's mistress with some of the money that he earned.[63]

Many less-skilled slaves attempted to provide amenities and comforts for their families. To cite one illustration, in 1827 Laura Randall of Jefferson County purchased "a dozen [chickens] from one of the Negroes at 25 cents apiece," permitting a small measure of generosity. For work well done Jud Poll, a slave at Wirtland, received $2 from the overseer to purchase an outfit for his future wife. According to Daniel H. Wiggins, some of the men at John Gamble's large Leon County plantation would use "rabbit meat for bait" to catch black fish for their families. Burrel hunted for wild game in Putnam County. He, too, received inducements in the form of rewards for working diligently.[64]

In some cases males acted to protect their families through extraordinary means, and examples are many. George, the property of John C.

Neal, abducted his wife, Lettus, their four children, and one of their grandchildren from W. C. Smith of Monticello. Jenny was believed to "have been seduced by a stout Negro man," with whom she left the Pensacola area. Dilsey, at large for three years from Jesse H. Billis, was said to be harbored around Shell Point by a man named "Power." Charles took wife Mary with him as he escaped from Jekyll Island, Georgia, to Florida, "where he . . . formerly lived." A family consisting of Hampton, wife Nanny, and five children fled Palatka and were thought to be going to Jacksonville, where they had "a large connection." Jim absconded with his loved one, giving his owner "reason to believe he is about Tallahassee, where he has been heretofore hired—his wife is a large dark complected woman, whom he decoyed off, and is doubtless with him."⁶⁵

Some men, on the other hand, skirted their responsibilities and took their marriages frivolously. Numerous slaves had more than one husband or one wife. Planter Achille Murat insisted that males generally "attach themselves to a woman and keep to her; but they are often inclined to change." The slave owner went on to assert that he knew of bond servants "who have married a dozen times, and have as many wives living, each of whom has as many husbands." What with Murat's many liaisons with slave women on his plantation, he certainly did not lead by example. The promiscuity of these male slaves may well have reflected an "assertion of masculinity in the face of feelings of inadequacy," but perhaps the behavior was based, in part, on observing the actions of their masters.⁶⁶

Where a parent offered his or her love and devotion to a child, the child typically reciprocated that love. Squire Jackson was "Very devoted to his mother," and he would often follow her in the cotton fields while she "picked or hoed cotton." Douglas Dorsey resented the brutal treatment of his mother by the cruel master's wife, and he decided to "put strychnine that was used to kill rats into her coffee that he served her." Fortunately freedom came and saved Dorsey from carrying out the deadly act. As mentioned earlier some children ran away toward home rather than engaging in today's practice of running away from home. When Hannah escaped from Jacksonville, for example, she was "believed to be headed for Tallahassee where her mother lives." One slaveholder at Jacksonville offered a $200 reward for the return of two escaped children in search of their "freed mother."[67]

The same affection and devotion could exist between siblings, who sometimes felt either a need to protect each other or to reunite after years of separation. Seeing his sister being brutally whipped, Aberdeen of El Destino plantation attacked the overseer with an axe. For his intransigence the bondsman received a "genteel floging" in front of the entire slave community. Douglas Dorsey's younger brother was sold to a Captain Ross and taken across the Suwannee River into Hamilton County. "Twenty years later [when] the brother was located by his family," an interviewer recorded, "he was a grown man, married and farming." Notwithstanding four decades of separation, the bonds of love and affection between brothers Isaac and Abraham Grant of Columbia County endured. Reunited with his brother at an A.M.E. church meeting at Tampa, Abraham, then a bishop, introduced Isaac by saying, "The last time I saw my brother forty years ago, this man (his master) had sold him to the Slave Traders, and he was going over the hill crying, following an ox cart while we children stood in a yard weeping at his going."[68]

Slaves in Florida differed little from servants elsewhere in their attempt to establish familial relationships. As Herbert Gutman noted, the slave family and kinship ties were the "central binding institutions within the slave communities." Despite the precarious nature of familial ties, bond servants sought to etch out a family life for themselves. "Although it was weak, although it was frequently broken, the slave family provided an important buffer," John Blassingame perceived, "a refuge from the rigors of slavery."[69] As Florida's slave population increased by the 1850s, slaves were better able to create some semblance of a private life for themselves. Indeed, slaves courted, established lasting relationships, and remained faithful and supportive to nuclear and extended family members, with many "marrying" each other for the second time after the Civil War. That some slaves, given the nature of slavery, could create and maintain any manifestation of family life stands as irrefutable testimony to their determination, character, and humanity.

RELIGION AND COMMUNITY

Religion served as a foundation for the triumph of shackled Africans and their descendants over spiritual and physical slavery. In Florida, as in other areas of the slave South, a mixture of Euro-Christian and African religious practices helped bond servants to endure many trials and tribulations and assisted in making life more bearable. Key, then, to understanding slavery in Florida is a comprehension of slave religion. This chapter considers Euro-Christian and African religious practices by bond servants, as well as the manner in which bond persons used those practices in their own way in the struggle to survive slavery.

Following their kidnapping in Africa and transportation to the Western Hemisphere, slaves retained their customary religious beliefs and, where possible, practices. As historian Robert Hall has shown, their descendants succeeded in continuing some African styles of worship into the twentieth century. Especially during and after the mid-1700s, though, whites systematically undertook to convert bond servants to Christianity within what was becoming the new United States. Ultimately, the process thus set in motion, as George P. Rawick explained, "blend[ed] the two" religious heritages into a new and unique form of religion.[1]

The motivations of whites in converting blacks to Christianity varied over time and from person to person. Importantly, out of the spirit of the Great Awakening of the mid-1700s, many people came to believe that converting the lowly "savage" slaves to Christianity would bring "civilization" to them. By the early 1800s the debate over the wisdom of such policies had been settled. Southern Baptists, Methodists, and Presbyterians commonly allowed bond servants to worship in their churches. Slaveholding adherents in these churches did not endorse conversion of their bond servants on the basis of equalitarianism; rather, they did so as paternalists who thought they knew what was best for their "people."[2]

Slave owners also knew what was best for themselves and for their ability to control their captive workers. Slave control thus constituted another significant cause for slave Christianity. Owners hoped that, with the cooperation of mostly white preachers, they could get slaves to believe that a better life in the afterworld could be achieved if they obeyed their "earthly masters" and only if they obeyed those masters. As Bertram Wyatt-Brown noted, the southern clergy defended slavery as a scripturally sanctioned institution. In Middle Florida, for example, planter's daughter Susan Bradford Eppes typically could recall that "negroes were preached to every other Sunday by a white preacher." Amon DeLaughter often recorded occasions when slaves on his mother's Madison County plantation were preached to by an itinerant white minister who had been a family friend for years. Large slaveholders such as Thomas Randall, Achille Murat, John and Robert Gamble, and William Wirt provided such preachers for their bond servants throughout the antebellum period. Sometimes they even attempted to ensure that services would continue after their deaths. Numerous slaveholder wills contained provisions for the religious instruction of their bond servants by white ministers. John Bellamy and William Bailey, to name just two, mandated religious instruction of their slaves at least "once or twice a month on the Sabbath day."[3]

Like their Middle Florida counterparts, East and West Floridians, including slave-owning holdovers from the Spanish colony and newly arrived Anglo-Americans, endeavored to influence the religiosity of bond persons. An important early initiative grew out of the difficulties encountered by the Methodist Church in converting whites who were heavily influenced by the Spanish past. The train of events began with the arrival at St. Augustine in 1823 of the Reverend Joshua Nicholas Glenn, the son of revolutionary hero James Glenn. The minister hoped to establish a Methodist society in the town, having been dispatched for that purpose by the church's South Carolina Conference. Glenn soon learned to appreciate the formidable challenge he faced at the center of Florida Roman Catholicism. Quickly, he redirected his efforts to recruiting bond servants. During the year, he baptized twenty-one blacks and admitted forty to church membership. In the process Glenn helped to plant Methodist loyalties within the heart of the East Florida slave community, a fact that would carry enormous consequences for Florida in the post–Civil War era.[4]

As preacher Glenn discovered, many East and West Florida planters adhered to the Roman Catholic faith and sought to convert their bond persons to Catholicism. Buckingham Smith of St. Augustine did so, echoing the actions of many of his fellow religionists. Glenn believed that some slaves had been forced to become Catholics. Others had rejected Catholic beliefs only to suffer as a result. Having endured penalties for their refusal to acquiesce to owner desires, slaves had adopted a sense of wariness regarding the white churches as a whole. "[Several slaves] have ben members of the Baptist Church [and] wish to have some conversation with me," the Methodist informed his diary. "In the evening Br Smith and I went to see the Black people who had sent for me in the morning They told us that they had been very much persecuted under the Spanish government Sometimes they war whiped Sometimes put in prison but held out faithful until this time —they also told us that it was not their wish to Join our church at preasant."[5]

Not just any type of Christianity suited Florida's slaveholders. They embraced the Pauline dictum, which they believed taught bond servants to be obedient to their masters. To them, acquiescent slaves constituted controllable ones. Former bond persons recalled countless conciliatory sermons preached by white ministers instructing them to obey their masters. "The [white] ministers admonished them to honor their masters and mistresses," Douglas Dorsey observed, "and to have no other God but them, as 'we cannot see the other God, but you can see your master and mistress.'" Mary Minus Biddle recalled, "The white minister would arise and exhort the slaves to 'mind your masters, you owe them your respect.'" Echoing Dorsey and Biddle, Margrett Nickerson asserted that "We had church wid de white preachers and dey tole us to mind our masters and missus and [we] would be saved, if not dey said we wouldn." For Bolden Hall the religious teaching to slaves boiled down to "obey their master and mistress at all time[s]."[6]

Religious indoctrination of enslaved blacks by owners occurred on many Florida farms and plantations (as it did throughout the South), and slaves were compelled to listen from tender ages. Slaveholders, their wives, or other members of slaveholding families joined in by taking on the paternalistic role of reading to their bond servants. Rebecca Bryant, the mother-in-law of Winston Stephens, often read the Bible to young and old alike on his farm. Winston's wife, Octavia, noted in January 1862 that her mother had all the bond servants "up here and read a chapter in the Bible [to them] etc and intends continuing it." Margrett Nickerson recalled a similar situation, where the slave owner's wife served as the Sunday school teacher for blacks on the plantation. She read to bond servants but did not "'low us to tech a book wid us hands." Squire Jackson, reminiscing about his childhood, recollected that such services interfered with happy pastimes. "Boys on the plantation would play ball and shoot marbles until church time," he told an interviewer.[7]

Slaves typically worshiped in the white-controlled churches of their masters.[8] Historian Robert Hall has shown that blacks generally attended "racially mixed formal churches" led by white clergymen. Blacks could be found at Roman Catholic, Presbyterian, and Episcopal services. Mostly, though, they reflected what was also the white community's preference by attending Methodist and Baptist churches. Often doctrinal and sectarian distinctions failed to move the slaves. Thus, Mary Minus Biddle, who grew up on a Columbia County plantation during the 1850s, might remember only that her master directed blacks to worship in "the 'white folks' church on Sundays."[9]

Arrangements for the slave presence in white churches came with all sorts of variations. At Tampa's Methodist church, some meetings were racially segregated, while others were not. "We have services in the morning for white people," Oliver Otis Howard explained in 1857, "in the afternoon for the *blacks* and in the evening again and presume the evening services are for both black & white." When congregations included both races, blacks were virtually always restricted to particular portions of the sanctuary. Mary Biddle and many others sat in the "rear of the church," and William Williams remembered slaves seated in the balcony when they worshiped with whites. At the First Presbyterian Church of Tallahassee, bond servants were permitted to sit in the north gallery. Somewhat to the contrary, Douglas Dorsey recollected that, on the Louis Mattair plantation in Suwannee County, "slaves were ordered to church to hear a white minister, [and] they were seated in the front pews of the master's church, while the whites sat in the rear."[10]

Hundreds of Florida churches owe their origins partly to founding members who were slaves. In 1838 four whites and two blacks established what later became known as Bethel Baptist Institutional Church in Jacksonville. Slaves also helped to start Concord Missionary Baptist around 1841 and Key West Baptist Church in 1843. Jim Seward stood among the first eight members of the Baptist Church of Christ at Peas Creek (Bartow), and others acted in the same capacity for the First Baptist Church of Tampa and the Union Baptist Church of Brooksville. These Baptist illustrations offer only a few examples that could be expanded in almost all parts of the state settled before 1865.[11]

A few slaveholders permitted their bond servants to build their own churches or places of worship. One early example arose during the development of Jefferson County in the late 1820s. Thomas Randall observed that his slaves, who had recently arrived in Florida from Maryland, were building their own little church before constructing places in which to live. "On the way to town, I discovered that near a beautiful grove of hickories North of the house . . . [the slaves] had formed an under enclosure with logs for seats and something like a pulpit for their religious exercises—this is the first I had seen of it." Tradition suggests that the origins of Bartow's First Providence Missionary Baptist Church also lay in the antebellum era. Slaves withdrew in the mid-1850s from Bartow's local white Baptist congregation and founded their own. Likely, other such churches existed at various times during the period, especially in East Florida.[12]

The number of churches founded by and for blacks increased in the Civil War years, even in the Middle Florida plantation belt. Members of Tampa's future Mt. Sinai A.M.E. Zion Church began meeting in a "discarded wooden shack . . . about three miles west of town." Cataline B. Simmons helped Sandy Cornish and Joseph Sexton to build Key West's A.M.E. Zion congregation not long before the Tampa church coalesced. Several A.M.E. churches have dated their beginnings similarly, including Marion County's Mt. Moriah (1860), Jackson County's Bethlehem (1861) and Mt. Olive (1862), and Madison County's Jeslam (1864). By war's end Robert Meacham had established at the state capital what became the banner church of African Methodism in Florida, Bethel.[13]

Although the overwhelming majority of slaves worshiped in white-controlled churches and normally listened to the preaching of white ministers, a surprising outcome could result. The sermons might teach obedience, but what the slaves heard was equality before God. They came to believe firmly that the souls of slaves were as precious as those of whites. Enslaved blacks thus found within the church powerful reassurance of their humanity. The thinking of a few went even further, prompting them to feel morally superior to their masters. Mary M. Biddle became one such person. "Yeah, wese jest as good as deys is only deys white and we's black, huh," she remarked. Biddle added, though, "She dar not let the whites hear this."[14]

Did nineteenth-century Florida slaves—who were, as one former slave claimed, "made to worship" in their masters' churches—genuinely believe in the Christian doctrines taught to them? The answer will never be known with any degree of certainty. Some bond servants, as John Boles found, "avidly accepted Christianity" and adhered to the religious lessons taught to them by whites. "I never witnessed a deeper humility than was exhibited by these poor slaves," one cleric recorded at St. Augustine in 1843. "These Blacks have a deep reverence for religion & all its sacraments." Others, including Mary Biddle, Douglas Dorsey, and Margrett Nickerson, simply did not accept what the churches taught. The idea of Sundays off meant a reprieve from work, and that fact could have motivated some slaves to worship with their masters. A few tried to negotiate conversion and adherence to the doctrines of Christianity in exchange for their freedom, or so the Methodist parson Joshua Glenn believed. "One poor african," he wrote, "[said that] he would not turn back from his [new] religion" if his St. Augustine master would grant him his freedom.[15]

What roles did enslaved blacks assume in the so-called white churches? The scarcity of source materials prohibits the question from being answered with certainty. It appears that whites generally restricted black involvement in any area of church life that concerned the use of power, authority, or discretion. The historian of the Sharon Baptist Church in Leon County, to offer an example, commented that "black members were not allowed to vote in business meetings, nor to serve on committees with whites." Slaveholders belonging to the First Presbyterian Church of Tallahassee did not allow their slaves any degree of equality within the confines of their edifice. No available records suggest that bond servants could sue or otherwise question their masters within the church for mistreatment. Ministers who encouraged such actions or any black presumption to authority faced censure. According to Barbara Rhodes, Tallahassee's Presbyterian minister H. N. Brinsmaid "caused great consternation and opposition among the members" when he preached against the evils of slavery. The members thereupon ousted him from their pulpit.[16]

The rule of slaveholder interest in the religious education of slaves carried with it many exceptions. Some masters did not care one way or the other. Amanda McCray's master, for instance, did not concern himself if or when slaves held worship services so long as the services "did not interfere with the work of the other slaves." Bolden Hall, who was held on a large Middle Florida plantation, experienced similar attitudes. He said that his master "did not interfere with . . . [the slaves'] religious quest." East Florida planters such as Zephaniah Kingsley gave bond servants a free hand when it came to private concerns such as religion and family matters. He claimed that he "never interfered with their connubial concerns, nor domestic affairs, but let them regulate these after their own manner."[17]

Among slaveholders could be found men who opposed any type of religious instruction for slaves. Some probably believed that blacks were not fully human beings and were incapable of learning or understanding the true tenets of Christianity. By the early 1830s others anxiously assessed the role that religion played in Virginia's Nat Turner insurrection. In those cases religiously inclined slaves found themselves having surreptitiously to find a way to worship. More than a few stole away to conduct secret religious meetings, thereby involving slaves in an act of conservative rebellion. These gatherings, as Robert L. Hall has observed, "threatened the slaveowner's control over the assembly of slaves." Owners did not always take such challenges to their authority lightly. Charlotte Martin's master did not allow his slaves to take part in any religious meetings. When the master caught her brother participating in one, the owner whipped the bondsman "to death."[18]

Because slaves sometimes interpreted religious teachings for themselves and at other times rebelled against their masters' authority by holding religious meetings on some plantations and farms, an "invisible church" existed and thrived. Many slaves rankled at the insistence of white ministers that they obey their "earthly masters." As mentioned earlier, Mary Biddle disagreed with the doctrines of her white preacher, insisting that respect between whites and blacks should be reciprocal. Margrett Nickerson also reflected the skepticism of some slaves toward the religious doctrine of whites when she said, "Dey never tole us nothing 'bout Jesus." Douglas Dorsey remembered a slave driver's wife who encouraged dissent. "[She could] read and write a little," he informed an interviewer, "[and] would tell the slaves that what the minister had just said was all lies."[19]

Sometimes the invisible churches operated simply at certain spots under trees or sites in the woods or in the slaves' own cabins. Bond servants could gather in these places, where whites could not hear them, for uninterrupted prayer and singing. Slaves on the plantation where Charlotte Martin worked had to steal away and meet in "secret to conduct religious services." Amanda McCray recounted that bond servants worshiped in an area called the "praying ground where 'the grass never had a chancet ter grow fer the troubled knees that kept it crushed down.'" Sarah Murray recalled that slaves in and around St. Augustine would conduct services in the woods, calling their gatherings "brush meetings." On the other hand, Squire Jackson remembered that "at [certain] times meetin's were held in a slave cabin where some 'inspired' slave led the services."[20]

At these secret meetings slave prayers often covered hopes and wishes that would have incensed most slaveholders. Certainly the enslaved blacks were not praying for the same things as their masters. Particularly, bond servants might plea for deliverance from bondage just as the Hebrews held in Egypt had done in the Bible. When a black Union soldier asked Claude Wilson's mother if she knew that freedom had come, the woman replied, "Yeh Sir, . . . I been praying for dis [day] a long time." Faced with such insurrectionary prayers, owners such as Judge Wilkerson endeavored repeatedly to stop the secret meetings. They did not want slaves believing that God's assistance in physically throwing off the shackles of servitude would be forthcoming.[21]

Sometimes bond servants would conduct their own brand of religious worship in the presence of unsuspecting whites. A remarkable example occurred in Jackson County during the Civil War and involved Henry Call, a slave preacher in the white Methodist Episcopal Church, South. At Cottondale (also known as the Bethlehem settlement), Call held prayer meetings on Thursday nights. At the conclusion of the meetings slaves engaged in a general handshaking that meant to them that they had joined the "African Methodist Episcopal" Church. Call asserted that he and three companions had organized an A.M.E. church "while the overseer looked on unaware of anything more than a prayer meeting or a handshaking was going on."[22]

When slaves controlled worship services, a high level of emotionalism characterized the occasion. As Albert J. Raboteau has shown, enslaved blacks retained part of their African religious culture, which was, as some whites perceived it, an unusual style of worship. During their "own services," bond servants exhibited excited behavior as they prayed, shouted, played music, and danced. They yearned, as Mary Biddle described it, for an "inspired" slave to lead them. "Many times the services were punctuated by much shouting [and praying] from the 'happy ones,'" Louis Napoleon commented. Willis Williams reflected what many slaves observed and experienced in worship services among other blacks. He claimed that black preachers "appealed to the emotions of the 'flock', and the congregation responded with 'amens', 'hallelheua', clapping of hands, shouting and screaming." Observing the scene at Tampa, Oliver O. Howard wrote, "Their singing is peculiar & very hearty." He added, "Some of them shout & some look very happy."[23]

Many slaveholders who favored quiet and sedate worship services viewed the intense emotional style preferred by their slaves with fear and suspicion. Even as tolerant a man as East Florida's Zephaniah Kingsley could succumb to such anxieties. The planter especially feared one slave "calling himself a minister." The man, in Kingsley's judgment, had taken "all authority over the negroes." He had done so through worship services or what the owner called "private nightly meetings." There, Kingsley insisted, the slaves got happy, danced, and beat drums all night long.[24]

Whether they sat in their masters' churches or in their own, or in a cabin or a secret place in the woods, bond servants combined African practices and Euro-Christian doctrine in their day-to-day worship, ending up with what Ira Berlin called a "new faith." That the African traditions survived should not come as a surprise. Peter H. Wood has shown that descendants of Africans in South Carolina maintained some African religious and cultural practices over long periods dating back to colonial times. The same was true for other states, such as Virginia, North Carolina, and Georgia, which supplied most of Florida's slaves. Ira Berlin classified many bond servants from these areas as low-country blacks who incorporated West African culture as reflected in "their language, religion, work patterns and much else." Although the majority of bond servants brought to Florida or else already living there in 1821 probably were third- and fourth-generation descendants, African religious practices would have evidenced themselves clearly in day-to-day life.[25]

If the persistence of tradition did not guarantee the survival of African religious practices in subsequent generations, the continuing presence in Florida of African natives would have done so. Florida's coastline had served slave smugglers well from the Second Spanish period through the antebellum era, adding large numbers of African natives to the state and regional population. As a result, in every part of Florida African natives lived until well past emancipation. One such man, Corporal Jaudon, was believed to be the oldest man in the state before his 1877 death in Leon County. Uncle Jack, who died at St. Augustine in September 1882, was "brought from Africa when a little boy" to become the slave of Buckingham Smith and "the faithful pastor of the church." Santa Quanta, who passed away at Archer in Alachua County later the same year, insisted that he was kidnapped in West Africa during 1778. "Me big boy in old country; some hair on face," he told friends. "Gola man catch me, tie and sell me to ship man." As late as 1860 a Virginian named James Evans reportedly grasped control of the abandoned Fort Myers to found his own smuggling enterprise. "Many believed [that] the real purpose of establishing a Depot," reported the deputy inspector of customs at Key West, "[was] for the reception of African Slaves."[26]

Slaves found that on the road to creating their new faith they could merge African beliefs with Christian doctrine more easily within the framework of the Baptist and Methodist Churches than in other denominations. Spirited congregational singing and the joyful sense of spiritual release common to Methodists and Baptists appealed to the African sensibility. The fact that these sects recruited a large part of their southern membership from poorer whites probably also made them more amenable to the spiritual needs of poor enslaved blacks.[27]

Water and how its use was integrated into church ritual often carried special mystical meaning for Africans, with rites of baptism looming as particularly important. In many African cultures water and springs symbolized rebirth, and water generally suggested life, fertility, and hope. Thus, a slave such as Louis Napoleon meant something special when he recalled that certain bond persons who accepted Christ were "prepared for baptism on the next visit of [the slave preacher] 'Father [James] Page.'" In this environment the Baptist practice of immersion especially called to mind African water rites. Louis Napoleon explained the procedure. "Candidates were attired in long white flowing robes, which had been made by one of the slaves," he recorded. "Amidst singing and praises they marched, being flanked on each side by other believers, to a pond or lake on the plantation and after the usual ceremony they were 'ducked' into the water," he continued. "This was a day of much shouting and praying." Often large numbers of slaves submitted themselves for baptism at the same time. Overseer Jonathan Roberson informed George Noble Jones in 1851, for instance, that "forty one (41) of your Negroes [were] Baptized last Sunday in the Canal above the Bridge by James Page."[28]

Some surviving African practices seemed so remote or "foreign" to white worshipers that they ascribed evil origins to the singing, drum beating, exhortations, and shouting. Ann Murray became one such person. She grew up on her mother's and stepfather's plantation during the 1850s and 1860s. Her suspicions of slave religious practices intensified over time. As of 1871 numerous of the family's former bond servants remained on the family lands. That year she penned the following words to her diary. "A drum [was] beating nearly all night last night, kept the dogs barking so that we could not sleep until late," Murray observed. "Negroes like to do everything at night in the dark, showing that their deeds are evil."[29]

Even if whites did not find evil in African religious practices, they nonetheless might be puzzled or intrigued by them, a situation that could stimulate anxieties on the plantation. The likelihood of this occurring tended to increase over time because the passing years brought more and more black preachers before slave congregations. Because they introduced African folk beliefs into services, the ministers sometimes struck whites as "witch doctors" or magicians. One of them stirred Zephaniah Kingsley's mind. The planter well remembered purchasing "Gualla Jack or Jack the Conjurer," who had been a priest in his African country, where "a dialect of the Angola tongue is spoken." As Kingsley put it, Jack had his "conjuring implements with him in a bag which he brought on board the ship." The planter added, "[He] always retained them."[30]

Many slaveholders besides Kingsley knew about "conjuring" and other African practices that constituted a part of slaves' religious services. Although they might not find them evil in origin, they still held them to be barbaric. Susan B. Eppes, who matured at a large Leon County plantation, considered enslaved Africans as heathens who practiced "Voo-Doo." She also argued that slaves were most superstitious, believing in "'de kunjer man' or 'de kunjer o' man,'" one who could be a terror or a best friend. The man could cast or break spells.

She helped to ensure that on her father's plantation slaves were taught about the "existence of a God—not a vengeful Voo-Doo" or conjure man.[31]

In fact, many slaves believed in African ways, giving them greater weight than they afforded to the master's Christian teachings. Governor Richard Keith Call's slave Delia was cursed, or so she and other slaves believed, by a conjure man. At eighteen, according the Ellen Call Long, Delia "began to droop" and soon died. "After the death," Long wrote, "the nurse . . . brought to my mother a small package of dingy cloth, in which was wrapped two or three rusty nails, a dog's tooth, a little lamb's wool, and a ball of clay." The governor's daughter continued:

> Trembling with awe, she said: "This is what killed Delia, ole Miss, I most knowed it was jest so. I most knowed as how she was conjured, and jest found dis under her mastrass where she die."
>
> On inquiry we found that she was the cause of jealousy to a companion negro girl, who had made threats towards her; and moreover, we learned, that every negro on the plantation had known all the time what power was at work upon Delia, but dare not, as they express it, "break the spell," for the evil spirit would have turned on the one that told it.[32]

Magic, witchcraft, and other beliefs, as well as conjuring, found a place in the worship services of blacks. "[Slaves] were duly schooled in all the current superstitions," Amanda McCray told an interviewer, "and listened to tales of ghosts and animals that talked and reasoned." Acie Thomas remembered being "taught that hooting owls were very jealous of their night hours and when they hooted near a field of workers they were saying: 'Task done or no done—night's my time—go home.'" Willis Williams added detail:

> Some wore bags of sulphur saying they would keep away disease. Some wore bags of salt and charcoal believing that evil spirits would be kept away from them. Others wore a silver coin in their shoes and some made holes in the coin, threaded a string through it, attached it to the ankle so that no one could conjure them. Some who thought an enemy might sprinkle "goofer dust" around their door steps swept very clean around the door step in the evening and allowed no one to come in afterwards.[33]

The culture could mix such practices with African traditions about age, respect for the elderly, and death to generate added seriousness, threat, and potency. Josephine Anderson recalled her family members telling her of the power of "old witch doctors" and babies born with a "veil" over their faces who could "see sperrits, an tell whas gonna happen fore it comes true." Other slaves believed in similar supernatural subjects and images. Amon DeLaughter recorded, for example, that one of the plantation slaves saw the "Ghost." Based on West African "Ancestral Worship," elders merited respect for they were poised between this world and the hereafter. Slaves considered as powerful any old or young bond servant who used sulphur, burned or wore bags of salt, or possessed other items to guard against magic or to ward off misfortune.[34]

People who believed in the supernatural power of such cultural and religious practices could literally experience pain, misfortune, or death as a result of them, and even relatively sophisticated members of planter society might honor some African ways. Susan Eppes offered a good example by relating that slaves on the plantation believed old Affie to be a witch. Therefore, slaves respected her, and nobody, including the master's family, bothered her. Affie did pretty much what she wanted, including staying away from the plantation for days, sometimes weeks, at a time.[35]

Funeral services among slaves, much as was true of their African forebears, were steeped in ceremony and ritual drawn from cherished African traditions. Robert Hall has explained that these "were often occasions for celebration, creating an intensely renewed sense of family and communal unity among the survivors." A contemporary illustration of an early-nineteenth-century burial echoes a number of West African traditions. The drawing shows a scaffold, an animal skin, and a variety of personal possessions utilized as part of the funeral ceremony.[36]

Another common custom was singing and praying through the night. Such ceremony marked Dolly's passing in East Florida in 1851. A newspaper account described what happened after the slave took to her death bed: "Her colored friends of all ages then flocked around her, bestowing those peculiar rites which among Southern slaves is singularly superstitious; but amid incantations, prayers, and day and night watchings . . . at last [came] the grim messenger [with] his inexorable summons, and the spirit of Dolly took wing to the House of her Eternal Master."[37]

Within the context of merged and merging African and Christian practices, black preachers often emerged as focal points for slave religion. As in most West African societies, they became significant figures and exercised undisputed leadership for a large segment of the bond servant population. Amanda McCray's interview preserves an account that illustrates how highly regarded the slave minister was on the 116-slave plantation where she lived: "The [Parramore] slaves had a Negro minister who could hold services any time he chose, so long as he did not interfere with the work of the other slaves. Slaves held the preacher in high regard since 'he was not obliged to do hard menial labors and went about the plantation "all dressed up" in a frock coat and store-bought shoes. He was more than a little conscious of this and was held in awe by others'."[38]

African American Christianity also allowed blacks to establish a level of independence with the rise of the black preacher. Bondsmen such as Robert Meacham, Thomas Warren Long, Richard Ellis, C. C. Simms, and James Page became particularly important and powerful religious figures among slaves in Florida, where the black minister occupied a key role in the struggle to help bond servants cope with their servitude. He enjoyed a special position within the community. A familiar sight on the farm or plantation, he could be trusted with the innermost secrets of slaves.[39]

A closer look at one such slave preacher, although not necessarily a typical one, offers insight as to their position and authority. As noted earlier, James Page was perhaps preeminent among Middle Florida's slave ministers. His life had started in Virginia. Born into slavery at Richmond on August 13, 1807, Page was purchased in 1828 as a body servant by a Richmond merchant named John Parkhill, who relocated to Tallahassee that same year. A Presbyterian elder, Parkhill arranged for Page to receive religious instruction. Unlike the majority of slaveholders in the South, Page's master and household were not indifferent to his Christian education. As Genovese aptly observed for some white Christians in the antebellum South, the Parkhills joined that "small but determined minority of slaveholders [who] defiantly taught their slaves to read." At least it is clear that they taught Page to read and write. The Parkhills did not seem to succumb to community pressure that swept most of Middle Florida against the education of bond servants. Over time Page earned Parkhill's trust. The owner often took the slave on his various travels, exposing the servant to many of Parkhill's religious ideas. By 1831 Page experienced a call to the ministry. If possible, and subject to the master's approval, he desired to testify about his faith as a Presbyterian, but because church rules excluded black preachers, Page turned to the Baptist Church. Baptist authorities not only allowed him to preach but permitted him significant freedom and latitude to carry his beliefs to his congregation.[40]

The ministry opened up Page's life to a much larger world and to a far greater freedom of movement than most slaves ever enjoyed. As Louis Napoleon recalled, Page was able "to visit all the plantations in Tallahassee, preaching the gospel. . . . Each plantation would get a visit from him one Sunday of each month. . . . The slaves on the Randolph plantation would congregate in one of the cabins to receive him when he would read the bible and preach and sing." Page's orbit quickly expanded beyond Leon County. For three decades he ranged widely in Middle Florida, and eventually the Baptist preacher traveled as far south as Key West and as far north as Thomasville, Georgia. Slaves eagerly awaited his arrival, anxious for exposure to his ideas and teachings. Page's ministry illustrates the remarkable potential exposure and influence of slave preachers but is all the more remarkable given that Page began preaching at a time when white concerns regarding black ministers were growing as a result of the 1831 Nat Turner insurrection; such concerns continued to grow until the Civil War began.[41]

To assert the influence and position of a minister such as James Page is not to argue that his teachings found universal acceptance within the slave community. Quite the contrary. Slaves proved time and again that they could respect an individual while rejecting some or all of his philosophy. Because of their close association with slaveholders, Page and other exhorters sometimes generated skepticism in the minds of listeners who thought that the preachers were being used as tools of the whites. Louis Napoleon suggested as much when he mentioned that some slaves declined to "accept Christ" when Page visited their plantations. Bolden Hall evidenced his own skepticism. "Occasionally the master—supposedly un-beknown to the slaves—would have an itinerant colored minister preach to the slaves," he remembered, "instructing them to obey their master and mistress at all times."[42]

The reaction to particular preachers varied according to the listener and his or her needs; it depended on the eye of the beholder. Two slaves could hear the same message, with one understanding it to be conservative and another considering it subversive. Thus, based on the place and those present, Page probably preached conservative and subversive sermons. Importantly, he and others like him were not as predictable as whites thought, nor were they as detached from African religious practices as whites and some blacks might have believed. With whites in attendance, preachers such as Page usually taught and preached salvation and obedience. At other times their words gained greater passion and appeal as they spoke directly to the hearts and souls of their fellow bond servants. As the skeptic Louis Napoleon acknowledged, many slaves touched by Page's words were caught up in exhortations, singing, and "much shouting from the 'happy ones.'"[43]

Having earned the trust of slaveholders, Page often was allowed to preach to black congregations without a white being present. The teachings he conveyed under such circumstances may have caused some slaves to challenge white authority. D. N. Moxley, an overseer for Leon County's George Noble Jones, thought so. He complained to the owner in 1854 that Page's sermons might offer a reason why he could not control some of the enslaved blacks. When several slaves ran away from the plantation or refused to work, Moxley concluded that the problem lay with Page's preaching and presence. The overseer informed the planter, "I have heard since I came to town that Jim Page and his crew bin the cass of all the fuss [on the plantation]." Jones thereafter barred Page from preaching on his lands.[44]

As mentioned earlier East Florida's Zephaniah Kingsley underwent a similar experience, and his reaction points out the potential for ministers to provoke controversy far more intense than that of James Page. Like Moxley, Kingsley believed at one point that he had lost control of his plantation because a slave "calling himself a minister," had completely taken "all authority over the negroes" from the overseer and himself. Kingsley, who usually ignored the religious affairs of his bond servants, may have exaggerated the point. He continued to complain that his slaves had become harder to manage, disobeyed his orders more frequently, and stole more of his food after the minister's arrival. The concerns were important ones. Kingsley and other slaveholders knew well the possibility of slave revolts if the "wrong" preacher took control over their bond servants. In 1828 the planter touched on the topic when he noted, "All the late insurrections of slaves are to be traced to influential preachers of the gospel."[45]

The importance, influence, and leadership of women who served the slave community as ministers have received little attention, but more than a few such individuals occupied the role of preacher. In Duval County, for example, bond servants would gather at the home of a slave woman known as "Mother Sam" to hear her teachings. Given the trust placed in her, Mother Sam attained a position of considerable importance. With her owner or another white person present, she would preach the Gospel to slaves, as well as baptize them in the St. Johns River at the foot of Jacksonville's Hogan Street. The nature and specifics of her private counsels, unfortunately, were not recorded.[46]

The slaves' religion mixed Christianity and African tradition in a manner that helped many bond servants to cope with the realities of life and suffering. It also afforded them a type of freedom within the confines of slavery that the master could not always touch. Slave ministers offered role models to a large audience of enslaved blacks. Their impact helped to ensure that by the 1850s the majority of Florida slaves had adopted a mostly Christian outlook. At the same time large numbers of enslaved blacks held on to all or a substantial part of their Africa-based beliefs. For those who accepted Christianity the religion served several purposes. It allowed enslaved blacks to view themselves and whites alike as equals under God. Significantly, many bond servants could look forward to having Sundays off from work if they worshiped with their masters. Others attending churches could pray for salvation in the hereafter, which gave them a reason for living until their work on earth was finished.[47]

African American Christianity did not grow in and of itself. Slaves incorporated over two hundred years of African and Christian religious practices to create what Ira Berlin called a "syncretic amalgam." It was a modified form of Christianity and represented as much the creation of a new faith as a partial adoption of the white man's religion. The Church, considered broadly, afforded bond servants reassurance of their humanity, while offering a system of priorities that ranked spiritual status far higher than earthly status. Their religion aided slaves in dealing with the psychological effects of slavery in order to survive spiritually as human beings.

MATERIAL
CONDITIONS
AND
PHYSICAL
TREATMENT

Scholarship on the material conditions of slaves' lives has expanded tremendously in recent decades, but Florida's particular experience has for the most part remained unexplored. Comprehending the institution of slavery in the state is impossible without an appreciation for how the quantity and quality of diet, shelter, clothing, medical care, and punishment affected human beings day to day. This chapter focuses on vital questions concerning material conditions and physical treatment. The examination reveals many similarities to the southern situation generally. As always, though, Florida's experience often traveled on a path of its own, and local exceptions sometimes could overwhelm the southern rule.

Before exploring the material and physical treatment of bond servants, it should be noted that not all slaveholders in Florida were whites. A number of examples illustrate that some slaves were owned by a few free blacks. Most typically, the black slaveholder held family members. For instance, Sampson Forrester, a onetime slave, had purchased his wife, Rose, from Hernando (now Pasco) County plantation owner William H. Kendrick. When the owner asked Rose whether she wanted to be sold, "she burst out crying and said, 'yes, sir, only to my husband.'" According to Lee H. Warner, George Proctor, a free black contractor in Leon County, may or may not have owned slaves but did agree to purchase his wife, Mary Chandler, from her owner for $1,300. Another Leon resident, Dorothy O'Cane, a fifty-nine-year-old free mulatto from South Carolina, listed ten slaves in 1860. Little is known about O'Cane, but some bond servants, if not all, appear to have been family members.[1]

At least one black slaveholder owned bond servants who were not family members. As historian Daniel Schafer has noted, Anna Jai Kingsley of Duval County held twelve slaves after being manumitted by her husband Zephaniah Kingsley Jr. Available evidence suggests that Anna, a onetime Spanish subject, treated her bond servants as persons rather than as governable objects.[2]

Overall, the ownership of slaves by free blacks at no time became a widespread phenomenon in Florida during the period from 1821 to 1865. In fact, it was rather atypical. African Americans largely owned blacks who were family members because Florida laws made it extremely hard or too expensive to liberate them. Since most were either family members or kinfolk, black slaveholders almost certainly treated their bond servants in a more humane fashion.

A look at Florida's laws concerning slave treatment would offer a good starting point for a general discussion of treatment of slaves. In one sense Florida mirrored other southern states in that it did not specify by statute the minimum quality or amount of food, shelter, clothing, and medical care that bond servants were to receive from their masters. On the other hand, the territory in 1828 adopted statutory provisions that related to the physical treatment of slaves. As examined later in this chapter, these and subsequent laws dealt mainly with the issues of prohibitions and punishments, but in criminalizing "cruel and unusual punishment" of bond servants the laws opened the door for some oversight of owner and overseer behavior, including the material conditions of slavery. As will be seen, that oversight was exercised, although only infrequently.[3]

As a practical matter the manner in which enslaved Africans were treated rested in the hands of their masters. Most exercised some reasonable judgment in deciding issues of concern to the slave's material condition. "If for no other reason," Julia Floyd Smith aptly noted, "self-interest prompted most planters to see that their slaves were properly cared for." She continued, "To provide them with adequate food and clothing was the first consideration." Such attitudes stemmed directly from the fact that slaves represented the single largest investment of slaveholders in Florida. A few owners went even further than most. Jefferson County's Bolden Hall recalled that his master "provided them with plenty of food and clothing." Similarly, Acie Thomas remembered that, on the plantation, the slaves always had "plenty of everything to eat."[4]

Overall, Florida's bond persons benefited from at least an adequate supply of food. The state's climate and agricultural diversity, coupled with owner concerns about their slaves' future increase and their ability to work, can be counted among the reasons. Florida produced large quantities of food for human and animal consumption, and, with the principal exception of cattle exports, much of the food and livestock remained in the state for the use of whites and blacks. "They planted for home use," explained Hillsborough County slave Stephen Harvell, "not to ship off." Of thirty-five testimonies that reflect the nature of slave life in Florida, the majority expressly report slaves as having adequate food supplies.[5]

Whether adequate supplies of food guaranteed adequate nutrition for slaves poses a separate question. Historian John Boles has argued of the southern slave experience that "the diet of everyone was monotonous and at times inadequate." Still, Florida may have differed somewhat from the common condition. The general availability of food, when tied to owner self-interest, seems to have resulted in at least a minimally nutritious diet for most bond servants. In some cases where owners neglected or refused to ensure an adequate diet for slaves, as James M. Denham has discovered, the owners "might also be subjected to extralegal punishment by community leaders." Bertram Wyatt-Brown has echoed Denham's assertion, suggesting that public exposure and pressure from community members may have persuaded most slaveholders to provide for their slaves. It became a matter of public honor for some masters to be perceived as paternalistic caretakers of "their people" in a patriarchal society.[6]

Without question, some enslaved Africans faced starvation in Florida. One case in point involved forty slaves. Things got so bad on the Jesse Watts plantation in the early 1850s that a Madison County grand jury publicly denounced Watts for not adequately providing for the care of his bond servants. Sadly, the public condemnation failed to have the impact intended, and one year later the owner again received censure. The grand jury deplored Watts's behavior, declaring that it provided "our enemies abroad their most powerful weapons for assailing our institutions [as a result of which] our whole country receives that odium which is only justly merited by a few." The jury went on to observe that a negligent master injures his "country" and "his neighbor," as well as himself. The public rebuke of Watts ultimately accomplished little. The material conditions for his slaves deteriorated over the decade to such a desperate point that a group of the bondsmen killed overseer M. D. Griffin, for which act three of the men were executed.[7]

As to what the slaves ate, Florida provided somewhat more variety than the South generally, but, much as in the rest of the region, pork and corn provided the bulk of the diet. Slaves preferred pork over other meats, and corn adapted itself fairly well to the Florida climate and grew bountifully alongside cotton. When owners or their agents issued provisions (usually once a week), adults typically received three and one-half to four pounds of pork and a peck of meal. The ration for children might differ depending on age and whether they were considered full or half hands, but most were allotted about the same amount as adults. Seasonal changes might bring some adjustment. In East Florida, for example, Zephaniah Kingsley gave every full working hand three and one-half to four and one-half pounds of bacon per week and a peck of corn meal. When other foods such as rice, peas, and other garden vegetables were available, though, less pork and corn could be expected.[8]

Many slaveholders, especially those with greater experience, paid close attention to the feeding of their bond servants. Thus, Elizabeth Wirt might inquire of her daughter Laura Randall, "Have you a supply of pork and fish, and meal for your Negroes." Or Thomas Randall might instruct, "It answers in this country to give the negro his peck of corn weekly and let him grind it at night by manual labor." The attention extended to making sure the food actually was turned over when expected. At Jefferson County's Chemonie plantation, for instance, slaves received weekly rations every Saturday or Sunday (in some other places on Monday). The overseer carefully noted the details for owner George Noble Jones's benefit. "Chesley and family three pecks of meal and six and half pounds of pork meat," he jotted on one occasion. On another he recorded, "Prophet, Joe, and Cinder" received "three pecks of meal and seven pounds of meat."[9]

Although pork and corn formed the mainstay of their diet, slaves consumed beef in large quantities, especially in East Florida, where cattle herds grazed in much of the settled and frontier portions of the peninsula. According to census records, the majority of farmers and planters in the region reported holdings in 1850 and 1860 that ranged in size from small to huge. As Stephen Harvell explained, "All over the country there was cattle." Zephaniah Kingsley certainly fed beef to his bond servants, having raised it on the Fort George plantation. In Putnam County Winston Stephens followed the same course, particularly during the Civil War years, when pork became relatively scarce. "I think you had better get Clark to buy you some two or three beeves," he directed his wife, "and kill one and mix the bacon and beef so as to make the bacon hold out. . . . I had rather do that than wait until all the bacon is gone and then have only beef."[10]

The slave diet usually omitted fresh milk, although certain areas tended to have greater available supplies than others. In the late 1850s at Tampa, for example, blacks and whites could obtain fresh milk once a herd of milch cows went into production. Sarah Brown Bryant recalled that her sister Liza would "milk the cows and churn the butter, and then [the master would] send the produce in by one of them to sell it from door to door." She also recalled that her sister had to carry the "great basket in which were the cans of milk and butter on her head" for at least "2 miles," selling it to people on her way to town.[11] Although most slaves lacked Sarah's access to fresh milk, more probably drank buttermilk if their systems could digest it. John Wesley Ellis remembered eating bread and drinking buttermilk while a slave in Jackson County. He recalled that the master would fill a trough with buttermilk and give the slaves a chunk of bread and make them "get up to dat trough [and eat] jes' lak lil' pigs."[12]

Reflecting similar conditions in Georgia and South Carolina, rice became a staple for many inhabitants. Any number of East Floridians grew the crop for their own consumption. Slave recollections often substantiated its importance. "[They] raised rice, cotton, peas, cabbage and all kinds of vegetables," Sarah Murray explained. Margrett Nickerson remembered, "Dere wuz rice, cotton, co'n, [and] tater fields to be tended to." When asked about food, Douglas Parish first mentioned "corn, rice, meat." At least 30 percent of former slaves whose reminiscences are available remembered eating and growing small quantities of rice where they lived and worked.[13]

Although not often mentioned as a supplement to the Florida slave's diet, some fruits could be offered. This appears to have been the case more in East Florida than in other parts of the state. Thanks to the warm climate and rainfall, fruits of one kind or another—but particularly oranges and grapefruits—were available to bond servants there for ten to eleven months out of the year. Stephen Harvell commented that most slaveholders passed on the planting of citrus groves, but "yard trees" usually grew oranges and other fruits for home use. Amanda McCray's memory paralleled Harvell's by recalling that she received fruit as a part of her plantation diet.[14]

Most bond people could supplement the food and supplies provided for them in a number of ways. As discussed in earlier chapters, many slaves pursued self-directed economic activities on a limited basis. One aspect of what may be called the "slaves' own economy" involved their garden plots. "Uncle Demps" at El Destino remarked that each slave was permitted access to one-quarter acre for the purpose. Some sold a portion of the crops, but they also supplemented their diets with the fresh vegetables they raised. Crops included black-eyed peas, watermelons, turnips, sweet potatoes, collard greens, corn, okra, and other items. Slaves might also keep chickens and tend them for eggs. Proprietors usually attended their gardens in the evenings, on Saturday afternoons, or on Sundays. Mary Biddle recalled that her father had to burn fires on scaffolds to light his fields enough to permit him to work at night. Some owners made allowances to ease the time problem. One overseer observed that he gave bond servants time off to cultivate their own crops, asserting that it "is a rule which we have, to give all the Negroes one day in the Spring to plant and one in the fall to reap."[15]

Available slave reminiscences suggest that the garden plots made a real difference in slave diet, at least when slave crops were used to supplement rations distributed by owners and their agents. Margrett Nickerson commented that slaves had plenty of peas, greens, and cornbread to eat. Shack Thomas could not recall a food shortage on the plantation, since the slaves had plenty of "corn meal, and bacon, and squash and potatoes." Claude Wilson grew up on "Corn bread, beans, sweet potatoes and collard greens." Sweet potatoes, peas, beans, squash, poultry, eggs, and various greens are mentioned time and again. Sarah Murray went so far as to declare, "[We] were fed the same food that the white people ate."[16]

Beyond the most common foods, slaves pursued other kinds of sustenance, as well. Besides pork, beef, poultry, and garden vegetables, they occasionally ate wild game. It might come in the form of venison, rabbit, squirrel, alligator, turkey, possum, or some other creature. Although the 1828 slave code prohibited possession of firearms by bond servants, planters occasionally allowed trusted slaves to have guns for such hunting. Burrel, one of Winston Stephens's slaves, carried a rifle to help him supplement the diet of his family and others on the Rose Cottage farm. Henry Wilson in West Florida allowed his slave Tom to do the same. Likely, the frequency of such practices came higher in East and West Florida than they did in the Middle Florida plantation belt.[17]

Slaves often fished. Daniel H. Wiggins noticed in 1842 that workers on a Jefferson County plantation ate "black fish" that they caught in a nearby stream. Mary Ann Murray, known also as Mary Gomez, recalled that they used to "catch trout more than a foot long" in and around St. Augustine. Burrel fished at the Stephens farm, along with the young boys, without white supervision and often supplied both the black and white families with the fruits of the catch. Zephaniah Kingsley permitted his slaves to fish along the St. Johns River and associated streams. Such examples reinforce the archeological discoveries of Larry McKee and Theresa Singleton, who have concluded from wild-food remains found in their digs that slaves often supplemented their diets with fish and wild game from rivers, creeks, and woods surrounding the plantation or farm.[18]

Sugar from sugarcane and molasses sometimes tantalized the slave's palate. In northeast Florida, where numerous sugar plantations dotted the landscape, bond servants commonly sweetened their foods with sugarcane juice. By the late 1840s the crop had expanded into the peninsula, grown on a large scale in today's Marion, Citrus, and Manatee Counties. Middle Florida also produced some sugarcane. "[The] cane was ground on the plantation and converted into barrels of syrup and brown sugar," Acie Thomas explained. "The cane grinding season was always a gala one," she continued. "There was always plenty of juice."[19]

Even with the general availability of food, conditions varied by owner, by season, by year, and by numerous other factors. When bond servants did not get enough to eat or grew tired of the monotony of their diet (or perhaps simply decided to engage in a small guerrilla action against slavery), they stole from their masters if they could. They paid a painful price when caught. Overseer Amon DeLaughter whipped Mary, Anne, Daniel, and Scot for stealing potatoes and other vegetables. He later flogged Birl and Isaac for "killing a hog" without his permission. Another overseer stopped Mugin from his "old trade of stealing chickens [at night]." Dick ceased stealing watermelons only after a dog seized him by the "seat of his pants." Thomas Randall and Louis Goldborough seemed constantly to be replacing chicken-coop doors after slaves had broken in and snatched the inmates. Octavia Stephens ached with frustration as animals disappeared from her farm. "You have lost another little pig and Henry one," she notified her husband on one occasion, "they 'came up missing.'"[20]

Preparation of food might be handled in several different ways. Often slaveholders concerned with efficient allocation of time required designated bond servants to cook and to apportion the food among the enslaved blacks. Margrett Nickerson's grandmother cooked dinner in large iron pots for all the hands on the plantation, for instance. She claimed there "was plenty of peas, greens, and cornbread" for the more than one hundred slaves to eat. Similarly, Patience Campbell observed her mother cooking dinner for the slaves in "large iron pots and pans in an open fireplace." On the small farm of George Bullock, one slave prepared meals for all thirteen bond servants plus the slaveholder's family. Leon County's Willis Williams recalled a similar situation, where his mother cooked meals for the master's family and the small slave population. Laura Randall noted in the late 1820s that slaves on the family's Jefferson County plantation were issued staples so that they could prepare their own morning and evening meals. On the other hand, the noon meal had to be prepared by a "cook specifically assigned to the task." This allowed less time away from fieldwork, but, as also occurred in West Africa, it allowed slaves to come together in a communal setting, if only for a brief period.[21]

Most planters allowed slaves to prepare their own meals at the end of each workday. Louis Napoleon and Claude A. Wilson agreed that at "'sun-down' the bondsmen would stop work and return to their cabins, [and] prepare their meals." Cooking and eating meals in their own cabins became important to slaves because it permitted them to spend "private" time with family and loved ones. With the variety of foods often limited, black cooks did what they could to "spice it up," but former slave Shack Thomas probably reflected the sentiments of many slaves when he said that the food remained simply "plain."[22]

If food for Florida's slaves generally proved at least minimally adequate, housing for the bond people left more to be desired. Medical doctors generally described the housing conditions as deplorable. Some of these physicians asserted that "the ugly appearances and uncomfortable condition of negro houses" contributed to the health problems of bond servants. Yet slaves depended greatly on these structures as a forum for many of their personal activities.[23]

Depending on the size of the plantation, its location, and the success of the slaveholder, slave quarters varied in size, construction, and quality. On the larger plantations many were situated away from the big house. This arrangement gave slaves a degree of privacy. The "quarters" could range in size from one or two cabins to small villages. A look into the past at conditions on one of East Florida's most historic places comes easily to today's student, for fortunately a good bit of information is available about the housing on Zephaniah Kingsley's principal East Florida plantation. There ruins of some of the buildings remain today. They remind us that the planter erected a series of structures made of tabby, arranging them in a semicircle. He located the quarters approximately one-quarter to one-half mile from his "big house." This permitted a semblance of privacy by keeping personal activities away from the owner's inquiring eyes. Most of these well-constructed houses consisted of one or two large rooms.[24]

Kingsley's village does not typify slave housing in Florida, however.

In line with regional patterns throughout the South, slave cabins normally were one-room wooden structures. Mary Biddle, to offer one example, described her living quarters as simply "a large one-room house built in the yard." John Finlayson of Middle Florida, who had over 180 slaves, put up rows of one-room cabins built with "whole logs notched together at the corners, with pine straw and mud to close the cracks."[25] Generally, slave carpenters covered the roofs of cabins with wooden shingles and hung shutters on the windows. Fireplaces in the early territorial period usually amounted only to dried mud and sticks, which constituted a serious fire hazard because many failed to draw properly.[26] During the 1840s and 1850s conditions for the bond servants (and whites, for that matter) improved, with many exterior chimneys made of brick and the fireplace openings inside consisting of either clay or brick. By then Douglas Parish could aver that his master "gave them comfortable quarters in which to live."[27]

Still, most slave housing during much of the antebellum period remained substandard. Slaves well remembered that reality. Squire Jackson said, for instance, that he was "born in a weather-beaten shanty in Madison, Fla. [on] September 14, 1841 of a large family." Claude Wilson's thoughts on the subject carried an understandable bitterness. He recalled inhabiting a "regular one room Quarters built of logs which was quite insignificant in comparison with palatial Dexter mansion on the plantation."[28]

With such substandard housing, daily living involved physical discomfort beyond that associated with slave labor and punishments. Slaves shivered in the winter and endured searing heat in the summer. Roofs leaked, and pests of all sorts found easy access to cabin dwellers. Fortunately, during the late 1840s and 1850s conditions improved slightly. A reform movement resulted in the replacement of dilapidated houses on some farms and plantations with better-built dwellings. The owners, acting primarily out of self-interest in terms of reducing labor loss resulting from the kinds of sickness associated with poor housing and hygiene, replaced old log cabins with frame buildings ranging in size from twelve by twelve feet to eighteen by eighteen feet.[29]

Our appreciation of the magnitude of slave housing problems elevates when we take into account the population of each tiny structure. The number of slaves to a house varied with size of the plantation, but typical structures became badly overcrowded when more than five bond servants lived in them. Census takers in 1860 recorded statistics that allow a glimpse of what slaves contended with in this regard. On the larger plantations a five-to-one ratio usually prevailed, whereas smaller farms offered slightly better conditions. Edward Haile of Alachua County possessed twenty cabins used by one hundred slaves, and David R. Williams had twenty-five cabins for 111 slaves. Leon County's William H. Branch dedicated thirteen cabins for use by fifty-six bond servants, and Fred R. Cotton of the same county had forty-eight cabins for 254 slaves. In Jackson County George W. Howard kept seventy persons in twelve cabins. For J. B. Owens the figures were eighteen cabins and eighty-nine servants. Somewhat unusual for Florida plantations at the time, Gadsden County's Joseph H. Seabrook and Jackson County's Benjamin Wynn averaged nine to ten individuals per cabin. On William Bellamy's Jefferson County plantation some families consisting of twelve members were crowded into one dwelling.[30]

Slave families found themselves compelled on many occasions to share their small homes, a circumstance that John Boles concluded was common in other parts of the South. George Noble Jones's plantation cabins were designed to house more than one family. At Winston Stephens's Rose Cottage, in Putnam County, three cabins housed eight slaves. A family of four lived in one; another held a mother, her daughter, and an unrelated female; and a single male occupied the third.[31]

Most cabins held few furnishings, at least when it came to furnishings provided by the owner. One former bond servant compared his provisions with those of his master. "The mansion was furnished with the latest furniture of the time," Claude A. Wilson remarked, "but the slave quarters had only the cheapest and barest necessities." The bare necessities for most slaves meant, for the most part, a bed and, perhaps, a simple wooden table and a chair or two. Wilson noted, for example, that his mother had "no stove, but cooked in the fire place using a skillet and spider."[32] Many former slaves remembered beds as the only furniture in their dwellings. When available at all, the frames often were constructed of wooden slats with ropes used as bedsprings. Willis Williams remembered an alternative arrangement.

"Boards were laid across for slats," he recorded, "and the mattress placed upon the boards." Mattresses—according to Wilson, Williams, Shack Thomas, and others—consisted of either chicken and goose feathers or moss. Sometimes only blankets or quilts cushioned a weary body. The bed, however comfortable or uncomfortable, usually stood in a corner of the one-room cabin on a dirt floor.[33]

With the tenacity they demonstrated in many areas of their lives, bond servants did not simply accept that the sparse furnishings provided by their masters were all that they could anticipate having for their family's use. Rather, they attempted to obtain more furniture through their own efforts. Claude Wilson gave the impression that, when his family left the plantation after the Civil War, they had enough furniture to fill a wagon pulled by several mules. Some of it may have been fashioned by family members, and some of it may have been purchased. Burrel, who could make money by fishing and hunting, seems to have bought furniture for his home. In Middle Florida, Murat plantation slaves who earned money for their garden crops presumably also added more furnishings to their cabins in the same manner.[34]

When it came to clothing themselves against the elements, Florida slaves may have fared better than many of their counterparts elsewhere in the South, although a milder climate deserves much of the credit. As was the case in much of the southern region, bond persons in the state generally received new or used clothes twice a year. Women might receive several dresses, two chemises, and a pair of shoes. For men two pairs of pants, two shirts, and a hat typically sufficed. According to Wilma King, enslaved parents had "little to say about what their children wore." Young children usually ran around naked, or boys wore only long shirts while girls wore frocks or dresses. They would not receive shoes until they were sent to the fields. Occasionally a supply of cast-off clothing might supplement typical allotments, as when Octavia Stephens's brother gave her old clothes "for the negroes."[35]

Slaves held on many farms and plantations routinely fashioned their own clothing, usually from cloth furnished to them by their masters. The type of cloth might range from light or heavy cotton material to the woolen fabric kersey to linsey and osnaberg. As Acie Thomas related, "Clothing were made during the summer and stored away for the cool winters." She added, "Young slave girls were kept busy knitting cotton and woolen stockings." By age seven or eight Patience Campbell had begun to spin and weave light cotton material for use on the plantation.[36]

Although slaves generally owned few clothes, runaway advertisements nonetheless suggested that, through their own ingenuity, some obtained more than the usual one or two changes of attire. As in the case of furniture, some bond servants likely purchased extras with whatever money they came by. Eulalia, for instance, boasted more than a couple of changes of clothes and other belongings; she "carried a large bundle of clothing of her own, consisting of some muslin, calico and checked homespun dresses, blankets, handkerchiefs, &c. Together with some utensils of blue Liverpool china" at the time she fled her St. Augustine residence. After George absconded from a Leon County plantation, he was described as having "plenty of clothing." When Jesse left a Gadsden County plantation, he "took with him a variety of good clothing."[37]

As for shoes, men and women received one pair during each winter, usually of the style known as brogans. "Campbell slaves did not have to go barefoot—not during the colder months, anyway," Shack Thomas explained. "As soon as the winter would come," he continued, "each one of them was given a pair of bright, untanned leather 'brogans', that would be the envy of the vicinity." Thomas's luck held with him when it came to shoes because not all slaves experienced such good fortune. Most owners concentrated on whatever shoes were available at the right price rather than on quality or comfort. Thus, Rabun M. Scarborough would purchase footwear whenever a good occasion arose, "thinking it best to get them while I can." He would wait "to give them out until cold weather." Others delayed until the last minute, then obtained whatever they could. As late as December 12 of one year, overseer Amon DeLaughter was still reminding himself to "get Negro shoes." Obtaining proper footwear became an even greater problem during slavery's final years, as Civil War shortages touched slaves as well as whites. Conscientious owners such as Ossian B. Hart of Tampa and Jacksonville sometimes traveled hundreds of miles to find acceptable goods to purchase.[38]

Although some enslaved blacks wore store-bought shoes, others crafted their own. That is what Patience Campbell's father ("a finished shoemaker") did, and his labors resulted in far more comfortable footwear. "After tanning and curing his hides by placing them in water with oak bark for several days and then exposing them to the sun to dry," she commented, "he would cut out the uppers and the soles after measuring the foot to be shod." Although not as adept at the trade as was Campbell, Squire Jackson remembered making "all the shoes he wore by hand from cow hides."[39]

Health problems plagued slaves in Florida. The semitropical climate brought with it many diseases and other problems, and poor housing, hard work in an exposed environment, and a diet sometimes less than nutritious compounded the difficulties of the slaves' lot. The terror of yellow fever and measles is discussed in chapter 4. Beyond those plagues cholera, pneumonia, colds, chills, fevers, intestinal disorders, and rheumatism chronically visited the slave quarters.

Reports of such health problems have survived from most regions during the antebellum period. Typically, overseer John Evans recorded that "old sucky has had pneumonia in its worst form." Octavia Stephens, during a sixteen-month period, repeatedly informed her soldier husband of the many illnesses her relatively few bond servants suffered. By way of example she covered Big Jane's fever, Jess's and Polly's whooping cough, that "Joe has had two chills," that Burrel "has a very bad cold," and Georgie's two fevers. Colds, intestinal disorders, and fevers struck widely among the El Destino plantation slave community in one four-month period. On the DeLaughter plantation, six slaves were stricken with typhoid fever, with Martha succumbing to the disease. During the warm months of May, June, and July, many slaves ailed continually on Middle Florida's Wirtland plantation. Overseer Kingsley B. Gibbs at East Florida's Laurel Grove plantation noted in early September 1841 that just about everyone had been "somewhat sickly on the place[,] the weather being very hot for the season."[40]

Injuries and accidents also beset enslaved blacks with regularity. Broken bones, cuts, hernias, burns, snakebites, and alligator attacks all figured prominently in slaves' lives. In Madison County overseer Amon DeLaughter noted that William had "cut" his leg and that June had died from burn injuries. Another bond servant had sustained a cut on the head. On November 18, 1856, he recorded that a "negro house" had burned to the ground, killing an entire slave family consisting of Prince, Harriet, and their baby. Such tales of injuries and accidents were echoed all over the state.[41]

When a slave fell seriously ill or suffered a serious injury, slaveholders in Florida and throughout the South usually sought the assistance of medical doctors. Susan B. Eppes remarked, for instance, that a physician had been "employed by the year" to treat bond servants on her father's plantation. Amon DeLaughter, reflecting similar actions by owners and overseers generally, called time and again on Dr. Norman G. McDonald and Dr. John Hunter Pope. The health of leased slaves also commanded owners' attention. As a matter of course, many would insert provisions in labor contracts that lessees were to seek "medical advice or attention" when the laborers became ill or were hurt. Drs. Byrd Charles Willis and Thomas Munroe shared a good bit of this business in Leon and Gadsden Counties. Unfortunately, the undeveloped state of medical science resulted in doctors treating whites and blacks by sometimes injurious methods, such as bleeding, cupping, and blistering. Medical treatment could result, and often did, in a terminal cure.[42]

When doctors were not available or when problems did not appear too great, slaveholders and overseers might try their hand at doctoring slaves. Thomas Randall proudly reported in 1828 from Jefferson County that most of the Wirt family slaves had been sick "since their arrival, and all in turn recovered . . . under my judicious treatment." Amon DeLaughter arranged to have a neighbor pull his "negros tooth" one Sunday. DeLaughter also would administer various concoctions, supposedly curative, to ailing slaves. Chemonie plantation overseer John Evans "bled England and [popped] a blister on the back of his neck" and administered "Calomel" before seeking a doctor's advice. Another overseer asked owner George Noble Jones to send a "Websters Medical Dictionary" so that he might treat slaves on the El Destino plantation.[43]

Bond servants, quite aware of the standards of treatment they otherwise might receive, sometimes felt more comfortable being treated by slave herb doctors. These individuals, highly regarded in the slave community, ministered to a vast range of illnesses and injuries. Squire

Jackson recollected that "'herb doctors' went from home to home" in the normal course of affairs. Willis Williams explained that some men spent a lot of time "around the 'grannies' during slavery [and] learned much about herbs and roots and how they were used to cure all manner of ills."[44]

With slaveholders the standards for physical treatment of slaves weighed perhaps as heavily as did standards for material conditions, but the slaveholders' interest focused most times on the limits of how and how much they might punish an errant slave. As mentioned earlier in this chapter, the territorial council in the 1820s barred "cruel and unusual punishment" of slaves, but the broad and vague language intimidated few of the harder hearts. Even given the statute, the law permitted a variety of vicious punishments such as cropping ears, branding, and nailing ears to posts. Masters, overseers, or any white person confronted by insolence or bad or insulting language could inflict punishment. Fines for going too far could range theoretically from $100 to $300.[45]

Whippings constituted the most common method for physical punishment of bond servants. Whites might whip slaves for just about any substantive infraction, including absconding, drunkenness, public disturbance, and other offenses. Especially in Middle Florida, the incidence of recourse to whippings apparently ran high. "The slaves . . . are generally treated with the greatest severity," a visitor to the region remarked in 1838. "A whip is the only language used with them." Most area planters staunchly defended the practice. "Let one of my negroes [rob me, and] he is whipped and corrected," declared Achille Murat. "The bodily pain once undergone, he feels no bad consequence from it." Some whites even could make light of the pain inflicted. Henry Wirt, according to his sister Ellen McCormick, once complained that "he had nothing to do for recreation except driving the hogs from under the house and occasionally flogg[ing] Clem," his personal bond servant.[46]

Southern lore has placed blame squarely on overseers for much cruelty inflicted with the lash, and examples available in Florida tend to support that claim. In one such instance D. N. Moxley gave a slave a "genteel floging." Reacting to reports of the torture, absentee owner George Noble Jones asked another one of his overseers to investigate.

After inquiries, the second overseer reported back to Jones, acknowledging that Moxley had laid the whipping on rather "thick." Whether Jones thereafter penalized Moxley in any manner is not known. In rare cases slaves were whipped for no reason at all, at least none apparent from the known circumstances. As mentioned already, such seems to have occurred with Clem, the hard-pressed bondsman of Henry Wirt.[47]

The majority of available Florida slave testimonies relate stories of whippings or else remembrances of other bond servants being flogged. George Edwards recalled whippings in East Florida, particularly in the St. Augustine area. The whip was used, although sparingly, on the Lenton Plantation according to Bolden Hall. Margrett Nickerson testified that her sister Holly "wouldn' holler and jes take [a whipping] and go on." Charlotte Martin's memories of slaves who "were severely flogged" remained vivid. And Sarah Brown Bryant still recoiled from thoughts of the whip used on her sister.[48]

The lash sometimes was wielded by women in order to make slaves stand in fear. Mary Biddle clearly recollected that her master's second wife "was always ready and anxious to whip a slave for the least misdemeanor." Douglas Dorsey echoed Biddle's assertion by stating his master's wife was "a very cruel woman, [who] would whip the slaves herself for any misdemeanor." Madison County's Nancy DeLaughter occasionally applied the whip herself rather than setting the overseer to the task. On July 30, 1855, for instance, she "whip[ped] Marendy." One year later DeLaughter flogged France.[49]

Whippings led on numerous occasions to the death of the victim. Douglas Parish's master told him that he "had seen overseers beat slaves to death."[50] Charlotte Martin grieved when her brother was "whipped to death for taking part in one of the religious ceremonies" on the plantation. Jefferson County overseer Guilford Dawkins lashed to death a slave named Jane. An overseer of Madison County, Nathaniel Sanders, beat the last breath from Charles. In Leon County an overseer named William killed a slave by severe flogging. A man named Amon hitched Sarah Bryant's sister Liza to a plow like a "horse or a mule" and whipped her as she pulled the implement. Liza finally succumbed to the "horrible treatment."[51]

The bodies of many slaves and, later, freedpersons bore the permanent scars of floggings. Runaway advertisements proved the assertion in the case of slaves. Of more than four hundred notices surveyed, at least 30 percent described individuals as having flogging scars. Another 150 bore either iron clogs, chains, iron collars, or pot hooks around their necks. Adam, a slave of Madison County's Augustus H. Lanier, evidenced, for example, "heavy scars on his back, some few on his breast and some on his arms." George ran away from his Middle Florida plantation twice in 1843 and at age twenty-eight already "his left leg, thigh and back showed marks caused by whipping." William B. McCall described Jesse, a mulatto, as having "a scar on his left cheek about the size of a ten cent piece, and also, one on his left knee, which causes him to limp a little when walking." Other punishments also carried physical manifestations. The ads mentioned individuals with toes removed and ears cropped. One man had been castrated. Some had been branded, usually on the breast and shoulder, with the master's initial or surname.[52]

Policies of masters determined the frequency and intensity of whippings, and some masters, especially in East Florida, minimized or avoided the practice. Douglas Parish's master was one such man. According to the ex-bondsman, the owner seldom punished his slaves and "never did he permit his overseer to do so." Parish continued, "If the slaves failed to do their work . . . He [the master] would warn them and show his black whip which was usually sufficient." Willis Williams was only a youngster of nine when freedom came, but he could not recall "any unpleasant experiences as related by some other ex-slaves." In fact, some slaveholders truly believed that they treated their bond servants well. A. Danforth, for example, reacted in surprise when his slave ran away. The master insisted that Titus had "no cause for absenting himself" from the estate.[53]

For those owners who whipped, the punishment could be inflicted in a variety of ways. Instruments used could range from switches to sticks to leather whips. Some owners also took advantage of chains, clogs, and other special devices to restrain bond servants. When Katy was captured after she had run away with her children, owner Peter Williamson of Jackson County tied a chain around her neck, secured her to the axle of a wagon, and whipped her as she was pulled through the streets of Pensacola. An English visitor to Middle Florida wrote in the late 1830s that he witnessed in the streets of Tallahassee "two negroes with heavy iron collars around their necks." The observer added, "These were captured run-aways; the collars which must have weighed seven to ten pounds had spikes projecting on either side." He concluded, "One of the poor creatures had hold of the spikes as he walked along to ease the load that pressed painfully on his shoulders."[54]

Punishments might not always involve whippings, but other techniques could prove equally painful and deadly. Henry Williams, a Nassau County overseer, killed a slave named John with "sticks, switches, and clubs." East Florida overseer George Thompson shot and killed a slave under his supervision. When George (who was mentioned as having such heavy scars) ran away for the second time, his pursuers shot him "8 or 9 times before he was subdued."[55]

Owners and others in charge of slaves sometimes were called before the bar of justice when punishments crossed certain boundaries and resulted in a public outcry. The case of Jackson County's Peter Williamson is an example. Having cruelly treated his slave Katy, the owner was summoned before a magistrate, indicted, and eventually convicted and fined $100. The following examples further illustrate that some malefactors might receive punishment for slave mistreatment. In 1829 Governor William P. DuVal sought to bring to justice Edward Robinson for the murder of Claiborn, a Gadsden County slave. The governor authorized a $200 reward for Robinson's capture. And the Orange County circuit court fined George Thompson, an overseer employed on a St. Johns Rivers plantation, $300 for killing a slave in his custody. On the other hand, in the early 1830s Lt. William H. Baker, an army officer in Pensacola, accidentally shot and killed Maria, a slave belonging to another officer. Baker was indicted and prosecuted. After the jury ruled the death of Maria accidental, Baker was found not guilty of manslaughter.[56]

Cases involving the wrongful death of another slaveholder's bond servant came before the courts as well. When Tom, who belonged to Henry Wilson, accidentally shot Sarah McNeil's bond servant Harry, McNeil sued Wilson for $600. On many such occasions when enslaved blacks were accidentally killed by another party, the owner received compensation for loss of property. The courts respected the property rights of slaveholders, and when slaves were injured or killed for no "justifiable reason," compensation resulted.[57]

With the enactment of the 1828 slave code, bond servants supposedly came under the protection of the law. But enforcement of these laws proved difficult indeed. With planters controlling the judicial system in most areas, treatment of bond servants rested in the hands of slaveholders. As such, they lived, in most cases, above reproach.[58] Intervention by the community or the state, it was argued, violated the principle that slaveholders held undisputed power over their bond servants. As James M. Denham has observed, "There was little motivation for rigorous enforcement of the law." Community pressure and the code of "Southern Honor" did little to stop or prevent some slaveholders from mistreating their slaves.[59]

In summary, the laws of Florida provided slaves some protection from extreme physical mistreatment. When a public outcry resulted from the mistreatment of a bond servant, perpetrators sometimes faced superior and circuit courts, justices of the peace, and magistrates. The justice system in Florida generally refused, though, to convict slaveholders or other whites for the murder or mistreatment of bond servants. Many times when a case arising from the death of a slave came before a court, the defendant would be punished only for manslaughter with a fine. When the courts ruled that a master should treat his bond servants more humanely by providing them with food, clothing, and shelter, the decisions proved hard to enforce. Through the laws masters held virtually absolute power over the bodies of their enslaved servants.

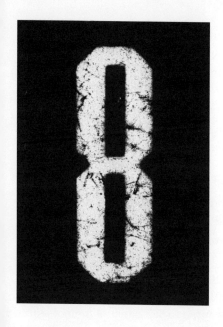

SOCIAL INTERACTION BETWEEN WHITES AND BLACKS

Although they lived largely in separate worlds, blacks and whites in antebellum Florida interwove the threads of their lives into a myriad of complex patterns. Masters and slaves could not escape each other. Slaveholders might have held indubitable power over their bond servants, but day-to-day existence demanded interdependence. To weave their way through the mazes thus created, blacks and whites often assumed roles that masked reality. Many times the roles, in turn, shaped relationships between the two groups in both the short and the long term. An understanding of the dynamics that made possible such a system requires careful examination of how and where the two worlds touched and how members of each race acted and reacted.[1]

White dependence on black slaves came in a multitude of forms, but it began in many cases with a white man's sense that he could judge his own success and social standing only by whether he owned slaves or, in many cases, how many slaves he owned. To an extent the question became one of self-image, as well as one of financial prospects. Thomas Randall offers a case in point. A migrant from Maryland in the late 1820s, he aspired to become a large Middle Florida planter and looked forward to the purchase of more and more slaves to help him achieve that status. He chafed at the challenge presented, particularly because, as he put it, "there is not the same certainty and convenience in procuring" slaves in Florida as in Maryland and Virginia. The high price of bond servants depressed him. He insisted that slaves he desired cost "25 to 50 percent" more than elsewhere. Even after ascending to the territorial bench, Randall remained committed to pursuing a life view that saw him first as a "planter" and only second as a "judge." By 1840 he neared at least partial satisfaction of his goal. That year he held fifty slaves. Hundreds of individuals such as Hardy Croom, Robert and John Gamble, William P. DuVal, and Achille Murat shared the same dreams and, at least for a time, success.[2]

Randall and his affluent friends possessed numerous advantages that aided their aspirations for slaveholding, but men of lesser means also shared their dreams. In East Florida small farmer Winston Stephens no less than Randall faced concerns about his self-image. He wanted to regard himself as a gentleman planter. His well-heeled future father-in-law, James Bryant, wanted to see him as a man of status as well. Accordingly, Bryant assured his daughter Octavia that, with wealth arising from his ownership of slaves, Stephens would rank as their social equal and placed a seal of approval on their subsequent marriage.[3]

Isaiah D. Hart shared the same ambitions as Randall, Stephens, and Bryant. An East Florida holdover from the Spanish era, he began his adult life virtually impoverished in the Patriot War's aftermath. He managed to overcome the situation by building a fortune based on a little slave stealing early in life, plus government positions and preferment in later years. He also emerged in 1821 and 1822 as the principal developer of Jacksonville. The status Hart longed for, though, was that of planter. In 1835 he signaled as much by advertising that he would exchange Jacksonville lots for more bond servants. His drive paid off. Five years afterward Hart could glow with pride at his two-thousand-acre plantation and his possession of fifty-seven bond servants. He called the plantation Paradise.[4]

Although dreams of planter status might sometimes take slaveholders and slaveholders-to-be on flights of fancy, such persons acknowledged their dependence on the peculiar institution, at least within their intimate circles. Ellen McCormick, for example, once turned her brother down for a loan, declaring that "[we] have to purchase negroes to supply ourselves with necessaries."[5] In Gadsden County Rabun Scarborough acknowledged to his wife their dependence on slave labor to keep the farm functioning during his Civil War absence. Further, Scarborough felt an "uneasiness" that his bond servants would make "but a small crop" without the presence of a white man on the farm. Similar comments dot Winston Stephens's correspondence to his wife and family members. His foreman, Burrel, naturally stood out: "tell Burrel to examine the new ground"; "tell Burrel not to get behind in his cleaning up"; "tell Burrel to continue his duty as a good servant"; "Let Burrel and Tom split rails"; "Let Burrel hunt the hogs about the Bluff"; and "I want Burrel to plant corn soon and I want him to prepare the land well."[6]

White dependence on black slaves extended beyond getting in the crops on large plantations. It included tending to slaveholder families and making sure that everything worked as it should within the plantation (or farm) world. It literally could come down to something as elemental as getting food on the table. Laura Randall admitted as much in a letter written from Jefferson County in 1827. She expressed to her mother in Maryland serious disappointment that their cook had not arrived from the "Eastern Shore," stating that the cook was "a very necessary article in this country." Until the slave took up residence a few months later, Randall's family lived basically on "fowl and water," that is to say, chicken soup. Multiplied one hundred times, such small needs amounted to large dependence, as Zephaniah Kingsley voiced in words with which many no doubt silently agreed: "It certainly is humiliating to a proud master to reflect, that he depends on his slave even for bread to eat," the East Florida planter observed. "But such is the fact."[7]

On any number of occasions dependence of whites on blacks reached such a level of significance that compromises resulted to the slaves' benefit. Such developments drew criticisms on the whites by others of their race. Jonathan Roberson, the sawmill overseer at El Destino plantation in Jefferson County, learned this lesson by exhibiting a reliance on bond servants under his control. Roberson allowed fifteen slaves to report to work after sunrise and to take breaks at their convenience. Presumably he did so in response to the slaves' insistence. Many times the overseer would not show up for days to supervise his workers. The slaves showed their ability and fidelity, but Roberson's public display of dependence on them did not sit well with the other overseer on the plantation, John Evans, who complained to the owner in no uncertain terms. In the event Roberson kept his job, enjoying a fifteen-year tenure despite the complaining of Evans and other overseers about his management style. Apparently, he persisted in that style and in his visible dependence on the bond servants.[8]

Just as masters relied on bond servants, slaves depended on their owners in countless ways. Especially, they counted on an ability to gain the approval and blessings of the slaveholder by good faith efforts. On the Thomas Folsom plantation hardworking slaves succeeded in that quest. The slaveholder responded by making sure his bond servants had, as Acie Thomas remembered, "plenty of everything to eat." With emancipation half of Folsom's slaves immediately left the plantation "glad of their freedom." Yet the remaining half stayed, believing that they could depend on Folsom for continued fair dealing.[9]

Whether individuals on either side of the Folsom plantation equation were role playing or else felt genuine care or respect for their opposites is hard to determine; certainly, many slaveholders convinced themselves rightly or wrongly that their actions had earned them a place in their slaves' hearts. Thus, Laura Wirt could believe that Lucy and Betsey felt "the most devoted affection" to her mother Elizabeth Wirt. George N. Jones had a similar perception that his slaves at Chemonie were always "anxious and glad to see him." At Tampa, shortly after the Civil War's end, Ossian B. Hart would argue that his slaves' personal regards for their master had outlasted slavery. "My former servants are all my friends," he declared, "because they know that I am theirs."[10]

During several armed conflicts—the Second Seminole War and the Civil War ranking as most important—the loyalty of Florida's slaves to their masters came under severe trial. The results demonstrated that most bond servants chose, when they could, the chance for freedom over any sense of affection or obligation to their owners. Masks that had rested firmly in place now could be discarded. Opportunities to leave masters especially arose in East Florida, although conditions in Middle and West Florida afforded limited possibilities. The percentages of those who remained behind despite the chance for freedom are not known with certainly, but thousands of bond servants "voted with their feet." One historian estimated that more than one thousand may have fled in East Florida alone during the opening stages of the Second Seminole War, even though slaves in the region tended to benefit from better conditions than those prevailing in Middle Florida. As a result of one Civil War incursion into Jackson County from Pensacola, another six hundred bond persons opted for a chance to leave masters behind. Leon County's Susan B. Eppes argued, though, that loyalty found more adherents than such examples might suggest. She recalled that some slaves "deserted them" through the Civil War years, but many stood "faithfully by their masters to the bitter end."[11]

Slaveholder perceptions of slave affection and loyalty affected the evolution of slavery as an institution. In the world of antebellum Florida, owners could easily convince themselves that they had earned undying affection and loyalty from their bond persons. Thus, they easily rationalized away the practice of routinely breaking the laws regulating slave life and behavior when it suited their convenience or inclination. They could always argue to themselves that their slaves were different because of the relationships and understandings forged by them as masters. This state of affairs facilitated more social interaction between blacks and whites by creating opportunities for mixing that otherwise might not have existed.

One aspect of planter willingness to break the law concerned flaunting legal proscriptions about slave literacy. Sometimes the needs of the farm, plantation, or business required literacy if blacks were to perform certain skilled tasks. Believing that he could "trust" his slaves, an owner simply convinced himself of the law's inapplication. Brian Rucker noticed the phenomenon among slaveholders in West Florida. "Some masters taught their slaves to read, write and cipher," he reported, "in order to better conduct the mechanical and commercial aspects of the business." The wife of the black driver on one plantation assisted her husband with the daily management schedules of bond servants. According to Douglas Dorsey, that was because she "could read and write a little." Banks Meacham taught his mulatto son, Robert, how to read and write. He even tried to enroll him in a private academy at Quincy until the other white parents rebelled at his temerity. As mentioned in earlier chapters, John Parkhill of Leon County instructed James Page how to read and write, and members of the Blount family did the same for their slave Stepney Dixon at Bartow in Polk County. Wills, letters, journals, and newspaper ads regarding slaves suggest that upwards of 15 percent of Florida bond servants had gained some proficiency in reading and writing before emancipation. As a result, the outside world moved closer to the slave, and the slave tended to maintain closer and more regular ties with the outside world.[12]

Although such relatively high rates of literacy or semiliteracy may appear surprising, knowledge of one unexpected source explains the reasons. Some black children picked up the rudiments of reading, writing, and counting from white playmates. On the farm or plantation youngsters of both colors, particularly boys, found common cause in passing time with happy diversions, at least until the slave boys and girls reached age ten to twelve. Thus, the situation of a white student's passing on teachings to a slave friend could occur frequently. Perhaps the most notable such case in United States history involved Frederick Douglass. Douglas Dorsey explained how the process might work in Florida. The young slave was told to carry the Mattair children's books to school for them. Willie Mattair, having become friendly as a result, liked to "teach Douglas what he learned in school." Eventually, Douglas gained a familiarity with the alphabet and with basic numbers.[13]

That white parents could react with passion to a black child's advances in literacy skills courtesy of their own white children is illustrated by a further look at Douglas Dorsey's experience. Having picked up a bit of learning, the young bond servant prided himself on his accomplishment. Mrs. Mattair felt quite different. Her temper flared on hearing the news. One day she called her son and Douglas into the dining room. In front of both boys she asked Douglas if he recognized certain alphabet letters and numbers on a piece of paper she held in her hand. He responded in the affirmative and began to call out the numbers and the letters. As an interviewer recorded, "When he reached the number ten, very proud of his learning, she struck him a heavy blow across the face, saying to him 'if I ever catch you making another figure anywhere I'll cut off your right arm.'" She then whipped both boys. To ease the soreness, "Willie would steal grease from the house and together [with Douglas] they would slip into the barn and grease each other's backs."[14]

As Douglas Dorsey could vividly avow if he were alive today, many white parents abhorred the kind of social interaction involved in white and black children playing together. They saw an immediate threat to the perception of slaves and slavery that they wished their children to adopt. East Florida's Rebecca Bryant was one. She grew concerned when Henry and George Bryant and Ben Gaines started a friendship with slave youngsters. Ultimately, she put a stop to the fun. In a letter Bryant explained her action. "It was necessary to do something," she asserted, "to keep them from such constant and familiar intercourse with the negroes."[15]

The extent to which most parents limited interracial playing on the farm or plantation cannot be measured precisely, but slave testimonies and reminiscences from slave-owning families suggest that such social interaction remained common despite whatever protests were lodged. Louis Napoleon happily recalled playing with the "master's three young boys" when he was a lad. Other ex-slaves, such as Acie Thomas, Sarah Murray, and Douglas Dorsey, remembered hours spent in pleasant pastimes with white children their age.[16]

Much of the confrontation and conflict on the farms and plantations of Florida stemmed not from children's play but from the sexual exploitation of female slaves by white males. That kind of social interaction took several forms. They related, in greater and lesser degrees, to the white men's perception of the black women's sexuality and fecundity. "The sexual exploitation of female slaves was rooted in the stereotypes surrounding black women," Deborah Gray White observed. "Unlike white women, who were thought to be prudish, pious, and domestic (an equally erroneous stereotype), black women seemed sensual and promiscuous, a notion formed when the Englishmen first met Africans."[17]

Perhaps the most common form of sexual exploitation concerned planter desires for the perpetuation of slavery through natural increase. Similar to the experience of other slave women who lived in the antebellum South, Florida's female bond servants found themselves expected to reproduce subject to their owner's will. Planters such as

George N. Jones pestered their overseers for information about pregnancies and new births. Octavia Stephens reflected the sentiments of many owners when she wrote her husband, "I am coming to the good news, now dont shout when I tell you that you are a negro and colt better off than when you left yes Sarah gave birth to a little girl on the morning of the 4th of July after a whole night of hard labour."[18] Slave memories ran harder on the subject. Douglas Parish recalled with disdain that his master purchased his mother "to be a 'breeder.'" Louis Napoleon's testimony took a similar course. He asserted that his mother "was known as a 'breeder' and was kept in the . . . Randolph mansion."[19]

Pressures exerted on them to act as breeders degraded slave women, as did other owner-imposed circumstances. The clothing provided to women, for instance, lessened their ability to command personal respect and to resist sexual exploitation. The climate and work conditions in Florida sometimes made a difficult situation worse. In the hot and humid weather, which could last from seven to nine months in West and Middle Florida and as many as ten months in the peninsula, slave women wore few clothes and usually no underwear. Whatever clothing was worn, special care had to be taken not to damage it because planters provided few, if any, replacements. Thus, while washing clothes and pursuing other domestic chores, bond servants pulled up their skirts. In the fields many worked with their skirts pinned up. In extreme cases, such as exemplified by cruel owner Jesse Watts's Madison County plantation, slave women and men labored almost naked.[20]

Exposure exacerbated white men's existing interest in black women as sexual objects, increasing what already amounted to widespread sexual exploitation of the bond servants to gratify white desires. Thus, a terrible situation was created for many black women. Evelyn Beasley of Tampa recollected the impact on her family. "Her mother was forced into companionship with this man," an interviewer related, "and although he appeared to have developed a real affection for her that lasted even after the slaves had been freed, she always hated him."[21]

Relationships between victimized slave women and the wives and other female relatives of the white men involved were poisoned easily by this form of sexual exploitation, sometimes leading to the separation of slave women from their children. "What must be the . . . desolate heart of [the slaveholder's] wife," Major Thomas Williams remarked at Fort Meade in 1857, "who, perhaps childless herself, sees around her, in the pale black & yellow faces of the slave children, in glaring contrast with the ebony of the mothers, the features of the husband repeated." Douglas Dorsey knew firsthand the problems that could result. His mother gave birth to a little boy "whose complexion was rather light." An argument then ensued at the plantation house. "Mrs. Matair began accusing Colonel Matair as being the father of the child," Dorsey recorded. "Naturally, the Colonel denied, but Mrs. Matair kept harassing him about it until he finally agreed to his wife's desire and sold the child." The onetime bondsman added, "It was taken from its mother's breast at the age of eight months and auctioned off . . . to the highest bidder."[22]

How widespread was the practice of this type of sexual exploitation of black women by white men in antebellum Florida? Clues can be extracted from the size of the reported population of mulattoes among slaves. Out of a slave population of 39,310 in 1850, for example, approximately 2,780 individuals (or 7.07 percent of Florida's black population) appeared to represent mixed racial origins. Ten years later the number and percentage of mulattoes had increased. Of 61,745 slaves a total of 4,741 persons were listed as mulattoes. That figure represented 7.67 percent of the total.[23]

The census figures may have underreported actual numbers of mulattoes because census takers depended on information from sometimes reluctant owners and overseers. Nonetheless, the practice of miscegenation proved quite common in certain areas of the state, especially in those regions of East and West Florida with strong Spanish heritages. Even without the Spanish influence the birth of mulatto children occurred often, for, as Wyatt-Brown has noted, "Miscegenation between a white male and black female posed almost no ethical problems for the antebellum Southern community." Laws against interracial sexual relations offered few obstacles. At least in the east and west, Daniel Schafer concluded, offenders "risked little more than gossip and ostracism."[24]

Some white males who exploited black females in a sexual manner occupied the highest levels of power and wealth in East Florida and, to a lesser extent, in other areas. These men suffered little in the way of overt public condemnation, even when they chose to cohabit with black women. Interracial unions appear to have been tolerated and, at times, accepted. White fathers frequently acknowledged their black offspring in public documents and elsewhere. In 1828, to cite one example, George J. F. Clarke of St. Augustine acknowledged his mulatto family, which included sons James, George, Joseph, John, and William. Whites in the area already "knew" of his "second" family before Clarke made his paternity a matter of public record when he tried to save his sons from paying a discriminatory poll tax.

Many similar examples appear in surviving public ledgers and files. Jacksonville's founder, Isaiah D. Hart, as Canter Brown has shown, "openly consorted with a black mistress until his death in 1861." Apparently, they shared one or more children. Other men such as Charles W. Clarke, Francisco X. Sanchez, and John Leslie fathered mulatto children and recognized them in their wills. Daniel Schafer found at least eleven Spanish holdovers who sired and acknowledged their black children in East Florida. Doubtlessly, many others await discovery or else chose to avoid declaring their paternity for the world to see.[25]

With its Spanish heritage West Florida witnessed patterns concerning sexual relations between slave women and white men that paralleled those in East Florida. Jackson Morton, who served in the United States Senate from 1849 to 1855 and in the Confederate Congress through the Civil War, seemingly fathered mulatto children with several slave women. Joseph Forsyth, a state senator in 1852, reputedly maintained a long, intimate relationship with one of his "loyal" female slaves. Forsyth ultimately manumitted the woman, giving her and her three children $6,000 for their transportation to the North and their maintenance and education afterward. John Hunt waited until his death to act. The will of this onetime member of the territorial council freed a slave woman and what were presumably his five children.[26]

A good number of Middle Florida planters, although less open about their liaisons than their counterparts in East and West Florida, kept slave mistresses and fathered mulatto children as well. Achille Murat, no less discreet than most of his friends, earned a notorious reputation for sexual encounters with slaves on his plantation. One such relationship ended tragically. A slave mother believed that Murat soon would sell her and the child that he fathered. Instead of parting with her child, the slave took the child's life and then took her own. Banks Meacham of Gadsden County also excepted himself from the rule of polite discretion. As mentioned earlier, he tried to enroll his mulatto son in Quincy's private academy. Meacham cared so much for his boy and treated him so well that the lad did not know if he was slave or free. Some owners, to the contrary, acted with a total disregard for the humanity of slave women and their mulatto children. These men might even offer the sexual services of their female slaves to friends and other visitors as a part of their desire to extend hospitality. Amon DeLaughter was such a person. While visiting friends and family, the Madison County man recorded in his diary that he would "hunt up a negro and go to bed."[27]

The scars of sexual exploitation continued to affect slave women well after slavery's end. They deeply resented bearing numerous children, which implied they were promiscuous and fair game for rape. Charlotte Martin reflected in old age on her former master. "[He] had sexual relations with his female slaves, for the products of miscegenation were very remunerative," she explained. "These offsprings were in demand as house servants." Ocalan Jenne L. Harris recalled her grandmother's stories about unwanted sexual liaisons with the master's son. "There was no relationship between the two, only a common bond in blood," Harris explained. "My grandmother didn't remember this with any pride."[28]

An example in East Florida demonstrates how tangled the web of sexual relations between whites and blacks could become. The tale began when two white brothers, John and William Parker, arrived in Florida from North Carolina about 1831. At the Second Seminole War's conclusion they relocated from Columbia to Hillsborough County, transferring their cattle operations a decade or so later into present-day Polk and Hardee Counties. William built his homestead at today's Homeland, a rural community near Fort Meade. The cattleman brought several slaves with him. They included Rachel Davis, then in her early twenties, and Rachel's sons Alfred, born in 1852, and Samuel, born in 1854. Subsequently, Rachel gave birth to a daughter, Eliza, during 1855 or 1856. All the children were mulattoes, apparently fathered by William Parker.[29]

The saga of Rachel Davis and her children took a dramatic turn in the mid-1850s after the Third Seminole War enveloped the southwestern and central peninsula. William Parker died from wounds received in a skirmish at Fort Meade on June 14, 1856. His brother John soon came into control of that part of William's estate that included Rachel and the children. John, who had served as Hillsborough County's sheriff and grazed large cattle herds on the open range, took Rachel as his own. In 1861 he apparently fathered her son Lloyd, who was followed by a daughter, Minerva, in 1862 and son, Corrie, in 1872. When Parker moved to Homeland during or soon after the Civil War, Rachel and the children came with him. She and her sons and daughters maintained at least some ties with the white Parkers, while prospering through marriage or else through citrus, cattle, and farming operations. Rachel died at Homeland on August 1, 1913. By then miscegenation had existed as an ordinary part of life for generations in the Parker and Davis families.[30]

As may have been the case with Rachel Davis and John Parker, some racially mixed unions involved varying degrees of fondness and attachment. As suggested earlier, East Florida especially offered a climate of some toleration and flexibility. White males at times publicly recognized relationships with black women and the paternity of the children from these unions. Duval County's Zephaniah Kingsley, for example, held his Senegalese wife, Anna Jai, in great affection and respect. He would entertain visitors at his plantation with his "coloured wife . . . at the head of the table surrounded by handsome and happy children." Kingsley asserted in his 1843 will that his wife was "one of the finest women I have ever known" and commented that she "has been true and faithful to me." The planter further noted that "she has always been respected as my wife and as such I acknowledge her, nor do I think that her truth, honor, integrity, moral conduct or good sense will lose in comparison to anyone."[31]

Kingsley's open acknowledgment of a slave woman as his wife constituted a rare situation, but the fact that their relationship involved reciprocal care and concern did not. Examples of similar relationships are many. Isaiah D. Hart, Kingsley's friend, grew strongly attached to his slave Amy Hickman. He praised her "long, faithful, kind and affectionate services to me," mandating that his executors "see that she has what I have left for her, and that they protect her in all her rights in all respects as fully as I could do if I were here present myself." Hart concluded his will with the words "Farewell Amy. Farewell my children."[32] William Ashley evidenced genuine feelings for his slave mistress, Nancy, with whom he lived openly at Tampa. He arranged, as late as 1873, to have her buried next to him in the town's Oaklawn Cemetery. The tombstone epitaph read: "Here Lie William Ashley and Nancy Ashley, Master and Servant; faithful to each other in that relation in life, in death they are not separated. Strangers, consider and be wise—in the grave all human distinctions of race or color mingle in one common dust."[33]

Given that some relationships between white men and slave women may have involved fondness, affection, care, or concern, black women always found themselves forced by circumstances to act at least partly out of the need to protect themselves and their children. Their concerns included economic considerations. So the mask may have remained in place for the slaves even in some of the supposedly affectionate liaisons. Whatever, more than a few black women benefited economically from liaisons with whites. Amy Hickman received valuable property from Isaiah Hart. The bequest included Jacksonville city lots, $2,000 cash, his bedroom and office furniture, and "my gold watch and chain which I now ware." Zephaniah Kingsley left Anna Jai well provided for with property and bond servants. He well realized that leaving her such desirable properties, not to mention acknowledging her as his wife, would draw public condemnation. In the circumstances he wrote, "I know that what I am about to do is going to bring down upon me tremendous criticism, but I don't give a damn." George J. F. Clarke also left property to his mistress and her children. White heirs often challenged such bequests. Isaiah Hart's son Oscar did so. As in Amy Hickman's case, though, courts sometimes allowed a freedwoman to prevail.[34]

The issue of miscegenation affected social relationships between whites and blacks beyond simply that of the man and woman involved. Often, as mentioned, white wives and children were drawn into the fallout of such a relationship, but competition between white and black males for the attention of black women also arose frequently. The competition became, at times, quite intense. Understandably, male slaves occasionally brought sexual liaisons between whites and blacks to the notice of authority figures. When Jonathan Roberson, the sawmill overseer at George Noble Jones's El Destino plantation, courted favors from one particular slave woman, for instance, other slaves reported the fact to field overseer John Evans. After Evans inquired of the woman about her relationship with Roberson, she informed him that the sawmill overseer had given her "gifts of whiskey on several occasions in exchange of certain favors." Evans probably took his findings no further. Over an eight-year period he, too, had carried on sexual relations with a slave, Mariah. He fathered at least two of her mulatto children.[35]

The public record reveals few sexual liaisons between white women and black men, but the numbers probably ran higher than the record suggests. The courting of one Marion County slave and a slaveholder's daughter resulted in marriage after slavery and six children. Nonetheless, black men clearly did not involve themselves in sexual relations with white women to the degree that white men did with black women. The few who did, if they were found out, paid a terrible price. If they were lucky, they made it to court on charges of rape. According to historian James M. Denham, at least eight slaves were prosecuted for rape or assault with the intent to rape. Of the eight, one won acquittal, one case did not reach a verdict, and six defendants were convicted and hanged. An unknown number of men simply were lynched. Dick, a Leon County slave, made it to court in 1840 but was lynched while his case was on appeal. Available documentation points to important class considerations in the cases that made it to trial. In many of the alleged rapes the women involved appear to have been lower-class whites.[36]

In Florida's violent and sometimes racially charged atmosphere, miscegenation resulted in tragedies beyond the lynching of accused rapists. The cases of the Duval County slave Celia and of an unnamed male slave from Marion County offer some perspective. In Duval County owner Jacob Bryan fathered eight mulatto children by his slave mistress, Sarah. On one occasion Bryan started to punish his daughter Celia, when the young woman killed him. The circumstances were these. Celia was working with a knife in her hand. When Bryan commenced the punishment, she fended him off with the knife, "with which she cut open his skull so as to produce instant death." Nine months later authorities hanged Celia for her crime. She expressed no remorse; rather, she denounced her mother, Sarah, as the cause of her death. In the meantime Bryan's friend Isaiah Hart, who served as executor of his estate, described Bryan's slave wife and mulatto children as the "only family which he made." The Marion County affair involved the slave who married the master's daughter. Reportedly, his life ended years after the marriage when her brothers killed him.[37]

Social relationships between blacks and whites fortunately involved happy occasions, as well as tragedies born out of sexual exploitation or lynchings. Particularly, members of both races regularly joined to celebrate certain occasions and holidays. Although never allowed to stand on an equal footing with whites, blacks were permitted to rub shoulders with members of the broader community in a variety of recreational and economic activities. Some occasions for social mixing were prompted or regulated by local, territorial, or state laws, whereas others arose out of custom. Overseer Amon DeLaughter of Madison County often recorded when he and other whites attended a "negro show at night." They did so for enjoyment and to keep watch. When whites married, slaves attended. DeLaughter noted one occasion when all the plantation hands were dressed "in big style." Where laws attempted to mandate a white presence at black events, they often fell far short of their purpose. One grand jury echoed many others when it bewailed the "great looseness or laxity that too generally prevails in the management of the Slave population." For the most part, though, the nature of contact between whites and blacks remained within reasonably anticipated or defined boundaries.[38]

Blacks regularly celebrated recurring holidays and other special events with whites. Generally, slaveholders released their servants from work for the Fourth of July, Thanksgiving, Christmas, and New Year. Those occasions often involved racially integrated gatherings. Acie Thomas's master, she recalled, gave enslaved blacks time off for frolics (dances), quiltings, and weddings. "There was always plenty of food," Thomas recorded, "masters vying with [one] another for the honor of giving his slaves the finest parties." Octavia Stephens reflected the special atmosphere that surrounded end-of-the-year festivities when she wrote in 1861, "we [and the] darkies had a Christmas frolic getting the pig out of the big pot it was cooked to pieces." Blacks and whites also cheered special occasions observed only locally. Pensacola's "Pad-Gaud" festival probably led the list, with Tallahassee's May Party coming in a respectable second.[39]

Social intercourse across the racial divide blossomed at times when blacks and whites frequented rustic versions of today's nightclubs. How much fraternization occurred is impossible to document, but it nevertheless caused great consternation among control-minded whites. One Jackson County grand jury condemned the "shanties" belonging to Dr. Horace Ely and another white scoundrel as a "public nuisance." The buildings provided cover for a "regular system of trading between negroes and white men." During one period Gadsden County slaves and whites frequented Elizabeth Miller's home to the "great annoyance of persons living or walking in that neighborhood."[40]

Alcoholic beverages were consumed at these party-type gatherings. John B. Harden of West Florida gained a reputation for selling liquor to both blacks and whites. Overseer Jonathan Roberson often fraternized with slaves under his control, drinking whiskey with them on many occasions. Daniel H. Wiggins recorded that slaveholders occasionally enjoyed large suppers with their slaves. The owner sometimes gave the bond persons "too much to drink," he insisted, which led to all-night altercations involving men and women. Jackson Countians complained repeatedly that a few white men were trading with blacks, giving them liquor. The slaves, they insisted, were "often seen drunk, and frequently caught with whiskey."[41]

Whites and blacks also gambled together, despite laws expressly forbidding the practice. Pensacola became a place, according to one early record, where "negro gambling houses and tippling shops resulted in manifold disorders to the interruption of the people of the city." Similar establishments graced most of the larger towns, especially in East Florida. Murray, a black army scout, routinely tested his luck in games of chance with white troops at Tampa during the Second Seminole War. A personal dispute growing out of one such game led to his violent demise at the hands of a white soldier. Racetracks provided another site for gambling. Because horse racing occupied a high position in Middle Florida planter esteem, numerous tracks and events drew

large crowds of blacks and whites. Trainers and jockeys for many owners were highly skilled slaves.[42]

Slaves engaged in social intercourse at whites-only occasions, even
though they did not attend as guests. Cooks and waiters, of course,
were usually bond servants, but so were the musicians. Because blacks
supplied the music, they probably shaped the way some whites danced
and the atmosphere within which they relaxed. Typically, a black en-
tertainer, "old Fred," was the star at one capital city event in 1849. A
decade later blacks still were playing the banjo and fiddling for whites,
as in the case of a dance on Achille Murat's plantation. During the
1840s, as Wiley Housewright discovered, "concerts by black perform-
ers were given in principal towns of Florida." Onetime slaves such as
Louis Napoleon and Douglas Dorsey remembered these talented people
who helped to bring about a cultural fusion. With their efforts the
African American banjo assumed its place alongside the Anglo-American fiddle.[43]

The two-way cultural diffusion of blacks and whites in Florida continued through the antebellum period and the Civil War. With some
social and recreational activities shared by the races, slaves possessed
a limited opportunity to express themselves without fear of retribution.
A certain amount of freedom was permitted. Clearly, most slaveholders made sure blacks remembered and stayed in their subordinate position in society. Yet miscegenation—mostly between white men and
black women—formed a common part of life in antebellum Florida.
Sexual relations over the racial divide occurred with frequency. Most
of it was exploitation or rape. In a few instances, though, genuine
affection grew between members of the two groups. In general, a
greater degree of cultural fusion and social cohesiveness resulted from
the interactions between whites and blacks in Florida, particularly in
East and West Florida, than might otherwise have been expected.

SOCIAL INTERACTION AMONG BLACKS

Bond servants in Florida managed to carve out some private time for themselves. The respite would take place once they had completed assignments or tasks, stopped work at day's end, or otherwise been relieved of their duties. Within the opportunity afforded by that free time, men, women, and children interacted in various ways. That they could etch out avenues of self-expression enhanced the bond servants' will to live and to face the daily harshness and seeming hopelessness of bondage. Raising a family, establishing kinship ties, practicing religious beliefs, and socializing sustained slaves in their struggle to endure the emotional and physical stress of bondage. This chapter explores aspects of slave life other than family and religion and examines how bond servants expressed themselves aesthetically. Particular emphasis is placed on their recreational and ceremonial activities.[1]

Recreation among bond servants linked them to black culture in general, offering individuals and groups creative ways to express themselves within the confines of the slave community. Black culture was exemplified under the rubric of recreation. This occurred whether the social intercourse involved language, storytelling, music, dance, or marriage and funeral ceremonies.[2]

Pathways of communication formed an important element of slave social and recreational interaction. When they attended parties, dances, marriages, and funerals, they communicated with each other in distinctive ways. Although most enslaved blacks knew at least some English, they likely spoke some other form of language as well, especially when not in the presence of whites. Based on their African heritage, where bilingualism was common, some slaves conceivably switched from standard English to some form of semi-Creole when they were among themselves. Since 50 percent of enslaved blacks in Florida from 1850 to 1860 came from the low country of South Carolina or Georgia, the likelihood of such bilingualism rises substantially. Runaway advertisements of the 1850s and early 1860s support this assertion. Many of them describe "African" negroes or persons who spoke little or broken English.[3]

Enslaved blacks who spoke English often did so with unique tones and dialects that owed much to their African past. Some planters took this to mean that, as in the case of Daniel in 1825, their slaves had a "speech difficulty." When Sandy absconded from a Middle Florida plantation in 1826, his owner described him as having a "stoppage in his speech, and is hard to understand." A St. Augustine slaveholder reported in 1835 the absence of his two slaves whom he had purchased in South Carolina. The man declared that John was "African born" and that George "stammers so much that at times it is difficult to understand what he says."[4]

The passage of time did not alter the confusion. In 1841 Jacob escaped from E. T. Jankes and spoke "thick like an African Negro." Some ten years later, John, a Gadsden County bond servant, absented himself from the plantation. His master described the runaway as "slow and low country spoken, having been raised in East Florida." An 1845 escapee was described as speaking "very broken" English. As late as 1860, Nimrod, who had absented himself from the plantation of Dr. F. Branch, evidenced a "muttering way of speaking."[5]

African words encouraged identification for slaves with a common heritage. Such words survived in the form of names. In 1842, for instance, planter Benjamin Chaires of Leon County placed a slave named Cuffe up for sale. Meanwhile, a runaway advertisement named an escaped bond servant from Tampa as "Cudgjo." These African day names meant, respectively, Monday and Friday. Chaires also listed other slaves for sale who had African/English names such as Phoebe, Joe, and Moses. In 1855 a bond servant whose name was "Congo" absconded from Leon County. At El Destino plantation in Jefferson County a bond servant named "Niger" served as a cooper in 1865. Planter Jesse Potts, like many other slave owners, held a bondsman named "Cato," a word likely derived from "Keta," a common name among the Yoruba, Hausa, and Bambara peoples in Africa.[6]

Numerous English-style names found in Florida plantation records, probate records, and runaway slave notices probably were homonyms of African names. The following sampling illustrates the point:

English	African	English	African
Abbey	Abanna	Joe	Cudjo
Abraham	Abra	Moses	Moosa
Billy	Bilah	Mingo	Mingo
Ben	Bungoh	Pat	Pattoe
Jack	Jaeceo	Sam	Samba

Some enslaved blacks substituted the African name for the English equivalent.[7]

Although most Florida slaves were born in the South, many still grasped fragments of their diverse West African culture. The knowledge came through stories of Africa passed from one generation to the next. Many of the tales could have been retained since the first cargo of Africans arrived in East Florida in 1763 and were then passed down to their descendants and kinship networks. Slaves at Pensacola during the 1760s spoke African languages. Uncle Jack and Santa Quanta, slaves who came directly from Africa, recalled stories told to them in Africa. They passed these stories down to their loved ones until well after slavery's demise. Slavers took Uncle Jack as a small boy and placed him on a ship bound for the Americas. Santa Quanta recollected leaving Africa around 1778. He lived in Georgia until brought to East Florida in 1847. The slave's master told the other slaves to leave him alone because he was "different." Quanta subsequently married Anna, a Gola woman, and then Jennie after the death of his former wife. He fathered eight children who would have heard his stories of

Africa many times. They would have believed him just as Josephine Anderson believed the stories told her as a young girl.[8]

The saga of capture and transportation to Florida, as illustrated by Uncle Jack's and Santa Quanta's recollections, occupied a hallowed place within family storytelling practices. Behind closed doors and in the comfort of his family, Leon County's Shack Thomas recounted that his West African father, Adam, would "spend hours after the candles were out telling him and his brothers about his capture and subsequent slavery." Thomas also recalled how his father and other Africans had been lured onboard a large ship by a seaman showing them "bright red handkerchiefs, shawls and other articles." Once onboard they were "securely bound in the hold of the ship, to be later sold some where in America."[9]

Douglas Dorsey also retained clear memories of his parents telling him of their enslavement. The act came at the hands of "people known as 'Nigger Traders' who used any subterfuge to catch Negroes and sell them into slavery." As Dorsey informed an interviewer, "Unfortunately, his mother Anna and his father were caught one night and were bound and gagged and taken to Jeff Davis's boat which was waiting in the harbor, and there they were put into the stocks." The boat stayed in port until it was loaded with blacks. Then it sailed for Florida, where Davis disposed of his human cargo.[10]

Many additional slaves passed on their stories of Africa to loved ones and others who would listen. Leon County's Corporal Jaudon, better known as "Daddy Jaudon," remembered belonging to the "Esco Gullah tribe" and being purchased first in Charleston, South Carolina. Subsequently brought to Florida, Daddy Jaudon never gave up his desire to go back to his homeland. He believed until he died at the age of 117 that, if he could find the path, "he could make his way back to Africa." Thomas W. Long, born in East Florida in 1832, became a minister of the A.M.E. Church and a state senator after slavery. Long clearly remembered his father's being "a native African of the Zulu Tribe." The father was, Long stated, "captured in a tribal battle at the age of fourteen years and sold into slavery."[11]

Clearly associated with their recreational or social discourse was the slaves' love of mimicry and humorous stories. Animal fables, trickster tales, proverbs, riddles, and folklore all represented expressions of black verbal art. Found in abundance in the nineteenth century, they were voiced or acted out on farms and plantations whenever slaves came together. Medical folklore especially took on importance, as slaves often were left to tend their own medical needs because of planter disinterest or the white doctors' miserable lack of proficiency. Thanks to West African beliefs passed down from one generation to the next, enslaved blacks knew of natural cures for just about any ailment or injury.[12]

African music, described as essentially rhythmic and percussive, permeated Florida's farms, plantations, and small towns. From generation to generation enslaved blacks displayed a talent for music and dance that had moved with them and their ancestors from Africa to the Americas. As one onlooker remarked of a black worker in Florida well after emancipation, "He can plunk almost any string instrument and produce lively, toe-tickling harmonies from a battered mouth organ." The man added, "Dancing comes as naturally to him as singing."[13]

Because African sounds and movements differed so markedly from those of traditional European and American music and dance, many whites heard nothing but noise and saw nothing but barbarity in them. A Middle Florida traveler in the late 1830s noted, "The crew of the boat on which I was, composed entirely of black slaves, was occupied on deck in part, with those foolish and ridiculous dances peculiar to Negroes while others raised their voices and sang almost savage melodies." Town officials reacted to white complaints at St. Augustine and Key West, among other places, by attempting to set curfews for performances. Key West's ordinance denied blacks the right "to play the fiddle, beat a drum, or make any kind of noise after bell-ring without permission of the mayor or alderman, under penalty of being whipped or put to labor on public streets."[14]

White reactions to African music often centered on dislike of the pounding drums, which may have provoked fears of slave revolt as much as they provoked aural sensitivities. Jefferson County planters Asa and Margaret May, for instance, abhorred the sound, a sentiment that rested with them well after slavery's end. They still were complaining about their "contract workers" in 1870. As Margaret recorded, "Drum beating nearly all night last night, kept the dogs barking so that we could not sleep until late." May continued, "Negroes like to do everything at night in the dark, showing that their deeds are evil." Given that blacks, whether slave or free, typically worked from "can't see to can't see," most of their recreational activities naturally occurred at night, a fact that escaped whites such as the Mays. Rather, such whites preferred to let their fears perceive the devil at play.[15]

Yet whites did not entirely fail to perceive the importance of music and dance to slaves. One Frenchman who toured Middle Florida in the late 1830s summed up best, perhaps, what some of the less-perceptive whites could not see. "Draw near to a plantation, and the noisy outbursts of laughter that you hear there will make you forget the overseer who goes about provided with his huge whip," wrote the comte de Castlenau. "Then come the rest days, and all the miseries of the week are forgotten in the wildest dances and the most ridiculous capers," the keen observer added.[16]

Duval County's Zephaniah Kingsley, the Randalls of Jefferson County, and others of their peers understood what de Castlenau was trying to explain. Sometimes criticized for the looseness of his slave-control policies, Kingsley commented that he "never interfered with their connubial concerns, nor domestic affairs, but let them regulate these after their own manner." Under this wise course of action slaves on the Kingsley plantations exuberantly pursued their "native dances" until their owner's demise. Laura Wirt Randall often would hear her family's slaves dancing and playing music. As time went on she grew accustomed to the "unusual noise in the night," since the "quarters of the Negroes being in the lower part of the yard—we hear them pretty frequently."[17]

As long as work schedules did not suffer, many owners permitted their slaves to sing, dance, and play music as late (or as early) as they desired. Louis Napoleon, among other ex-bondsmen, clearly recalled slaves gathering "at one of the cabin doors [and] they would sing and dance to the tunes of a fife, banjo or fiddle that was played by one of their number." Weekend nights especially witnessed boisterous festivities. Zephaniah Kingsley's bond servants eagerly anticipated, in his words, "[the] dancing, merriment and dress for which Saturday afternoon and night, and Sunday morning were dedicated." Usually participants-to-be prepared in advance for events. Octavia Stephens recognized as much when she informed her husband, "The darkies are to have a party tonight."[18]

Slaves delighted in carrying their music and dance out into the broader community, and town streets often served as stages for impromptu performances. A visitor at Tallahassee commented on that fact in 1838. "Negroes travel by night with their hands over their heads, sometimes 10 or 15 in a company serenade a neighborhood with their rustic songs," he informed a friend. "The most gifted gives out one tune, all then join in, and such music I have never heard," he continued. "The Negroes were seldom still before midnight, dancing, fiddling, on one or two strings."[19]

Occasionally, the festivities proved a bit much even for normally sympathetic whites. One traveler recorded his observations of events on the Randall plantation in 1841, when the "frolicking of the Negroes" disturbed the family during much of one Sunday night. Thomas Randall already had been reeling from stress. He recently had lost his judgeship and was struggling financially in the aftermath of the Panic of 1837 and the collapse of Middle Florida's Union Bank. Now his temper boiled over. He set out to end the all-night dancing, singing, playing of drums, and clapping of hands as quickly as he could. Apparently, he failed. The traveler then quoted Randall's overseer George Roney as later declaring, "He is determined to break it up or quit the place."[20]

Likely Randall, even when the victim of a fiery temper, did not treat the fiddler too badly. As a general matter, talent at fiddling came highly prized among blacks and whites. When Douglas Dorsey recalled the old songs of slavery days, he remembered them played "to the tune of an old fiddle." A Tallahassee man noted in the 1830s, "The Negroes were seldom still before midnight—dancing, fiddling on one or two strings—a Negro is on the que vive the minute the fiddle squeaks." Runaway slave advertisements mentioned fiddlers, often describing the slaves as "artful and intelligent." Owners and their children in later years often first remembered that someone fiddled when they recollected family slaves. In a typical manner Margaret Watkins Gibbs recorded her recollections of slaves on the plantation of her father William Joel Watkins near Bartow in Polk County. "Among our Negroes was Andy [Moore], the fiddler," she began. "The slaves had dancing and plenty of singing."[21]

The bond servants' style of dancing endured as a part of their day-to-day existence on the plantations and farms of Florida during slavery and after. The forms and types represented a wide variety. Douglas Dorsey remembered "the Green Corn Dance" and "Cut the Pigeon Wing." Laura Randall referred to a peculiar frolic done by slaves as the "jig dance." On at least one occasion Pensacola residents complained about "Congo Dancing" in the absence of laws barring the frolicking of blacks in that particular city. Zephaniah Kingsley believed one type of dancing that took place on his northeast Florida plantation to be unique.[22]

When dances were held, fashion displayed itself within the limited means of those held in bondage. Blacks attired themselves in an array of clothing, ranging from distinctively colored cuffs and collars to simple homespun pants and dresses. Many times slaves would dye or add colorful patches to otherwise dull trousers, jackets, and petticoats. Claude A. Wilson recalled that many clothes were dyed with "red oak bark, sweet gum bark and shoe make roots." Mary Biddle remembered the process used for dying regular white clothing. "The dye was made by digging up red shank and wild indigo roots," she explained, "which were boiled."[23]

Runaway slave notices offer a further glimpse of the clothing that might have adorned dance goers. When Ben ran away from his master, he wore "cotton canaburg pants, and an old dark colored coat with no sleeves." The master of Jesse described him in 1830 as being "well clothed, as he took with him a variety of good clothing." When Jim and his wife Martha absconded from a Middle Florida plantation, the former was described as wearing "blue cloth clothes with a white hat." One East Florida slaveholder described his female fugitive as wearing a "cloak of fine grey Bath coating." When the body of bond servant Smart was fished from the Withlacoochee River in 1855, it was wrapped in a "black thin coat, white drawers, shoes."[24]

Fashion at dances and other social events included headgear, probably in deference to the African belief that the head should be covered. Male and female slaves commonly wore handkerchiefs. When George absconded from an East Florida plantation, his master described him as wearing a "red silk handkerchief on his head." Another slaveholder noted that his female bond servant wore a "coloured handkerchief round the head." When Milly absented herself from an East Florida plantation, she wore a "blue and white plaid home-spun Frock, and plaid Handkerchief."[25]

Some blacks adopted Anglo-American forms of headgear. Many fugitives were described as wearing straw, palmetto, raccoon, leather, woolen, and beaver hats. Woolen hats were favorites. When John left a Jefferson County plantation, his master notified others that he was wearing a "Kersey Coat and cap, Cotton Drill Pants and old vest." Jim wore a white hat when he left a Middle Florida plantation. In 1840 an East Florida slaveholder described one of his fugitives as wearing a "fine palmetto hat with a black ribbon." When Ivy absented himself from a not-too-distant location, he wore a "felt hat." On the other hand, when Charles absconded in the same region, he sported more typical headware, that is, "a common negro woolen cap, without [a] front." Smart and Bazzell covered their heads similarly, with "black wool hats."[26]

Hairstyles, as well as clothing and headgear, made cultural statements at dances, just as they did day to day. Many women braided and plaited their hair or wore it twisted like twine in an African fashion. So many women wore their hair in plaits that a slave woman might command an increased purchase price as an "excellent . . . Plaiter." Men also chose plaits at times, and both men and women sometimes wore their hair long or in a bush style. Runaway notices routinely commented on hairstyles as a distinctive feature. Thus, in 1856 an owner described Rosie as wearing her "hear in plaits" and another commented on George's "long plaited hair."[27]

Besides the great care taken with clothing, headgear, and hairstyles as fashion and cultural statements, no ensemble was complete without some form of jewelry. Bead-and-brass-wire earrings, bead armbands, silver and gold ear bobs and drops, iron-ring bracelets, and other items of jewelry were commonly associated with Africans. Slaves arriving in South Carolina and Georgia during the seventeenth and eighteenth centuries from Africa often wore them. Bond servants in nineteenth-century Florida continued the tradition. As early as 1823 one slaveholder described his female fugitive as having "a hole in the middle of the upper lip made probably to wear a ring." Another indicated that one of his slaves wore "a ring in his left ear." In 1845 one runaway wore "a small ring in one ear."[28]

If dances and parties offered opportunity for happier times, a wedding could prove positively joyous. As mentioned earlier, whites sometimes attended such ceremonies or even officiated at them. On many occasions, though, blacks celebrated wedding vows within their own community and traditions. The choice usually lay first with the man. "If a slave saw a woman whom he desired he told his master," Mary Biddle explained. "If the woman in question belonged on another plantation, the master would consult her master: 'one of my boys wants to marry one of your gals,' he would say," she continued. "As a rule it was agreeable that they should live together as man and wife."[29]

Before many slave couples commenced living together, they performed their own wedding ceremonies, often with the assistance of a black preacher. The presence of a black minister represented the custom on George Noble Jones's Middle Florida plantations and on those of many of his planter peers. Popular preachers might travel widely to unite couples. The Baptist James Page, for example, covered much of the plantation belt in his rounds, performing marriages throughout Middle Florida and elsewhere before and after freedom came. The ceremony usually was a simple one. "Mos folks dem days got married by laying a broom on de floor an jumpin over it," Josephine Anderson recalled. "Dat seals de marriage, an at de same time bring em good luck."[30]

Other recreational activities besides music, dance, and weddings also helped to fill the lives of Florida bond servants. According to Mary M. Biddle, "The slaves from the surrounding plantations were allowed to come together" on special occasions such as a "big candy pulling, or hog killing and chicken cooking." Squire Jackson recalled boys on the plantation playing "home ball and shoot[ing] marbles" on Sundays. Stephen Harvell claimed that "log rollings" were big events among slaves in the central and southern peninsula.[31]

Sundays offered many slaves an opportunity to make money for themselves by trading their goods at rural markets or else in town, and they attempted to enjoy such occasions to the fullest. Trading and traveling to trade thus provided a forum for interaction between bond servants that provided pleasure and social interaction among blacks on the one hand and could spark concerns among control-minded white citizens on the other. So perturbed did some of Gadsden County's leading citizens grow in 1837 that they denounced, through the grand jury, the whole idea of slaves trading on Sundays. "We believe this custom is highly demoralizing," they pronounced. "[It] tends to corrupt and derange the habits of our slave population, and render the Sabbath a day of amusement, dissipation, and debauchery." Such protests notwithstanding, Sunday trading excursions continued unabated, for the most part, through the antebellum period.[32]

One negative and potentially damaging aspect of Sunday trading days, weekend parties, and weeknight gatherings concerned the consumption of alcohol. At many parties and dances, some bond servants consumed such a quantity of alcoholic beverages that they became rowdy or worse. By way of example, John Gamble of Leon County customarily gave his enslaved blacks a big dinner at the completion of the harvest season. At one such occasion a white guest observed that Gamble's slaves "had plenty to eat and a great deal too much to drink, and they danced, quarrelled, and fought throughout the night." William D. Moseley experienced alcohol-related problems with a few of his bondsmen. He noted in 1850 that he found Bryant "badly cut by Jim in a drunken frolic produced by drinking whiskey to excess on Saturday." The same Gadsden County grand jury that denounced Sunday trading by slaves added, "The Negroes make use of that opportunity to pilfer from their masters and others, those articles which are readily exchanged for spirituous liquors."[33]

To avoid the kinds of problems that Gamble and Moseley experienced from allowing slaves too much alcohol, some owners attempted to keep their bond persons from drinking. John Warren made it clear that he and his wife did not want anyone trading with their slaves—"especially in spirituous liquors"—without express written permission. Some citizens believed in the necessity of a ban on giving any "spiritious liquors" to slaves because, once the bondsmen had gotten used to alcohol, they might "pilfer from their masters and others" to get it. Bond servants Randall and Milly did just what some masters feared they would do to obtain liquor. According to Susan B. Eppes, the two "stole the key from the smoke house and planned to exchange bacon for whiskey in Tallahassee, and planned to have a big party." Citizens of Pensacola berated John B. Harden for conducting a private liquor business, doing so because the customers he appealed to included "darkies as well as the weary and idler."[34]

As some of the drinking disputes well illustrate, interactions between slaves were not always congenial. Human emotions ruled in the quarters as they did in the big house, and blacks naturally fell victim to their share of altercations, quarrels, and disagreements. Ed, one of Nancy DeLaughter's Madison County slaves, ran a McGehee family bond servant named Randolph from the DeLaughter quarters. He saw him as a threatening competitor. Overseer Amon DeLaughter's diary reveals many similar entries regarding arguments between slaves. He recorded, for example, "Ed & Kesiah have a fuss about their children." Obviously in the aftermath of a lover's quarrel, Darian asked the overseer to "make Charlotte go home with him." On several occasions DeLaughter noted that "Frank and Ed fuss, as well as Harriet and France at night." On one of George N. Jones's Jefferson County plantations similar conditions prevailed. In one instance Rose argued with her husband, Renty, over his infidelity. She consequently left him.[35]

As would be expected, arguments between slaves sometimes led to shootings, stabbings, and even death. On the DeLaughter plantation Jack and Prince argued and ultimately fought, with the former cutting the latter on the head. From Tampa, Laura Lancaster reported in June 1857 of the trouble in which her mother's servant George found himself. "He unfortunately *cut* and *wounded badly* a fellow servant," she wrote, "and *as yet we cannot* tell how the affair will terminate." A Jackson County occurrence saw Bryan killing his fellow slave Toney. In Jefferson County Ben stabbed his cousin Tom "in a scuffle." On Christmas Day 1856 Lewis killed another slave in Leon County. L. A. Thompson's bond servant Ned killed a different Lewis, this one the property of William Burroughs, in an argument that raged while they walked together down a Tallahassee road.[36]

Deaths from whatever cause brought slave families and the slave community together. "Funeral rites in traditional African societies," as Robert Hall has noted, "were often occasions for celebration, creating an intensely renewed sense of family and communal unity among the survivors." Sadly, some whites viewed these unique rituals merely as slaves frolicking instead of mourning the dead. The death of Molly, an aged slave woman, demonstrates the survival of some African cultural ways that whites viewed as unusual. Molly passed away at the age of 116 in 1851. She probably had been brought to the colonies from Africa in the mid-1700s, and she had served as a cook for several army officers during the American Revolution. In preparing for Molly's passing, a newspaper reported, "Her colored friends of all ages then flocked around her, bestowing those peculiar rites which among Southern slaves is singularly superstitious." The rites included "incantations, prayers, and day and night watchings." A reflection of the African past, an ancestor deserving reverence had to be buried properly by members of the community, whether whites understood or not.[37]

In summary, Florida bond servants gained some opportunity through free time to buttress mental and emotional strength not only through their family and religious institutions but also through their recreation and other communal exercises. Slaves expressed themselves through storytelling, dances, fashion, playing games, and other activities. Enslaved blacks and their descendants often communicated with each other in unique ways about which masters knew or, perhaps, cared little. Although such activities sometimes resulted in danger or harm, more often they permitted a measure of joy in lives otherwise circumscribed by bondage.

25. Most of Florida's enslaved blacks lived in log cabins of one sort or another. The one shown here, although the photograph was taken after emancipation, illustrates this typical form of housing. Courtesy Photographic Collection, Florida State Archives.

26. In addition to whipping intransigent slaves, many owners punished them by forcing them to sit or stand in stocks. The punishment continued to be administered following emancipation, as this Apalachicola man learned in 1866. He was locked in the pillory for seventy minutes for assaulting a white man. Courtesy Photographic Collection, Florida State Archives.

27. Slaves played the banjo or fiddle at social gatherings of both whites and blacks. This tradition survived slavery, as indicated by the tunes of this black fiddler in 1873. Courtesy Photographic Collections, Florida State Archives.

28. Personal relationships sometimes crossed racial lines, especially in areas of Florida where Spanish traditions persisted. Most often these relationships involved sexual exploitation of black women by white men. Exceptions existed, though, as may have been the case with South Florida cowman John Parker and his slave Rachel Davis. This photograph is of Rachel's daughter, Eliza Davis Allen, who was born in Polk County in 1856. Courtesy Canter Brown Jr.

29. Corrie Davis, son of bond servant Rachel Davis and cattleman John Parker. Courtesy Canter Brown Jr.

30. This nineteenth-century burial incorporated animal skin, a scaffold, and other worldly possessions of the deceased, linking Florida slave practices to particular African traditions. Commonly the assemblage of pots, bottles, and other material objects also marked black graves. Courtesy Photographic Collection, Florida State Archives.

SALE ON WEDNESDAY, JUNE 20.

Commissioner's
SALE.

In pursuance of a decree made at April
Term, 1842, of the Superior Court of the Middle District of Florida, in and for the County of Leon, sitting in Chancery, made in a certain cause between **JOSEPH CHAIRES**, Executor of Ben Chaires, deceased, Petitioner for the foreclosure of a Mortgage, and **ROBERT H. BERRY**, defendant, and by virtue of the execution issued to me to enforce said decree, I shall, on the 29th day of June, 1842, at the Plantation called the **FAUNTLEROY PLACE**, on the public road leading from Tallahassee to Blocker's Cross Road, in said county, Leon, within legal hours, proceed to sell at public outcry highest bidder for cash, the following

SLAVES

included in said Mortgage, viz

Charles, Shine, Ed and Mitchell, Edmund Roberts, Moses, Jane Joe, Phœbe, Delia, Henry, Harriett, Carter, Fanny, Mary, Ann, Tom, Sarah, Charles, Molly, Kate, Lindon, March, John, Alexander, Graywood, Lary, G , Newton, Cuffe, Castelo, Silla, Dilly ia, Ginny, Sarah, Beck, Nancy, Patie inah, Sally, Ana, Henrietta, Betsey, ah, Priscilla, Jim, Victoria and Adam and issue after 20th April, 1840.

CHARLES S. SIBLEY,
Commissioner in cery, and Elisor in said case,
Appointed by of said Court to make said sale.
Tallahassee, May 27, 1842.

31. Some slaves maintained African names, as indicated in this 1842 Leon County sales advertisement. Courtesy Photographic Collection, Florida State Archives.

32. Abraham escaped from slavery and became the trusted adviser of the Seminole chief Micanopy. He would negotiate with the president of the United States in the 1820s and, later, play a crucial role in the Second Seminole War of 1835 to 1842. Courtesy Photographic Collection, Florida State Archives.

33. Selina Rollins lived in the Alachua County community of Micanopy, named after one of the highest ranking Seminole chiefs. She was born in the area during the Second Seminole War and remained there until her death around 1925. Courtesy Photographic Collection, Florida State Archives.

Left, 34. An artist's representation of John Horse, also called John Cavallo or Gopher John. John Horse emerged as a war leader of Black Seminoles during the Second Seminole War. Courtesy Photographic Collection, Florida State Archives.

Below, 35. An 1850s drawing of a Florida delegation consisting of Seminoles and Black Seminoles. *Left to right:* Billy Bowlegs, Chocote Tustenuggee, Abraham, John Jumper, Fasatchee Emathla, Sarparkee Yohola. These men undertook a state visit to Washington, D.C., to negotiate with federal authorities. Courtesy Photographic Collection, Florida State Archives.

Right, 36. Ben Bruno, like Abraham, served the Seminoles as an interpreter. Where Abraham also advised the chief Micanopy, Bruno counseled Billy Bowlegs. Courtesy Photographic Collection, Florida State Archives.

Below, 37. An early-twentieth-century representation of blacks and Seminoles together in Florida. Courtesy Photographic Collection, Florida State Archives.

BEN BRUNO, NEGRO SLAVE AND FAVORITE.

38. House slave named "Mauma Mollie," who was carried from Africa to South Carolina on a slave ship. She became the nursemaid to John and Eliza Partridge of Jefferson County, who purchased her during the 1830s. Courtesy Photographic Collection, Florida State Archives.

39. Nursemaid "Aunt Jane" cared for Dr. J. D. Palmer's daughter Sarah during the 1850s. Earlier she had survived the Second Seminole War Indian attack on Indian Key. Courtesy Photographic Collection, Florida State Archives.

40. From the 1500s to 1865, slave runaways found refuge in Florida, often by asso-
ciating with Indian tribes such as the Seminoles or by creating their own communities. The tradition persisted after the Civil War, as illustrated by this 1873 drawing. Courtesy Photographic Collection, Florida State Archives.

41. Abolitionists failed to infiltrate Florida to any great extent during the antebellum period, but individuals sometimes acted to free enslaved blacks in the state.
This is an artist's representation of Jonathan Walker, described as an abolitionist
and slave stealer. Walker received an SS brand (denoting slave stealer) and was
confined to a pillory at Pensacola in the 1840s. Courtesy Photographic Collection,
Florida State Archives.

Massacre of the Whites by the Indians and Blacks in Florida.

The above is intended to represent the horrid Massacre of the Whites in Florida, in December 1835, and January, February, March and April 1836, when near Four Hundred (including women and children) fell victims to the barbarity of the Negroes and Indians.

42. Described by some historians as possibly the largest slave insurrection in the antebellum South, the Second Seminole War of 1835 to 1842 witnessed blacks fighting for their freedom in Florida. As one general put it, the conflict was a "Negro war." This artist's representation of the fighting was published during the war's early stages. Courtesy Photographic Collection, Florida State Archives.

$50 REWARD!

My Boy, NIMROD, formerly owned by Dr. E. Branch, having run away from my plantation on the Hillsborough River, I offer the above reward of FIFTY DOLLARS to any person who will return him to me, or safely lodge him in jail and inform me of the fact, so that I may get him into my possession.

Nimrod is stout built, of low stature, having a downcast countenance, and a muttering way of speaking. He has a very large foot and hand for a person of his age, being about fifteen or sixteen years old. His color is that of a dark mulatto.

EDMUND JONES.

Tampa, Nov. 17, 1860. 37-tf

Above, 43. Typical runaway slave advertisement. From the *Tampa Florida Peninsular,* November 17, 1860.

Right, 44. During the Civil War slaves assisted—voluntarily or otherwise—both the Union and Confederate armies. Charity Stewart reportedly made soap for the Confederates during the war. Later she remained on a Jefferson County plantation, where she died at the age of 93. Courtesy Photographic Collection, Florida State Archives.

Right, 45. Tony Davis served his master at the front during the Civil War. With the peace he returned to the plantation of his birth in Leon County and raised a family, passing at the age of 93. Courtesy Photographic Collection, Florida State Archives.

Below, 46. An artist's rendition of an escaped slave who joined the Union army. This illustration of the black infantryman is representative of black Union soldiers who fought in Florida. Courtesy Library of Congress.

THE ESCAPED SLAVE IN THE UNION ARMY.—[SEE PAGE 422.]

47. Runaway slaves were called "Contrabands" by the Union. This illustration depicts con
trabands attempting to get to a Union boat in their escape from slavery during the Civil Wa
Courtesy Photographic Collection, Florida State Archives.

INTERACTION
BETWEEN
BLACKS AND
INDIANS

Before the United States flag ever flew over Florida, blacks had already involved themselves in multileveled and long-lasting relationships with its resident population of Native Americans. By 1821 the Spanish colony had been renowned for generations as a haven for fugitive slaves—or "maroons," as they came to be called—and as a nightmare for slaveholders to the north. Unlike the situation that would develop in Texas, a territory otherwise similar in many ways, Florida's Indians generally acted as friends and allies of blacks until about 1838. Nonetheless, the relationship that developed between blacks and Seminoles, Creeks, and Mikasukis ultimately played a prominent role in the expulsion of most Native Americans and maroons from Florida. This chapter concentrates on the sometimes crucially important interaction of blacks and Indians, with particular emphasis on the Seminoles from 1821 to 1858.[1]

In the triracial Florida world fugitive slaves and their descendants rested at the root of much of the impending conflict between whites and Indians, certainly the Seminoles. Runaways themselves from Alabama and Georgia, Seminoles were casualties of war spawned by the expanding colonial frontier. Gifted with a name that meant runaways, they occupied a situation similar to that of black runaways. Both blacks and Seminoles sought refuge from the intrusion and control of Europeans, especially the British and Anglo-Americans. Over time blacks and Seminoles realized that they needed each other, although for reasons unique to each group. The Seminoles required blacks to help them keep their lands, and blacks allied with the Seminoles to enable them to preserve their freedom.[2]

The cooperation between blacks and Seminoles shaped the social interaction and cultural contact between the two groups. Spaniards probably introduced the maroons to the Seminoles. Fugitive slaves from the Carolinas began escaping to Florida as early as the seventeenth century, joining blacks, who, in some cases, could trace their Florida roots back to the early sixteenth century. The Seminoles pulled away from the Creeks in Georgia and relocated in Florida only during the mid-1700s. Quickly the two groups began to associate with one another, their relationships growing closer as the years passed. Early records called the maroons "slaves" of the Seminoles, but anthropologists now describe them as vassals because, as in feudal systems, reciprocal obligations defined the relationship. Whatever language is used, the fact remains that blacks and Seminoles allied with each other and with the Spanish in resisting incursions of Anglos into Florida. As a result, Seminoles and blacks engaged in interracial cooperation under the Spanish long before large numbers of Anglos came to dominate the peninsula. Not surprisingly, American authorities found it difficult during the 1820s and the 1830s to implement a divide-and-rule strategy to conquer the Indians and blacks.[3]

Regardless of a black's status as slave, vassal, fugitive, or free, trading among blacks and Seminoles encouraged intimacy and interaction. At least as early as 1808 two groups were seen trading in and around St. Augustine. The Spaniards even employed Africans to trade with the Seminoles. The free mulatto Juan Bautista Collins, for example, traveled to the Seminole heartland in today's Alachua County to exchange various wares for cattle.[4]

The close cooperation evidenced itself spectacularly during the Patriot War of 1812 to 1814. In that conflict Georgia frontiersmen, many of whom lived near the St. Marys and St. Johns Rivers, tried to take East Florida from the Spanish. An engagement in what is today

Alachua County saw blacks and Seminoles successfully turn back a heavily armed force. Conscious of their own losses and vulnerability, though, the allies sought greater security by relocating their homes to the southwestern peninsula. Seminoles largely settled around the headwaters of the Peace River (Talakchopco hatchee), whereas blacks relocated closer to the Tampa Bay area to maintain a separate identity and basic control over their own lives. This large settlement of blacks, located on the Manatee River at present-day Bradenton, apparently was called Angola. One white party also referred to it as the "Sarrazota, or Runaway Negro Plantations."[5]

The black refugee population at Angola continued to grow after the War of 1812. Following their defeat at the Battle of New Orleans in January 1815, British officers returned to Florida four hundred black warriors whom they had recruited as soldiers. Seemingly, eighty of the veterans were taken to the Manatee River, whereas the remainder with some Indian allies were ensconced in an Apalachicola River fortification. General Andrew Jackson and many planters, eyeing development of a cotton empire in southwest Georgia and southeastern Alabama, viewed the fort as dangerous. They believed it would attract runaway slaves and be a base from which raids could be conducted into the United States. Jackson ordered United States Army forces to destroy the Negro Fort. In 1816 a hot cannonball ignited a gunpowder magazine, blowing up the settlement. More than two hundred men, women, children—blacks and some Indians—died in the blast. Survivors fled eastward toward the Suwannee River, where additional black veterans, other black warriors, and their families had gathered.[6]

The First Seminole War of 1817 to 1818 quickly followed the Negro Fort's destruction, with Andrew Jackson directing efforts that would unite Seminoles and blacks in their own defense and spur the growth of Angola. Having moved eastward from the Apalachicola, Jackson's men in April 1818 trapped the black warriors and their families against the west bank of the Suwannee River, narrowly missing Seminoles who had escaped into the peninsula. Heavily outnumbered, the black men fought fiercely to allow their families to escape. The desperate action succeeded, and many veterans of the fight settled with their families at the Manatee. Others joined Seminoles in villages that lay within the hammock lands of today's Hernando and Pasco Counties. Red Stick Creeks, whom Jackson originally had chased out of Alabama, settled along the upper Peace River in now-abandoned Seminole towns. Despite the relative success of Jackson's Florida campaign, whites still had not broken the strong alliance between blacks and Seminoles. If anything, a stronger bond of unity welded members of these two darker races.[7]

As discussed in chapter 1, Jackson was not yet done with the Red Stick Creeks or the black warriors. In 1821, just after the general had agreed to accept Florida's provisional governorship, his Lower Creek allies raided the peninsula. They attacked Seminole villages from the Suwannee down to modern Pasco County. Driving further south, they ultimately destroyed Angola. Likely three hundred blacks were dragged back into American slavery, and the remainder of Angola's population of perhaps seven hundred to eight hundred divided between refuges in the Bahamas and the Florida interior. The raid compounded for blacks and Seminoles the importance of lessons already learned. In unity lay strength.[8]

By the time American authority over Florida had been secured in 1821, violent, destructive, and sometimes fatal experiences had bonded the maroons and the Seminoles. The numbers of blacks remaining in Florida's interior are not known with certainty, but estimates of one thousand to fifteen hundred appear plausible. Some of them had been "freed" by the Spanish, whereas others were "slaves," in the sense discussed, of the Seminoles or the Red Stick Creeks. They have been referred to by several names other than maroons. The terms have included Indian Negroes, Indian Blacks, Seminole freedmen, Afro-Seminoles, Negro-Indians, black Indians, black Muscogulges, Seminole Negroes, and Black Seminoles. Students of the subject usually prefer the latter term. "Seminole blacks [or Black Seminoles] remains a useful term," explained historian Kevin Mulroy, "constituent members being Africans or their descendants, whose association with Seminole Indians played a large part in their history and the construction of their identity."[9] It is important to keep in mind, though, that as much as 75 percent of the Black Seminoles actually were "maroons." This is so because they either were fugitives from slavery or the descendants of fugitives whose communities were initially concealed in the peninsula and inaccessible to whites.[10]

Adhering to prescribed arrangements, the Seminoles treated captives, runaways, and free blacks the same. A philosophy that stressed consonance and stability, as well as the favorable way Spaniards treated blacks, influenced the system. The form of vassalage that the Indians applied to blacks probably reflected an earlier sabana system that the Spaniards had used with other Florida Indians in working the land. For one thing, Seminoles recognized the rights of blacks to control their day-to-day affairs. They agreed to the maroons' living in villages apart, sometimes at a substantial distance from Indian towns. As early as 1820 an observer explained the agricultural scheme used by the Seminoles. Blacks "raise corn for their subsistence," he recorded; "if they have a surplus it goes to the families of their master."[11]

As such a vassalage system would anticipate, Seminoles acted toward blacks more as patrons than as masters. The maroons gave a percentage of their crops, horses, cows, and hogs to their Seminole neighbors in exchange for land and protection from whites. The system worked well and remained substantially unaltered through the mid-1830s. Typically, a white writer noted in 1837 that blacks worked and managed "their stocks and crops as they please, giving such a share of the produce to their masters as they like."[12]

Yet some whites, reflecting their worldview, wanted to believe that Seminoles held blacks as "slaves" in the truest sense of the word, a perspective that many early historians adopted. A newspaper article reported, for example, that Micanopy, leader of the Seminoles, "owned one hundred negroes . . . and was raising large and valuable crops of corn and cotton." In truth some Seminole Indians indeed had purchased black bond servants from the British and the Spanish as symbols of prestige. Following emigration from Florida, some Seminoles in the West attempted to control Black Seminoles as slaves. Nonetheless, the facts available reveal realities of life prior to the Second Seminole War that encompassed a very different relationship. "The Seminoles certainly did not establish a clear-cut master slave relationship," concluded one historian. The distinguished scholar Kenneth M. Porter added, "[Blacks were] in no case treated as chattels."[13]

There were some claims by blacks of mistreatment by Seminoles. Individual Seminoles doubtlessly treated their "slaves" more harshly than did others. Presumably, some took advantage of blacks and, despite the common practices of most, compelled them to work hard in the fields or otherwise abused them. In the early 1830s, for example, Lydia operated a kind of crude inn or stopover within the Indian lands on the military road between Fort Brooke and Fort King, about one day's ride north of Tampa Bay. In earlier years, though, she had risked reenslavement by relocating to the St. Johns River area. "She came there from the Indian Nation in consequence of the Indians having killed one of her sons," explained "a Negro man named Kent." Micanopy, on the other hand, proved no harsh slave master, despite what the white press sometimes suggested. Generally noted by firsthand observers for his kindness, the chief probably treated blacks much more humanely than did most white slaveholders in East Florida. His system reflected, for the most part, the typical Seminole practice. As Seminole agent Wiley Thompson described in 1835, he allowed blacks to make a contribution to their "owner annually, from the product of his little field."[14]

The greater number of complaints that have surfaced against the Indians have related to experiences during the Second Seminole War. They have included stories of floggings of blacks and other forms of ill treatment. Such occurrences represented circumstances during and after 1838, when the maroons worked out favorable emigration plans with United States authorities at, what some Seminoles and Creeks believed, the Indians' expense. Other stories originated with slaves who rebelled at the Second Seminole War's outset and sought refuge in Indian lands. Many of these bond servants had departed their plantations willingly, a fact that, on capture, they did not want to delve into too deeply. Accordingly, many preferred to relate tales of a servitude under the Indians that was harsher than slavery under the whites, hoping that their owners might go easy on them.[15]

Blacks possessed certain advantages in dealing with the Seminoles that helped to ensure decent treatment. Most important were their agricultural skills. The Indians chose not to depend on an agrarian way of life, preferring, if they could, to hunt and to graze cattle. They desired to spend little time growing crops or supervising blacks in the manner of white slaveholders. They welcomed their arrangements with maroons. "The Indian owner never presumed to meddle [in the affairs of blacks]," commented one Indian agent.[16]

As mentioned, the Black Seminoles typically lived away from Seminole towns and villages, at least when they were not under threat from outsiders. "The Negroes dwell in towns apart from the Indians," explained William H. Simmons in the early 1820s, "and they are the finest looking people I have ever seen." The practice allowed the maroons to maintain their separate identity and control over their daily lives. They continued to live in their traditional way until at least the Second Seminole War's commencement. A chronicler of the territory confirmed that fact when he noted during the conflict's early stages that "slaves" of the Seminoles (together with other blacks) "live in villages separate, and in many cases, remote from" the Seminoles.[17]

The names of a good number of black settlements are known. Perhaps the single most important one was Peliklakaha in Sumter County, a village controlled by Abraham and sometimes called Abraham's Town. As will be discussed, he became "sensebearer" (or chief counselor) to Micanopy during the 1820s. Others named in documents included Suwannee Old Town, King Heijah's Town or Payne's Negro Settlement, Buckra Woman's Town, and Mulatto Girl's Town. The disruptions caused by the 1821 Creek raid on Angola severely hit many of these places and spurred the growth of others in its aftermath.[18]

Other black villages or settlements also proved important to the maroons. Historian Canter Brown has pointed to two places, in addition to Peliklakaha, that played crucial roles in times to come. In 1818 or 1819 the Creek chief Oponay had established one village on Lake Hancock north of present-day Bartow in Polk County. Called Minatti, it housed Oponay's slaves and, later, some of Angola's refugees. The 1821 raid also had disrupted Buckra Woman's Town in the Big Hammock, which lay within today's Hernando and Pasco Counties. Sister to the dead Seminole chiefs King Payne and King Bowlegs, Buckra Woman mothered the future Seminole chief Billy Bowlegs. By 1823 she had transferred her cattle operations and black vassals to a village situated on a creek that flowed westward into Peace River about fifteen miles below Minatti (three miles south of Fort Meade). The stream retains the name Bowlegs Creek. Buckra Woman called the village Tobasa or Wahoo.[19]

In their separate communities maroons, or Black Seminoles, continued to identify with their black heritage. Naturally, their cultural ways differed greatly from those of the Seminoles. The differences helped to form the maroons' unique ethnicity and defined them as a people. Circumstances tended to reinforce the black heritage over time. Runaway slaves from South Carolina and Georgia continued to reach the maroon refuges during the 1820s and early 1830s. Some Florida bond servants meanwhile seemingly passed back and forth between white territory and Indian lands without too much trouble. Sampson Forrester, for example, was "captured" twice by the Seminoles and held by them for years before he "escaped." The traffic moved at times from inside Indian lands to white areas. Among others, John Caesar and Abraham, who spoke English and Spanish among other languages, often passed through the slave quarters of farms and plantations to the north and east of the Indian lands, interacting with bond persons who lived there. Reportedly, many male slaves on the farms and plantations of East Florida also "had wives among the Indian Negroes, and the Indian Negroes had wives among them." Presumably the traffic reinforced the continued exposure to African American cultural ways within Indian lands and helped to mold the nature of slavery in the upper peninsula.[20]

Some cultural distinctions can be discerned from surviving records. Physically, fashion differences could be observed. Whites mentioned, for instance, that some Black Seminoles wore hats of a type other than traditional Indian headbands and feathers, probably an African and African American tradition passed down through the generations. Portraits of Abraham show him wearing something akin to a turban without feathers, possibly a fancified version of a handkerchief wrapped about his head. Language made a difference, too. No matter how long blacks lived around Seminoles, whites identified them as talking in a particular "Negro dialect." Religious exercises likely included "ring-shouts" and the call-and-response form of worship. Florida maroons may have retained, as well, the African American marriage ceremony of "jumping the broom," at least in some form. As far as familial arrangements went, maroon leaders for the most part were endogamous but practiced polygamy, which followed West African tradition. A few Florida maroon leaders such as Abraham did not strictly practice endogamy, having Seminole women among their several wives.[21]

How blacks named themselves and their communities differed from the Seminoles and showed African influence, illustrating a measure of cultural solidarity with slaves throughout Florida. As mentioned in the previous chapter, some blacks retained West African day names, such as Cuffy or Cuffe (Monday) and Cudjo or Cudjoe (Friday). Several settlements bore the names of black women. Buckra Woman's Town, sometimes spelled "Bucker Woman's Town," referred to an African-derived expression even though the village's owner was a Seminole. *Buckra* was a pejorative term, stemming from the Ibo word for "white man," used by slaves to describe their white southern plantation masters. Abraham's home of Peliklakaha presumably drew its name from the Kongo. The Suwannee River, home at times to Black Seminoles, owed its name, evidence suggests, to the Bantu word *nsub-wanyi*, meaning "my house, my home."[22]

The maroons may have clung to important parts of their African cultural heritage, but close association and daily interaction with the Seminoles led, as would be expected, to significant acculturation. Seminoles learned from blacks how to construct different types of houses and how to grow rice. Micanopy reportedly delighted in the merits of Peliklakaha, so much so that he spent a good part of his time there. Black Seminoles—including leaders such as Abraham and John Horse—spoke the Seminoles' native tongue, as well as their own "Negro" dialects. Although some Black Seminoles kept their African American day names, as in the case of King Cudjo, they might adopt Seminole appellations, too. Abraham proudly used his war title, "Souanaffe Tustenukke." Maroons took Indian dances and blended them with African ones. Songs received the same treatment.[23]

Blacks and the Seminoles and other Native Americans sometimes evidenced the intimacy of their association through miscegenation. Governor Richard K. Call, a large Middle Florida planter, knew from firsthand accounts that Indians "intermarried" with blacks in the peninsula, contrary to reports published at various times. The inevitability of sexual amity among blacks and Seminoles became more assured as the former began to increase in numbers among the Indians immediately prior to and then during the early stages of the Second Seminole War.[24]

In later years former slaves proudly traced their descent from such mixed ancestry. William M. Adams of Texas, for instance, recorded that his father, a "Black Creek Indian," was born in Florida. Samuel Jackson similarly remembered his family lineage. Jackson insisted that he "inherited his travelling [or tracking abilities] from his Indian grandmother." Frank Berry, correctly or incorrectly, claimed to be Osceola's grandson. Berry's elders told him that his "grandmother, serving as a nurse at Tampa Bay[,] was captured by the Indians and carried away to become the squaw of their chief."[25]

The exact number of racially mixed black and Indian families or the extent of miscegenation remains a mystery, but marriage and cohabitation between the two groups may have been less common on the Florida frontier than some studies have suggested. Miscegenation certainly occurred. If surviving records do not mislead, though, the practice seems to have applied mostly in relationships within the leadership circles of both groups, which suggests attempts to cement personal or clan alliances. About 1812, under Spanish rule, to cite the first of several examples, John Cavallo or John Horse, who would emerge into the spotlight during the Second Seminole War, was born to the Seminole chief or subchief Imotley and an African or African American mother. The chief Econchatomica (Red Ground Chief), accounts indicate, lived to see a black granddaughter. Chief Micanopy wed two women, one of whom was a "half-breed Negro woman." One of Osceola's wives, at least one account argues, was the daughter of a runaway black and a Seminole chief. King Philip fathered a black Seminole son, John Philip. And the greatest of all Black Seminole leaders, Abraham, wed the widow of a former Indian chief.[26]

When the several factors that have been discussed are considered together, it is easily seen that the maroon presence in Florida resulted in the development over time of a distinctive culture that retained strong influences from African roots. These roots were combined with the fruits of experiences on the southern plantations and contact with Native Americans, Spaniards, and the English. The language of maroons epitomized this evolution and accomplishment. It differed from that of whites and Indians alike but contained a good measure of English. It also blended African, Spanish, and Muscogulge words and phrases to form something new and representative of a unique culture. As seen, it also left legacies for today's Floridians in the names of significant places and things.[27]

The maroon presence in Florida brought the Seminoles, as well as the blacks, many rewards, but it also caused trouble for the Indians. The Seminoles provided land and sanctuary to blacks or else helped to protect them where they lived apart. For those efforts whites attacked the Indians, claiming they harbored runaway slaves, and clamored for the return of their property. Before discussing the legitimacy of the slaveholders' claims, one point should be made. Slaveholder demands for the return of slaves who arrived in Florida prior to ratification of the Adams-Onís Treaty in January 1821 were disingenuous at best. That pact, which solemnized the transfer of Florida from Spain to the United States, specified that the "inhabitants" of Florida "shall be . . . admitted to the enjoyment of all privileges, rights, and immunities of the citizens of the United States." It provided further for payment by the United States of claims against Spain. The claims related mostly to runaway slaves and were paid by the government in due course. If anyone "owned" the pre-1821 runaways, it was the United States government.[28]

After the treaty took effect, the trickle of runaways into Florida never abated. At times the flow appeared more like that of a stream.[29] Runaway slave notices told the story. One slaveholder noted the flight to freedom of his bond servants, Charles and Mary. Charles could speak "Minorean [Minorcan] and Seminole," and the couple probably were headed to "Musketo" to live among the Indians. A decade later another slaveholder declared that William Jones and Christopher Chambers were trying "to get to the Indian nation," where they could find asylum. One runaway slave became "one of the most distinguished leaders" among the Seminoles during the Second Seminole War. Primus, the bondsman of Florida's Erastus Rogers, absconded to the Seminole lands to join his wife, who was living there. The path to freedom continued to beckon even during the middle period of the

Second Seminole War. On one occasion United States soldiers captured "50 to 60 negroes more," who were attempting to make their way to the Seminoles.[30]

Seeing their property disappearing and feeling the continuing threat to their estates, slaveholders from Florida, Georgia, South Carolina, and other slave states thundered against the Seminoles and dispatched slave catchers to recapture their "lost property." Many of the agents sought assistance from United States forces stationed at Fort Brooke on Tampa Bay. Its commander through most of the 1820s, Virginia-born Colonel George Mercer Brooke, at first lent help, although he did so without enthusiasm. As the years passed, Brooke's attitudes changed. He witnessed privations that included persons "dying for the want of something to eat." He grew furious over questionable claims and the cruel treatment of captured runaways. Congressman Josiah Giddings explained Brooke's subsequent actions. "So flagrant were these outrages upon the Indians and negroes," he wrote, "that Colonel Brooke . . . at that time commanding in Florida, took upon himself the responsibility of addressing the [Indian] Agent, advising him not to deliver negroes to the white men, unless their 'claims were made clear and satisfactory.'" To his eternal credit Brooke also informed the agent that his troops would no longer aid the slave catchers' efforts.[31]

The absconding of slaves to the safety of the Indian territory hit East Florida slaveholders especially hard. As a St. Augustine newspaper noted in 1824, "Serious complaints have frequently been made by the planters, that their negroes are harboured among the Indians with impunity; and it is said that many decline settling in the Territory because they are liable to the loss of their negroes by elopement." The combined threat of Seminoles and maroons continued to color political and economic debates as the fires of race and Indian war began to burn. According to one 1837 account, the public mood then suggested "That the Peninsula of Florida is the last place in the limits of the United States wherein the Indian should be allowed to remain, for obvious reasons." A principal obvious reason was that "if [they were] located in Florida, all the runaway slaves will find refuge and protection with them."[32]

The seven-year Second Seminole War, which commenced in December 1835, may be seen at least in part as a result of slaveholder anger with Seminoles for harboring maroons and the Black Seminoles' resisting or avoidance of recapture. The events leading up to the outbreak of fighting and the war's early stages illustrated graphically the intimate association that had grown up between blacks and Seminoles. They showed, as well, the reliance placed on the wisdom of black leaders by Seminole chiefs as they faced key decisions.[33]

During the decade that preceded 1835, blacks emerged as the leading counselors or "sensebearers" to most of the principal Seminole chiefs. Intelligence counted, and so did language skills. As trader Horatio Dexter pointed out, "[The black leaders] speak English as well as Indian." John Caesar, for instance, filled the role of adviser to King Philip, the chief who ranked second to Micanopy in authority among Seminoles. Cudjoe stood close to Micanopy's future successor, the young Billy Bowlegs. One man who knew them both described Cudjoe as Bowlegs's "waiting man." Bowlegs's half-brother Alligator maintained close ties to John Cavallo or John Horse, so close that many army men referred to John as "Pease Creek John," reflective of Bowlegs's and Alligator's Peace River cattle grazing headquarters. Finally, and also at Peace River, the war chief Harry of the village of Minatti planned and cooperated with the Red Stick Creeks who lived below him at Talakchopco (today's Fort Meade). Harry would have dealt particularly with the Red Sticks' rising young war leader, Osceola.[34]

No Black Seminole stood higher in the councils of power than did Abraham. Born between 1787 and 1791, he spent his youth as a slave at Pensacola. He learned English well and developed a strong sense of poise. "He walks like a courtier of the reign of Louis XVI," one army officer commented. Apparently Abraham escaped at some point because he enlisted with other blacks in the British army during the War of 1812's latter stages. He may have been at the Negro Fort when it was destroyed, probably fought at the Battle of the Suwannee in 1818, and likely fled from there to Angola on the Manatee River. By the mid-1820s he had emerged as an adviser to Micanopy. He traveled with the chief and other Indian leaders to Washington in 1827 and helped them negotiate with President John Quincy Adams. Micanopy "freed" him for his valuable services. "This negro Abraham exercised a wonderful influence over his master," recorded a military official at the time; "he was a very shrewd fellow, quick and intelligent, but crafty and artful in the extreme."[35]

With the passage of years Abraham's skills as counselor and middleman—and his influence among the Seminoles—grew. An 1837 Fort Brooke visitor described his abilities. "Abram, the negro chief, seems to be Micanopa's *Prime Minister*," the visitor wrote. "He is said to be a shrewd diplomat—a perfect non-commital—talks a great deal and fluently, but is astonishingly successful in avoiding every expression which might be turned against him, and commit his Prince." The facility, together with diplomacy, tricked white officials time and again into believing that Abraham would side with them or else sell out the Seminoles. They repeatedly discovered to their chagrin the enormity of their error.[36]

The white officials believed that Abraham had assisted them in convincing the Seminoles to emigrate pursuant to Andrew Jackson's Indian Removal Act. In truth he and other black leaders—fearful of re-enslavement despite promises to the contrary—were planning armed resistance in cooperation with Red Stick Creeks. Many Seminoles at first proved reluctant to join the effort because they stood to lose their cattle and whatever other wealth they retained if fighting were to occur. Abraham pressed Micanopy for support, a factor that became all the more important when, in the early 1830s, Micanopy achieved election as supreme chief of Florida's Indians. Abraham sought allies elsewhere. He and John Caesar fanned out to the plantations above and to the east of the Indian lands, alerting slaves to the upcoming war and encouraging them to rebel and join the fighting once it had begun. As a correspondent reported in early 1836, "[Abraham] engaged in effecting a junction with the negroes now under arms."[37]

Abraham's hard work paid off in late 1835 and early 1836. As Harry and Osceola conducted raids aimed at forcing an attack that would unite the Seminoles with the blacks and Red Stick Creeks, Abraham succeeded in gaining Micanopy's ear. Particularly, he convinced the chief to concentrate forces in late December 1835 across the military road stretching from Tampa Bay to Fort King. The counselor had been tipped off by slaves at Fort Brooke that a column of soldiers commanded by Major Francis L. Dade was approaching the Indian lands, and he feared that they had selected his town of Peliklakaha as one of their targets. When Dade hove into sight, Micanopy at Abraham's urging rose, fired, and killed the officer, touching off the Dade Massacre and the Second Seminole War. Reportedly, "Abraham and his band" finished the deadly work. About the same time, John Caesar and King Philip attacked plantations to the east and north, murdering inhabitants, burning crops and buildings, and liberating slaves to join the fighting. Ultimately, as many as 750 to 1,000 or more slaves may have sided with the Black Seminoles. If so, Abraham, John Caesar, Harry, Cudjoe, John Horse, and their allies had launched quite possibly the largest slave rebellion in United States history.[38]

The opening assaults of the Second Seminole War overwhelmed available military forces, and American military leaders found themselves out-generaled by the blacks and Indians. Only after a series of setbacks and some utter disasters did army headquarters in late 1836 finally turn over command in Florida to a man who understood the place occupied by black leaders, counselors, and warriors in the conflict's broader scheme. His name was Thomas S. Jesup. "Throughout my operations I found the negroes the most active and determined warriors," he later recorded, "and during the conferences with the Indian chiefs I ascertained that they exercised an almost controlling influence over them." Eventually, even Florida's political leadership came to accept Jesup's insight. "[Blacks] wield great influence among [the Indians]," Governor Richard Keith Call commented, "which they never failed to exercise against the white man, with whom he could expect only slavery and inequality."[39]

In line with his perceptions of the Black Seminoles and the war, Jesup's opening moves hit hard at the maroons. On the way to take command he attacked and burned a black village on the Oklawaha River, seizing forty-one persons. In January 1837 fifty-two more blacks fell into his grasp near the Withlacoochee River. The same month Jesup's men killed John Caesar and captured eight more near Lake Apopka. As the toll of black casualties continued to mount, Jesup planned to negotiate a quick settlement to the war.[40]

Having attacked black combatants and their families so harshly, Jesup now developed a policy aimed at ending the war by guaranteeing blacks that they would be protected from slave catchers and allowed safe passage with the Seminoles and other Indians in their movement to the West. His was a carrot-and-stick approach, but his emigration policy addressed a central issue of the fighting. The war revolved to a great extent around the question of what would happen to the maroons. It was, as Jesup declared, "a negro and not an Indian War."[41]

Tragically, as it turned out, the general misjudged the determination of the black combatants. "The warriors have fought as long as they had life and such seems to me to be the determination of those who influence their councils—I mean the leading negroes," he ultimately acknowledged in frustration. "I have required . . . immediate emigration," he explained to high authorities. "There would be no difficulty in making peace . . . were it not for that condition," he continued. "The negroes who rule the Indians are all averse to removing to so cold a climate."[42]

Still, by the spring of 1837 Jesup had compelled his opponents to sign a peace pact. Abraham helped with the negotiations, as did John Horse and others. Jesup gave his word that all allies of the Seminoles would be sent to the West. To ensure the sincerity of the blacks and Seminoles, the general retained some as hostages while John Horse and others gathered up their supporters and families. Jesup also set in motion plans to betray the Black Seminoles. Responding to slaveholder demands, he acted, as explained by Congressman Josiah Giddings, to make "an *arrangement* with the chiefs, by which the slaves belonging to the *citizens of Florida*, captured during the war, should be given up."[43]

Whether subsequent events occurred because Jesup's betrayal plans leaked or because the whole idea of surrender had been a sham to gain time and a respite from fighting, the peace process soon exploded in the general's face. On June 5 Osceola, John Horse, and other warriors attacked the emigration camp at Tampa Bay. "All the Negroes disappeared at once," one historian commented, "and the Indians followed them into the swamps." A furious Jesup quickly and radically switched policies. Within days he informed volunteer soldiers that "[the Indians'] *negroes,* cattle and horses, as well as other property which they possess, will belong to the corps by which they are captured." Congressman Giddings summed up the policy change. "From this time forward," he wrote, "[Jesup] lent his energies, and the power of the army, to the object of capturing and returning slaves."[44]

The impact of the new policies gradually wore down the black combatants, although the fighting persisted through 1837 and into 1838. In fact, the year 1837 ended with the conflict's largest pitched battle, the Battle of Okeechobee. Arguably, the blacks under John Horse and their Indian allies won, but starvation had commenced to exact a greater toll than could the soldiers. Jesup's temper had calmed, as well, permitting him to view the situation more objectively. Where he earlier had toyed with leaving the Seminoles in Florida and sending the blacks back into slavery, he now realized that "the two races . . . are identified in interests and feelings" to the extent that he must address black demands. The general finally concluded that "should the Indians remain in this territory, the negroes among them will form a rallying point for runaway negroes from the adjacent states." To get the Seminoles to emigrate, Jesup accepted that the blacks, whether "legally" held by the Indians or recent runaways "legally" owned by whites, would have to leave, too, or the war would continue as before.[45]

Once Jesup's thinking had reached that point, he finally found a way to implement his divide-and-conquer strategy regarding the Seminoles and Black Seminoles. In the late winter and spring of 1838 he assured black warriors, anxious for their families' survival, that they would not be reenslaved by white masters if they separated themselves from the Seminoles and Creeks, if necessary, and departed for the West. By June most Black Seminoles had agreed to surrender. Subsequently, they were transported to Arkansas. Their departure from Florida marked a crucial turning point for Florida's history and the course of the Second Seminole War.[46]

Effectively, the agreements of 1838 resulted in a shift in the role of many Black Seminole leaders from supporting the Indian war to serving the needs of the United States Army. Once in the West, they discovered their promised freedom to be elusive, as Creeks and Seminoles attempted to claim them as slaves. Gaining official recognition of independent status required them to return to Florida. John Horse's case is illustrative. For a promise of manumission papers he came back to the territory in 1839 to serve as an army guide and interpreter and to help persuade the remaining Indian fighters to emigrate west. He performed his duties so well that he became the trusted interpreter for Colonel (later General) William Jenkins Worth. John Horse assisted the general with sensitive negotiations. Scholar Kenneth W. Porter wrote of him, "During the last two years of the war [he] was very nearly the 'indispensable man' in the army's relations both with the Indians who were still 'out' and those who had finally consented to 'come in.'" On the ship from Florida John Horse took with him and carefully guarded a paper dated February 22, 1842. The prized writing specified that "[John Horse,] his wife and increase, Indian negroes, are regarded as having established a right to their freedom from all further services for their former Indian Master."[47]

Given these events and the subsequent role of Black Seminole leaders in United States Army operations, the relationship between blacks and Florida's Indians understandably became rather tenuous after 1838. With the majority of Florida maroons secured in the West the remaining Seminoles probably felt that their black comrades had struck a good bargain at their expense. The bonds of amity strained further when blacks served as guides and interpreters for whites. Blacks who had lived among the Seminoles knew how to reach their remote villages and could easily lead troops to the Indian hideouts. Seminoles and military men understood that fact well. Colonel William S. Harney, for example, employed a black guide to take his forces "to the Everglades." Another officer, Ethan Allen Hitchcock, deeply appreciated what another guide accomplished. "That Negro was the only man in America, black or white," he declared, "who could have performed that service in a part of the country never before visited [by whites]."[48]

Angry and resentful, the Seminoles took their revenge when they could. The black guide Billy, who accompanied Lieutenant Colonel Josephus Guild in search of blacks and Seminoles, was killed by Indians who believed he willingly betrayed his onetime allies. After capturing the Negro interpreter Sandy and one other man in 1839, the Seminoles allowed them to live for only four days. "They then tied them to a pine tree and inserted in their flesh slivers of light wood," explained an onlooker, "setting them on fire, and at the same time placing torches at their feet." The account continued: "In this way it was five or six hours before they died." Even following the war's end Sampson

Forrester kept a wary eye open. "While [the Indians] had buried the hatchet, as far as the public at large were concerned, they still had a small one ground up for Forrester, who they kindly promised to kill on sight for 'deserting' them," an early account noted. "Forrester, however, had ideas of his own on this subject," the account added, "and courted the society of a double-barreled shotgun very closely for some time."[49]

That the involvement of maroons in events leading up to and through the Second Seminole War had a significant impact on slavery in Florida is beyond question. Some of the effects in East Florida have been discussed already. It should be remembered that fears of race war and black-supported Indian war also terrified Middle Florida planters and their families. That apprehension, in turn, prompted demands for harsher slave codes and enhanced day-to-day restrictions on slave life by the men who controlled territorial government. As early as 1827 Jefferson County's Laura Randall lived with fear. She recorded on November 3 that she "was dreaming all night about Indians." The day before she had visited the place where "the scene of the Indian massacre [of the Carr family] had occurred the last winter." She continued, "It will be some time before I shall be free from apprehensions of some night assault from these fiends."[50]

The anxieties grew as war approached and flared. In 1835 overseer Louis Goldsborough recoiled at the killing of a "white boy and Judge Randall's slave named Tom." He observed that as long as there were Indian problems, "neither our negroes nor others can work with the same heart of life they [would do] otherwise." Four years later the area was still enduring raids that resulted in the deaths of whites and slaves. The possibility of an Indian and black triumph loomed as a real one. Goldsborough eventually determined that "if Osceola came, and I find myself forced to abandon Wirtland to his mercy . . . I shall take all the Negroes to Pensacola."[51]

The Second Seminole War's conclusion in 1842 halted the hostilities but only temporarily. The remaining Seminoles, Creeks, and Mikasukis—with their few surviving black allies—bided their time, still determined not to leave Florida. As whites continuously pushed toward the Everglades in the early 1850s, some bands decided on armed resistance. Their resistance culminated from 1855 to 1858 in the Third

Seminole War, also known as the Billy Bowlegs War. The hostilities focused primarily on the Tampa Bay region and the Peace River area and were mainly skirmishes instead of battles. Although blacks played no central role in the conflict, a few probably involved themselves. Such was the case with Ben Bruner [Bruno]. He served Chief Billy Bowlegs well as an interpreter and adviser.[52]

The Bowlegs War also touched the lives of slaves owned by white frontier settlers. As in the Second Seminole War, blacks who acted to protect whites were subjected to the same type of treatment as their masters. At Fort Meade, for example, Indians attacked the Tillis family. In the confusion Mrs. Tillis ran for the safety of her cabin, leaving sons Dallas and Calhoun at the mercy of the warriors. Aunt Line was more concerned for the children than was their mother. She risked her own life and was "painfully wounded" in the forehead while rescuing the boys.[53]

The Indians sometimes acted against the interests of slaves in another way. With the power of the Fugitive Slave Law of 1850 behind them, some whites employed Seminoles to catch runaway slaves. Attempting in extremely difficult circumstances to keep whites from infringing on their South Florida lands, the Indians felt pressure to distance themselves from blacks by agreeing to serve the slaveholders. Billy Bowlegs undertook in 1853 to cooperate to a limited extent. "I told [Bowlegs and others] that they must bring in the runaways," an official reported from Fort Myers on November 2. "Bowlegs said if they came to his town where he could catch them without endangering any of his people, he would bring them in." The official added, "He said he did not intend to take the trouble to hunt them—he saw no good need for helping the White people of Florida to get their slaves." Some of Bowlegs's compatriots proved more amenable. "One of the negroes was brought back a few days ago by the indians," the same official had recorded in June. "[He] says he ran away from his master in Georgia eight weeks ago."[54]

By the Third Seminole War's conclusion, the beacon of freedom that had flared brightly to guide southern slaves for almost three centuries to refuge in Florida's vast wilderness flickered only dimly. Billy Bowlegs had left Florida in the spring of 1858, and in his place a slave-smuggling operation assumed the buildings at abandoned Fort Myers.

Black fugitives from Georgia and the Carolinas, as well as from the plantations and farms of Florida, occasionally still fled to the southern peninsula. Their fight continued until near the Civil War's end. "COM-MITTED TO JAIL ON SATURDAY, 5th inst., a Negro man, who says his name is Moses, and that he belongs to Mr. Wm. B. Reynolds, who resides near Ocala, Fla.," read a typical advertisement published in 1859. Unfortunately for the runaways, few Seminoles or other blacks remained to ease their path or to protect their sanctuary. An era of fundamental importance to African Americans in Florida and the South had passed away.[55]

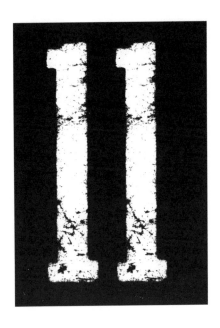

SLAVE

RESISTANCE

The scholarship of slavery has passed far beyond the days when writers painted portraits of the institution that offered happy slaves singing in the fields or bond people tearful at the thought of the old master heading off for the Civil War. Today it is known that slaves throughout the South resisted bondage in ways great and small. As the distinguished African American sociologist W. E. B. Du Bois pointed out, "Gradually the whole white South became an armed and commissioned camp to keep Negroes in slavery and to kill the black rebel." Given Florida's heritage as a refuge of freedom, its vast hidden places, and its flexible colonial traditions, it is no wonder that resistance in the territory and state equaled or exceeded that found elsewhere. The story of that tremendous struggle occupies the following pages.[1]

Slaves tended to fall into one of three categories at any given point in time. Owner Jesse Potts described the first category in referring to his slave Cato as "loyal." That was the state in which most slaveholders would have desired their bondsmen to remain. A second classification involved persons who did not surrender to slavery nor rebel with violence against it. Rather, they attempted to retain some dignity and self-respect in times of crisis by running away, at least for a time, rather than caving in to slaveholder demands. Laurence accomplished this when he surprised his owner by fleeing because he did not want to drive a load of cotton to the port at St. Marks. Eventually, Laurence returned, received "a little punishment," and went back to work. The third category involved those who resisted slavery overtly, sometimes with violence. Celia Bryan knew well about this pathway, for she murdered her owner with a hoe when he tried to punish her. Despite the laws and hegemony of the slaveholding class, rebel bond servants sometimes killed their masters, committed arson, conspired to commit or carry out mass rebellion, or undertook other activities to demonstrate their physical resistance to servitude. Yet the "average" slave's life in Florida probably consisted of both resistance and accommodation.[2]

Therefore, most Florida slaves usually fit more closely within the second of the three categories. Still, some individuals surrendered psychologically to their servitude, becoming extensions of the master or other whites. Willis Williams may have been one such individual. His recollections of slavery involved primarily positive things. He remembered his master as nothing but kind. Williams insisted that he had endured no "unpleasant experiences as related by some other ex-slaves." His owner, he asserted, never flogged bond servants, and Williams especially had liked the idea of sitting in the balcony at the same church attended by his white owner.[3]

One of the Partridge family slaves in Jefferson County may have belonged to the same category as Williams; at least her owners thought so. "We buried either in [18]57 or [18]58 our faithful old 'Mauma' Mollie," Henry Edward Partridge recorded, "her who had nursed nearly all of the children of the family; been a friend as well as a faithful servant to my Mother; in whose cabin we had often eaten the homely meal of fried bacon & ash cake and where we always had welcome and sympathy and whom we loved as a second mother." Partridge added, "Black of skin but pure of heart, she doubtless stands among the faithful on the right of the King." The possibility always exists, though, that Mollie was something other than she appeared to the Partridges. As Randolph B. Campbell has observed, "It is impossible to distinguish between those who internalized the behavior patterns of the loyal servant and those who engaged in conscious accommodation for the purpose of getting along with masters."[4]

But many more slaves rebelled against bondage or otherwise adopted a noncooperative attitude rather than surrendering to it. One interesting possibility suggests itself. In the territory and state, West and East Florida enjoyed a reputation for having a less-harsh slave regimen and a more flexible pattern of race relations. On the other hand, bond servants clearly outnumbered whites in Middle Florida, a situation that may have helped slaves there endure the psychological and emotional scars of servitude better than their West and East Florida counterparts. In Middle Florida bond servants more easily could share each other's support. The numbers were impressive. In 1850 four out of five Middle Florida residents were bond persons. Ten years later three out of five people in the region remained in bondage.[5]

For slaves who chose such a path resistance could take many forms. The most common one usually occurred when planters failed to allow a degree of independence within the slave community and bond servants became uncooperative by performing their various duties poorly. The objective of most bond persons was not the immediate overthrow of slavery or immediate personal freedom. Rather, it centered on maintaining a relationship for the time being in which both master and slave compromised on what was considered an acceptable level of punishment, food, work, shelter, and free private time. "Slaveholders [and their bond servants] constantly struggled over responsibilities and rights within this system of inordinately unequal power," Ira Berlin has explained.[6]

Enslaved blacks often protested or demonstrated their disenchantment with conditions of servitude simply by complaining or grumbling about their work assignments. Greater forms of resistance could carry undesirable costs. If a planter consistently fared badly because of poor slave performance, for instance, eventually he or she would have to sell some or all slaves. The division could result in the separation of families and the loss of loved ones. Consequently, the majority of slaves understood their responsibility to perform work assignments in a normal fashion, but they reserved the option to voice frustrations when agreed-upon arrangements were ignored. Examples easily come to hand of bond servants complaining when overseers and masters worked them beyond a certain customary limit. Slaves might challenge an overseer's authority by going directly to the owner with their complaints. When George Noble Jones's laborers felt that they had been overworked, they sought to undermine the overseer's authority by taking their gripes directly to Jones during one of his intermittent visits. "Your negroes behave badly behind my back and then run to you," the overseer lamented, "and you appear to beleave what they say."[7]

Not all bond servants belonged to a master so willing to listen, of course. Winston Stephens's East Florida slaves certainly never found ears so receptive as Jones's. After his black driver, Burrel, criticized the amount of work he and other slaves had to perform, Stephens expressed glee that his wife had spoken "so short" to him. The Putnam County man added, "If they trouble me I will hire the whole of them out and you may tell . . . [Burrel] so."[8]

Many slaves, although comprehending that their lives were interwoven with that of the master, nonetheless expressed day-to-day dissatisfaction with servitude through poor work performance. Here a continuing war of wills existed between the master and the slave. Although the planter held virtually absolute power, neither he nor the authority that supported him could ensure effective control of the quality or quantity of work performed. Enslaved blacks knew the ways of their masters quite well, and forcing bond servants to work at a certain pace or to complete assignments at a given time did not always prove fruitful. Louis Goldsborough's experience provides an example. One of his slaves, who had twenty years' experience packing cotton, caused the overseer the kind of problems that other owners and overseers experienced regularly. When Goldsborough pressed the man too hard to pack cotton too quickly, the slave packed the cotton wet. The firm of consignment in Liverpool, England, informed the overseer of the fact to his embarrassment. Goldsborough administered a flogging in front of the plantation's slave community, but the slave had made his point as well.[9]

Even with the threat of severe punishment or the administration of it, many slaves refused to be worked beyond a certain level. Margrett Nickerson's sister, for one, would not be overworked. Margrett recalled that Holly stood back on "non' uv em, when dey'd git behin' her, she'd git behin' dem; she wuz dat stubbo'n and when dey would beat her she wouldn' holler and jes take it and go on." At Goodwood plantation in Leon County the overseer acknowledged that a particular bond servant "was a good hand." Still, the man was "hard to manage." Pine Hill's Affie was the same way. She would leave the Leon County plantation when faced with "any kind of work which she found disagreeable." At Jefferson County's El Destino the overseer routinely flogged slaves for "coming up short" on their cotton picking. Once he did so, four slaves took to the woods, denying him their labor for a couple of days. But like most bond servants throughout the South, the four fugitives returned to their master on their own accord.[10]

Resistance to work assignments was by no means limited to field hands. Middle Florida house servants, although benefiting from easier chores than field-workers, still rebelled against certain tasks. William Wirt complained that one slave, probably believing that she had done enough work for a given day, became unmanageable and started working to her own "liking." Another house servant on the same plantation rejected the amount of work assigned to her and ultimately had to be "ejected from the kitchen." In at least one case a Columbia County house servant rebelled against the whole idea of being a house servant and demanded to be set to work in the fields. Claude A. Wilson told the story to an interviewer. "[His] mother was very rebellious toward her [house] duties and constantly harassed the 'Missus' about letting her work in the fields with her husband," he recorded, "until finally she was permitted to make the change from the house to the fields to be near her man."[11]

Realizing that overt opposition to a master's control might lead to punishment, slaves developed a less easily detected form of demonstrating dissatisfaction. They feigned illness. It is impossible from the vantage point of the early twenty-first century to distinguish between those bond servants who were indeed sick and those who pretended to be and thereby resisted the work system. As discussed earlier, Florida abounded in health hazards for everyone. Still, slaves learned early that concocting an illness was one simple, yet difficult-to-disprove, route for evading the work routine. Perhaps it was an overseer none too skilled at managing his slaves who reported to his employer, "I beleave that I am further behind this year gathering cotton than I ever been but I cant help it." He continued, "I am doeing all I noe . . . so much sickness."[12]

More often than men, slave women reported themselves sick or injured. "The most common form of female self-defense," Deborah White has noted, "was feigning illness." Some chronically complained of sickness most of the time. A few went too far and tipped off the master. Chemonie plantation's overseer A. R. McCall reported, to cite one example, that Ellen was not sick but trying to "deceive" him. Alexander Randall reflected McCall's sentiments when he declared that Nelly "is not much sick . . . And supposes herself privileged [by not having to work]." Owners did not always prove so perceptive. A quiet-acting, reserved slave at Chemonie became so overjoyed by the news of her freedom that she dropped her crutches and began to walk. This revelation understandably disgusted the former master because he had excused the bond servant from doing any "real work" for seven years. Because most slaveholders entertained concerns about any condition that would limit a woman's childbearing potential, they generally made some allowances for illnesses as long as the illnesses seemed credible.[13]

Slave women did not monopolize the idea of pretended ailments; men fabricated sickness when they wanted "time off" from work as well. Records hint that on one of George N. Jones's plantations slaves took turns feigning illness. The overseer of the El Destino mill found that four or five of the slaves under his control normally were "sick." During one four-month period, about one-third of the workforce typically was confined to the quarters because of "illness." Just possibly, Washington, who lived on Charles W. Bannerman's plantation, may have won the prize for longevity of resistance through feigned illness. His master's diary records him as sick for a good part of the period from 1846 to 1855.[14]

The number of slaves who became ill rose during the planting and harvesting seasons when the hardest work faced the farm or plantation's workforce. Again, real illness constituted an important factor, but the impact of pretended ailments cannot be discounted. What, for instance, actually was occurring when, in September 1839, Ellen Wirt Voss complained that "almost every man, woman, and child with two exceptions have been sick"? Or when Louis Wirt recorded that his mother's bond servants were constantly sick during the warm season?

What had Charlotte meant to convey to Henry Wirt in 1843? In that instance, Wirt informed a relation, "I think Charlotte [a slave] told me there was more sickness during the months of May, June, and July among the negroes than she had ever known."[15]

Resistance could evidence itself in petty theft as well as in feigned illness, especially when a battle of wills developed between an owner and slaves over the bounty that the bond servants had produced. Food rations offered one important subject of disagreement. When a dispute occurred, some slaves habitually showed their dissatisfaction simply by helping themselves to additional food and livestock without the master's permission. The slaves probably perceived their actions as taking what they had worked for, although most masters saw the practice as stealing. Attempting to reduce this type of tension, insightful slave owners allowed bond servants to cultivate their own gardens, to fish and hunt wild game, and sometimes to sell their goods for cash or other products. When these arrangements could not be worked out, though, slaves relied on their own accounting system.[16]

Potential objects of theft varied widely. Wiley took pigs from Edward Bradford. George N. Jones's sugar houses were hit so often that the overseer begged for new (and better) locks. Daniel and Scot stole potatoes from Nancy DeLaughter, and Birl and Isaac went after hogs. One overseer believed (probably rightly) that Mugin was up to his "old trade of stealing chickens [at night]." Dick achieved a certain reputation for stealing watermelons and stopped his thefts only after a dog seized him by the "seat of his pants." And two "trusted" slaves of the Eppes family, Molly and Randall Junior, conspired to steal bacon from the smokehouse. Charles, a slave belonging to O. M. Parmon, may have exceeded the accomplishments of most. Citizens of the St. Augustine vicinity reacted in alarm in 1830 to reports that he had committed "some extensive robberies." The list ran on and on.[17]

Because it contradicted the law and most slaveholders' wishes, learning to read and write offered one passive form of resistance for enslaved blacks. Literate bond servants could take advantage of their skills by writing passes or teaching other slaves how to read and write without the master's permission. Literacy meant they might be able to gain some knowledge of current events to disseminate in the quarters. Slave owners knew the practice was common. William Alsop described one fugitive as being "very intelligent." The owner continued, "He . . . can read and write and will probably forge passes for himself." A stout slave man may have ushered off Jenny, according to another runaway notice, and "no doubt [supplied her] with forged passes." Madam Widow Marmillon took pains to note in a separate advertisement that her slave "reads and writes and may have made a false certificate of liberty."[18]

When passive or mild resistance failed to meet the needs of the moment, some slaves escalated the level of opposition and resorted to retaliation on a more violent scale. The decision could come unexpectedly and quick. Four women at El Destino plantation discovered this possibility when an enraged friend came to their assistance. The story began when the women came up short with their cotton picking. The overseer prepared to whip them, but they ran away before he could do so. After they were captured and returned to the plantation, the overseer began to flog one of the runaways. Her brother Aberdeen thereupon attacked the overseer with an axe. Fortunately for the overseer, the slave driver, Prince, quickly stopped the assault. In Jefferson County similar circumstances produced deadlier results. Faced with a whipping, Simon killed his master, Richard Cole, by beating him to the ground and then throwing him into a creek. In Madison County a slave of William Pearce murdered him to stop a flogging. A detailed account of the incident survives. "When [Pearce] got up from the table, he went out into the back yard and called the fellow out of the kitchen, and told him to come to him," it reads. "Manifesting a great deal of submission, he obeyed; but so soon as he got within striking distance, drew an axe, which he had concealed and split in twain the head of his master—scattering the brains in every direction."[19]

Enough acts of group violence occurred to cause real concern to slave owners and to Florida society in general. The bond servants typically acted only after prolonged abusive treatment. One notorious example occurred in Madison County in 1860. After being deprived of adequate clothing, shelter, and especially food for over a year, slaves on Jesse Watts's plantation killed overseer M. D. Griffin. A historian described the event: "Griffin was struck down from behind with an ax," wrote James M. Denham. "His body was placed in a wheelbarrow, tied in a sheet, attached to an anvil, and then sunk in twenty feet of water."

After they had accomplished their work, eleven slaves made their escape. Eventually, six men were convicted of the crime. Three—William, Coleman, and Addison—were hanged, whereas the remainder received pardons.[20]

Such extreme attempts at resistance were not confined to Middle Florida counties such as Madison. East Florida slaves violently expressed objections to conditions of servitude, particularly as the plantation belt extended itself in the 1850s into the peninsula. Marion County planter William J. Keitt fell victim to direct action in 1860, the same year that overseer Griffin died. A state senator and brother of South Carolina secessionist Lawrence M. Keitt, the planter raised the ire of four bond servants, although the specific reasons are not known. "His body was found bathed in blood, and his throat cut from ear to ear," the local newspaper reported. Of the four slaves, only Lewis paid for the crime with his life. He died knowing that, by the murder of so prominent a man, he had set off widespread fears among the planter class in Florida and elsewhere. "No longer can we open the door to the [wayfarer] and offer a Southern cheerful hospitality," commented Keitt's sister-in-law. "The midnight dagger and the poisoned bowl may, many days after, come to us." The *Ocala Florida Home Companion* agreed, labeling the incident "a public calamity." At least twenty-two black males and one female were executed under judicial process in antebellum Florida for committing murder against whites, usually an overseer or slaveholder.[21]

In just the manner suggested by W. J. Keitt's sister-in-law, slaves sometimes adopted more exotic, but still deadly, approaches. They vented their frustrations and anger without resorting to the use of an axe, knife, or gun. Women, particularly cooks, found potential in the use of poison. Such was the case on Thomas Randall's Belmont plantation in 1832. There Sally and two other women seethed at mistreatment they received from a callous overseer. They responded by trying to kill him through tainting his food. Perhaps it was the overseer and the slaves' good fortune that the three women subsequently were sold.[22]

If the murder of an individual living on an isolated farm several miles outside the village of Ocala could stir fears and passions to the extent that W. J. Keitt's demise accomplished, how much more panic might be generated from a full-scale slave revolt. Such an event was the form of slave violence that most terrorized southern whites. Volumes have concentrated on the Stono Rebellion, the Nat Turner uprising, and other revolts that occurred outside Florida, including the closely watched and bloody rising of slaves on the French island of Saint-Domingue (Haiti). Some historians have suggested, though, that no significant slave revolt occurred in the United States between Nat Turner's 1831 struggle and the Civil War's beginning three decades later. Yet, as discussed in chapter 10, what probably constituted the largest slave uprising in the annals of North American history ravaged Florida from 1835 to 1838 during the Second Seminole War. That armed resistance, unlike other rebellions, had no religious overtones. It simply represented a fight to the death for freedom and a direct challenge to the institution of slavery by perhaps one thousand or more individuals.[23]

Because historians have only just begun to accept that the Second Seminole War was a massive slave revolt, it is easy to understand that little analysis of that rebellion on Florida and the institution of slavery has been made. The historian Canter Brown has examined the revolt's reverberations on Florida society. The development of Florida's slave code, its fight over statehood, the nature of its political system, and divisions that evidenced themselves over the issue of secession all involved legacies of race war according to Brown. He concluded, "Local customs, conditions, and events had substantial impact upon the evolution of slavery and relations between the races." Future research may add greater depth to Brown's findings and extend the range of the revolt's echoes into the racial violence that plagued Florida in the late nineteenth and twentieth centuries.[24]

Incidents such as slave revolt or murder aside, most slaves found in their hearts more humanity than was afforded to them by the whites and recoiled at the idea of violent resistance. Instead, when circumstances compelled them to act, they took flight. W. E. B. Du Bois believed these developments were crucial factors that affected the southern slave system. "Even the poor white, led by the planter, would not have kept the black slave in nearly so complete control had it not been for what may be called the Safety Valve of Slavery," he observed, "and that was the chance which a vigorous and determined slave had to run away to freedom." Du Bois added, "It is certain from the bitter effort to increase the efficiency of the fugitive slave law that the losses from runaways were widespread and continuous."[25]

Because secure refuges and determined allies beckoned to Florida bond servants who were considering escape, the incidence of running away in the territory and state was probably higher than in other slave states. White Floridians certainly thought so. In 1834 the *Tallahassee Floridian* reflected the already intense concerns of many whites. "There are few things which have been subjects of greater complaint for the last two or three years than runaway negroes," its editor proclaimed. He complained that they "are permitted to go at large, and plunder the public." Ten years earlier a St. Augustine journalist had expressed dread that the problem of runaways might keep new settlers from relocating. "It is said that many decline settling in the Territory," he wrote, "because they are liable to the loss of their negroes by elopement." Susan Bradford Eppes summed up the situation when she reflected, "It grew to be quite common to hear of run-a-way negroes."[26]

The dynamics of slave flight to peninsular havens has been considered at length in chapters 1, 4, and 10, and Civil War–era runaways will be examined in chapter 12; but the subject has several other facets. First, which slaves were most likely to attempt escape? The answer is complicated. One factor concerned how long a bond servant had been living at a specific place. Slaves who had been on a farm or plantation for only a brief period tended to be the most prone to escape. Other factors also were important. Of the runaways considered in one study, 75 percent were young males. They averaged twenty-nine years of age. Some left when new masters or overseers took control of the enterprise; others fled out of anger or frustration. Some absconded out of a simple desire to be free. Slaves ran away throughout the year. Donorena Harris concluded that more left the plantation in February, April, May, and June than at any other time, but contemporary sources indicated to the contrary that more fled during June, July, August, and September. Of the 742 slaves who fled Florida farms and plantations from 1821 to 1860 who were studied, 148 or 20 percent were repeaters. A few could be described as habitual offenders.[27]

Importantly, many bond servants escaped not so much because of ill treatment but to return to a previous home where family members and loved ones presumably still lived. After Achille Murat purchased Chester, the bond servant tried to make his way back to Hanson County, North Carolina. William and Maria escaped from C. C. Williams of Tallahassee, and they were said to be heading to Tennessee where they once lived. Joshua Croom of Jefferson believed that Hector and Simon would try to make their way back to Muscle Shoals, Alabama, where they once resided. Ned, who belonged to Leon County's William Treadwell, set off toward his old home in South Carolina.[28]

Some historians have noted that the majority of slaves who escaped usually did so alone. These contentions mirror the Florida situation during much of the period from 1821 to 1865. Escapees such as Byrd, David, Caesar, William, George, Rose, Sophia, Robin, Maria, John Butler, and others left their masters unaccompanied. Most solitaires were attempting to get back to a previous home or loved ones. Forty-year-old Allen, for example, wanted to return to St. Marys, Georgia, where he "formerly lived." July left the *Carolina* steamer alone in search of his wife who lived in Palatka. Dick fled Leon for Gadsden County to return "to Asa Munson on the Ocklockney [River]." Thomas Randall's Rebecca, he believed, tried to make her way back to South Carolina where she once lived. And after fugitive Sandy broke out of jail in Leon County, he quickly departed for St. Augustine.[29]

Somewhat surprisingly, about 30 percent of runaways apparently left their owners in twos, and 15 percent absconded in larger groups. East Florida experienced a higher number of slaves fleeing in twos and larger groups than Middle Florida. Abraham Brown and Georgia ran away from a sawmill on Barkers' Island along the St. Johns River. Edward and James Wanton remained at large from James Riz's place near Palatka for about two months. Tony, a field hand, and Jim, a carpenter, took their leave from the St. Augustine area, and a Negro couple made their escape from Jacksonville in 1829. Three escaped slaves made their way to the Indian lands in 1823 from St. Augustine. Cracker Jim, John, Primus, and Allen absented themselves together from an East Florida plantation. Five blacks left a Marion County plantation in 1856. A family of seven—including Hampton, his wife, Nanny, and their five children—escaped from Palatka around September 1850. Charles and Abraham ran away from a plantation at Cabbage Hammock in Palatka in 1846. The largest group of slaves to escape together, presumably, involved the twelve fugitives sought in Monroe County during 1848. The party included men, women, and children.[30]

Fewer slaves ran away from Middle Florida in such small groups. Isaac and Jack left D. A. Gaillard in Jefferson County, attempting to return to Columbus, Georgia, where they "were both purchased." Kidder Moore of the same county advertised for the capture of Joe, Bob, Bryant, and Rachael in 1847. Edmund and his pregnant wife Rebecca escaped from Leon County's Samuel Parkhill. Once captured in Georgia, they subsequently broke out of jail and set out for Virginia, where they had been purchased by a slave trader. Dr. Ash advertised for the capture of June, his wife, Tyre, and Frank in 1837. Jim and Martha, who left owner Thomas Green, headed to Tallahassee where they had once lived and worked. On one occasion two girls, one fifteen and the other twenty, left the region together. George and William escaped their Gadsden County plantation on a Sunday, probably headed for North Carolina. And a group of six men—including "Jim, Willis, Reuben, Bass, Harve, and Thad"—escaped from a Jackson County estate. The largest group of fugitives from Middle Florida may have been a three-generational family. It consisted of George, his wife, Lettus, their four children, and one grandchild.[31]

Most runaway episodes involved bond servants who absconded for only a short period and then returned from one day to one week later to take their punishment. Winter, of Chemonie plantation, left the premises for four days because he did not want to be whipped for coming up short on his cotton picking. William Moseley caught a little girl and returned her to his neighbor's plantation the same day that she had departed. According to A. R. McCall, "Mariah got the Devil in her and walk[ed] of[f]." When she returned, the driver gave her ten lashes with his whip. In a highly unusual case Edward Bradford's slave Affie earned a reputation as a habitual fugitive who stayed at large for up to three months at a time.[32]

Although many fugitives absented themselves for only a brief time, some runaways stayed at liberty for months and even years. If the slave resided in East Florida, chances were that he or she would remain at large far longer than did Middle Florida runaways. One study suggests that East Florida fugitives often sustained their absences for one month or more, which is not surprising in light of the refuge's proximity to nearby Indian lands. Many instances are known. In one case Harry and Daniel were still missing from Alachua County after two months. Charles and Abraham, who absconded from Palatka, remained away for over three months. Clarissa, from Jacksonville, absented herself for over one year. Pompey stayed out for over fifteen months. After a two-year absence from Judge O'Neill of Fernandina, John was discovered and asked to surrender. Allegedly, the slave catcher killed the bond servant when he attempted to use a gun.[33]

The actual places sought by Florida's slaves varied according to several factors. Young married slaves were more likely to remain within the territory or state, especially as Florida became more settled and slave kinship networks grew locally. Ties of family and affection, after all, rated high as a cause of slave flight. Hannah's experience reflects that fact. Purchased by an East Florida slaveholder, she fled several times, "believed to be headed for Tallahassee where her mother lives." Middle Florida's runaways often remained in that region, where most of Florida's slaves resided. Thus, George and John were thought to be "lurking at Black Creek where they have Wives." One owner offered a handsome $200 reward for the return of two children who had run away to seek their "freed mother." Abram of Leon County determined to look "for his wife," and Levenia left Tallahassee for Quincy, where "she has a husband."[34]

Escapees with fewer familial ties to bind them to Middle Florida usually did not linger in the region. Most often they moved on to the central or southern peninsula. Aware of traditional alliances forged among slaves, free blacks, and Seminole Indians from the late eighteenth to the mid–nineteenth centuries under both Spanish and British rule, many Middle Florida slaves tried to make their way to the Black Seminole and Indian settlements. That story is discussed at greater length in chapters 1 and 10.[35]

As suggested by previous examples, Florida fugitives sometimes undertook ambitious journeys to escape slavery. In 1848 a family of three—Dick, his wife, Margaret, and their five-year-old son, Charles—fled recently formed Marion County and attempted to reach New Orleans by canoe. They failed and were captured. Cornelius Beasley of St. Augustine postulated that his slave Harrison would go to South

Carolina "in pursuit of his wife." A group of slaves from Middle Florida tried to make their escape to North Carolina. When Lee decamped, his master believed he would go to Columbus or Atlanta, Georgia, for in "one of those . . . [places is] his mother."[36]

Some runaways looked beyond the peninsula for a haven in the Bahamas. The tradition had been established as early as 1821. In that year survivors of the destruction of the Manatee River maroon refuge Angola fled to the Keys and were taken by Bahamian fishermen to Andros Island. Others followed, particularly after the British Empire abolished slavery in the mid-1830s. Several slaves escaped from St. Augustine in 1842 on boats belonging to the local harbor pilots. They headed for freedom to the Bahamas, robbing and murdering a Key Biscayne man en route to their destination. After reaching the islands, the runaways remained safe under British jurisdiction despite pleas from planters for their return to Florida. Some twelve years later another group of twelve slaves escaped by boat from Key West to Andros Island.[37]

Cooperation among members of the slave community facilitated flight by bond servants. Whites were convinced this was true. John R. Lloyd traced Charlotte to "certain negro quarters" and issued a public warning to all persons "under the severest penalty of the law" against harboring her. Dilsey's master believed, after she already had been away from the plantation for "about 3 years," that she still was harbored by a man named Power. When Ivy absented himself from a St. Augustine farm, he received clothing from unknown blacks. According to a runaway notice, he had gone away with only a "Jacket and trowsers made of White Plains, Osnaburgh shirt Felt hat, coarse shoes & a plaid cloak." On his journey to freedom Ivy received another set of clothing resembling the coat "worn by U.S. Soldiers." Jupiter's owner believed that the escaped preacher had been housed and fed by other bond servants. He was "no doubt prowling around the neighborhood." An angry A. Watson believed that his slave Ben had been fed and given protection. He broadcast that he would "apply the law of Judge Lynch to my own satisfaction, on those concerned in his concealment."[38]

Inevitably, some planters came to believe that their runaways were being assisted by abolitionists, although these reformers were never a threat to the institution of slavery in Florida. Irrational fears nonetheless prompted public meetings and demands for protective legislation. One Jacksonville gathering in 1835 condemned fellow citizens even for reading abolitionist literature: "We consider as dangerous all persons who may be subscribers to or who shall take any Abolitionist paper or pamphlets, or seditious or incendiary publications, and will view all such persons as inimical to our institutions and meriting summary punishment." One Leon County planter who had problems with slaves absconding from his lands had similar fears. He warned, "The community are requested to look out for Abolitionists as I have strong reasons for believing their interference with these servants."[39]

Whether the individual held remotely abolitionist thoughts or not, white assistance with slave flight almost always was an individual act. There were few, if any, well-planned conspiracies to aid the escape of large numbers of slaves. In handing out punishments, though, planter-influenced juries declined in most instances to see a lesser threat. "They saw little difference between those they considered misguided fanatics seeking to free slaves on humanitarian grounds," explained historian James M. Denham, "and those who used force or persuasion to steal slaves for resale elsewhere." Irwin Granger of Jefferson County assisted Ben with his unsuccessful escape. The jury found him guilty of "unlawfully, willfully, [and] maliciously" knowing and aiding a slave with his runaway attempt. When James Kelly was found guilty merely for "aiding runaway slaves," he received sixty days in prison for his crime. William Pittman only "uttered" abolition sentiments. Residents still hauled him before Judge A. H. Bush's Jackson County court.[40]

In many such cases involving suspected abolitionists or persons sympathetic to runaways, no records exist on the sentences meted out to the guilty party. Seemingly, unofficial punishments substituted for official ones in many cases. According to former slave Shack Thomas, some alleged abolitionists simply were run out of town. In one celebrated 1844 case the defendant likely wished he was so lucky. Jonathan Walker, a true Boston abolitionist, abetted the escape of seven Pensacola slaves. All culprits were apprehended and returned. The slaves went back to their respective masters, and Walker stood trial and was found guilty of "aiding and abetting" runaways. The court ordered that he be placed in the pillory, branded on the hand with the letters SS, imprisoned for fifteen days, and fined $150.[41]

Sometimes when slaveholders believed abolitionists were aiding slaves' escape, the bond servants in fact were being ushered off by real criminals. Slave stealing appears to have been a common problem in Florida, and at times that fact actually offered some comfort to slaveholders. Mary Roberts of Jackson County, for example, wanted to believe that Harry had been "carried off by some person" instead of absconding on his own. A. Danforth believed that Titus had "no cause for absenting himself, and taking no clothes except such as he wore off, it is believed that he may have been stolen." A group of men took one of Colonel Fleming's bond servants. The wily slave pretended to be lame, though, and "was dropped off on the road of escape." More typically, a small party of W. H. G. Saunders's bond servants concealed themselves on Fleming's Island while their owner chose to think that they had been stolen.[42]

Slave stealers and runaways had a relatively easy time of it because slave patrols operated only sporadically in the state. Statutes required patrols or the local militia to deal with complaints concerning slaves, free blacks, and Indians. Yet day-to-day reality posed another situation entirely. In a refrain often heard in Florida, the Leon County grand jury in 1853 condemned "the entire neglect of the patrol duty in the county." Historian James M. Denham explained. "The law empowered patrols to police locales against the late-night ministrations of blacks, yet in most counties these patrols were often neglected." Denham added, "Local magistrates and justices of the peace enforced laws regulating patrols, but public apathy made their task difficult."[43]

Still, patrols seemed to operate at least on some level during crisis times. During the Civil War, particularly, patrols monitored Florida more frequently than previously had been the case. Shack Thomas of East Florida recalled that patrols gave "him a lot of trouble every time he didn't have a pass to leave [the plantation]." As Thomas remembered, being captured by a patrol commenced a thoroughly unpleasant experience for slaves. Once runaways were in custody, he recollected, they would be "gagged and tied in a squatting position and left in the sun for hours." He had seen other slaves "suspended by their thumbs for varying periods." Louis Napoleon had similar memories. If patrols caught a slave "going off without a permit from the master," he recorded, "they were whipped with a 'raw hide.'" Sometimes patrols operated on a "bring 'em back dead or alive" philosophy. Madison County's Amon DeLaughter recorded in 1861, for instance, that a slave of McGehee had been killed by the patrollers or "regulators."[44]

Lax slave patrols aided runaways, but owners also sometimes contributed to the ease of slave flight by their overconfidence. The more secure masters became of their power over the slaves, the bigger the gap grew between what they actually knew about their bond servants and what they thought they knew. Mistaken perceptions of attitudes were epidemic because, despite owners' thoughts, bond servants usually did not accept their condition, maintaining their own concept of freedom. Susan Bradford Eppes found herself just one of many who discovered the true state of affairs. During the Civil War's waning days, she got an unexpected surprise when she asked Emelina, one of her trusted and reliable bond servants, to cook. Eppes claimed that Emelina replied, "Take dem keys back ter your mother and tell her don't never 'spects ter cook no more, not while I lives . . . tell her I's free, bless de Lord."[45]

Not all whites accepted such illusions as easily as did Eppes. Many slaveholders understood fairly well the character and overall disposition of their bond servants. Ellen McCormick was one. She did not want to buy "Charles" from her father William Wirt, for instance, because she had "no confidence in his fidelity or attachment if the temptation to run away, or leave me in a free state were offered him." D. N. Moxley, who did not spare the whip, recognized that he simply could not manage Die well enough to get her to work effectively for him, whatever her seeming disposition might be. So he dispatched her to Chemonie plantation. The overseer there succeeded where Moxley had failed. "I have not had cause to strike her a lick," he recorded. "I wish [Moxley] would let her stay here," the man continued. "She will work for me without any trouble."[46]

In summary, most of Florida's bond servants found ways to survive slavery, physically and psychologically. Many individuals simply tried to live their lives in a way that would allow them some dignity, space, and independence of the master. They did not seek every opportunity to rebel openly or violently against their lot. Slave resistance irritated masters, but it could also exact a high price from slaves in terms of punishment and the possible separation of family and loved ones through sale. Slaves rebelled in more subtle ways. They might neglect their work, complain or grumble about assignments, or feign illness at times when they felt that the slaveholder or overseer had crossed certain agreed-upon boundaries. They might also, and often did, run away. Their absence was often only temporary, with many returning on their own to the farm or plantation. In some cases slaves in Florida remained away for months and years or else permanently. Violent rebellion did sometimes occur. Most important, what some historians have called the largest armed slave insurrection in United States history may well have occurred in Florida between 1835 and 1838. That conflict, which constituted one part of the Second Seminole War, helped to mold the nature of the territory and state's slave society, as well as many of Florida's political, governmental, and social institutions.

SLAVERY
AND THE
CIVIL WAR

The Civil War found Florida totally unprepared and badly divided. Four years of calamity followed that dramatically affected slaves' lives, demanded great sacrifices of many, and ultimately led to emancipation. Forty-four percent of the state's population of 140,000 suffered bondage, but geography and history piled the greatest challenges on the minority of slaves who lived outside the plantation belt. Still, the war years produced change for all and set the stage for a new world that would begin in 1865. The Florida slaves' Civil War story has only recently been documented and merits further exploration.[1]

Civil War action struck Florida early and hard. Secession in January 1861 came as a surprise to many in a state where large numbers of Unionists proclaimed adherence to the United States, especially in East Florida. Secession convention members wisely had declined to put the measure to a popular vote. Nonetheless, the administrations of governors Madison Starke Perry and John Milton, the latter man a Middle Florida planter, faced immediate crises in dealing with federal military installations at places such as Pensacola, Key West, and St. Augustine, the state's first-, second-, and fifth-largest towns. As it turned out, Key West never fell from Union hands. Pensacola and St. Augustine rested in them by 1862, as did Fernandina. Jacksonville yielded to United States forces on three earlier occasions before its final occupation in early 1864. Cedar Keys eventually became a Union camp, and coastal towns such as Tampa and Apalachicola also experienced visitations, although not permanent occupations.

In fact, beginning in early 1862 the Union could have worked its will anywhere in the state had it chosen to do so. That February General Robert E. Lee ordered withdrawal of most Confederate troops. "The effect of the order is to abandon Middle, East and South Florida to the mercy of the Lincoln Government," lamented Governor Milton in March. He subsequently patched together a quilt of home guard forces and more-or-less irregular troops to protect the plantation belt, receiving only moderate assistance from Confederate authorities. Fortunately for Milton and Florida's other Confederate sympathizers, the Lincoln administration chose not to concentrate its efforts on taking the state. Middle Florida was left relatively secure, whereas West and East Florida were opened to devastating military incursions and the evils of an internal civil war.[2]

The situation resulted in major disruptions of the institution of slavery in East and West Florida. In the east, particularly, the proximity of Union troops held out a beacon of hope for freedom that the state's bond servants had not seen since the negotiated surrender of most Black Seminoles in 1838. In time the northeastern coastal counties and the St. Johns River region, where federal gunboats patrolled, witnessed a steady stream of men, women, and children seeking freedom from bondage. Duval County, to cite one example, contained approximately two thousand slaves. By war's end owners had lost over half of them to the protection of United States forces. For many "black Floridians," as Daniel Schafer noted, "freedom became as close as the St. Johns River."[3]

Union raiding parties added to the toll on slavery. In just one of the series of incursions, loyal troops time and again marched in 1864 from Fort Myers up the state's interior through the rich cattle grazing prairies along the Peace River. In cooperation with naval units they also seized coastal towns and villages. The soldiers aimed to destroy Confederate properties and supplies, disrupt rebel operations, and liberate bond servants. From the cattle gathering center of Fort Meade one secessionist voiced a familiar complaint. "They took all [the] horses and wagons—loaded up with provisions, corn, fodder and meat—took the Negro men and all firearms," he declared, "and went back to Fort Myers."[4]

The Peace River raids help to demonstrate the human side of the seizure of "contrabands," as the Union men called the bond persons. Contrabands were important in the history of Civil War Florida. The men, women, and children who entered Union lines or cast off the shackles of slavery with the assistance of raiders usually remained in Florida. Among them were individuals who would help to transform the state in the war's aftermath. Joseph Sexton was among the slaves taken from Fort Meade. Within one year following freedom Sexton could be found hard at work helping to pioneer the African Methodist Episcopal Zion Church in the state and, later, in the Bahamas. In the process he would emerge as a great advocate for quality education and for the decent treatment of African Americans.[5]

The story of the Peace River raids replayed itself many times in the peninsula and in West Florida. "The boats left the next day, taking all the negroes they could," observed a Tampa women after her town's occupation. A Key West correspondent reported after a raid through Hernando County: "The result of this expedition was the capture of seven prisoners, fifteen horses, and thirteen negroes." The language could have applied elsewhere. In the Panhandle the Choctawhatchee River area experienced such warfare with the same results. "[The Yankees] made a clean sweep of negroes, horses, mules, oxen, turkeys, chickens, corn, meat, and everything they could find to eat," recorded a local man. "They did not ask the negroes if they wanted to go," he continued; "they ordered them to hitch up the teams and make ready to go."[6]

Slaves discovered that the protection of the United States government did not mean a life of ease and comfort. Conditions at the refugee camp on Egmont Key at Tampa Bay's mouth reflected the quality of some Union efforts. Fear prevailed. There was dread by "Negroes and white refugees of an attack by rebels," a naval officer detailed in his journal. Mosquitoes, hunger, and exposure to broiling heat and winter cold in the absence of remotely suitable housing compounded the problems. "Quiet contrabands—troublesome mess arrangements," the officer tersely noted. Finally, when transport arrived to relocate refugees, whites always received preferential treatment. Of conditions late in the war at Jacksonville, a missionary related, "We are besieged night and day, with a crowd of these poor outcasts, who [sleep] on our piazzas and [bivouac] in our yard." An indomitable human spirit won out in most cases, despite the trials. "I think they do as well—perhaps better—than any other class of people under the same circumstances," another missionary concluded.[7]

Joining the United States Army or Navy offered men a chance to fight for freedom and also to earn a little money for themselves or their families. In northeast Florida alone one thousand or more men stepped forward once the chance was afforded to them in the fall of 1862 and thereafter. Often circumstances required them to leave without their families and loved ones, who remained on farms and plantations behind Confederate lines. Thomas Warren Long's experience provides an illustration. When he ran away from his master, John Roberts, in late 1862, twenty-three-year-old Long initially felt compelled to go without his wife and children. But after joining the Thirty-third United States Colored Infantry (USCI), the now-free man went back to Jacksonville. There Long "stole his wife and two daughters." He then returned to Fernandina and rejoined his regiment, which he served with distinction.[8]

In significant ways Thomas W. Long's experience echoes that of many of his fellow slave soldiers and of the units in which they fought for freedom. Daniel Schafer has reported that their median age was twenty-four on enlistment. Two-thirds of them had been involved in agriculture of one sort or another, although 10 percent were skilled craftsmen. They were actively engaged, as was Long, in Florida operations by early 1863. Before the war's end they had joined the ranks of numerous regiments. The units included the First, Second, and Third South Carolina Infantry, the Fifty-fourth Massachusetts, and the Second, Eighth, Twenty-first, Thirty-fourth, Thirty-fifth, Ninety-ninth, and 102d USCI regiments, as well as Long's Thirty-third.[9]

The Florida men who believed that liberty could be achieved for all slaves with a Union victory proved more than willing to risk and give their lives for the United States. They participated in engagements large and small in most areas of the state, including the well-known battles of Olustee and Natural Bridge. Colonel Thomas Higginson described the Florida soldiers as bold and brave fighting men. At Olustee on February 20, 1864, the Eighth and Thirty-Fifth USCI and the Fifty-fourth Massachusetts, including Florida recruits, fought, as one Union soldier described, "like devils." The Eighth suffered 60 percent casualties. Approximately 203 Union men were killed there and 1,152 wounded, some of them Floridians. At the Battle of Natural Bridge just south of Tallahassee in early 1865, over three hundred blacks died in the state's last significant fighting during the war.[10]

Black Union soldiers sometimes paid a terrible price even after the fighting stopped. At Olustee those who were wounded or taken prisoner faced hard-hearted treatment or even execution at the hands of Confederate soldiers. After the battle the rebels killed blacks left on the battlefield disabled but alive. Confederate soldiers apparently had taken seriously the directive of Colonel Abner McCormick of the Second Florida Cavalry. "Do not take any negro prisoners in this fight," he ordered. One white Union veteran insisted that the southerners "bayoneted without mercy." He continued, "A Rebel officer happened to see [one negro] and, dismounting from his horse, placed his revolver close to the negro's head, and blew his brains out." William Penniman of the Fourth Georgia Cavalry heard gunshots and asked a Confederate officer what was happening. The officer replied, "Shooting niggers sir."[11]

Some runaway slaves who joined the Union army served in special roles as informants, guides, and river pilots. When Union troops landed along Pablo Creek, for example, they were led by Israel, a runaway slave from Jacksonville. His presence was prized because he was "thoroughly acquainted with all of the country." Isaac Tatwell, a northeast Florida fugitive and former slave pilot of the steamer *St. Mary's,* gave Union officers valuable information about coastal defenses. At Pensacola two black cooks who had escaped from the Fifteenth Confederate Cavalry gave significant details to the Union army concerning the enemy's location and strength.[12]

Numerous slaves from northeast Florida also joined the Union navy. Early in the war the Gulf Blockading Squadron had begun using blacks long before other naval squadrons. When it was reconfigured into the West Gulf Blockading Squadron and the East Gulf Blockading Squadron in 1862, Secretary of the Navy Gideon Wells directed that its officers resort to the expediency of enlisting contrabands "as no more [white] men can be sent to you." Soon the presence of black recruits from Florida became evident.[13]

One key service of black sailors from Florida helped Union naval forces to undermine the ability of rebels to preserve foods. What the men did was to provide information concerning Confederate saltworks along the coastline. In the days before refrigeration salt formed an essential element in the preservation of fish and other meats. Some blacks knew exactly where these enterprises were located because they had previously worked at them. Mary Minus Biddle, for example, recalled that fellow slaves made salt at Cedar Keys, which, thanks to information related by blacks, the Union was subsequently able to target for destruction.[14]

Slaves who joined either the Union army or navy soon found that their liberators easily discriminated against them on racial grounds. Black soldiers and sailors faced unequal treatment when it came to wages, assignments, and overall treatment. Secretary of the Navy Gideon Wells decided, for instance, that blacks would "be allowed . . . no higher rating than boys, at a compensation of $10 per month and one ration per day," wages far below those of white sailors. For most of the war black soldiers earned less than 60 percent of what white soldiers received. An Augusta, Georgia, newspaper—admittedly not an unbiased source—reported that blacks who had joined the army at Fernandina tried to escape because "they are worked hard, get little rest and food, and no pay." Blacks, as opposed to whites, were required to work at Fort Taylor at Key West and Fort Jefferson in the Dry Tortugas during yellow fever epidemics because officials labored under the misimpression that they were immune to the dreaded disease. Scores of blacks died. In fact, health care of all kinds posed problems greater for blacks than it did for others. Squire Jackson saw this firsthand. He ran away with his brother to join the army. He recalled that, upon reaching the Union camp, he saw "wounded colored soldiers stretched out on the filthy ground." The sight of these wounded men and the inadequate medical attention given them by the Federals proved so repulsive that he decided not to enlist.[15]

Poor treatment and other factors led on occasion to discipline problems. The majority of black Florida recruits followed the rules and regulations of the Union forces, but a few did not. Even old grudges could get a recruit in trouble. Long-legged Jake found out that when he returned to Jacksonville to get even with his former master A. M. Reed. Jake seethed at Reed for selling his wife to buyers from Georgia. Union officers placed the soldier in confinement for threatening to kill Reed and burn his house down. By that time the onetime bond servant already had placed a loaded gun to the head of a man who had shot at him when he escaped from Reed's plantation. Late in the war three black soldiers were executed for allegedly taking advantage of a white woman. According to Esther Hawks, similar crimes were more common among white soldiers, but they largely went unpunished.[16]

Slaves and contrabands also worked as laborers for the United States military effort, even though they did not serve in the military. In July 1862 the Federals passed the Second Confiscation Act, which allowed Union soldiers to free slaves of disloyal owners and to impress them into service. Yet impressment never became a real issue because blacks voluntarily served in sufficient numbers. Some slaveholders who were Union sympathizers hired their bond servants out to the military. In such a capacity slaves helped to fortify Forts Jefferson and Taylor. With a critical shortage of white laborers the Union accepted these black workmen with open arms. Owners received from $20 to $36 per month for their bondsmens' services. The Federals also provided the slaves with food, shelter, and medical care. Some bondsmen may have been allowed to keep a portion of the money for themselves.[17]

East Florida slaves who did not run away to join the United States Army or Navy or otherwise labor directly for the government or military assisted the Union cause in other ways. In Jacksonville bond servants who had helped to establish one of Florida's earliest black churches, Bethel Baptist Institutional, used the edifice as a hospital for the care of Union soldiers. Amanda McCray recalled that she assisted the Federals by cooking for Union soldiers. Clarissa Anderson allowed her slave Lettie to prepare meals for the Federals at St. Augustine. Aunt Eliza also served food to Union solders at Fort Jefferson. Even on the plantations many bond servants tried to do their part from afar. In some instances they simply stopped cultivating corn and other crops for human consumption. At least two East Florida planters predicted as early as 1862 that slaves would harvest crops no longer.[18]

Blacks throughout Florida thus found themselves laboring on be-half of the war effort, but sometimes the work was forced and in aid of the Confederates. Florida and Confederate authorities compelled hundreds of black Floridians to toil on war-related projects. Although many were required to assist local efforts earlier, the Confederate Congress provided for the impressment of slaves on February 17, 1864. The War Department fixed Florida's quota at five hundred. Although masters were to receive pay for slave hire up to $25 per month, some did not want to lend their bond servants to such work. Confederate service usually involved heavy labor that often was dangerous. The enslaved blacks were forced to depend on the Confederate govern-ment for their food, clothing, and shelter, and the response many times left much to be desired. A number of owners feared that slaves might use the opportunity away from the farm or plantation to flee to the Union army.[19]

Confederate sympathizers and others who found themselves with unemployed slaves on their hands outnumbered those who leased to the Confederate or state government. Particularly, Middle Florida of-fered a population willing to bargain. Individuals in other areas also were inclined to take advantage of offers, despite the misgivings of others. Robert Watson discovered that to be true at Tampa. Given per-mission to hire slaves from Confederate sympathizers in 1862, he easily met his quota. "We pay two dollars each a month for servant hire," he commented; "they cook and wash for us and keep our house in order." Although Watson's task proved an easy accomplishment at Tampa, Florida officials nonetheless found themselves regularly threatening to impress slaves in order to meet needs.[20]

A large group of slaves who worked in and around the Confederate army were body servants for their masters, men who then were serving as rebel officers. George W. Witherspoon was one such man. Fifteen years of age at the war's onset, the Gadsden County slave attended Robert Witherspoon during two years of Confederate service. Union forces captured George at Knoxville, Tennessee, but he escaped and returned to Quincy. Henry Call of Jackson County similarly experi-enced Confederate army life. His young master died at the Battle of the Clouds near Chattanooga, Tennessee, in November 1863. "After the battle, Henry Call went among the dead in search of his master," one account reported. "After he had found him and buried him, he was sent back to Cottondale, Florida."[21]

Most slaves who served with the Confederate army did so as a result of impressment. "Negroes could [work for] the Southern army if they desired," Patience Campbell explained; "none of them wished to do so but preferred to join northern forces and fight for the thing they desired most, freedom." However reluctant slaves might be, rebel officials realized in the conflict's opening months the strategic necessity of involuntary black labor. As early as October 1861 local Confederate officers tried to conscript slaves to do the "dirty and smutty work" at Fort Steele on the St. Johns River.[22]

The Confederacy employed slaves to build and maintain other fortifications as well. Attempting to keep control of the Apalachicola River for Confederate ships in 1862, officers in gray urged Governor Milton to send slaves to help strengthen area defenses. They desired "50 negroes immediately, with overseers, to go on with necessary work." Their message noted, "We left 50 negroes there already at work." According to one official, the Confederacy had received an additional 137 slaves from Tallahassee by June 1863 to continue the arduous task of securing and reinforcing the Apalachicola River defenses.[23]

Slaves were made to perform all sorts of additional duties for the Confederacy. Officials commanded Acie Thomas "to haul food and ammunition to different points between Tallahassee and a city in Virginia." Thomas asserted that it became common for Confederate soldiers to visit plantations and demand a "certain number of horses and slaves for service." Some slaves served the Confederacy by laboring as longshoremen or else manning blockade running vessels. Thomas Valentine did so for Captain Robert Johnson until apprehended by a Union warship in October 1863. James McKay received a Confederate commission to secure as many "Negroes as can be had" for cattle drives. Others made salt. Sarah Brown Bryant operated salt works on the Alafia River, and Andy Richardson spent time in the same business at Bayport.[24]

The value of their work notwithstanding, Confederates tended to treat slaves poorly. Blacks routinely faced harsh words and often endured cruelty, even when working directly on the war effort. In 1863 rebel cavalrymen recaptured several runaways in West Florida and hanged them. In the same region five cavalrymen rode up to the house where three of their slave cooks lived and yelled, "Turn out, you sons of bitches, and get us some breakfast." Although inexcusable, a separate incident at least concerned military blacks rather than civilians. It occurred during a Confederate raid on the Pensacola area in 1863. On that occasion a Rebel officer spread the word that he was "only after the negro soldiers; [and] that he would not fire on the white pickets, but that every black picket that could be seen would be shot."[25]

Some slaves, women in particular, openly objected to aiding the southern cause, even indirectly. Among other places, Polk County witnessed such incidents. William J. Watkins, according to his daughter, "used the men and women to plant everything possible to help the southern army and especially the families of the men about us who were in the southern army." When the slaveholder loaned out one of his slaves to do laundry for a woman whose husband had joined the Confederacy, the negotiation proved unacceptable. The young bond servant quickly returned from the farm to which she had been sent. "Missis L. she say your father he sending us to wash to help her husband fight to keep us slaves," the slave sharply informed her mistress.[26]

Rare indeed was the slave man or woman who truly desired to assist the Confederacy in any way. To do so meant the perpetuation of involuntary servitude. Exceptions existed, however, and a few bondsmen served the Confederacy willingly. According to Dr. Etheldred Philips, Union blockaders patrolling the Apalachicola River in December 1862 had to force a black pilot to leave a Confederate boat. Philips asserted that the slave preferred to lose his life rather than betray his country. Aleck willingly served as a scout for his Manatee County master, Captain Archibald McNeill. The slave's service allowed the Confederate officer to elude capture by the Federals. Most of the slaves known to have served the Confederate cause in so willing a manner appear to have acted out of deep personal attachment and loyalty to their masters.[27]

Conditions in West Florida differed from the rest of Florida. Although the region stretched from the Perdido River to the Apalachicola, half of its inhabitants resided in Escambia and Santa Rosa Counties. The region held fewer than 8 percent of Florida's slaves and only 15 percent of the population. Yet during the course of the war many of

SLAVERY AND THE CIVIL WAR : 239

the few slaves who remained worked for the military at Pensacola, whether Union or Rebel. "The Confederacy utilized its slave labor resource by employing slaves in war industries, the construction of defensive works, [and numerous other tasks]," historian Brian R. Rucker has found. Black regiments, including a few recruits from the region, served out of the Union-controlled Fort Barrancas during the war's later years. For the most part they built fortifications and bridges and performed other manual tasks. A few West Florida black Union soldiers saw action under Brigadier General Alexander Asboth during his Jackson County raid of September 1864.[28]

Although conditions tended toward the turbulent in East and West Florida, Middle Florida's slave community felt little direct impact from the war. Even so, slaves there were aware of the conflict and its course. Regardless of how hard Florida slaveholders and the larger white society tried to keep news away from bond servants, the majority gleaned some information. Adam Sanks, for example, remarked about the widespread availability of war news among the slaves. He noted that some who could read communicated the facts to other slaves. By accident or design they came across newspapers at plantation houses and elsewhere. Slaves generally knew of the fighting between the blue and gray, a fact that Confederate general Joseph Finegan recognized. "There was a communication network between negroes within Union lines in east Florida and the slaves behind Confederate lines," he commented in the spring of 1863. "Many slaves have escaped, because messages were conducted through the swamps and under cover of the night and could not be prevented." Slaves who could read and write forged passes for others to escape to Union lines. Of surviving Florida slave interviews, only Douglas Dorsey's indicated anything to the contrary. He declared that slaves on the Mattair plantation had "hardly been aware that there had been a war going on."[29]

Squire Jackson's reminiscences illustrate just how news was picked up and how adept slaves were in misleading their owners about their knowledge. He recalled an incident with his master that occurred after he had learned to read and write. "One day as he was reading a newspaper, the master walked upon him unexpectedly and demanded to know what he was doing with a newspaper," an interviewer recorded. "He immediately turned the paper upside down and declared 'Confederates done won the war,'" the account continued. It concluded, "The master laughed and walked away without punishing him."[30]

Men serving as teamsters proved valuable sources of information for their fellow slaves. Often called "Black wagoners," men such as Acie Thomas worked for the Confederacy and knew firsthand about some aspects of the conflict. He would have found it easy to pass the news of the war on to other teamsters, who, in turn, would have told other blacks. The wagoner on Kidder Meade Moore's plantation in Jefferson County enjoyed opportunities to receive and relay information. While working away from the plantation, he traveled near and far, hauling goods for his master.[31]

Beyond knowledge of the conflict, Middle Florida's bond servants shared with their East and West Florida counterparts a distinct awareness of how whites responded to the war. They witnessed white boys and men departing for military service. More than a few saw white wives weeping for the safe return of their husbands or else at news of their capture or death. As the war began to turn in the North's favor, some slaves began to speak out more openly and in a manner that should have alerted owners to their astute perceptions and personal sentiments. Sarah Brown Bryant related to an interviewer a revealing story:

> One day during the war, Sarah went into the [John T.] Lesley home in Tampa and found Margaret Lesley rocking her daughter India. Both were crying. Sarah asked why they were crying. [Mrs. Lesley] replied that her husband and the father of her child was away in the war and he might be killed. Sarah then asked [Mrs. Lesley] if she remembered when [Sarah] was first brought to Tampa she would cry for her mother. And they would spank her. She said she told Mrs. Lesley not to cry, as it would not do her any good.[32]

Other slaves also watched as whites went to war. Neil Coker knew the North and South were at war because she saw many "Federal troops, both whites and Negroes," pass by her master's plantation on the well-traveled Bellamy Road. Cowhunter Stephen Harvell recollected similar events. About twenty-one years of age at the time, he especially remembered Confederate soldiers camping on his master's property before scouting for Yankees. Louis Napoleon watched as his master's "oldest sons went to the war with the Confederate army," along with the white driver. Willis Williams's master did not enlist, but his "eldest son Charlie" volunteered for Confederate service. Others encountered slave body servants returning with the personal belongings of their deceased owners. Lewis, for example, buried the remains of Captain George Parkhill in Richmond, Virginia. The slave then brought his master's personal property to his loved ones in Florida. As mentioned earlier, Henry Call of Jackson County journeyed home under the same circumstances.[33]

At times bond servants appeared to have a better grasp of wartime realities than did the owners. Some slaveholders believed that the peculiar institution would persist indefinitely, even as the Union troops advanced toward victory. At least they continued to write wills distributing their slave property as if the war and its impact on slavery were not a matter of concern. Leon County's Dr. Edward Bradford and Escambia County's David Williams, for example, were among the many who willed family members their slaves late in 1863. They acted after the effective date of the Emancipation Proclamation and the Confederate disasters that summer at Gettysburg and Vicksburg. William Ham and A. J. Hewlitt of Alachua County bequeathed bond servants to their heirs in 1864 and 1865. Jesse Mims of Escambia and Ben Hopkins of Putnam County took the theme even further. They preferred to forget that the war had freed African Americans by 1866; their wills dated in that year distributed bond servants to family members. Many other slaveholders in East Florida and even more in Middle Florida were bequeathing their slaves to family members and loved ones late in the war.[34]

From 1863 to 1865 slaveholders continued to hire out or provide for the hiring out of their bond servants, often for terms that extended well beyond emancipation. Thomas H. Triplett's will specified in August 1863 that slaves were to be hired out in the "interest of my wife and children." Sarah Green's slaves were rented out after August 1864. Some slaveholders and estate administrators either hired out or made plans to lease bond servants during the early months of 1865. As late as April, William E. Kilcrease's administrator had hired out slaves until year's end. Legal advertisements made evident the fact that many owners intended to continue the practice as long as they possibly could or else simply refused to believe that slavery's end had come.[35] As late as 1864 and early 1865, there were many willing buyers of slaves. Columbia County's Frank Raulerson sold Abram and Isaac Grant in 1864. Sarah Murray's master disposed of all his slaves except her family to buyers and speculators when he heard that Union soldiers would be coming to the area during the "last days of the war." Advertisements for slaves still were appearing in some Florida newspapers in June 1865. In the conflict's waning months women slaves were more vulnerable to sale than were healthy men. "Many female slaves discovered they were disposable property," explained historian Tracy Jean Revels, "as families unwilling to sacrifice prime field hands often sold women and children to pay wartime debts." The Kilcrease estate administrator in Gadsden County conveyed a slave woman and her child in January 1865, to cite just one example.[36]

Past arguments have suggested that rising slave sales prices during the war years evidenced southern confidence in the Confederacy and the continuation of slavery. The inflation actually reflected continuing depreciation in the value of Confederate currency. Willis Williams and Claude A. Wilson recalled that increasingly worthless paper money "called 'shin plasters' flooded the southland during Civil War days." Slaveholder assessments offer an idea of the figures involved. In 1860 the Kilcrease administrator assessed a male slave at $3,500. Jonathan Robinson, also of Gadsden County, valued the worth of his thirty-eight-year-old male at $4,500 in 1863. In 1864 Abram Grant brought $6,000 and his brother Isaac $5,000 in Confederate currency. By 1865 bond servants were being valued at an average of $4,200 each on the Kilcrease plantation.[37]

Most slaveholders could not simply ignore the realities of war as did some of their Middle Florida peers. They kept a keen eye on developments and acted prudently to preserve their holdings. Often the owners did so by relocating their slaves when Union troops first neared their vicinity. Many northeast Florida owners transferred slaves, as well as their own families, early on. They moved their bond servants to the "interior," that broad stretch of territory that ran from Jackson County on the west to Columbia, Alachua, and Marion Counties on the east. "It may not be long before we may have to move from here or submit to the reign of Yankeeism," the Reverend Edward F. Gates wrote from Waukeenah in 1862. "The people from the eastern section of the state are scattered through here pretty thick." Stephen Bryan took his slaves and those of his neighbor to unoccupied land near Ocala. Jacksonville planter Samuel Fairbanks refuged his slaves in Clay County as early as 1862. Adam Sanks remembered his fellow slaves being run hurriedly out of St. Augustine when Northern soldiers came to town. Some owners tried but failed in the effort. Before most of his slaves could escape to Union lines, A. M. Reed "started all the negroes . . . for the interior." The planter nonetheless lost the majority of his slaves before the trip was ended.[38]

Southwest Florida's owners likewise sought to outmaneuver Union troops, although most did so, early on at least, in less of a crisis atmosphere. Edmund Jones, Hillsborough County's largest slaveholder, moved his twenty-six bond servants to Polk County in 1862. Daniel Stanford did the same with his nine slaves. The next year George Wells added sixteen more. Feeling greater need for dispatch than Jones, Stanford, and Wells were John C. Cofield and his partner. They were Manatee County's largest owners. Exposed in a coastal county easy to access from Union-held Key West, the two men fled with their 190 bond servants to Louisiana as soon as they heard that war had broken out. As actual fighting neared the plantation-heavy Hernando County area in 1864, many planters shifted their holdings to Marion and Sumter Counties. As a local official informed the governor when raiders attacked near Brooksville, "A good deal of time has been lost in scouting after the enemy and running Negroes from their reach."[39]

As shown by John C. Cofield's example, some Florida slaveholders were prepared to remove their bond servants from the state altogether. George Washington Scott, a Tallahassee planter, instructed his family to remove their slaves to Albany, Georgia, should the Union threaten the capital city. Others followed suit. Bennard Overton fled with his slaves to Virginia because he believed that the state's coastline was better protected than that of Florida. Afraid that two of his bond servants might escape to the Federals, Etheldred Philips, a slaveholding Unionist, thought it wise to secure them in North Carolina. West Florida's few slaveholders typically thought it best to remove their families and slaves to southern Alabama. Some refuged at Brooklyn in Alabama's Conecuh County.[40]

In a few instances slaveholders from other Confederate states reversed the process and brought their bond servants to Florida for safekeeping. William J. Watkins of Charlotte County, Virginia, had selected a suitable relocation site in southern Polk County by late 1861. His family and slaves, including the Andy Moore and Royal Reed families, arrived early the next year. Laura Hood recalled that when the "Yankees came through" Georgia, Henry Banks refuged his bond servants in Florida. Other slaveholders from Alabama and as far away as Virginia also brought their slaves to the Confederate stronghold of Middle Florida. Still, the number of slave relocations was never high. Nor did Florida experience a large influx of slave refugees from other places.[41]

Whether slaves were refuged in or out of the state, bond servants experienced disrupted lives. Many felt sharply the trauma of being separated from family and kinfolk. Even freedom could not overcome the bonds of kinship and affection in some cases. When the Union army approached one slave and granted him liberty, he refused to leave the area. The man wanted to find his wife, who had been refuged in North Carolina.[42]

The effect of slave relocations was to concentrate Florida slavery even more in Middle Florida and its eastern extension in Columbia, Alachua, and Marion Counties. Even there, where the war's brutal impact remained a distant thunderclap, the passing years brought changes of enormous dimensions. Lines of authority shattered, and slaves grew increasingly restive. A pot had been set to boil that, had the war not ended as it did, would have boiled over on its own.

One major change that affected Middle Florida slaves concerned who exercised supervision over them. With many white males either conscripted or volunteering for Confederate service, white women found themselves shouldering the burden of managing farms and plantations. To say that this dynamic strained the master-slave relationship in a region where slaves greatly outnumbered whites is an understatement. By mid-1862 a Tallahassee editor realized that a full-blown crisis lay at hand if the government did not stop the flood of men into the military. "Many men could serve the Confederacy better out of military service than in it," the man opined. "It is a mistake for planters and overseers to desert their plantations," he continued. "The governor should take immediate steps to see that at least one white male adult was left on each plantation."[43]

The Confederacy permitted draft exemptions for certain planters and overseers into early 1864, but thereafter the military's insatiable appetite for men guaranteed that women would continue the new order on farms and plantations. Historian Drew Gilpin Faust described it as "white women . . . assum[ing] direction of the region's 'peculiar institution.'" Although husbands routinely instructed wives by mail as to plantation affairs, the women maintained day-to-day responsibility. They found the job difficult at best. Octavia Stephens, for one, often had to exert her power to its full extent to gain slave cooperation. "I blazed out at Burrel last Saturday about wishing the old beef gone," she informed her husband in late 1861. "I guess he thought I was 'spunky' all of a sudden, but I did not care, I told him I was tired of hearing grumbling." The struggle increased in intensity as wartime privations hit hardest on those in the quarters rather than those in the main house. As one example, men stirred in anger when the clothing allotted to their wives deteriorated beyond shabbiness. Squire Jackson's temper late in life still rose as he compared the white mistress's homespun dresses to slave women's attire. He described it as "grass skirts woven very closely with hoops around on the inside to keep from contacting the body."[44]

As Octavia Stephens discovered, slaves became visibly troublesome in the absence of most white men. Countless individual acts of defiance marked the war years, increasing as the conflict dragged on from year to year. Even Governor John Milton suffered, although he remained at home. At his Jackson County plantation Flora and Jane became quite unmanageable. Jane simply ignored her tasks or did them poorly. Flora left the Miltons' baby unattended, allowing him to scatter his toys asunder. When the governess tried to punish them for their insubordinate behavior, they retaliated to the point that she was frightened almost to tears.[45]

Increasing numbers of slaves ran away in defiance of the new conditions, and some became so unruly as to alarm entire communities. Laws were tightened and punishments escalated without apparent success. One of the legislature's first acts in the fall of 1861 attempted to address an already deteriorating situation by reorganizing and consolidating the patrol system. Local authorities succeeded at maintaining patrols at some places and times, but the absence of adult men undermined the efforts. Madison County's Amon DeLaughter recorded the new level of punishments. When patrollers caught three slaves trying to escape, they administered 150 lashes to one, 50 to another, and returned the third to his master with a reprimand. Many of those absconding attempted to reach Union lines, but others remained behind to stay near loved ones. By 1862 their numbers around Tallahassee had grown. When combined with slaves taking temporary liberty, the situation, town fathers feared, was ripe for a wave of lawlessness. After a series of robberies stoked the fires, the *Florida Sentinel* encouraged residents to take up arms to protect themselves from this danger and other potential forms of slave unrest.[46]

Although no large-scale rebellions occurred in Florida during the war years, rumors of slave insurrection plots circulated as early as November 1860. Some whites expected a large-scale insurrection, many of them having experienced the phenomenon during the Second Seminole War. Accordingly, they took every rumor seriously. "I am afraid to go to Waukeenah on account of the negroes," young Katie Gates informed her father from Gainesville in late 1862. "I am afraid they will uprise and kill all of the white people." The murder of a white man named Plummer in Jacksonville by three slaves at the war's outbreak suggested to some that an insurrection already was planned. When the numbers of runaways from the northeastern counties mounted, Confederate General R. F. Floyd urged Governor Milton to take the drastic step of declaring a state of martial law. The fears persisted.[47]

The ever-present and building tensions and the accumulation of privations notwithstanding, Middle Florida's slaveholders should have been pleased by the overall behavior of their bond servants. Once again the state's black bond servants proved their humanity and decency in the face of white insensitivity and outright cruelty. Virtually all white families lived securely on their farms and plantations. Bloody portraits of slave revolts on Saint-Domingue and Jamaica, not to mention the Second Seminole War, could boast no mirror image in the wartime plantation belt. Although increasingly restive, slaves who lived too far from Union lines to bring their families safely within United States protection remained in place, worked as circumstances required, and waited for the changes to come. The situation could not have continued indefinitely, but it did not need to.

As the wait continued, Florida's black population turned for solace to religion and the comfort of music. Slave ministers such as Methodists Robert Meacham, Henry Call, Allen Jones, and Joseph Sexton and Baptists Cataline B. Simmons, Samuel Small, John A. Potter, and James Page began to lay foundations for the growth of organized black churches in the postwar era. In their humble sanctuaries, in military camps, and on farms and plantations, the sounds of music often filled the air. Many songs and tunes reflected traditional rhythms. "Often in the starlit evening I have returned from some lonely ride . . . ," recorded a Union officer, "and, entering the camp, have silently approached some glimmering fire, round which the dusky figures moved in rhythmical barbaric dance the Negroes call a 'shout', chanting, often harshly, but always in the most perfect time, some monotonous refrain." He added, "These songs, are but the vocal expression of the simplicity of their faith and the sublimity of their long resignation." Later, tunes such as "John Brown's Body" and "My Country 'Tis of Thee" became standards where slaves had access to them. "At this moment the camp resounds with the John Brown hymn, sung as no white regiment can sing it," noted a Federal soldier, "so full of pathos and harmony."[48]

The call of freedom naturally found its voice in the wartime music. One song heard in Jacksonville resounded often within the state's limits or was echoed by similar tunes. Fortunately, its words have been preserved:

Blow, boys blow
Blow dis naggar off to New Yak,	Blow Boys Blow
Dere he walk de streets,	Blow Boys Blow
Dere he kiss de gals,	Blow Boys Blow
Dere he read de papers,	Blow Boys Blow
Dere he cut his capers,	Blow Boys Blow.[49]

Pressing against anxieties born out of fears of disappointment, anticipations of freedom percolated more and more strongly as Union triumph neared. "[We] prayed for [the] victory of the Northern Army," Claude A. Wilson observed. Most slaves carefully hid such sentiments from their masters, but the hopes they expressed had been present in many hearts since Abraham Lincoln's election. Prince Lampkin carried with him memories of the day at Fernandina when the new Republican administration took office in 1861. "They all refused to work on the fourth of March," an account detailed, "expecting their freedom to date from that day." On the Parramore plantation, according to Amanda McCray, residents of the quarters first heard of the war from their black minister, who "held whispered prayers for the success of the Union soldier." When a trooper asked Claude Wilson's mother whether she knew about her freedom, she answered, "Yeh Sir . . . I been praying for dis a long time."⁵⁰

By early 1865 many slaves awaited a particular sound that would chime freedom at long last. "Word was sent around among the slaves that if they heard the report of a gun," Louis Napoleon explained, "it was the Yankees and that they were free." Apparently, plans did call for signaling the war's end with guns, for blockading vessels blasted tributes to southern capitulation with barrages of cannon fire, and the state's occupied towns rocked with the same kind of celebration. At Jacksonville 250 rounds heralded the new era, an unmistakable signal. From the towns and coastal zones the reverberations passed into the interior in mid and late April. Louis Napoleon recalled that when slaves caught the guns' music in the air, they started to cry and say "dem de Yankees." Margrett Nickerson echoed a similar story. "When the big gun fiahed," she noted, "de runerway slaves comed out de woods from all directions." Nickerson added, "de was all very glad." The tone of response, Willis Williams commented, was "jubilant but not boastful."⁵¹

The formalities of emancipation followed slowly, sometimes taking several weeks. Mary Ann Murray of St. Augustine, better known as Mary Gomez, remembered the experience in a Union-held area. "All the slaveholders were ordered to release their slaves and allow them to gather in a large vacant lot west of St. Joseph's Academy," she related, "where they were officially freed." On May 20 at Tallahassee, General

Edward McCook accepted the state capital's surrender. Word of the approaching ceremony circulated widely. One slave recalled that others immediately "dropped the plows, hoes and other farm implements and hurried to their cabins." He added, "They put on their best clothes 'to go see the Yankees.'" A participant in the Tallahassee celebration commented, "The soldiers and Negroes were in ecstacy; the [white] citizens were not so enthusiastic." By that time United States soldiers, many of them black Floridians, had begun to fan out into the countryside to spread the word. Acie Thomas recounted that "a soldier in blue came to his plantation and brought a[n] [emancipation] 'document' that Tom, their master[,] read to all the slaves."[52]

The difficulty of transportation in the rural state and the relatively small numbers of United States troops available for the task blocked some slaves from learning of freedom for quite a time. A number of owners, in the meantime, acted to keep their bond servants in the dark, hoping to retain them as slaves for their own pecuniary benefit. Bolden Hall experienced such a delay. He insisted that his former master knew that slavery had ended early in 1865 but "kept them until May [of that year] in order to help him with his crops." Still, others tried to encourage the newly freed men and women essentially to ignore the news. According to a Polk County minister, "We advised them all to make the very best arrangements they could with their former owners to secure for themselves and their families permanent homes." The freedmen responded, he acknowledged, "with contempt."[53]

African Americans in Florida, as in other states of the South, thus demonstrated their will to become free. They had refused passive acceptance of slavery, whether in villages or towns or on the plantations, farms, or front lines. Slaves in northeast Florida and to a lesser extent in West Florida actively resisted slavery and showed their desire for a Union victory by joining Federal forces. Bond servants in Middle Florida did not have the same opportunities to escape and join Union forces available to their counterparts in the east and west. Still, they tried to hinder the progress of the Confederacy in other significant ways. Claude Wilson's mother reflected the sentiments of most Florida slaves when the day of jubilee finally arrived. "[I have been] praying for dis a long time," she said. Sadly, their struggle for full justice, freedom, and equality in America had only just begun.[54]

"To President Lincoln
on Issuing the Emancipation Proclamation"

Thou has spoken!—Let the earth resound
 With hallelujahs to our gracious God!—
The gladsome news—four million men will soon
 No longer groan beneath the tyrant's rod!

Thy words are echoed by ten million hearts
 From hill to dale—to the islands of the sea:
They are Redemption's chartered harbingers,
 When men—no longer slaves, but free shall be!

Thou hast spoken! and a million arms
 Are gleaming brightly from the battle van;
And banner proudly waving on the breeze—
 Presaging victory to thy ripening plan!

Thou hast spoken! and thy name shall glow
 Forever on Columbia's altar bright;
For thou has stayed a vile, despotic tide,
 And bravely battled for the trampled right!

May thy footsteps ever lead thee upward—
 Upward to that bright, celestial land:
Where safely sheltered from the storms of life,
 Thou'lt join the heroes of the Patriots' band.[55]

—John Willis Menard
Florida State Representative, 1874

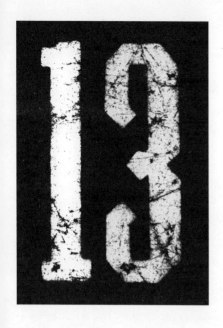

CONCLUSION

Although Florida entered the union of states in 1845, fifteen years ear-lier it already had become one of the South's fastest growing slave territories in terms of percentage increases. The seeds that would give flower there to an Old South economy and way of life already had been planted for generations. Anglo-American colonists had begun filtering into the once and future Spanish colony during its occupation by the British from 1763 to 1783. When the Spanish Empire granted conces-sions to Norte Americanos in the early 1790s, increased numbers of United States citizens relocated. Spanish ways transformed the new-comers in significant ways, but recent arrivals transformed the colony even more. By the early 1800s Florida had become a part of the United States in all but name.

The changeover in Florida's status to United States territory be-came official in 1821, launching substantial immigration, especially in the rich lands that lay between the Apalachicola and Suwannee Rivers. There wise investors hoped to make or enhance fortunes with large cotton plantations. Those who settled this new land of Middle Florida hailed mostly from the older southern states of Maryland, Virginia, and North and South Carolina, as well as from the growing nearby slave states of Georgia and Alabama. Thanks to these settlers, the

Middle Florida counties of Jackson, Gadsden, Leon, Jefferson, Madison, and—to a lesser extent—Hamilton quickly prospered, emerging by the 1850s as some of the wealthiest in the Old South.

The planters faced many challenges along the way. There were threats posed by conflicting Spanish traditions regarding slavery and race relations that survived in East and West Florida. Rapidly, they addressed the problems by taking control of local and territorial governmental policy-making institutions. In Middle Florida, with the exception of Gadsden County, slave owners soon held over 95 percent of all local political positions. Their hegemony included control of the territorial council by the late 1820s. By 1845 they dominated office holding at all levels of government through most of the newly minted state. In the process slaveholders also reached out to direct Florida's economic and social destinies. Slavery had become a securely planted institution in the peninsula, as well as the panhandle.

The vision of an Old South Florida dominated by the Middle Florida planter class reached fruition for many of the original settlers and their heirs by the 1850s. The labor of slaves permitted them to claim credit by 1860 for the production of over 95 percent of all cotton grown in the state. Numerous white families enjoyed the pleasures of an affluent lifestyle. Clinging to their privileged status, the planters and their political agents prepared to defend the institution of slavery at almost any cost. By the Civil War's eve they still met with political opposition from some East and West Floridians, but they virtually had eliminated all opposition to the institution of slavery.

Meanwhile, slavery and slaves had influenced the character and development of Florida in crucial and enduring ways. Questions of race and servitude had played key roles in virtually every event of importance from the 1810s through the Union challenge to Confederate authorities at Pensacola in 1861. The clash between Spanish and Anglos during the Patriot War of 1812, for instance, stemmed partly from a difference in attitudes about free and enslaved blacks and their treatment in northeast Florida. Florida's willingness to serve as a haven for runaway slaves from the United States had sparked Andrew Jackson's 1818 incursion into the territory, which triggered what history called the First Seminole War.

Those early events were a prelude to what followed. Jackson's invasion prompted many runaway slaves or other maroons to seek sanctuary deeper in the peninsula. By 1835 several all-black towns and villages—most notably Peliklakaha and Minatti—coexisted alongside Seminole or Creek communities. Their presence, in turn, stirred fears of planters, who saw armed free blacks as a threat to slaveholding in general and the continued immigration of white planters in particular. In part the Second Seminole War of 1835 to 1842 sought to rid Florida of the free blacks, together with their Indian allies. To do so, the United States waged the most costly "Indian War" in its history. With at least one thousand black warriors among the Seminoles, Thomas Jesup aptly noted that the fight was "not an Indian War, but a Negro War." After some seven years the majority of Seminoles and their black allies had been killed or had surrendered. The survivors were transported west of the Mississippi River, ending the planters' nightmare.

The Second Seminole War's end ushered in an era of rapid expansion for slavery and the plantation economy. It endured, with ups and down, for almost two decades. Bond servants were brought to Middle Florida in large numbers. From 15,500 territorial slaves in 1830 the total ran to more than 39,000 after statehood. By the time Florida seceded from the Union the slave population had passed sixty-one thousand. In 1861 well over two-thirds of those held in bondage lived and worked in Middle Florida. East Florida contained 17 percent of all slaves, whereas West Florida's total amounted to only 8 percent.

With the post–Second Seminole War expansion came the spread of the plantation belt into such nearby East Florida counties as Columbia, Alachua, Marion, and Hernando. Still, slavery did not expand as rapidly in the central and southern peninsula as it did in Middle or northeast Florida. Thus, in 1860 the institution certainly had not reached its natural limits in the state. A climate less hospitable to cotton culture, the survival of Spanish traditions, and the character of the peninsula's white residents spoke directly to why slavery grew there so slowly. Many settlers who came into the region between 1821 and 1860 did not identify so closely with the institution of slavery as their counterparts elsewhere in the state. The large majority, called "Crackers," carved out an independent existence by living off the land, subsistence agriculture, and cattle grazing. Most owned no slaves. Of those who did, holdings usually included one or two adult slaves and, perhaps, their children. A significant number of the children were fathered by owners or other white men.

The frontier-like central and southern peninsula excepted, slaves made up the backbone of Florida's economy. In Middle Florida the bond servants toiled on large and small units. With a great deal of encouragement from owners, they continued to reproduce themselves. Given prohibitions on slave importation and the importance of their labor contributions, bond persons increased appreciably in value by the start of the Civil War. With small planters and farmers also using slave labor to cultivate crops for human and animal consumption, Florida's agricultural economy had become reasonably self-sufficient by 1860. To a limited extent slaves addressed their own issues of self sufficiency. At least those bondsmen living in rural areas were allowed to cultivate their own garden patches of cotton and food crops. They could consume the results or sell them for money of their own.

The organization of slave labor varied greatly. Depending on a unit's size, slaves could work according to the task or the gang system. Within the Middle Florida plantation belt the latter predominated, although in East and West Florida the task system enjoyed great popularity. On the largest units both systems operated as suited the plantation's needs and, over time in some places, the desires of the workers. On smaller units bond servants performed a variety of chores, usually working alongside their masters. Here master and slave lived in close proximity, whereas on larger farms and plantations slave quarters were often located at some distance from the main house.

The hiring or leasing of bond persons eventuated as an important element of the Florida economy and institution of slavery. By 1830 owners clearly perceived that the lease system offered another highly functional and flexible way of ensuring a reasonable return on investments in slaves. The majority of West Florida bond servants, primarily in Escambia and Santa Rosa Counties, engaged in little agricultural labor but were leased out to various industries and the military. In Middle Florida leased bond servants were rented out primarily as agricultural workers. In northeast Florida they performed agricultural and nonagricultural tasks, many involving highly honed skills.

Work demanded most but not all of a slave's time. Bond servants typically labored long hours and performed many chores, but they also enjoyed some free time. Many especially looked forward to taking a half day on Saturday and all day Sunday off to supplement release time during evening hours. Thanksgiving, the Fourth of July, and Christmas week were regarded throughout the state as holidays. In various places and at various times other accommodations were made to allow bond persons time for personal tasks such as planting and harvesting gardens.

A rural life and agricultural labor proved the destiny of most Florida slaves, but exceptions abounded. A minority of bond servants, perhaps 5 to 10 percent of the total, worked as skilled craftsmen or house servants on farms and plantations or lived in the state's three or four principal towns. Generally, these laborers performed tasks less taxing physically than those expected of field hands. Compared to agricultural workers, they faced less exposure to the elements but probably worked longer hours. Some slaves held positions of serious responsibility, serving as drivers, wagoners, mechanics, and seamstresses. Although prohibited by law from doing so, a large number of bond servants—especially in East Florida—were allowed to hire their own time and seek profitable employment for themselves. Compelled to act (partly from fears of imminent or actual slave revolt and race war), Florida lawmakers regulated slave life in a manner that mirrored the practices of other southern states. Frequently, they exceeded other states in harshness. The slave code prohibited "cruel and unusual punishment" of enslaved blacks yet afforded slave owners virtually unchecked authority to do whatever they wanted. What slaveholders wanted included punishments. Accordingly, masters exercised hegemony over bond servants by inflicting a broad variety of punishments, particularly whippings. When the punishment or other mistreatment exceeded accepted boundaries enough to spark an outcry within the community, an appearance in court might be required of the owner. Usually, slaveholders received a warning and charges otherwise were dropped. In general, slaves lived at the mercy of their masters. No law effectively protected them.

The slave code guaranteed minimal material conditions of slaves' lives. On the other hand, the strictures proved just as unenforceable as those against excessive punishments. Most courts simply did not want to interfere in the business of slaveholders and allowed them to use their own judgment in the treatment of bond servants. Reflecting the southern pattern, Florida slaves typically lived in small, uncomfortable, and otherwise inadequate housing, although conditions improved slightly during the 1850s. They were allotted clothing and shoes made out of the cheapest materials, and quantities never matched the need based on the brutal nature of slaves' work. More fortunately, slaves generally benefited from food adequate to provide nutrition and energy to perform their assignments. Because bond servants were investments to be protected, masters normally obtained the services of a physician when slaves suffered serious illnesses.

The family served within the slave community as a vital institution that afforded personal comfort, as well as helpful protection from the psychological pressures of bondage. The large majority of bond servants held significant kinship ties, some going back four or more generations in Florida. Demographics assisted in facilitating marriage and family because, generally speaking, parity existed between males and females between the ages of ten and fifty. Despite a constant threat of separation, bond servants depended on the nuclear and extended family for support and for survival. Coresidential consensual and nonconsensual unions existed throughout the state. Surviving records often reflect single women with children as heads of their families. To some extent the records mislead. Many slaveholders owned more than one plantation or had relatives or friends who owned plantations and farms. As a result they often permitted marriage off the land of residence. In such circumstances males were listed elsewhere than with their families. Despite absences from their families because of sale or separation, black men had a presence and were recognized as having a major role in the slave household. Notwithstanding the nature of servitude, slaves sought and, to a point, carved out family lives for themselves that provided support and a sense of worth in a society that largely treated them as objects.

Much like the family, religion played a prominent role in the lives of bond servants. Some enslaved blacks believed in the sermons of white ministers that charged slaves to be loyal and obedient to their masters. Other slaves questioned or rejected the doctrines as failing to recognize the equality of all human beings in the eyes of God. Worshiping primarily in the churches of their masters, Florida bond servants still proved able to mix Euro-Christian and African religious practices in ways that helped them to endure the harshness of bondage. Large numbers practiced Christianity, but they did so with an African style of worship and with an understanding of the experience based on African concepts. Some bond servants believed in voodoo and hoodoo, superstition, and conjuring that existed largely outside the realm of Christianity. These beliefs coexisted with Christianity day to day and became part of the cultural milieu of black religious worship services. A high degree of emotionalism characterized black worship, a practice sometimes present among poor southern whites.

Blacks and whites, blacks and other blacks, and blacks and Indians interacted in complex and ever-evolving ways. Blacks and whites depended on each other for survival. Some masters and their bond servants held very close ties. Sometimes whites had two families, one white and the other black. Some black women consented to these liaisons, but the majority effectively were raped. Although in violation of the law, whites sometimes taught individual blacks to read and write. White children played with black youngsters up to about the age of twelve, when the master-slave relationship changed. At certain times of the year blacks and whites celebrated special events together.

Blacks within the slave quarters interacted and socialized in a variety of ways. They built ties of culture and heritage through the use of African-influenced language. They utilized several recreational outlets such as storytelling, music, and dance. They also celebrated weddings and participated in religious functions. On sad occasions blacks came together to perform various unique rituals for those who had passed away.

The experience of Florida slaves interacting with Indians dated back to the early 1500s. By 1835 blacks and Seminoles had forged alliances that many white settlers thought threatened their very existence. As a result the Second Seminole War was fought, leading to the death or removal of Black Seminoles. The legacy of their presence remained important, though. In the years before 1838, communications between Black Seminoles and the slaves on East Florida's farms and plantations had been open and easy. Therefore, East Florida's slave culture evolved subject to heavy influences from free maroons, a circumstance that altered it substantially from the slave culture that marked Middle Florida. Additionally, the light of freedom that shone out of Black Seminole towns and villages never fully died out, and slaves from throughout Florida and other parts of the South ran toward it through the 1850s and most of the Civil War.

Blacks reacted in different ways to their enslavement. On the one hand, some bond servants acted as loyal workers who apparently loved and identified with their masters. On the other hand, some slaves rebelled in ways large and small against their bondage at every opportunity. The majority of slaves simply tried to endure, in great part to preserve family ties and to protect loved ones. These bond servants nonetheless committed individual acts of defiance that could not be punished as threatening the foundation of society or of slavery. The most common form of slave resistance was work slowdown or sabotage. As for overt acts, running away constituted the main type of resistance. In Florida the majority of bond servants who absconded from their masters were male slaves. Whether they received concessions or not, the majority of slaves expected them from their masters and became rebellious when agreed-upon boundaries were violated. The overwhelming majority of bond servants clearly wanted freedom. They used whatever resources they could command in the meantime to survive and to mold their world. Bond servants thought and felt as human beings who sought to live, work, and raise families. The whites treated them largely as commodities.

In Florida and in other southern states, slave owners reacted to fears of abolitionists and the potential for large-scale uprisings among their bond servants. Just prior to and during the Civil War there were attempts to increase the use and effectiveness of slave patrols, particularly in Middle Florida. Actually, few abolitionists ever ventured into Florida, or, if they did, they remained relatively quiet. Nonetheless, abolitionists took much of the blame for what amounted to common slave stealing.

The course of the Civil War essentially destroyed slavery in much of East and West Florida, and the conflict's end destroyed the peculiar institution in Middle Florida. Well over a thousand slaves in the east and west fled to the protection of Union lines and enlisted in the

United States Army or Navy or else served as spies, guides, and cooks and in other capacities. Middle Florida rested uneasily but did not experience violent slave revolt. Instead, the fabric of slavery began to tear with the stresses of wartime life, leaving the institution tattered at best. By midwar the majority of Middle Florida slaves knew that a Union victory meant liberation for them, and they contributed to the Union cause in many small ways. Blacks served the Confederacy; but of those who did, most were impressed as laborers. When the day of jubilee arrived in May 1865, Florida slaves celebrated "in ecstacy."

If any fact remains clear from the slave's experience in Florida during 1821 to 1865, it is that Florida could not have existed and grown as it did without the hard work, courage, sacrifices, and sometimes genius of black men and women. History has been written without crediting their achievements. Public markers and descriptive brochures talk of this plantation or that beautiful antebellum home or the march of the frontier or the Indian wars as a product of white effort and enterprise. Yet it was the black worker or black builder or black cowhunter or Black Seminole who often came first, endured the worst, and stayed in place despite all obstacles until the job was done. Praise is due these unsung men and women whose names largely have been lost. They deserve to be remembered.

"Florida"

Sweet ocean goddess, divinely fair and free,
Outstretching far into the summer sea,

As if to catch the constant ocean breeze
That swiftly speeds over the gulf and seas!

Thou art a fairy land—a "Land of Flowers,"
With towering pines and vine-clad bowers—

With boundless lakes and broad, majestic streams,
That bask forever in bright, sunny gleams.

Dear sunny land of orange and balmy sky,
Where summer reigns and flowers never die!

Thrice bless'd are thou, with trees forever green,
And varied fruit, with air and clime serene.

Long hast thou groaned 'neath burdens of the Past,—
Ravaged by wars and by oppression blast:

But now take hope—thy future shall be bright,
Thy chains have fallen, and ended is thy night.

Thy wasted fields and trees will yield again:
Redoubled harvests shall thy sons regain.

Thy hidden wealth, and healing balmy clime,
And charming scenery, varied and sublime,

Must lure from every clime, from every land,
Uncounted thousands to thy shores of sand.

And these will summon forth, with skilful toil,
The hidden treasures of thy wasted soil.

Take hope and rise, land of the fig and pine!
Thy woes are ended and new life is thine.

Labor and Liberty, and wealth and power,
Henceforth will be thy allotted dower![1]

—John Willis Menard
Florida State Representative, 1874

ABBREVIATIONS

PKY	P. K. Yonge Library of Florida History, University of Florida, Gainesville
SAEFH	*St. Augustine East Florida Herald*
SAFH	*St. Augustine Florida Herald*
SAFH&SD	*St. Augustine Florida Herald and Southern Democrat*
SAHSRL	St. Augustine Historical Society Research Library
SAN	*St. Augustine News*
SAR	*St. Augustine Record*
SLF	State Library of Florida, Tallahassee
SN	*Slave Narratives: A Folk History of Slavery in the United States, from Interviews with Former Slaves,* Federal Writers' Project
TDT	*Tampa Daily Times*
TF	*Tallahassee Floridian*
TF&A	*Tallahassee Floridian and Advocate*
TF&J	*Tallahassee Floridian and Journal*
TFP	*Tampa Florida Peninsular*
TFS	*Tallahassee Florida Sentinel*
TP	*Territorial Papers of the United States*
TSF	*Tallahassee Star of Florida*
TSJ	*Tallahassee Southern Journal,* 1846
TFW	*Tallahassee Florida Watchman*
UWF	University of West Florida, Pensacola

NOTES

PREFACE

1. Peter H. Wood, *Black Majority*; Betty Wood, *Slavery in Colonial Georgia*; Edmund S. Morgan, *American Slavery*; Ripley, *Slaves and Freedmen*; Boles, *Black Southerners*; Owens, *This Species of Property*; Webber, *Deep like the Rivers*; Raboteau, *Slave Religion*; Levine, *Black Culture*. See also Elkins, *Slavery*; Lane, *Debate over Slavery*; Fogel and Engerman, *Time on the Cross*; Van Deburg, *Slave Drivers*; Scarborough, *Overseer*; Creel, *Peculiar People*; Fox-Genovese, *Within the Plantation Household*; Faust, *Mothers of Invention*; and Malone, *Sweet Chariot*.

2. Although the following older studies may require revision in light of contemporary scholarship, they offer a glimpse of slavery in various southern states: Ballagh, *Slavery in Virginia*; Bassett, *Slavery in the State of North Carolina*; Brackett, *The Negro in Maryland*; Coleman, *Slavery Times in Kentucky*; Flanders, *Plantation Slavery in Georgia*; Klingberg, *Negro in Colonial South Carolina*; Chase C. Mooney, *Slavery in Tennessee*; Sellers, *Slavery in Alabama*; Sydnor, *Slavery in Mississippi*; Joe Gray Taylor, *Negro Slavery in Louisiana*; Orville W. Taylor, *Negro Slavery in Arkansas*; Rosser Howard Taylor, *Slaveholding in North Carolina*; Trexler, *Slavery in Missouri*.

3. Julia Floyd Smith, *Slavery and Plantation Growth*. Several theses and articles, although somewhat dated, offer information on and insight into slavery in Florida. See Hering, "Plantation Economy in Leon County," and Julia F. Smith, "Cotton and the Factorage System"; Edwin L. Williams Jr., "Negro

Slavery in Florida"; Appleyard, "Plantation Life in Middle Florida"; and Bates, "Preliminary Study."

4. Escott, *Slavery Remembered,* 9–10. See also Bailey, "A Divided Prism"; Blassingame, "Using the Testimony of Ex-Slaves"; Woodward, "History from Slave Sources"; and Mormino, "Florida Slave Narratives."

5. Mormino, "Florida Slave Narratives," 407.

6. A number of excellent studies describe, analyze, and explain the many dimensions of slavery without adhering to any particular theoretical model. See, e.g., Randolph B. Campbell's *Empire for Slavery* and Joyner's *Down by the Riverside.* For an interesting discussion of the two basic historiographical approaches used by scholars from the 1960s to the present in describing slavery in the United States, see Young, *Domesticating Slavery.*

1. RACIAL CONTACT AND THE AFRICAN PRESENCE

1. Jane L. Landers, "Free and Slave," 167; *Black Society in Spanish Florida,* 104–6, 117, 150–53.

2. Jane L. Landers, "Free and Slave," 167; see also Gannon, "First European Contacts," 16–17.

3. Jane L. Landers, "Free and Slave," 168; "Traditions of African American Freedom," 18–19; "Africans in the Land of Ayllon," 105–23. Some scholars believe that the first African to set foot in Florida was Esteban, a member of an expedition that landed near Tampa Bay in 1528; however, Juan Garrido and Juan Gonzalez (Ponce) de Leon, two blacks, had accompanied Ponce de Leon on his voyages to Florida as early as 1513 and again in 1521. See, e.g., Richard R. Wright, "Negro Companions," 217–28; Berlin, *Many Thousands Gone,* 65; Jane L. Landers, *Black Society in Spanish Florida,* 10–12.

4. See, e.g., Mullin, *Africa in America*; Tannenbaum, *Slave and Citizen*; Genovese, "Treatment of Slaves," 202–10; Scott, *Slave Emancipation in Cuba.*

5. Jane L. Landers, "Africans in the Land of Ayllon," 105–23; "Free and Slave," 169; Richard R. Wright, "Negro Companions," 217–28. See also the excellent study by Berlin, *Many Thousands Gone,* 64–65, as well as Lyon, *Enterprise of Florida*; TePaske, *Governorship of Spanish Florida,* 135–54; and Chatelain, *Defenses of Spanish Florida,* 59–75.

6. Jane L. Landers, *Black Society in Spanish Florida,* 6, 101–6, 127–29; "Acquisition and Loss," 85–87; "Traditions of African American Freedom," 19–20; "Gracia Real de Santa Teresa de Mose," 13; Corbett, "Migration," 414–18, 420–21; Canter Brown Jr., "Race Relations in Territorial Florida," 289. See also Peter H. Wood, "Changing Population"; Kuethe, "Status of the Free Pardo," 105–17; McAlister, *"Fuero Militar" in New Spain.*

7. Jane L. Landers, *Black Society in Spanish Florida,* 2, 7; Canter Brown Jr., "Race Relations in Territorial Florida," 289–90; Fugitive Negroes of the En-

glish Plantations to the King, June 10, 1738, SD 844, microfilm reel 25, John B. Stetson Collection, PKY.

8. Jane L. Landers, "Spanish Sanctuary," 296–330; "Gracia Real de Santa Teresa de Mose," 13–14; Dunlop, "William Dunlop's Mission," 24; TePaske, "Fugitive Slave," 2–12.

9. Arnade, "Raids, Sieges, and International Wars," 111–12; Jane L. Landers, "Gracia Real de Santa Teresa de Mose," 9–30; "Spanish Sanctuary," 296–302; "Traditions of African American Freedom," 22–23; "Acquisition and Loss," 88; TePaske, "Fugitive Slave," 2–12; I. A. Wright, "Dispatches of a Spanish Official," 144–93; Hurston, "Letters of Zora Neal Hurston," 664–67; Berlin, *Many Thousands Gone*, 72–76. On the use of Florida as a sanctuary for South Carolina slaves, see Giddings, *Exiles of Florida*, 1–27; Morgan and Terry, "Slavery in Microcosm," 122; Siebert, "Departure of the Spaniards," 146; Robert L. Gold, "East Florida Spaniards in Cuba," 216–17; James Leitch Wright Jr., "Blacks in British East Florida," 426–42.

10. Schafer, "'Yellow Silk Ferret,'" 72–73. See also Grant to Richard Oswald, November 21, 1764, Ballindalloch Castle Muniments, #659, Edinburgh, the papers of James Grant–Secretary, National Register of Archives, Scotland; Littlefield, *Rice and Slaves* 63; Peter H. Wood, *Black Majority*, 82–84; Fabel, "British Rule in the Floridas," 134–35; Kay and Cary, *Slavery in North Carolina*, 23–24.

11. Schafer, "'Yellow Silk Ferret,'" 75–76; Berlin, *Many Thousands Gone*, 142–46. See also Coclanis, *Shadow of Dream*, 80–81; Clowse, *Economic Beginnings*, 122–32, 167–71, 220–21, 231–35, 256–58; Peter H. Wood, *Black Majority*, 35–62; Clifton, "Golden Grains of White," 266–83; Hilliard, "Antebellum Tidewater Rice Culture," 94–110; Wilms, "Development of Rice Culture," 45–57; Chaplin, "Tidal Rice Cultivation," 29–61.

12. James Leitch Wright Jr., *Florida during the American Revolution*, 1–44.

13. Schafer, "'Yellow Silk Ferret,'" 85, 90–91; Jane L. Landers, "Free and Slave," 174–75; "Traditions of African American Freedom," 24–25.

14. Jane L. Landers, "Traditions of African American Freedom," 22–23; "Free and Slave," 178.

15. Jane L. Landers, "Free and Slave," 180; Alexander, "Ambush of Captain John William," 286; Patrick, *Florida Fiasco*, 194; Gannon, "First European Contacts," 16–17; Jones and McCarthy, *African Americans in Florida*, 9–10; Bickel, *Mangrove Coast*, 44–59, 182–83; Canter Brown Jr., *African Americans on the Tampa Bay Frontier*, 9; *Florida's Peace River Frontier*, 5–9.

16. Covington, "Negro Fort," 80. See also Covington, *Seminoles of Florida*, 28–49; Jane L. Landers, "Free and Slave," 180; "Traditions of African American Freedom and Community in Spanish Colonial Florida," 34; Mahon and Weisman, "Florida's Seminole and Miccosukee Peoples," 191; Hall, "African Reli-

gious Retentions," 48; Klos, "Seminole Removal Debate," 128, 134, 144; James Leitch Wright Jr., "First Seminole War," 565–69; Hawes, "Cannonball."

17. Canter Brown Jr., "Sarrazota," 5–6.

18. Ibid., 15–19; Canter Brown, Jr., *African Americans on the Tampa Bay Frontier*, 9–20; Covington, "Negro Fort," 79–81; Giddings, *Exiles of Florida*, 53; "'Defenses of the Floridas,'" 248; *Charleston City Gazette and Commercial Advertiser*, quoted in *Philadelphia National Gazette and Literary Register*, December 3, 1821; John Lee Williams, *Territory of Florida*, 299–300. On the Battle of the Suwannee in April 1818, see Giddings, *Exiles of Florida*, 46–54. On the name *Angola*, see Jose Maria Caldez and Joaquin Caldez case files, Spanish Land Grants (Unconfirmed Grants), microfilm file 2.1, John Germany Public Library Special Collections Department, Tampa.

19. Canter Brown Jr., "Sarrazota," 12–17; *Charleston City Gazette and Commercial Advertiser*, quoted in *Philadelphia National Gazette and Literary Register*, December 3, 1821.

20. Julia Floyd Smith, *Slavery and Plantation Growth*, 9–27; Canter Brown Jr., "Race Relations in Territorial Florida," 299–300. See also Sidney Walker Martin, *Florida during the Territorial Days*.

21. Genovese, *Roll, Jordan, Roll*, 27. See also Blassingame, *Slave Community*; Rawick, *Sundown to Sunup*; Fogel and Engerman, *Time on the Cross*; Canter Brown Jr., "Sarrazota," 5–19.

22. Coker and Parker, "Second Spanish Period," 153. See also Fabel, "British Rule in the Floridas," 136.

23. *Fifth Census; or Enumeration of the Inhabitants of the United States as Corrected at the Department of State*, 1830, 156–59. See also Harper, "Antebellum Census Enumerations," 42–44.

24. Jane L. Landers, "Free and Slave," 181; Hill, "George J. F. Clarke," 197–253; Jane L. Landers, *Black Society in Spanish Florida*, 123–24, 150–53, 242; James Leitch Wright Jr., *Creeks and Seminoles*, 81–88; Barr and Hargis, "Voluntary Exile," 4; *St. Augustine Florida Herald* (hereafter *SAFH*), May 12, 1830; May, "Zephaniah Kingsley," 145–59; Schafer, "Neither Freemen nor Slaves," 599.

25. Jane L. Landers, "Free and Slave," 177; Julia Floyd Smith, *Slavery and Plantation Growth*. See also Rivers, "Slavery in Microcosm," 235–45; "Dignity and Importance," 404–18; "Slavery and the Political Economy," 1–19; "Madison County," 233–44.

26. Baptist, "Migration of Planters," 527–44.

27. Julia Floyd Smith, *Slavery and Plantation Growth*, 10. See also Rivers, "Slavery in Microcosm," 235–45; "Dignity and Importance," 404–18; "Slavery and the Political Economy," 1–19; "Madison County," 233–44.

28. Jane L. Landers, "Free and Slave," 181; Canter Brown Jr., "Race Relations in Territorial Florida," 290; Manley and Brown, *Supreme Court of Flor-*

ida, 105; *St. Augustine East Florida Herald* (hereafter *SAEFH*), November 27, 1824; Mahon, *Second Seminole War,* 29; Julia Floyd Smith, *Slavery and Plantation Growth,* 113; David Y. Thomas, "Free Negro," 336.

29. Canter Brown Jr., "Florida Crisis," 421–38; "Race Relations in Territorial Florida," 301; Bates, "Legal Status," 160–61.

30. Mahon, *Second Seminole War,* 69–86; Canter Brown Jr., *Florida's Peace River Frontier,* 36–42; "Race Relations in Territorial Florida," 303.

31. Mahon and Weisman, "Florida's Seminole and Miccosukee Peoples," 193; Klos, "Seminole Removal Debate," 129; Canter Brown Jr., "Sarrazota," 5–19; Boyd, "Events at Prospect Bluff," 55–96; "Horatio S. Dexter," 81–92; *American State Papers: Indian Affairs* (hereafter *ASPIA*) 2:439.

32. Rivers and Brown, "Indispensable Man," 1–23; Canter Brown Jr., *African Americans on the Tampa Bay Frontier,* 19; "Race Relations in Territorial Florida," 289, 304; *Florida's Peace River Frontier,* 34–59; Porter, "Negro Abraham," 17–18; *Black Seminoles,* 66–67; Peters, *Florida Wars,* 108; *American State Papers: Military Affairs* (hereafter *ASPMA*) 7:820–22; Giddings, *Exiles of Florida,* 97–114; Jesup quoted in Porter, "Negroes and the Seminole War," 444. See also Mulroy, *Freedom on the Border,* 28–29.

33. Rivers and Brown, "Indispensable Man," 1–23; Klos, "Seminole Removal Debate," 138–43. On the Black Seminoles in the west, see Porter, *Black Seminoles,* and Mulroy, *Freedom on the Border.*

34. Schafer, "U.S. Territory and State," 221; Dodd, *Florida Becomes a State,* 31–47, 63; Doherty, *Whigs of Florida,* 1–8; *Tallahassee Floridian* (hereafter *TF*), April 4, 1840.

35. Schafer, "U.S. Territory and State," 221–25.

36. Ibid., 223–24.

2. On Middle Florida's Large Plantations

1. See Rawick, *The American Slave,* vol. 17 of *Florida Narratives* (hereafter *AS-FN*), 243, 252. On the scope and potential uses of the Florida slave narratives, see Mormino, "Florida Slave Narratives," 411–12.

2. See, e.g., Julia Floyd Smith, *Slavery and Plantation Growth*; Boles, *Black Southerners*; Randolph B. Campbell, *Empire for Slavery,* 115–54; Kolchin, *American Slavery,* 121.

3. Catharine Wirt to Louis Goldsborough, January 3, June 8, 1839, and Ellen Wirt McCormick to Catharine Wirt, October 1, 1843, Wirt Papers.

4. Randolph B. Campbell, *Empire for Slavery,* 115–16.

5. *Fifth Census; or Enumeration of the Inhabitants of the United States,* 1830, 156–57; *Sixth Census of the United States,* 1840, 454–55; *Seventh Census of the United States,* 1850, 391–401; *Population of the United States in 1860,* 50–54; *Agriculture of the United States in 1860,* 225; *Statistics of the United States (Including Mortality, Property, etc.) in 1860,* 340–41.

6. U.S. Decennial Censuses, 1830 and 1840 Florida censuses (population schedules) and 1850 and 1860 Florida censuses (slave schedules); *Tallahassee Floridian and Journal* (hereafter *TF&J*), February 12, 1854; Stampp, *Peculiar Institution*, 201–6. See also Rivers, "Slavery in Microcosm," 235–45; "Dignity and Importance," 404–18; "Slavery and the Political Economy," 1–19; "Madison County," 233–44.

7. Shofner, *Jefferson County*, 85–89; John Gamble diary, passim; Laura Randall to Elizabeth Wirt, December 17, 1827, Thomas Randall to William Wirt, September 23, 1833, Wirt Papers.

8. See Amon DeLaughter journal, April 14, 1854–November 1, 1860; *AS-FN*, 329.

9. *Sixth Census of the United States, 1840*, 337–45; *Eighth Census of the United States, 1860*, 57; *Compendium of the Enumeration of the Inhabitants and Statistics of the United States, Sixth Census, 1840*, 337; *Compendium of the Seventh Census, 1850*, 408; *Agriculture of the United States in 1860*; De Bow, *Industrial Resources*, 1:149; Gray, *History of Agriculture*, 2:739, 756; *Tallahassee Florida Sentinel* (hereafter *TFS*), January 9, 1844; *TF&J*, November 17, 1849; D. D. Smith, *John (Virginia) Smith*, 1–2; J. Randall Stanley, *History of Gadsden County*, 56; Julia Floyd Smith, *Slavery and Plantation Growth*, 139. For the history of tobacco in the Tidewater Chesapeake region and the transformation of the culture to Middle Florida (particularly Gadsden County), see Walsh, "Slave Life."

10. *AS-FN*, 242–47, 250; Amon DeLaughter journal, April 14, 1854–November 1, 1860; Thomas Randall to William Wirt, April 13, 1828, Wirt Papers.

11. Julia Floyd Smith, *Slavery and Plantation Growth*, 66–67; "Cotton and the Factorage System," 36–48; *AS-FN*, 246; Shofner and Rogers, "Sea Island Cotton," 373–80. As in other parts of the South during the antebellum period, large planters dominated the cotton culture in Middle Florida. See, e.g., Mandle, "Plantation Economy," 1:214–28. Hine, Hine, and Harrold, *Odyssey*, 119–26.

12. See Amon DeLaughter journal, passim; Phillips and Glunt, *Florida Plantation Records*, passim.

13. Paisley, *Red Hills of Florida*, 169–70; Murat, *United States of North America*, 98; Amon DeLaughter journal, April 14, 1854–November 1, 1860; *AS-FN*, 213; Joyner, "World of the Plantation Slaves," 52.

14. Deborah Gray White, "Female Slaves," 109.

15. Julia Floyd Smith, *Slavery and Plantation Growth*, 53–77; Rivers, "Slavery in Microcosm," 235–45; "Dignity and Importance," 404–18; "Slavery and the Political Economy," 1–19; "Madison County," 233–44.

16. Rivers, "Troublesome Property," 111–13; Julia Floyd Smith, *Slavery and Plantation Growth*, 71–72; Phillips and Glunt, *Florida Plantation Records*, 31–33, 563–68; Eppes, *Negro of the Old South*, 1–2; Amon DeLaughter journal,

April 1, 1854–November 1, 1860. The gang and task systems had been used by Carolina and Georgia planters during the seventeenth and eighteenth centuries. Once in Florida, the planters usually employed one or the other system, and some used both systems. See Philip D. Morgan, "Task and Gang Systems," 191–92; "Work and Culture," 563–99.

17. Amon DeLaughter journal, April 1, 1854–November 1, 1860; AS-FN, 243, 251; Phillips and Glunt, Florida Plantation Records, 566–68; Abbey, "El Destino and Chemonie Plantations," part 1, 179–213, part 3, 3–46.

18. Murat, United States of North America, 98; Catharine Wirt to Louis Goldsborough, January 3, June 8, 1839, Wirt Papers; Rivers, "Troublesome Property," 112; Shofner, History of Jefferson County, 127.

19. King, Stolen Childhood, 22.

20. Laura W. Randall to Elizabeth Wirt, October 4, 1828, and Henry Wirt to Elizabeth Wirt, October 20, 1843, Wirt Papers.

21. Rivers, "Dignity and Importance," 418; AS-FN, 213, 242–43, 250, 329, 335; Amon DeLaughter journal, April 1, 1854–November 1, 1860.

22. See the following Leon County slaveholder wills in Leon County will records, Book A: Margaret Cotton, May 28, 1846, 223–27; Richard Whitaker, March 14, 1855, 189–93; Canada Summersett, October 25, 1859, 165–67. See also AS-FN, 214, 339. Children and young females sometimes were trained to become house servants, as in the case of Emeline on Leon County's Pine Hill Plantation. Mother to Susan Bradford Eppes, n.d., folder 2, Pine Hill Plantation Papers; Fox-Genovese, Within the Plantation Household, 152–53.

23. Phillips and Glunt, Florida Plantation Records, 24–27, 117, 120–23; Boles, Black Southerners, 113–15; Scarborough, Overseer, 5–6; Abbey, "El Destino and Chemonie Plantations," part 1, 188–200.

24. Much like other overseers in Middle Florida and throughout the South, Amon DeLaughter, John Evans, and D. N. Moxley often failed to please their employers. Amon DeLaughter journal, 76; Phillips and Glunt, Florida Plantation Records, 150; Julia Floyd Smith, Slavery and Plantation Growth, 53–61; Rivers, "Troublesome Property," 112; Franklin and Schweninger, Runaway Slaves, 235–38.

25. AS-FN, 243.

26. Phillips and Glunt, Florida Plantation Records, 150; Julia Floyd Smith, Slavery and Plantation Growth, 57.

27. Seventh Census of the United States, 1850, 391–401; Population of the United States in 1860, 50–54.

28. Tallahassee Floridian and Advocate (hereafter TF&A), November 21, 1829, March 13, 1832; Jefferson County, board of commissioners minutes, May 1851; Florida, Laws of Territorial Florida (1832), 32, 143–45.

29. TF&J, December 4, 1852, April 16, 1853; Denham, Rogue's Paradise, 120–40. See also Scarborough, Overseer.

30. *TF&J*, December 4, 1852, April 16, 1853; Denham, *Rogue's Paradise*, 120–40; Blassingame, *Slave Community*, 163; Kolchin, *American Slavery*, 103; Parish, *Slavery*, 32. See also Van Deburg, *Slave Drivers*.

31. Deposition of Richard Saunders, Case 1214-A, 168–701, Leon County Court House, Tallahassee, Florida; Rogers and Clark, *Croom Family and Goodwood Plantation*, 121. For more information, see Chapter 6.

32. Eppes, Pine Hill Plantation Papers, 12; Phillips and Glunt, *Florida Plantation Records*, 562–68; *TF*, June 15, 1839; Owens, *This Species of Property*, 6.

33. McRory and Barrows, *History of Jefferson County*, 87; Eppes, Pine Hill Plantation Papers, 72; Helen M. Edwards memoirs, n.p.; Paisley, *Red Hills of Florida*, 169–83; Amon DeLaughter journal, passim; Julia Floyd Smith, *Slavery and Plantation Growth*, 20–21; Shofner, *Jefferson County*, 40; Willoughby, "Apalachicola Aweigh," 178–94; *Fair to Middlin'*, 19–31; Owen, "Apalachicola," 1–25; Ellen Call Long, *Florida Breezes*, 35; *Magnolia Advertiser*, April 8, 1829.

34. *AS-FN*, 166; Rivers, "Baptist Minister James Page," 43–54; Lykes, *Gift of Heritage*, 7–10.

35. John Gamble diary, passim; Amon DeLaughter journal, passim; Denham, *Rogue's Paradise*, 129.

36. Linsin, "Skilled Slave Labor," 188–89; Julia Floyd Smith, *Slavery and Plantation Growth*, 53–55.

37. Shofner, *Jefferson County*; *Jackson County*; Eppes, Pine Hill Plantation Papers, 12–81; *TF&J*, November 29, 1853; Shofner, *Jefferson County*, 98, 128–29; William Kilcrease probate records, file 1005, books 1–6, and Cyrus Dearborn probate records, file 362, Gadsden County probate records; Rivers, "Slavery in Microcosm"; "Dignity and Importance"; "Slavery and the Political Economy"; "Madison County."

38. Thomas Randall to William Wirt, September 23, 1833, Wirt Papers; Eppes, Pine Hill Plantation Papers, 22; *Quincy Sentinel*, December 11, 1840, November 14, 1843; *TF*, November 7, 1835.

39. Entry of November 22, 1827, Laura Randall journal, Catharine Wirt to Louis Goldsborough, January 3, June 8, 1839, Ellen W. McCormick to Catharine Wirt, October 1, 1843, Wirt Papers; *AS-FN*, 242.

40. Shofner, *Jackson County*, 148; William Taylor will, reel 4, Jackson County probate records; *AS-FN*, 213–14; wills of W. P. Barnes, Elizabeth Henry, and John Pratt, Gadsden County probate records; *Quincy Sentinel*, November 11, 1840; *Jacksonville East Florida Advocate*, October 12, 1839; *Jacksonville Florida Republican*, June 3, 1851; *St. Augustine East Florida Herald*, June 7, 1823; *St. Augustine Florida Herald*, June 13, 1833, April 3, 1834; *Tallahassee Southern Journal*, June 2, 1846. See also Blassingame, *Slave Community*, 311; Randall M. Miller, *Dear Master*, 139; Murat, *United States of North America*, 99; Parish, *Slavery*, 31.

41. Ellen McCormick to Mother, September 8, 1842, Wirt Papers.

42. Ibid., Elizabeth Wirt to Catharine Wirt, January 3, 1839, Ellen McCormick to Catharine Wirt, June 14, September 10, 1843; *AS-FN*, 242; Hine, Hine, and Harrold, *Odyssey*, 127.

43. Eppes, Pine Hill Plantation Papers, 9; misc. papers in William Kilcrease file, Gadsden County will and probate records.

44. *AS-FN*, 165, 244, 252; Amon DeLaughter journal, passim; Eppes, Pine Hill Plantation Papers, 5.

45. *AS-FN*, 330; Eppes, Pine Hill Plantation Papers, 12–13; entry of November 28, 1850, in Moseley, "Diary"; Murat, *United States of North America*, 99; Shofner, *Jefferson County*, 133.

46. *AS-FN*, 213; Eppes, Pine Hill Plantation Papers, 12–13; Ellen Call Long, *Florida Breezes*, 197. Kidder M. Moore remembered her father giving slaves a big dinner and gifts during Christmas time. See Helen M. Edwards memoirs, 1, 3–5.

47. Ellen Call Long, *Florida Breezes*, 197; Murat, *United States of North America*, 98; John Gamble diary, 1835, 1851, passim. On the development of the slave's economy, see Berlin and Morgan's introduction in their *Cultivation and Culture*; Breen and Innes, *'Myne Owne Ground'*, 81–82.

48. John Gamble diary, 1835, 1851, passim; Amon DeLaughter journal, passim; Rivers, "Troublesome Property," 114–15.

49. Bates, "Legal Status," 160; Edwin L. Williams Jr., "Negro Slavery in Florida," 93; Canter Brown Jr., "Race Relations in Territorial Florida," 295–97; Julia Floyd Smith, *Slavery and Plantation Growth*, 48; "An Act for the Punishment of Slaves, for Violation of the Penal Laws of the Territory," Florida, *Laws of Territorial Florida* (1833), 182–83; *AS-FN*, 215.

50. Bellamy, "Slavery in Microcosm," 345; *Quincy Sentinel*, July 31, October 16, 23, 1840, January 27, 1843; *TF&A*, April 6, December 28, 1830, February 28, 1832; *Tallahassee Southern Journal*, June 2, 1846; *TF&J*, September 29, 1855.

51. Laura Randall to Elizabeth Wirt, January 17, February 3, 1828, Laura Randall to Elizabeth Wirt, October 4, 1828, Thomas Randall to William Wirt, December 12, 1828, May 4, 1831, January 10, 1832, Elizabeth Wirt to William Wirt, June 28, 1827, Ellen McCormick to Mother, October 12, 1842, Ellen McCormick to Catharine W. Randall, May 15, June 8, 1845, Wirt Papers; Louis Goldsborough to Elizabeth Goldsborough, August 28, 1836, January 9, 1837, Goldsborough Papers; *TF*, December 12, 1835, November 12, 1836, June 8, 1839, January 2, 1841; Andrew Young Inventory, April 26, 1842, Jackson County probate records, Book C, 689–91; Moseley, "Diary," 2, 4, passim; Jeremiah D. Reid will, April 17, 1856, Madison County will records and letters testamentary, Book B, 88–95; Samuel Parkhill will, December 15, 1841, Case Style no. 48, Leon County will records. See also the following wills of slaveholders in Jefferson County will records and letters testamentary, Book B: John B. Morris will, June 17, 1847, 9–11; John Doggett will, September 25, 1849, 45; William S.

Murphy will, July 13, 1863, 130–31; and Thomas H. Triplett will, August 30, 1863, 127–28. As to problems arising from the lease system, see case file, *Gideon Green v. Harp and Kerr,* March 10, 1832, Leon County records of civil actions; Hughes, "Slaves for Hire," 260–86.

52. Jonathan Robinson probate records, file 1529, Gadsden County probate records; Robert S. Edmund will, August 13, 1850, Gadsden County will records, Book A, 219–24; Canter Brown Jr., "Race Relations in Territorial Florida," 296–97; Wade, *Slavery in the Cities,* 143–79, 209–42; *Southern Cultivator,* April 1854, 105–7, June 1858, 378; Book of Sales of Personal Estates, 1846–1860, 6, Leon County probate records; Edwin L. Williams Jr., "Negro Slavery in Florida," 93–110, 182–204; Bancroft, *Slave Trading,* 145.

53. Louis Goldsborough to Elizabeth W. Goldsborough, August 28, 1836, Goldsborough Papers; *TF&A* April 6, 1830, February 28, 1832; *TF,* December 12, 1835, November 12, 1836, June 8, 1839, January 2, 1841. In Middle Florida railroad companies frequently hired bond servants. *TFS,* February 24, 1855; Rivers, "Dignity and Importance," 416–18.

54. John G. Gamble wills, May 19, 1844, and December 4, 1852, case style 167 and 229, Benjamin Chaires Sr. will, June 12, 1835, case style 31, John Parkhill Sr. will, October 1, 1855, 200–203, case style 229, Leon County probate records; John Shepard will, February 19, 1846, Leon County will records, Book A, 159–61. The will and probate records of Leon, Gadsden, Jackson, Jefferson, and Madison Counties contain many similar examples. See also Linsin, "Skilled Slave Labor," 189; *Memorial of the Tallahassee Railroad Company,* 23d Cong., 2d sess., S. Doc. 267, 1; Williams, "Negro Slavery in Florida," Pt. 2, 194–95; *TF&J,* April 3, 1858; Chatham, "Plantation Slavery in Middle Florida," 78; misc. items in Thomas A. Bradford Papers; Bancroft, *Slave Trading,* 145; *TFS,* February 24, 1855; Julia Floyd Smith, *Slavery and Plantation Growth,* 21.

55. Genovese, *Political Economy of Slavery,* 247; *Sixth Census of the United States,* 1840, 344.

56. Wade, *Slavery in the Cities,* 244–45; Rivers, "Slavery in Microcosm," 228–34; Linsin, "Skilled Slave Labor," 189; Groene, *Ante-Bellum Tallahassee,* 31; Canter Brown Jr., "'Hopes I Cherished,'" 3; Lee H. Warner, *Free Men,* 55.

3. ON MIDDLE FLORIDA'S SMALL PLANTATIONS

1. *Fifth Census; or Enumeration of the Inhabitants of the United States,* . . . 1830, 156–59; *Sixth Census; or Enumeration of the Inhabitants of the United States,* 1840, 454–55, *Seventh Census of the United States,* 1850, 391–401; *Population of the United States in* 1860, 50–54; U.S. Decennial Censuses, 1830 Florida census (population schedules); *Agriculture of the United States in* 1860, 225; *Statistics of the United States (Including Mortality, Property, etc.) in* 1860, 340–41. The term *planter* usually refers to an individual who owned at least

twenty slaves and five hundred acres or more. See Stampp, *Peculiar Institution*, 30.

2. Louis Goldsborough to Elizabeth Goldsborough, January 1837, Goldsborough Papers; Julia Floyd Smith, *Slavery and Plantation Growth*, 15–27, 153–70; Rivers, "Dignity and Importance," 404–5, 418; "Troublesome Property"; "Slavery in Microcosm," 236–37; "Slavery and the Political Economy," 2–4; "Madison County," 233–36.

3. Denham and Brown, *Cracker Times and Pioneer Lives*, 46. The paragraphing of this quotation has been changed from the original in the interest of clarity.

4. Womack, *Gadsden*; J. Randall Stanley, *History of Gadsden County; Sixth Census of the United States*, 1840, 337–45; *Eighth Census of the United States, 1860,* 57: *Compendium of the Enumeration of the Inhabitants and Statistics of the United States, Sixth Census,* 1840, 337; *Compendium of the Seventh Census,* 1850, 408; *Agriculture of the United States in 1860,* 18–21.

5. *AS-FN*, 58–59.

6. Entry of October 1841, David L. White diary. According to census reports, Judge David L. White's holdings did not exceed eight slaves during much of the antebellum period. *AS-FN*, 350.

7. Rabun Scarborough to Sister [his wife], November 8, 29, 1861, Scarborough Letters.

8. *TFS*, January 9, 1844; *TF&J*, November 17, 1849; De Bow, *Industrial Resources*, 1:149: *Compendium of the Seventh Census,* 1850, 408; *Agriculture of the United States in 1860,* 18–21; Gray, *History of Agriculture,* 2:739, 756; Shofner and Rogers, "Sea Island Cotton," 373–80.

9. *AS-FN*, 350; D. D. Smith, *John (Virginia) Smith,* 1–2; J. Randall Stanley, *History of Gadsden County,* 56; Julia Floyd Smith, *Slavery and Plantation Growth,* 139.

10. Julia Floyd Smith, *Slavery and Plantation Growth,* 68; *Agriculture of the United States in 1860,* 99.

11. Rabun Scarborough to Sissy, November 8, 1861, Scarborough Letters.

12. *Compendium of the Seventh Census,* 1850, 408; *Agriculture of the United States in 1860,* 18–21.

13. See also the reminiscences of Douglas Parish and Patience Campbell in *AS-FN*, 58–60, 257–61.

14. Rabun Scarborough to Sissy, November 8, 22, 1861, Scarborough Letters; David L. White diary, July 1835–June 1842.

15. Faust, "Slavery in the American Experience," 23.

16. David L. White diary, July 1835–June 1842. Rabun Scarborough held approximately eighteen male and female slaves of varying ages, but he drew few distinctions concerning the types of work they performed on his small farm in Gadsden County. Scarborough Letters.

17. Julia Floyd Smith, *Slavery and Plantation Growth*, 69; David L. White dairy, July 1835–June 1842.

18. David L. White diary, July 1835–June 1842. During this general period George Bullock held only six slaves and about two hundred acres of land. His holdings never exceeded ten slaves and 250 acres during the antebellum period. See U.S. Decennial Censuses, 1830, 1840, 1850, and 1860 Florida censuses, Jackson County (population schedules), 1850 and 1860 Florida censuses, Jackson County (slave schedules).

19. *AS-FN*, 347; David L. White diary, July 1835–June 1842.

20. King, *Stolen Childhood*, 21.

21. *AS-FN*, 58–60, 257–61, 347–54.

22. Ibid., 257–58.

23. David L. White diary, July 1835–June 1842; *AS-FN*, 257–61, 347–54. Regarding small slaveholders who held skilled slaves whom they also utilized for other tasks, see Jesse Potts will, August 4, 1829, Book A, 93, and Cyrus Dearborn will, March 14, 1835, Book C, 1, 82–84, also probate file no. 362, Leon County will records and Leon County Courthouse, and John W. Malone will, May 15, 1837, Book C, 125–26, also probate file, no. 1184, Gadsden County probate records and Gadsden County Courthouse, Quincy, Florida.

24. *AS-FN*, 58–60, 257–61, 347–54; David L. White diary, July 1835–June 1842.

25. *AS-FN*, 347; Francis H. Rutledge will, November 28, 1866, Leon County will records, Book A, 517.

26. Cyrus Dearborn will, March 14, 1835, file no. 362, and John W. Malone will, May 15, 1837, file no. 1184, Gadsden County Courthouse.

27. Julia Floyd Smith, *Slavery and Plantation Growth*, 56. Small slaveholders, regardless of where they resided in Florida, usually worked alongside their bond servants. Canter Brown Jr., "Race Relations in Territorial Florida," 294–96; *Florida's Peace River Frontier*, 136–54; *African Americans on the Tampa Bay Frontier*, 24–29; Solomon and Erhart, "Race and Civil War," 321–22.

28. Canter Brown Jr., "'Hopes I Cherished,'" 2–3.

29. Rabun Scarborough to Sissy, November 8, 15, 18, 22, 1861, Scarborough Letters.

30. *AS-FN*, 58–60; Julia Floyd Smith, *Slavery and Plantation Growth*, 78–100; Rivers, "Troublesome Property," 111–16.

31. Canter Brown Jr., "'Hopes I Cherished,'" 1–36.

32. *AS-FN*, 347–54.

33. David L. White diary, July 1835–June 1842.

34. *AS-FN*, 257–61.

35. Genovese, *Roll, Jordan, Roll*, 391; Linsin, "Skilled Slave Labor," 183–96.

36. Cyrus Dearborn will, March 14, 1835, file no. 362, Gadsden County probate records.

37. Linsin, "Skilled Slave Labor," 195; John Rix will, May 20, 1839, Book A, 419–20, Sampson Pope will, January 11, 1840; Book D, 286–92, Jackson County will records.

38. Julia Floyd Smith, *Slavery and Plantation Growth*, 73.

39. *AS-FN*, 347–54.

40. Julia Floyd Smith, *Slavery and Plantation Growth*, 81; Rivers, "Troublesome Property," 114–15.

4. IN EAST AND WEST FLORIDA

1. Brown, *Florida's Peace River Frontier*, 63–68; Keuchel, *History of Columbia County*, 59; Ott and Chazal, *Ocali Country*, 41–59; Stanaback, *History of Hernando County*, 20–27; *Georgetown (S.C.) Winyah Observer*, January 3, 1851, February 4, July 28, 1852.

2. Genovese, "Treatment of Slaves," 202–10; Scott, *Slave Emancipation in Cuba*; Tannenbaum, *Slave and Citizen*; Jane L. Landers, *Black Society in Spanish St. Augustine*; "Traditions of African American Freedom," 17–41.

3. Jane L. Landers, "Gracia Real de Santa Teresa de Mose," 9–30; "Traditions of African American Freedom," 21–23.

4. Schafer, "Neither Freemen nor Slaves," 587–610; Canter Brown Jr., "Race Relations in Territorial Florida," 287–93; Landers, *Black Society in Spanish St. Augustine*; Foner, "Free People of Color," 406–30; *SAEFH*, June 7, 1823; Sidney Walker Martin, *Florida during the Territorial Days*, 25–47. See also Marvin Harris, *Patterns of Race*; Jordan, *White Man's Burden*; Fields, *Slavery and Freedom*; Knight, *Slave Society in Cuba*; Genovese, *Roll, Jordan, Roll*; Degler, *Neither Black Nor White*. Regarding slaveholders who fought to adopt the Spanish three-caste system and more relaxed relations with people of color in East Florida, see William Graham Davis, "Florida Legislative Council"; Lisenby, "Free Negro in Antebellum Florida"; Kingsley, *Treatise*; "Address to the Legislative Council of Florida on the Subject of Its Colored Population"; Schafer. *Anna Kingsley*; May, "Zephaniah Kingsley," 145–59; Bennett, *Twelve on the River*, 89–113; Stephens, "Zephaniah Kingsley," 71–76.

5. Schafer, "Neither Freemen nor Slaves," 587–610; Coker, "Pensacola 1686–1763," 117–33; "Financial History," 1–20; "West Florida," 49–56; "Pedro de Rivera's Report," 1–22.

6. Schafer, "Neither Freemen nor Slaves," 587–610; Coker, "Pensacola 1686–1763," 117–33; "Financial History," 1–20; "West Florida," 49–56; "Pedro de Rivera's Report," 1–22; Rucker, "Blackwater and Yellow Pine," 1:1–88.

7. Schafer, "Neither Freemen nor Slaves," 589–90; "Plantation Development," 172–83; Rutherford, "Settlers from Connecticut," 41; Janice Borton Miller, "Rebellion in East Florida," 173–86; Susan Parker, "Men without God or King," 140. See also Murdoch, *The Georgia-Florida Frontier*; Patrick, *Florida Fiasco*.

8. Giddings, *Exiles of Florida*, 16–56; Canter Brown Jr., "Sarrazota," 6–8.

9. Entry of October 5, 1841, Kingsley B. Gibbs journal; Rucker, "Blackwater and Yellow Pine," 2:594–606.

10. Blakey, Lainhart, and Stephens, *Rose Cottage Chronicles*, 24; Kingsley B. Gibbs journal, 22–23; Murat, *United States of North America*, 98; Rivers, "Troublesome Property," 111–14.

11. Rucker, "Blackwater and Yellow Pine," 2:597; *Pensacola Gazette* (hereafter *PG*), August 15, 1835, October 14, 1837; Bateman and Weiss, *Deplorable Scarcity*, 33; Polk, "Pensacola Commerce and Industry," 62–63; Starobin, *Industrial Slavery*, 25–26.

12. Canter Brown Jr., *Ossian Bingley Hart*, 13–23.

13. *Fifth Census; or Enumeration of the Inhabitants of the United States*, 1830, 157; *Sixth Census; or Enumeration of the Inhabitants of the United States*, 1840, 455; *Seventh Census of the United States*, 1850, 399–400; *Population of the United States in* 1860, 52–54.

14. Leslie A. Thompson, *Manual*, 593; *Fifth Census; or Enumeration of the Inhabitants of the United States*, 1830, 157; *Sixth Census; or Enumeration of the Inhabitants of the United States*, 1840, 455; *Seventh Census of the United States*, 1850, 399–400; *Population of the United States in* 1860, 52–54.

15. Leslie A. Thompson, *Manual*, 593; *Fifth Census; or Enumeration of the Inhabitants of the United States*, 1830, 157; *Sixth Census; or Enumeration of the Inhabitants of the United States*, 1840, 455; *Seventh Census of the United States*, 1850, 399–400; *Population of the United States in* 1860, 52–54; Rucker, "Blackwater and Yellow Pine," 2:594.

16. *AS-FN*, 94, 178; *St. Augustine Record* (hereafter *SAR*), October 21, 1934.

17. *AS-FN*, 32.

18. *TFS*, March 12, 1850; Julia Floyd Smith, *Slavery and Plantation Growth*, 68–69; *SAR*, October 21, 1934, May 23, 1987; Buckingham Smith will, April 17, 1869, St. Johns County will and probate records.

19. Julia Floyd Smith, *Slavery and Plantation Growth*, 68–69; Blakey, Lainhart, and Stephens, *Rose Cottage Chronicles*, 62.

20. Blakey, Lainhart, and Stephens, *Rose Cottage Chronicles*, 61, 94, 100; *AS-FN*, 33.

21. Blakey, Lainhart, and Stephens, *Rose Cottage Chronicles*, 100.

22. Ibid., 255–56; Canter Brown Jr., "Very Much Attached to Tampa," 66; "Luke, a slave, plaintiff in Error, Vs. The State of Florida," in *Florida Reports* (1853), 185–96; Schafer, "Neither Freemen nor Slaves," 602. For an interesting discussion of white attitudes toward blacks during the antebellum period and beyond, see Fredrickson, *Black Image*.

23. Kingsley B. Gibbs journal, 22–23; *AS-FN*, 358; *SAR*, October 21, 1934.

24. *St. Augustine Evening Record*, February 14, 1930.

25. Stephen Harvell interview, 4, box 7, folder 3, Florida Negro Papers.

26. John H. McIntosh biographical file, Biographical files, St. Augustine Historical Society Research Library (hereafter SAHSRL); John H. McIntosh, St. Johns County Deed Records, Book N, 104–7, also in file no. 1501-1518, St. Johns County will and probate records; John H. McIntosh will, January 3, 1853, file no. 1502-D, A. B. Nance will, June 24, 1848, file no. 1547-D, Francis Richard II will, March 6, 1826, file no. 1756-D, Duval County will and probate records; Winston Stephens grew sugarcane, as well as cotton. Blakey, Lainhart, and Stephens, *Rose Cottage Chronicles*, 211.

27. *SAFH*, April 3, 1834; *Tampa Florida Peninsular* (hereafter *TFP*), November 1, 1856.

28. Schafer, "'Yellow Silk Ferret,'" 72.

29. *AS-FN*, 97, 355.

30. See the following in the Duval County probate records: I. D. Hart will, September 27, 1861, file no. 900-D; A. B. Nance will, June 24, 1848, file no. 1547-D; Francis Richard II will, March 6, 1826, file no. 1756-D.

31. Schafer, *Anna Kingsley*, 9–10; Blakey, Lainhart, and Stephens, *Rose Cottage Chronicles*, 89, 93.

32. *AS-FN*, 97; *SAR*, October 21, 1934, May 13, 1987; Buckingham Smith will, April 17, 1869, Book A, 98, St. Johns County will and probate records.

33. *AS-FN*, 94, 178.

34. Ibid., 34; Hawes, "One-Time Slave"; *Tampa Morning Tribune*, July 19, 1927; Sarah Brown Bryant interview, in box 7, folder 3, Florida Negro Papers; Brown, *Children on the Tampa Bay Frontier*, 29.

35. Joe G. Warner, *Biscuits and 'Taters*, 18; Stephen Harvell interview, 2, 3, 5, box 7, folder 3, Florida Negro Papers.

36. Stephen Harvell interview, 2, 3, 5; *Bartow Courier- Informant*, December 4, 1895, September 9, 1896; Canter Brown Jr., *Florida's Peace River Frontier*, 136–39, 178, 394; Hamilton, "Dempsey Dubois Crews," 9.

37. Graham, *Awakening of St. Augustine*, 20–21; Fennell, "Blacks in Jacksonville," 37–38; Oliver O. Howard to Lizzie Howard, March 29, 1857, Oliver O. Howard Papers; William W. Rogers, *Outposts on the Gulf*, 30.

38. Graham, *Awakening of St. Augustine*, 20; Canter Brown Jr., *Genealogical Records*, 49–50; *Florida's Peace River Frontier*, 178, 188.

39. *Seventh Census of the United States*, 1850, 401; *Population of the United States in 1860*, 54; Canter Brown Jr., *Florida's Black Public Officials*, 43–54.

40. *Seventh Census of the United States*, 1850, 401; *Population of the United States in 1860*, 54; Martin Richardson, "Pensacola"; Canter Brown Jr., *Ossian Bingley Hart*, 68–70; *Savannah Daily Georgian*, May 14, 1853.

41. Graham, *Awakening of St. Augustine*, 11–13; Thomas Frederick Davis, *History of Jacksonville*, 105–6; *TF&J*, November 6, 27, 1858; *Savannah Morning News*, September 25, 1857; *New York Herald*, August 14, 1864.

42. Maria Louisa Daegenhardt Archer reminiscences.

43. See the following items in the Duval County probate records: John D. Bellechasse will, June 13, 1853, file no. 117-D; John Lewis will, February 6, 1855, file no. 1275-D; James Buckland will, April 9, 1836, file no. 78-D; Samuel S. Browning will, July 10, 1835, file no. 76-D; James Long will, September 27, 1848, file no. 1269-D; John Creichton will, November 7, 1838, file no. 342-D; George Fleming will, March 29, 1851, file no. 911-D; Thomas C. Blanchard will, January 30, 1856, file no. 360-D; Joshua Hickman will, August 29, 1837, file no. 850-D; James D. Pelot will, February 9, 1841, file no. 1598-D. See also Robert J. Bigelow Papers; *SAFH*, January 17, 1824, May 12, 1830, April 3, 1834, July 8, 1835; *TF*, January 8, 1842; *Jacksonville East Florida Advocate* (hereafter *JEFA*), October 12, 1839; *Jacksonville Standard*, February 24, March 10, 1859; *Jacksonville News* (hereafter *JN*), December 13, 1851; *Jacksonville Florida News* (hereafter *JFN*), December 23, 1848, February 25, 1850, October 13, 1855; *Jacksonville Florida Republican* (hereafter *JFR*), January 31, 1856.

44. Graham, *Awakening of St. Augustine*, 20; *Boston Daily Journal*, September 12, 1862; Amy Dru Stanley, *Bondage to Contract*, 18–20.

45. William W. Rogers, *Outposts on the Gulf*, 30; Graham, *Awakening of St. Augustine*, 20.

46. Graham, *Awakening of St. Augustine*, 20; *Boston Daily Journal*, September 12, 1862; *St. Augustine News* (hereafter *SAN*), November 19, 1842; Canter Brown Jr., "Race Relations in Territorial Florida," 292–93; *JFN*, January 29, 1848; *JFR*, August 11, 1855; I. D. Hart will, September 27, 1861, file no. 900-D, A. B. Nance will, June 24, 1848, file no. 1547-D, Francis Richard II will, March 6, 1826, file no. 1756-D, Duval County will and probate records. One Jacksonville ordinance required slave mechanics to pay an annual fee of $10.50. Common laborers had to pay $5.50, and female laborers paid $3.50. Jacksonville, *Ordinances of the Town of Jacksonville of 1859*, 43.

47. *JN*, January 19, August 7, 1850, December 19, 1851, May 15, 22, 29, June 5, 1852, February 10, 1858; *JFR*, November 7, 1850, September 25, 1851; *Jacksonville Standard*, May 3, 1860; *SAEFH*, February 1, 1823, January 17, 1824; *SAFH*, July 8, 1835, March 29, 1837; *SAN*, June 19, 1840; *St. Augustine Florida Herald and Southern Democrat* (hereafter *SAFH&SD*), September 17, 1841; *JEFA*, September 1, 1840.

48. Blakey, Lainhart, and Stephens, *Rose Cottage Chronicles*, 281–83.

49. Dibble, *Antebellum Pensacola*, 3:64; "Slave Rentals," 101–13; Rucker, "Blackwater and Yellow Pine," 2:606.

50. Rucker, "Blackwater and Yellow Pine," 2:606; Dibble, *Antebellum Pensacola*, 3:61–67; Griffin, "Cotton Mill Campaign in Florida," 265–66; Rucker, "Arcadia and Bagdad," 158.

51. Gosse, *Letters from Alabama*, 251–52; Walker, *Trial and Imprisonment*, 23–33; *PG*, November 7, 1834, August 19, 1837, July 14, 1838, August 24, 1839, July 25, August 29, 1840, June 29, July 27, 1844, April 19, 1851, June 4, 1853,

March 18, 25, 1854, August 8, 1857. For a description of the slave females between the ages of fifteen and twenty and of the skills it took to do their jobs, see *PG*, August 15, October 10, 1846. For a more general overview, see Eaton, *Growth of Southern Civilization*, 72–73.

52. Blakey, Lainhart, and Stephens, *Rose Cottage Chronicles*, 1–31; *AS-FN*, 178–79, 356.

53. Kingsley B. Gibbs journal, 24.

5. THE FAMILY

1. For provocative discussions of the slave family in the U.S. South and Southwest, see, Philip D. Morgan, *Slave Counterpoint*; Berlin, *Many Thousands Gone*; Malone, *Sweet Chariot*; Blassingame, *Slave Community*; Genovese, *Roll, Jordan, Roll*; Breen and Innes, *'Myne Owne Ground'*; Gutman, *Black Family*; Kulikoff, *Tobacco and Slaves*; Deborah Gray White, *Ar'n't I a Woman?*; Burton, *In My Father's House*; Manfra and Dykstra, "Serial Marriage," 18–44; Stevenson, *Life in Black and White*; Randolph B. Campbell, *Empire for Slavery*; Hudson, *To Have and to Hold*.

2. Kolchin, *American Slavery*, 148–50; Parish, *Slavery*, 78–79; Faust, *James Henry Hammond*, 112, 243; "Culture, Conflict, and Community," 83–98; Bleser, *Hammonds of Redcliffe*, 68; Kingsley, *Treatise*, 14–15; Faust, "Slavery in the American Experience," 7.

3. Faust, "Slavery in the American Experience," 4; Philip D. Morgan, *Slave Counterpoint*, 498–500. See also Stevenson, *Life in Black and White*; Dusinberre, *Them Dark Days*.

4. John Solana and Harriet Alvarez marriage license, June 15, 1839, St. Johns County marriage records.

5. *AS-FN*, 167. For an interesting study of the problems enslaved blacks encountered trying to maintain coresidential family arrangements and the alternative household structures that consisted, in large part, of female-headed families, see Stevenson, *Life in Black and White*, 206–25.

6. *AS-FN*, 257.

7. Phillips and Glunt, *Florida Plantation Records*, 124; Thomas Randall to William Wirt, May 4, 1831, January 10, 1832, Wirt Papers; Gamble Family Papers, passim; Rivers, "Dignity and Importance," 419; Faust, *James Henry Hammond*, 5–19.

8. Thomas Randall to William Wirt, December 20, 1828, November 20, 1829, Wirt Papers; Blassingame, *Slave Community*, 173; Rivers, "Dignity and Importance," 414; Gutman, *Black Family*, 11–28, 128–33, 285–90, 354–59; Oakes, *Ruling Race*, 176–79.

9. *Fifth Census of the United States*, 1830, 157–59; *Sixth Census of the United States*, 1840, 454–57.

10. *Fifth Census or Enumeration of the Inhabitants of the United States*, 1830,

157–59; *Sixth Census; or Enumeration of The Inhabitants of the United States,* 1840, 454–57; *Seventh Census of the United States,* 1850, 396–400; *Population of the United States in* 1860, 52–54. See also Klein, *Slavery in the Americas;* Cohen and Greene, eds., *Neither Slave nor Free;* Knight, *Slave Society in Cuba;* Corwin, *Spain and the Abolition of Slavery in Cuba;* Aimes, *History of Slavery in Cuba.*

11. See, e.g., James H. McArvers will, March 13, 1842, Book A, 150–52, in Book C, William E. Kilcrease will, May 26, 1860, 164–71, Jesse Potts Sr. will, August 4, 1829, 245–46, Gadsden County will and probate records; John Doggett will, September 25, 1849, Book B, 45, Jefferson County will and probate records; Allen G. Johnson will, December 20, 1854, Bryant Sapen will, January 7, 1858, Book B, 12–15 and 17–18, Frances Ross Inventory, December 28, 1863, Bryant Sheffield deed, February 18, 1853, Book D, 115–17, 176–77, Hamilton County will records; John Rix inventory and appraisement, May 25, 1839, John Randolph appraisal, July 18, 1842, Book A, 419–20, 686, Andrew Young will, April 26, 1842, Book C, 691, Jackson County will records; Achille Murat will, March 8, 1847, and John Finlayson will, February 23, 1865, Book B, 85–87, 155–58, Jefferson County will records; George T. Ward will, August 26, 1859, John Parkhill will, October 1, 1855, Book A, 37–39, 200–203, John B. Whitehead will, January 24, 1857, Book B, 269–74, and Benjamin Chaires Sr. will, June 12, 1838, 571–73, case style no. 31, Leon County will and probate records; Redden W. Parramore will, January 14, 1852, Jeremiah Reid will, April 17, 1856, Book B, 23, 88–95, John Lipscomb will, August 27, 1856, Richard J. Mays will, March 28, 1864, Edward Tabb will, October 1, 1857, Book C, 37–41, 85–87, 107–9, Madison County will records. Notes or copies of these and other surveyed probates, inventories, and appraisements are on file for review at the Florida A&M University Black Archives, Research Center and Museum. Edward Bradford to Dear Sir, January 26, 1863, box 515, file 3, Miscellaneous Manuscripts, Special Collections, Strozier Library, Florida State University.

12. Parish, *Slavery,* 87. Former slave Patience Campbell knew both her parents and recalled that they lived on separate plantations; see *AS-FN,* 28.

13. Blassingame, *Slave Community,* 173–77; Oakes, *Ruling Race,* 176–79; Manfra and Dykstra, "Serial Marriage," 18–44; Gutman, *Black Family,* 11–18, 128–33, 145–55, 285–90, 317–19, 354–59, 418–28; Genovese, "American Slaves and Their History," 112. The spouses of some Florida bond servants may have lived on other plantations as far away as Georgia, South Carolina, and Arkansas because some planters operated several plantations in different states. Former slave Adeline Johnson (Alias Adeline Hall) provides an example. Born and raised in South Carolina, she recalled that her master had been one of the rich men who also owned plantations in Georgia, Florida, and Arkansas before the Civil War. Similarly, ex-slave Charley Watson, also born and raised in South Carolina, remembered that his master had plantations in Georgia and

Florida. For more information see Federal Writers' Project, *Slave Narratives* (hereafter *SN*), vol. 2, pt. 3, pp. 36, 188. Planter George Noble Jones owned two plantations in Florida, called El Destino and Chemonie, while simultaneously owning a large plantation where he resided near Savannah, Georgia. Phillips and Glunt, *Florida Plantation Records*.

14. *Fifth Census of the United States*, 1830, 157–59; *Sixth Census of the United States*, 1840, 454–57.

15. *Sixth Census of the United States*, 1840, 454–57; *Seventh Census of the United States*, 1850, 396–400; *Eighth Census of the United States*, 1860, 52–54.

16. *Fifth Census of the United States*, 1830, 157–59; *Sixth Census of the United States*, 1840, 454–57; *Seventh Census of the United States*, 1850, 396–400; *Eighth Census of the United States*, 1860, 52–54.

17. Plantation records, estate dispersals, tax lists, probate records and inventories suggest that the majority of slaves lived in households composed of simple nuclear families with a 25 percent probability that the family included two parents and their children. During the 1860s more three-generational kinship ties developed in Middle Florida. For examples of wills, inventories, and appraisements that grouped Florida slaves into single, two-parent, or extended-family units, see William E. Kilcrease will, May 26, 1860, Book C, 164–71, Gadsden County will records and in file no. 1005 Gadsden County Courthouse; Allen G. Johnson will, December 20, 1854, Book B, 12–15, William Reed will, June 30, 1849, Book C and D, 245–46, 387, 430–31, and Philemon Bryan will, October 15, 1858, Book D, 32–34, Hamilton County will records; John B. Whitehead will, January 24, 1857, Book B, 269–74, Wright Saunders will, October 10, 1855, Book A, 206–8, case style no. 12, John W. Cotten will, August 1, 1840, Book A, 82–85 and case style no. 84-A-E, and Augustus Fisher will, June 15, 1857, case style no. 280-A, Leon County will and probate records; Joseph M. White will, September 28, 1836, and letter of administration, April 5, 1843, Book A, 30–31, 82, Wesley Adams will, April 28, 1854, Mary Edwards will, August 10, 1847, and John Finlayson will, February 23, 1865, William Bailey Jr. Will, July 16, 1862, William Budd will, June 27, 1862, Book B, 58–59, 85–87, 155–58, 160–61, 162–65, Jefferson County will and probate records; Jacob Robinson will, December 8, 1840, Book A, 18–25, James Williams inventory and appraisal, November 1, 1849, Richard Smith Inventory, March 28, 1847, and Annutticus Gaskins, an appraisal, January 1, 1848, and January 13, 1849, distribution of slaves, Book B, 533, 575–76, 619, 664, Simmons Baker appraisement, December 10, 1853, Book C, 194–207, Francis R. Ely letter of testamentary, November 12, 1859, Book D, 624, Jackson County will records; Michael Duskin will, March 3, 1845, James Dell will, November 30, 1848, Ransom Cason Sr. will, November 12, 1853, Bennet M. Dell will, February 21, 1855, and Nancy R. Lewis will, February 25, 1856, Book A, 19–24, 25–32, 35–38, 50–66, 78–79, M. E. D. Dell estate appraisement, March 5, 1858, John Younger will, December 10,

1860, William Ham will, November 9, 1864, Book B, 2, 15–22, 58–59, Alachua County will and probate records; Thomas V. Wright appraisement, December 17, 1861, Book 1, 17, Clay County probate and will records; Gabriel Priest will, September 3, 1861, and Ben Hopkins will, February 21, 1862, and June 13, 1866, Book B, 129, 159, 419–21, Putnam County will records; S. L. Sparkman deed, February 19, 1848, Book A, 76–77, and Leroy G. Lesley will, April 25, 1861, Book C, 170–71, Hillsborough County will records. Notes or copies of these and other surveyed probates, inventories, and appraisements are on file for review at the Florida A&M University Black Archives, Research Center and Museum. See also Malone, *Sweet Chariot*.

18. *Fifth Census of the United States, 1830*, 156–57; *Sixth Census of the United States, 1840*, 454–55; *Seventh Census of the United States, 1850*, 391–401; *Population of the United States in 1860*, 50–54; *Statistics of the United States (Including Mortality, Property, etc.) in 1860*, 340–41; U.S. Decennial Censuses, 1830 and 1840 Florida censuses, Jackson, Gadsden, Leon, Jefferson, and Madison Counties (population schedules); U.S. Decennial Censuses, 1850 and 1860 Florida censuses, Jackson, Gadsden, Leon, Jefferson, and Madison Counties (slave schedules).

19. Julia Floyd Smith, *Slavery and Plantation Growth*, 122–52; Rivers, "Slavery in Microcosm," 235–45; "Dignity and Importance," 404–18; Slavery and the Political Economy," 1–19; "Madison County," 233–44.

20. See, e.g., Green Chaires will, November 12, 1860, Book A, 336–39, Wright Saunders will, October 10, 1855, case style no. 12, and Augustus Fisher will, June 15, 1857, case style no. 280-A, Leon County will and probate records; John Morris will, June 17, 1847, Emmala Bellamy will, April 30, 1851, John Doggett will, September 25, 1849, Wesley Adams will, April 30, 1854, Martin Palmer will, January 1, 1857, John B. Braden will, February 6, 1855, and Bethelham Bird will, December 30, 1863, Book B, 9–11, 34–36, 45, 58–59, 82–83, 90, 125–26, Jefferson County will and probate records; John G. Bleach will, December 6, 1847, file no. 87-D, Jacob Bryan inventory, February 28, 1848, file no. 99-D, Isaiah D. Hart will, September 27, 1861, file no. 900-D, George Fleming inventory, March 29, 1851, file no. 911-D, James Long will, September 27, 1848, file no. 1269-D, John Lewis will, February 6, 1855, file no. 1275-D, John Mizell will, November 3, 1838, file no. 1371-D, A. B. Nance appraisement, June 24, 1848, file no. 1547-D, Mary E. Smith will, March 4, 1859, file no. 1901-D, and Robert R. Turner will, December 12, 1862, file no. 2097-D, Duval County probate records. Notes or copies of these and other surveyed probates, inventories, and appraisements are on file for review at the Florida A&M University Black Archives, Research Center and Museum. See also Stevenson, *Life in Black and White*, 239.

21. Phillips and Glunt, *Florida Plantation Records*, 71, 74, 111–13, 115–16.

22. Eppes, *Negro of the Old South*, 49–51.

23. Kingsley, *Treatise*, 8–9. For more on slave and free black families, see Roark and Johnson, "Strategies of Survival"; Stevenson, "Distress and Discord," 103–24; Gutman, *Black Family*, 3–14.

24. Amon DeLaughter journal, 18, 30; *AS-FN*, 97.

25. Phillips and Glunt, *Florida Plantation Records*, 63, 74, 151–52.

26. Louisa Anderson to Catharine W. Randall, December 1841, Ellen McCormick to Elizabeth Wirt, October 12, 1854, Wirt Papers; John Gamble diary, passim.

27. Slave marriage permit record, SAHSRL; *St. Augustine Evening Record*, February 14, 1930.

28. Blakey, Lainhart, and Stephens, *Rose Cottage Chronicles* 123; Phillips and Glunt, *Florida Plantation Records*, 152.

29. See, e.g., William E. Kilcrease will, May 26, 1860, Book C, 164–71, and John W. Malone will, January 17, 1844, Book C, 164–65, file no. 993, Gadsden County will and probate records; Jeremiah Reid will, April 17, 1856, Book B, 88–95, John Lipscomb will, August 27, 1856, Book C, 37–41, Madison County will records; George T. Ward will, January 8, 1863, Book A, 37–39, and John B. Whitehead will, January 24, 1857, Book B, 269–74, John W. Cotten testamentary, August 21, 1845, Book A, 82–85, case style no. 84-A-E, Leon County will and probate records. Notes and copies of these and other surveyed probates, inventories, and appraisements are on file for review at the Florida A&M University Black Archives, Research Center and Museum.

30. Jeremiah Reid will, April 17, 1856, Book B, 88–95, Madison County deed records; Rogers and Clark, *Croom Family*, 120–25; Joyner, "World of the Plantation Slaves," 61; Deborah Gray White, "Female Slaves," 117; Joyner, *Down by the Riverside*, 127–40.

31. Notes on or copies of the surveyed wills are available for review at the Florida A&M University Black Archives, Research Center and Museum. See also, Brown, *Women on the Tampa Bay Frontier*, 20–21.

32. *AS-FN*, 2–4, 242, 251–55, 257, 327, 347, 356; *TF*, June 15, 1839; *Tampa Daily Times* (hereafter *TDT*), April 17, 1924.

33. *AS-FN*, 26–29, 180; Francis Richard II will, March 6, 1826, file no. 1756-D, Duval County probate records.

34. Moseley, "Diary," 65; Blakey, Lainhart, and Stephens, *Rose Cottage Chronicles*, 19, 52–54; *SAR*, October 21, 1934; *AS- FN*, 3–4; A. B. Nance appraisement, June 24, 1848, file no. 1547-D, Duval County probate records.

35. Philip D. Morgan, *Slave Counterpoint*, 512.

36. *St. Augustine Evening Record*, February 14, 1930.

37. Julia Floyd Smith, *Slavery and Plantation Growth*, 116–18; Blassingame, *Slave Community*, 173–77; Gutman, *Black Family*, 144–84; *JFR*, July 24, October 9, 1851; *JN*, December 19, 1851; *TFP*, December 11, 1855; Jesse Potts will, August 4, 1829, Book C, 245–46, will records, Gadsden County; John B. White-

head will, January 24, 1857, Book B, 269–74, Leon County will records; Edward Tabb will, October 1, 1857, Book C, 107–9, Madison County will records.

38. *TFS*, December 9, 1851; *TFP*, December 14, 1855, March 21, April 11, 1857; Andrew Branning estate inventory and appraisement, June 23, 1828 file no. 71-D, George Fleming estate inventory, March 29, 1851, file no. 911-D, Martha M. Ortega will, June 8, 1858, file no. 1575-D, Rebekah E. Read estate inventory and additional documents, July 27, 1851, file no. 1760-D, Daniel I. Turknett will, March 10, 1858, file no. 2092-D, Duval County probate records; Sarah Brown Bryant reminiscences, box 7, file 3, Florida Negro Papers; *TDT,* July 27, 1923; *Tampa Sunday Tribune,* June 5, 1988.

39. For a sampling of such wills see the following: Martin Palmer will, January 1, 1857, Book B, 82–83, John W. Malone will, January 17, 1844, Jesse Potts will, August 4, 1829, Book C, 164–65, 245–46, Gadsden County will and probate records; John Braden will, February 6, 1855, Julius High will, September 30, 1852, Robert D. Sturge will, August 26, 1861, Book B, 90, 103–4, 116, Jefferson County probate records; Allen G. Johnson will, December 20, 1854, James Bell will, July 17, 1853, George Powledge deed, February 13, 1840, Josiah Baisdin will, July 1, 1834, Henry Stephens will, January 19, 1849, Book B, 12–15, 47–48, 76–77, 133, 206, 300–307, Shaderick Sutton deed, January 20, 1844, William M. Reed will, June 30, 1849, Book C, 115, 245–46, Francis Ross appraisement, December 28, 1863, Bryant Sheffield will, February 18, 1853, Book D, 115–17, 176–77, William Roberts will, September 12, 1843, Books D and E, 43, 339, Hamilton County will records; Reddin W. Parramore appraisement, January 14, 1852, Jeremiah D. Reid will, April 17, 1856, Book B, 23, 88–95, Alexander Moseley will, August 30, 1844, William Taylor will, June 23, 1853, Richard J. Mays will, March 28, 1864, Nancy DeLaughter will, June 28, 1864, John Sapp will, December 1, 1852, Edward Tabb will, October 1, 1857, Book C, 1–6, 80, 85–87, 89–91, 100–102, 107–9, Madison County will records; William Parramore will, August 21, 1829, Daniel Campbell will, June 18, 1832, Malcolm Nicholson will, November 18, 1838, Daniel Shall will, July 9, 1840, James H. McArvers will, March 13, 1841, Book A, 20–23, 52–53, 124–25, 134, 150–52, Gadsden County will records; Joseph M. White will, September 28, 1836, Book A, 30–31, Achille Murat will, March 8, 1847, Paul Ulmer will, May 14, 1850, John F. Dewitt will, December 30, 1854, Mary Sattonstall will, November 29, 1851, Mary Edwards will, August 10, 1847, Theodore Turnbell will, December 25, 1857, Sarah B. Green will, August 30, 1860 and August 17, 1864, William S. Murphy will, July 13, 1863, William Bailey Jr. will, July 16, 1862, Book B, 5–7, 38–39, 64, 71, 85–87, 92–93, 110, 150, 130–31, 160–61, Jefferson County will records; Joesph Allen will, June 10, 1839, James Pritchett will, October 1, 1839, William Turner will, December 13, 1840, James Whitehead will, August 31, 1847, John Shepard will, February 19, 1846, John Moore will, February 10, 1855,

Green Chaires will, November 12, 1860, Book A, 5, 8, 23–25, 113–17, 159–61, 260, 336–39, William Harris will, December 20, 1827, case style no. 1, Benjamin Fitts will, June 23 1829, case style no. 2, Wright Saunders will, October 10, 1855, Book A, 206–8, case style no. 12, Benjamin Chaires Sr. will, October 1, 1835, case style no. 31, John W. Cotten testamentary, August 1, 1840, Book A, 82–85, case style no. 84-A-E, John G. Gamble will, May 19, 1844, and John Gamble will, December 4, 1852, case style nos. 167 and 229, Leon County will and probate records; Bennet Ferrell petition, December 30, 1839, John Rix inventory and appraisement, May 25, 1839, John Randolph appraisal, July 18, 1842, Book A, 321–22, 419–20, 686, Charles McKay inventory, July 3, 1845, Thomas King inventory, February 28, 1846, Edward Pittman inventory and appraisal, December 21, 1846, Daniel Smith inventory, December 29, 1846, Samuel Robinson inventory and appraisal, December 1, 1842, James Williams inventory and appraisal, November 1, 1849, Anutticus Gaskins appraisal and distribution of slaves, January 1, 1848, January 13, 1849, Richard Smith inventory, June 20, 1848, Joseph Russ appraisal, December 21, 1848, William H. Robinson appraisal, May 10, 1849, Terry Watson estate (hired-out slaves), January 27, 1838, Book B, 301–2, 406–7, 512–13, 517, 536, 575–76, 619, 624–26, 664, 697, 757, 803, Andrew Young will, April 26, 1842, Book C, 691, Benjamin Dickson inventory and appraisal, January 31, 1858, Francis R. Ely letter of testamentary, November 12, 1859, Book D, 44–46, 624, Jackson County will records.

40. AS-FN, 95; James H. McArvers will, March 13, 1841, Book A, 150–52, Gadsden County will records. In over 75 percent of those probates in which slaves were listed or inventoried, slave owners had no compunctions about separating children from family members. See, e.g., the following sampling of Middle Florida slaveholder probate records: William Kilcrease will, May 26, 1860, Book C, 164–71 and file no. 1005, Cyrus Dearborn will, March 14, 1835, Book C, 1, Gadsden County will and probate records; James Whitehead will, August 31, 1847, Book A, 113–17, Benjamin Chaires Sr. will, October 13, 1838, case no. 31, John Gamble will, May 19, 1844 and December 4, 1852, case nos. 167 and 229, Leon County will and probate records; Joseph R. Rawls will, July 7, 1841, Book A, 111–12, John Braden will, February 6, 1855, Book B, 90, Jefferson County will and probate records; John Randolph appraisement, July 18, 1842, Book A, 686, Jackson County will and probate records; John Sapp will, December 1, 1852, Book B, 100–102, William Taylor will, June 23, 1853, Book C, 80, Madison County will and probate records.

41. Daniel Campbell will, June 18, 1832, and Eliza James will, September 30, 1836, Book A, 52–53, 85, Gadsden County will records; John Moore will, February 10, 1855, Book A, 260, Leon County will records.

42. Rogers and Clark, *Croom Family*, 140; Thomas Triplett will, August 30, 1863, Book B, 127–28, Jefferson County will records.

43. Rucker, "Blackwater and Yellow Pine," 2:594–607. Probate Records for Santa Rosa County are not available, but see sampling of probate records for slaveholders in Escambia County will records, Book 1: Joseph Noriega will, October 30, 1824, 7–9; Levi Waters will, June 11, 1824, 12–13; Francisco Touard will, April 30, 1825, 13–14; Mareana Bonifay will, September 16, 1825, 15–17; Dorothy Walton will, January 26, 1828, 29–32; Rusalini Perez will, April 10, 1830, 46–49; John Conley will, October 6, 1830, 50–51; Vic lure Le Lassier will, April 10, 1833, 61–63; Pedro De Alba will, October 28, 1835, 66–71; Elizabeth Foster Birland will, May 10, 1835, 72–73; Marguaritta De La Rua will, June 16, 1840, 108–9; Henry Michelus will, May 23, 1841, 112–13; Maria Vellen will, March 9, 1846, 130–32; Byrd E. Willis will, August 26, 1846, 133–36; Sarah A. Davis will, October 29, 1846, 136–39; Enginio Sierra will, March 15, 1849, 147–53; Sarah Francis will, September 4, 1849, 170–74; Eunice Alba will, February 24, 1851, 177–79; Samuel Clifford will, March 1, 1851, 190–91; Nathaniel L. Mitchell will, August 18, 1851, 191–95; John Morgan will, March 10, 1853, 209–10; John J. Balada will, October 16, 1854, 212–13; Charles Evans will, January 27, 1856, 220–21; Susan Jones will, March 20, 1857, 223–24; David Williams will, April 6, 1863, 266–69; Jesse Mims will, January 22, 1866, 270–71.

44. "Old Wills and Letters of Testamentary," 57, Hillsborough County probate records; Francis Richard II will, March 6, 1826, file no. 1756-D, I. D. Hart will, September 27, 1861, file no. 900-D, A. B. Nance appraisement, June 24, 1848, file no. 1547-D, Charles R. Thompson will, November 25, 1855, file no. 2085-D, Duval County probate records; John H. McIntosh, St. Johns County deed records, Book N, 104–7; *TFP*, October 4, November 1, 1856; Schafer, "Neither Freemen nor Slaves," 587–610; Livingston, "Dempsey Dubois Crews," 8–11; Stowell, ed., *Balancing Evils Judiciously*, 39–75.

45. Mary Hobkirk will, September 12, 1835, file no. 841-D, Duval County probate records; Nancy DeLaughter will, June 29, 1864, Book C, 89–91, Madison County will records; John B. Whitehead will, January 24, 1857, Book B, 269–74, Leon County will records; Abraham Dupont will, June 17, 1852, Book 1, 256, 294, 402, St. Johns County will and probate records.

46. John B. Whitehead will, January 24, 1857, Book B, 269–74, Leon County will records; Abraham Dupont will, June 17, 1852, Book 1, 256, 294, 402, St. Johns County will and probate records.

47. Shofner, *Jefferson County*, 137. See the following wills of slaveholders who hired bond servants out for the purpose of ensuring payment of costs for the education of the masters' children, among other things: in Book B, Jefferson County will records, John B. Morris will, June 17, 1847, 9–11, John Finlayson will, February 23, 1865, 155–58; in Book C, Gadsden County will records, Cyrus Dearborn, March 14, 1835, William E. Kilcrease inventory and appraisment, May 16, 1860, 1, 164–71; in Book A, Leon County will records,

Joseph Allen will, June 10, 1839, 5; James Pritchett will, October 1, 1839, 8; William Turner will, December 13, 1840, 23–25; in Book C, Madison County will records, Edward Tabb will, October 1, 1857, 107–9; Virgil Bobo will, October 22, 1848, 23–26, Benjamin Lanier will, November 3, 1857, 63–64; in the Duval County probate records, Samuel S. Browning will, July 10, 1835, file no. 76-D, James Buckland will, August 9, 1836, file no. 78-D, Francis M. Richard III will, November 30, 1852, file no. 1757, Jefferson P. Belknap will, November 1, 1865, file no. 133-D, John Lewis will, February 6, 1855, file no. 1275-D. See also Blakey, Lainhart, and Stephens, *Rose Cottage Chronicles*, 282; Julia Floyd Smith, *Slavery and Plantation Growth*, 77. Occasionally owners as prominent as William D. Moseley and Benjamin A. Putnam were indicted for allowing slaves to hire themselves out. See *State v. William D. Moseley* (1858), Putnam County case files; Putnam County circuit court minutes, Book 1, 328, 364, 365, 370, 383, 393, 395, 428.

48. Julia Floyd Smith, *Slavery and Plantation Growth*, 129–30; McDuffee, *Lures of Manatee*, 31–38; Blakey, Lainhart, and Stephens, *Rose Cottage Chronicles*, 80; Schafer, "Freedom Was as Close," 157–84; John Gamble diary, entry of January 26, 1847; Thomas Randall to William Wirt, April 13, 1828, Wirt Papers; Phillips and Glunt, *Florida Plantation Records*, 151–53; Rivers, "Troublesome Property," 104–27.

49. *TF&J*, January 15, 1859; *TF*, June 8, September 28, 1839, September 9, 1848, December 20, 1851; *JFN*, October 13, 1855; Canter Brown Jr., "Race Relations in Territorial Florida," 296–98.

50. For a sampling of bond servants who absconded in search of relatives or loved ones, see, e.g., these runaway ads: *JFR*, October 30, 1850, October 9, September 25, 1851, July 4, 1855; *JN*, June 5, 1846, March 19, 1847, March 4, June 10, 1848, October 30, 1852, January 1, 1853, October 13, 1855; *Jacksonville Courier* (hereafter *JC*), April 2, 16, June 25, August 6, 1835, January 4, 1851; *SAEFH*, October 16, 1824, April 11, 1826; *JEFA*, October 12, 1839, September 1, 1840; *TF*, May 11, 1833, August 22, October 17, 1835, November 1, 1837, February 3, April 7, May 26, September 15, 1838, February 9, April 6, June 1, 8, August 2, September 28, 1839, January 15, 1840, November 1, 1845, March 6, 1847, February 20, 1858; *SAN*, June 19, 1840; *Tallahassee Florida Watchman* (hereafter *TFW*), October 6, 1838; *Tallahassee Star of Florida* (hereafter *TSF*), May 21, 1840, September 1, 1843; *Apalachicola Gazette*, February 2, 1839; *SAFH* February 10, 1830, May 17, June 16, 1832, July 29, 1835, June 16, 1838; *St. Augustine Ancient City*, March 13, 1852; *TFS*, April 15, May 5, October 15, 1841, February 18, March 4, 1842, June 3, 1855; *St. Augustine Florida Gazette*, September 15, 1821; *Tallahassee Florida Intelligencer*, October 6, 1826; *Tallahassee Florida Advocate*, November 1, 1828; *TF&A*, October 6, 1829; September 7, 1830; *TF&J*, October 27, 1849, April 12, May 10, 1851, June 12, July 31, 1852, May 20, 1854;

Quincy Sentinel, July 3, September 18, 1840, January 1, 8, 1841, May 9, 1843; *Pensacola Floridian,* March 23, 1822. See also Granade, "Slave Unrest in Florida."

51. *TFS,* May 5, 1839, March 4, 1842; *Quincy Sentinel,* January 8, 1841; *Jacksonville St. Johns Mirror,* March 7, 1861; *JC,* August 6, 1835.

52. Denham, *Rogue's Paradise,* 217; *TFS,* February 18, 1842; *JN,* March 4, 1848.

53. *JFR,* October 9, 1851; *SAFH,* November 29, 1832; *TF,* August 4, 1838; Moseley, "Diary," 23.

54. Canter Brown Jr., "Race Relations in Territorial Florida," 299; Blakey, Lainhart, and Stephens, *Rose Cottage Chronicles,* 52–53; Phillips and Glunt, *Florida Plantation Records,* 63, 74; Thomas Wirt to William Wirt, December 26, 1840, Thomas Randall to William Wirt, December 26, 1840, Ellen McCormick to Elizabeth Wirt, October, 12, 1842, H. Louisa Anderson to Catharine Wirt Randall, December 1, 1842, H. Louisa Wirt to Elizabeth Wirt, July 14, 1844, November 26, 1844, Wirt Papers; Rivers, "Dignity and Importance," 414.

55. *TF,* January 18, 1834; Amon DeLaughter journal, passim.

56. H. Louisa Anderson to Catharine Wirt Randall, December 1, 1842, Ellen McCormick to Elizabeth Wirt, October 12, 1842, Wirt Papers; Blakey, Lainhart, and Stephens, *Rose Cottage Chronicles,* 52; Rivers, "Baptist Minister James Page," 43–54.

57. Hattie Reed to D. Bryant, March 22, 1863, and O. Stephens to D. Bryant, April 2, 1863, in Reed, "Diary of A. M. Reed"; Schafer, "Freedom Was as Close," 157–84; Berlin and Rowland, *Families and Freedom,* 48–50.

58. 1870 Florida census, Jefferson County (population schedule); Leon County marriage records, "Register of Marriage Licenses (Colored), 1865–1868," 236, Book 10; Canter Brown Jr., "'Hopes I Cherished,'" 3–4, 35–36; *Genealogical Records,* 69–70; *TDT,* July 20, 1923; Polk County marriage records, "Marriage License Record for Colored Persons," 2.

59. *AS-FN,* 107–19, 347–52; Blakey, Lainhart, and Stephens, *Rose Cottage Chronicles,* 94.

60. Deborah Gray White, "Female Slaves," 113; *Ar'n't I a Woman?,* 91–141; Rawick, *Sundown to Sunup,* 39, 199–210; Owens, *This Species of Property,* 39–41; Webber, *Deep like the Rivers,* 152; Mann, "Slavery, Sharecropping, and Sexual Inequality," 283–85.

61. *AS-FN,* 33, 336.

62. Rogers and Clark, *Croom Family,* 113–28; Pine Hill Plantation Papers, 72; John Finlayson will, February 23, 1865, Book B, 155–58, Jefferson County will records.

63. Murat, *United States of North America,* 98; Rivers, "Baptist Minister James Page," 43–54; Lykes, *Gift of Heritage,* 10.

64. Laura Randall to Mother, November 19, 1827, Wirt Papers; Shofner, *Jefferson County,* 130; John Gamble diary, passim; Blakey, Lainhart, and Stephens, *Rose Cottage Chronicles,* 93; Coles, "Florida Diaries," 478–97; Daniel H. Wiggins diaries, entry of May 31, 1841.

65. *Pensacola Floridian,* March 23, 1822; *TSF,* May 21, 1840; *JC,* April 2, 1835; *TF,* May 11, 1833.

66. Murat, *United States of North America,* 97; Philip D. Morgan, *Slave Counterpoint,* 536.

67. *AS-FN,* 94–95, 178; *JFR,* January 4, 1851; *JFN,* July 3, October 30, 1852.

68. Phillips and Glunt, *Florida Plantation Records,* 110; *AS- FN,* 95; Kealing, *African Methodism in Texas,* 199–203; Charles S. Long, *A.M.E. Church in Florida,* 110–11; *Jacksonville Florida Times-Union,* February 27, 1896, March 4, 1896; *Tampa Morning Tribune,* March 3, 1896, January 5, 1901. After many years of separation former slave Harrison Beckett claimed his father, born in Florida and taken to Texas, returned to Florida ten years after freedom came to find out about his kinfolks and the real name of his family. Former slave Robert Solomon recalled that his father went back to Florida and Georgia to locate members of his wife's family. See *SN,* vol. 3, pt. 1, pp. 56, 208.

69. Gutman, *Black Family,* 260; Blassingame, *Slave Community,* 103.

6. Religion and Community

1. Hall, "African Religious Retentions," 48; Rawick, *Sundown to Sunup,* 39. See also the following studies that focus on African American religion among antebellum American slaves: Raboteau, *Slave Religion;* Boles, *Masters and Slaves;* Blassingame, *Slave Community,* 130–48; Mathews, *Religion in the Old South,* 185–236; Genovese, *Roll, Jordan, Roll,* 159–284; Hall, "Do, Lord, Remember Me."

2. Joyner, "World of the Plantation Slaves," 73–81; Berlin, "Slaves' Changing World," 57–59; Rivers, "Madison County," 238; "Slavery and the Political Economy," 8.

3. Pine Hill Plantation Papers; Eppes, *Negro of the Old South,* 3–4; Amon DeLaughter journal, passim; Murat, *United States of North America,* 97–98; Wyatt-Brown, *Yankee Saints and Southern Sinners,* 165; William Bellamy will, April 12, 1851, William Bailey Jr. will, July 16, 1862, Jefferson County will records, Book B, 34–36, 160–61; Rivers, "Slavery in Microcosm," 244; "Dignity and Importance," 415. Anderson Peeler, a white minister from the Florida Conference of the Methodist Episcopal Church, South, preached to bond servants at Aucilla, and John Gamble encouraged his slaves to listen to white ministers. *TF&J,* January 11, 1854; John Gamble diary, passim.

4. "Diary of Joshua Nichols Glenn," 137; Thrift, *Florida Circuit Rider,* 29–33; Canter Brown Jr., *Florida's Black Public Officials,* 1–69.

5. Buckingham Smith will, April 17, 1869, St. Johns County will and probate

records; "Diary of Joshua Nichols Glenn," 137. See also the diary excerpts of a Massachusetts traveler who witnessed blacks and whites worshiping together in a St. Augustine Catholic church. Thompson, "Massachusetts Traveler," 129–41.

6. Berlin, "Slaves' Changing World," 58; *AS-FN*, 35, 98, 166, 252.

7. Blakey, Lainhart, and Stephens, *Rose Cottage Chronicles*, 89–90; *AS-FN*, 4, 178.

8. George M. Foster, *Methodist Episcopal Church in Ocala*, 5, 12–13; J. Randall Stanley, *History of Gadsden County*, 63; Pennington, "Episcopal Church in Florida," 3–17; Cushman, *Goodly Heritage*; Browning, "History of Concord Baptist Church"; Provence, "Historical Sketches"; Joiner, *History of Florida Baptists*; J. Randall Stanley, *History of Jackson County*, 82; Rosser, *History of Florida Baptists*, 28; Brooks, *History Highlights of Florida Methodism*, 30; Hall, "Do, Lord, Remember Me," 302–31; "Yonder Come Day," 411–32; McIlwain, *Presbyterianism in West Florida*, 41; Kirk, "Southern Presbyterian Church in Florida," 55.

9. Boles, *Black Southerners*, 157–62; Rhodes, *At First*, 35; *AS-FN*, 35.

10. The act of incorporation of the First Presbyterian Church in Tallahassee contained an article reserving the gallery for blacks. *AS-FN*, 98, 165, 252, 352; McCord, "First Hundred Years," 27; Oliver O. Howard to his wife, March 29, 1857, Oliver O. Howard Papers.

11. Rice, "Negro Religion," 5–6; *New York Globe*, August 18, 1883; *130th Anniversary*; Fennell, "Blacks in Jacksonville," 62–67; Browning, "History of Concord Baptist Church," 6–7; Canter Brown Jr., *Florida's Peace River Frontier*, 102; *Tampa before the Civil War*, 128, 151–52; Roger Rice Landers, "Freedmen's Bureau."

12. Thomas Randall to William Wirt, April 13, 1828, William Wirt to Laura and Thomas Randall, n.d., 1828, Wirt Papers; Lewis, "Bartow, West Bartow," 51–52.

13. Hall, "Black and White Christians," 85–86; Maloney, *Sketch*, 35; "Tampa Church," in *Negro in Florida's Cities*, n.p.; Walls, *African Methodist Episcopal Zion Church*, 202; Brady, *Things Remembered*, 15; *Guide to Supplementary Vital Statistics*, 2:434, 442, 498, 552, 580; Canter Brown Jr., "'Hopes I Cherished,'" 3–4.

14. *AS-FN*, 35; Boles, *Black Southerners*, 157–58.

15. *AS-FN*, 97–98, 252–53, 352–53; Shippe, *Bishop Whipple's Southern Diary*, 21; Boles, *Black Southerners*, 157; "Diary of Joshua Nichols Glenn," 156.

16. Rhodes, *At First*, 25–26; Boles, *Black Southerners*, 158; Bryant, *Indian Springs*, 59; Hall, "Black and White Christians," 85.

17. *AS-FN*, 165, 214; Kingsley, *Treatise*, 14.

18. Hall, "Black and White Christians," 81; *AS-FN*, 166; Davis, *Nat Turner*

before the Bar of Judgment, 4–10, 43, 60–76, 130–73; Hall, "Religious Symbolism of the Iron Pot," 125–29.

19. *AS-FN,* 35, 97–98, 252; Rivers, "Troublesome Property," 107.

20. *AS-FN,* 35, 166, 215; *SAR,* October 21, 1934.

21. *AS-FN,* 166–67, 360.

22. Charles S. Long, *A.M.E. Church in Florida,* 55–57.

23. *AS-FN,* 35, 245, 353; Oliver O. Howard to Lizzie Howard, July 22, 1857, Oliver O. Howard Papers. See also Raboteau, *Slave Religion.*

24. Kingsley, *Treatise,* 14–15; Margaret Murray May diary, 78, 116.

25. Berlin, "Slaves' Changing World," 58; Baptist, "Migration of Planters to Antebellum Florida," 527–44; Peter H. Wood, *Black Majority,* 167–81; Philip D. Morgan, *Slave Counterpoint,* 631–58; Schafer, "'Yellow Silk Ferret,'" 75–79.

26. *Tallahassee Weekly Floridian,* May 22, 1877; *Fernandina Florida Mirror,* September 16, November 25, 1882; Theodore Bissell to Harrison Reed, April 1, 1864, Florida Direct Tax Commission Records, RG 59, NA; Hall, "African Religious Retentions," 44; U.S. Decennial Censuses, 1830 Florida census (population schedule); Du Bois, *Suppression of Atlantic Slave Trade; Harper's Weekly,* June 2, 1860, 344–46; Mooney, *American Naval Fighting Ships,* 4:408; Silverstone, *Warships of the Civil War Navies,* 93; Holder, "At the Dry Tortugas," 183; *New York Times,* March 13, 1862; Solomon and Erhart, "Race and Civil War," 327–29.

27. Genovese, *Roll, Jordan, Roll,* 189–90; Heyrman, *Southern Cross,* 46–52, 217–25; Montgomery, *Under Their Own Vine,* 19–25.

28. *AS-FN,* 245; Phillips and Glunt, *Florida Plantation Records,* 31; Rivers, "Baptist Minister James Page," 47; Joiner, *History of Florida Baptists,* 17. Some of the interactions between blacks and whites in one particular Baptist church can be found in the Pigeon Creek Baptist Church minutes, entry of July 20, 1822; Hurston, "Negro in Florida"; Lomax, "Negro Baptizings," 386–90; Baldwin, "Festivity and Celebration," 391–98.

29. Margaret Murray May diary, 116.

30. Kingsley, *Treatise,* 13.

31. Eppes, *Negro of the Old South,* 175.

32. Ellen Call Long, *Florida Breezes,* 181.

33. *AS-FN,* 213, 353.

34. Ibid., 4–6; Amon DeLaughter journal, passim; Mulira, "Case of Voodoo," 34–68; Creel, "Gullah Attitudes," 69–97; *Peculiar People.*

35. Cannon, "Voodoo Death," 169–81; Eppes, *Negro of the Old South,* 98.

36. The picture is in the FSA collection. See also Philip D. Morgan, *Slave Counterpoint,* 642.

37. *JFR,* June 3, 1851.

38. *AS-FN,* 214.

39. Rivers, "Baptist Minister James Page," 43–54; "Troublesome Property," 107–9; Joyner, *Down by the Riverside*, 169–71; Berlin, "Slaves' Changing World," 59; J. Randall Stanley, *History of Jackson County*, 82; Phillips and Glunt, *Florida Plantation Records*, 31; *New York Globe*, August 18, 1883.

40. Rivers, "Baptist Minister James Page," 43–54; "Troublesome Property," 107–9; Genovese, *A Consuming Fire*, 25; Chatham, "Plantation Slavery in Middle Florida," 63–65.

41. Rivers, "Baptist Minister James Page," 43–54; "Troublesome Property," 107–9; Genovese, *A Consuming Fire*, 25; Chatham, "Plantation Slavery in Middle Florida," 63–65; *AS-FN*, 244–45.

42. *AS-FN*, 165–66; Amon DeLaughter journal, October 15, 1854, 10; Woolridge, "Slave Preacher," 28–37.

43. *AS-FN*, 245.

44. The overseer of the mill bondsmen at El Destino, Jonathan Roberson, had allowed slaves to be baptized by James Page several years prior to the arrival of D. N. Moxley in 1854. Phillips and Glunt, *Florida Plantation Records*, 31, 108, 118–19.

45. Kingsley, *Treatise*, 13–15.

46. *130th Anniversary*, 3; Barbara Ann Richardson, "History of Blacks in Jacksonville," 20–21.

47. Hall, "African Religious Retentions," 42–70.

7. MATERIAL CONDITIONS AND PHYSICAL TREATMENT

1. Lee H. Warner, *Free Men*, 44–49; *JFT-U*, July 27, 29, 1883; *Tampa Journal*, December 8, 1888; Canter Brown Jr., *African Americans on the Tampa Bay Frontier*, 29; *Agriculture of the United States in 1860*, 225; *Statistics of the United States (Including Mortality, Property, etc.) in 1860*, 340–41; Ellis and Rogers, *Favored Land*, 38.

2. Schafer, *Anna Kingsley*, 19–42.

3. Randolph B. Campbell, *Empire for Slavery*, 134–35; Joyner, "World of the Plantation Slaves," 85–88; Leslie A. Thompson, *Manual*, 511; Denham, *Rogue's Paradise*, 129; Duval, *Compilation*, 223; Bates, "Legal Status," 166; Edwin L. Williams Jr., "Negro Slavery in Florida."

4. Julia Floyd Smith, *Slavery and Plantation Growth*, 80; *AS- FN*, 165, 330; Kingsley B. Gibbs journal, entry of December 25, 1841, 24; Rivers, "Troublesome Property," 104–27.

5. U.S. Decennial Censuses, 1850 and 1860 Florida censuses (agricultural schedules); Phillips and Glunt, *Florida Plantation Records*, 62–63; Stephen Harvell interview, 2, box 7, folder 3, Florida Negro Papers; *AS-FN*, 335–36, 356–57.

6. Boles, *Black Southerners*, 85; Denham, *Rogue's Paradise*, 129; Wyatt-Brown, *Honor and Violence*, 12, 16–17, 22, 187–206.

7. *TF&J*, December 4, 1852; *TFS*, December 7, 1852; Jefferson County circuit court minutes, Book A, 455; Amon DeLaughter journal, 113; *TFP*, May 5, 12, 26, 1860; Boles, *Black Southerners*, 88; Denham, *Rogue's Paradise*, 129, 136.

8. Julia Floyd Smith, *Slavery and Plantation Growth*, 80; Boles, *Black Southerners*, 88; Blassingame, *Slave Community*, 158–59; Franklin and Moss, *From Slavery to Freedom*, 130–31; Genovese, *Roll, Jordan, Roll*, 544–45; Shofner, *Jefferson County*, 128–29; *Jackson County*, 150; *AS-FN*, 165; Amon DeLaughter journal, 111; Kingsley B. Gibbs journal, 7–22; Kingsley, *Treatise*, 14–16.

9. Elizabeth Wirt to Laura W. Randall, November 13, 1827, Thomas Randall to William Wirt, March 20, April 7, 17, 1833, Wirt Papers; Abbey, "El Destino and Chemonie Plantations," 292–329.

10. Blakey, Lainhart, and Stephens, *Rose Cottage Chronicles*, 226; Stephen Harvell interview, 3, box 7, folder 3, Florida Negro Papers; Kingsley B. Gibbs journal, entry of December 25, 1841, 24; Rivers, "Troublesome Property," 115; Amon DeLaughter journal, 48.

11. Sarah Brown Bryant interview, box 7, folder 3, Florida Negro Papers; *TDT*, July 27, 1923; Hawes, "One-Time Slave."

12. *TDT*, April 17, 1924; Boles, *Black Southerners*, 91–92; Shofner, *Jefferson County*, 129.

13. Sidney Walker Martin, *Florida during the Territorial Days*, 113; *SAR*, October 12, 1934; *AS-FN*, 25, 58, 250.

14. Stephen Harvell interview, 2, box 7, folder 3, Florida Negro Papers; *AS-FN*, 213.

15. *AS-FN*, 33; Kingsley B. Gibbs journal, entry of December 25, 1841, 24; Kingsley, *Treatise*, 12; Berlin, "Slaves' Changing World," 53; Phillips and Glunt, *Florida Plantation Records*, 48.

16. *AS-FN*, 33, 250, 338, 356–57; *SAR*, October 12, 1934; Boles, *Black Southerners*, 89.

17. Blakey, Lainhart, and Stephens, *Rose Cottage Chronicles*, 50; *TF&J*, October 22, 1859: Leon County circuit court minutes, Book 6, 295; Denham, *Rogue's Paradise*, 137.

18. Daniel H. Wiggins diary, entry of April 17, 1842; *SAR*, October 21, 1934; Coles, "Florida Diaries," 496; Singleton, "Archaeology of Slave Life," 172; McKee, "Plantation Food Supply," 111; Reitz, Gibbs, and Rathbun, "Archaeological Subsistence on Coastal Plantations," 163–91; Kingsley, *Treatise*, 14; Amon DeLaughter journal, 153.

19. *AS-FN*, 97; John Lewis will, February 6, 1855, file no. 1275, Duval County probate records; Schene, "Robert and John Grattan Gamble," 61–73; *SAEFH*, March 22, 1823, April 3, 1834; Schafer, *Anna Kingsley*, 20; Blakey, Lainhart, and Stephens, *Rose Cottage Chronicles*, 211; Scarborough Letters, 15; *AS-FN*, 329; Amon DeLaughter journal, 15, 24, 46, 54, 76; Phillips and Glunt, *Florida Plan-*

tation Records, 174; Laura H. Randall to Mother, November 26, 1827, Wirt Papers.

20. Amon DeLaughter journal, 16, 60; Louis Goldsborough to Elizabeth Gamble Wirt, January 2, 1833, Louis Goldsborough to William Wirt, February, 1834, Louis Goldsborough to wife, August 31, 1855, Louis Goldsborough Papers; Joshua Hoyet Frier journal, 35–36; Kingsley, *Treatise,* 14; Blakey, Lainhart, and Stephens, *Rose Cottage Chronicles,* 233–34.

21. Laura Randall journal, entry of November 22, 1827, Wirt Papers; *AS-FN,* 58–59, 250, 347–48.

22. *AS-FN,* 244, 338, 355.

23. *Southern Cultivator,* May 1857, 140–42, June 1857, 144, August 1857, 237–43; *De Bow's Review,* January 1858, 63–64, November 1858, 571–72, April 1860, 597–99, July 1860, 112–15; Amon DeLaughter journal, 104.

24. Julia Floyd Smith, *Slavery and Plantation Growth,* 89–90; Amon DeLaughter journal, 104; Eppes, *Through Some Eventful Years,* 55; Singleton, "Archaeology of Slave Life," 155–75; Schafer, "'Yellow Silk Ferret,'" 89.

25. Julia Floyd Smith, *Slavery and Plantation Growth,* 87.

26. *AS-FN,* 32.

27. Ibid., 259.

28. Ibid., 178, 355.

29. Phillips and Glunt, *Florida Plantation Records,* 47–48; Rare Slave Papers, Black Archives, Research Center, and Museum.

30. Julia Floyd Smith, *Slavery and Plantation Growth,* 90; Berlin, "Slaves' Changing World," 48–49; *Slaves without Masters,* 252; John Brown, *Slave Life in Georgia,* 191; Steward, *Twenty-Two Years a Slave,* 19; Vlach, "Plantation Landscapes," 21–50; Rare Slave Papers, Black Archives, Research Center, and Museum; *Southern Cultivator,* January 1856, 17; Blassingame, *Slave Community,* 254; *Slave Testimony,* 278, 294; Shofner, *Jackson County,* 150; U.S. Decennial Censuses, 1860 Florida census (population schedules). See also Griffin W. Holland Papers.

31. Phillips and Glunt, *Florida Plantation Records,* 47–48; Blakey, Lainhart, and Stephens, *Rose Cottage Chronicles,* 52; Boles, *Black Southerners,* 86; Rare Slave Papers, Black Archives, Research Center, and Museum.

32. *AS-FN,* 356.

33. Ibid., 339, 350, 356.

34. Ibid., 360; Blakey, Lainhart, and Stephens, *Rose Cottage Chronicles.* 50; Murat, *United States of North America,* 98.

35. Julia Floyd Smith, *Slavery and Plantation Growth,* 80; Boles, *Black Southerners,* 86; Joyner, "World of the Plantation Slaves," 55–56, 70; Deborah Gray White, "Female Slaves," 108–10; Blakey, Lainhart, and Stephens, *Rose Cottage Chronicles,* 240. See also Shane White and Graham White, *Stylin,* 5–36.

36. Boles, *Black Southerners*, 86–87; Rabun Scarborough to sister, February 14, 1862, Scarborough Letters, 24; *AS-FN*, 59, 330; Julia Floyd Smith, *Slavery and Plantation Growth*, 82.

37. *SAEFH*, March 1, 1823; *TSF*, May 21, 1840; *TF&A*, July 13, 1830; *TF&J*, February 20, 1858.

38. Rabun Scarborough to Sister (his wife), October 7, 1861, Scarborough Letters, 9; *AS-FN*, 339; Amon DeLaughter journal, December 12, 1854, November 5, 1857, 13, 72; Ossian B. Hart to Catharine S. Hart, June 5, 1863, Dena E. Snodgrass Collection; Canter Brown Jr., *Ossian Bingley Hart*, 126–28.

39. *AS-FN*, 59, 181.

40. Rogers and Clark, *Croom Family*, 124–25; Thomas Randall to William Wirt, April 13, October 14, 1828, Elizabeth Wirt to Laura Randall, October 12, 1837, Louis Goldsborough to William Wirt, February 1, 1834, Ellen McCormick to Elizabeth Wirt, April 15, 1842, Louisa A. Wirt to Elizabeth Wirt, July 14, 1844, Wirt Papers; Amon DeLaughter journal, 48, 71, 75, 95–96, 110; Blakey, Lainhart, and Stephens, *Rose Cottage Chronicles*, 75, 119, 150–51, 156, 197–98, 225; Phillips and Glunt, *Florida Plantation Records*, 79, 95–96; Kingsley B. Gibbs journal, entries of September 1, 1841, June 19, 1842, April 30, 1843; Charles W. Bannerman diaries, entries of October 1, 1846, September 11, 23, 27, October 9, 1847.

41. Amon DeLaughter journal, 48, 71, 75, 95–96, 110.

42. Ibid., 94; *TF&A*, March 2, 1830; Julia Floyd Smith, *Slavery and Plantation Growth*, 97–98; John Hollingsworth diary, passim; John M. W. Davidson physician's journal, passim; Phillips and Glunt, *Florida Plantation Records*, 93–96; Amon DeLaughter journal, 25; Pine Hill Plantation Papers, 5; Hammond, *Medical Profession*, 400, 445–46, 502–3, 691–92; unlike Charles Manigault, who refused to spend money on medical care for his enslaved blacks at Gowrie, a rice plantation in Georgia, slaveholders in Florida would generally pay for the services of medical doctors when bond servants were seriously ill or injured, see Dusinberre, *Them Dark Days*, 84–121; Richard H. Steckel, "Slave Mortality," 86–114.

43. Genovese, *Roll, Jordan, Roll*, 62; Amon DeLaughter journal, 58, 93–94, 117; Joyner, "World of the Plantation Slaves," 58; Thomas Randall to William Wirt, April 13, 1828, Wirt Papers; Phillips and Glunt, *Florida Plantation Records*, 87–90.

44. *AS-FN*, 181, 353; Joyner, "World of the Plantation Slaves," 58–59; Deborah Gray White, "Female Slaves," 112.

45. Bates, "Preliminary Study"; David Y. Thomas, "Free Negro," 335–45; Leslie A. Thompson, *Manual*, 511; Duval, *Compilation*, 223; Denham, *Rogue's Paradise*, 121.

46. de Castlenau, "Essay on Middle Florida," 240; Murat, *United States of North America*, 96; Ellen Call Long, *Florida Breezes*, 164; *SAR*, October 21,

1934; Canter Brown Jr., "Race Relations in Territorial Florida," 296; Ellen McCormick to Catharine Randall, January 29, 1843, Wirt Papers.

47. Phillips and Glunt, *Florida Plantation Records*, 110.

48. Ibid., 39, 114, 165–66; *SAR*, October 21, 1934; Sarah Brown Bryant interview, box 7, folder 3, Florida Negro Papers; *TDT,* July 27, 1923; Hawes, "One-Time Slave."

49. Phillips and Glunt, *Florida Plantation Records*, 35, 94; Amon De-Laughter journal, 24, 48.

50. Phillips and Glunt, *Florida Plantation Records*, 259.

51. Sarah Brown Bryant interview; *TDT,* July 27, 1923; Hawes, "One-Time Slave."

52. See, e.g., *SAFH*, May 7, 1834, April 1, 1835; *TFW,* October 6, 1838; *TF&A,* July 30, 1830; *TSF,* September 1, 1843; *TF&J,* January 22, December 30, 1851, January 29, 1853.

53. *AS-FN,* 258, 347–48; *PG*, May 20, 1837.

54. Groene, *Ante-Bellum Tallahassee,* 112–13; *Territory v. Peter Williamson* (1829), Escambia County criminal case files; Denham, *Rogue's Paradise*, 129–30, 138.

55. *TSF,* April 20, September 1, 1843; affidavit of Duncan M. Bryant, March 4, 1856, in *State v. Henry W. Williams* (1856), Florida Comptroller Vouchers—Criminal Prosecutions, RG 350, series 565, folder 8, FSA; Leon County superior and circuit court minutes, Book 4, 61, 65.

56. *Territory v. Peter Williamson* criminal case file; *PG,* March 10, 1829; *Tallahassee Florida Advocate,* March 21, 1829; *SAFH,* April 8, 1829; Escambia County superior court minutes, Book 1, 417, 419; *St. Augustine Ancient City,* July 30, 1853; Orange County minutes of the circuit court, Book A, 79; *Territory v. William H. Baker* (1831), Escambia County criminal case files; *TSF,* April 20, 1843; Leon County superior and circuit court minutes, Book 4, 61, 65; William P. DuVal to William Wilson, November 28, 1829, Florida, Territorial Auditor Vouchers, RG 352, ser. 584, box 1, folder 2, FSA; *Key West Register and Commercial Advertiser,* February 19, 1829; *TFS,* June 4, 1844; Pine Hill Plantation Papers.

57. *Sarah McNeil v. Henry Wilson* (1821), Escambia County civil case files; *PG,* November 27, 1830; Escambia County superior court minutes, Book 1, 530–31.

58. Genovese, *Roll, Jordan, Roll,* 27, 37–43; Canter Brown Jr., "Race Relations in Territorial Florida," 287; Rivers, "Dignity and Importance," 404–30; "Slavery in Microcosm," 235–45; "Madison County," 233–44; "Slavery and the Political Economy," 1–19.

59. Denham, *Rogue's Paradise,* 130; Wyatt-Brown, *Honor and Violence,* 187–213; Genovese, *Roll, Jordan, Roll,* 40.

8. Social Interaction between Whites and Blacks

1. See Genovese, *Roll, Jordan, Roll*; *World the Slaveholders Made*; Blassingame, *Slave Community*, 284–322; Owens, *This Species of Property*; Kolchin, *American Slavery*, 70–105, 118–27; Joyner, *Down by the Riverside*, 52–57; Deborah Gray White, *Ar'n't I a Woman?* 62–90; Denham, *Rogue's Paradise*, 120–40; Rivers, "Troublesome Property," 112–22.

2. Thomas Randall to William Wirt, July 11, September 22, 1828, Thomas Randall to Madam [Elizabeth Wirt], n. d., Thomas Randall to William Wirt, May 4, 1831, Wirt Papers; John Gamble diary, passim; Schene, "Robert and John Grattan Gamble," 61–73; Shofner, *Jefferson County*, 120–48; Julia Floyd Smith, *Slavery and Plantation Growth*, 38, 67, 87, 124, 127–28.

3. James W. Bryant to Tivie [Octavia Bryant], October 23, 1859. Bryant-Stephens Family Papers; Blakey, Lainhart, and Stephens, *Rose Cottage Chronicles*, 29; *JN*, March 6, 1846.

4. Brown, *Ossian Bingley Hart*, 13–40; *JC*, January 1, 1835.

5. Ellen McCormick to mother [Elizabeth Wirt], October 12, 1842, Wirt Papers.

6. Rabun Scarborough to sister, October 7, November 8, 15, 18, 29, 1861, January 13, 1862, Scarborough Letters; Blakey, Lainhart, and Stephens, *Rose Cottage Chronicles*, 87, 90–93, 160–61, 168.

7. Laura Randall to mother, November 26, 1827, February 9, 1828, Wirt Papers; Kingsley, *Treatise*, 16.

8. Phillips and Glunt, *Florida Plantation Records*, 71, 74, 111–13, 115–16.

9. Henry Wirt to Elizabeth Wirt, October 20, 1843, Wirt Papers; Phillips and Glunt, *Florida Plantation Records*, 331–32.

10. Louisa A. Wirt to Elizabeth Wirt, July 14, 1844, Thomas Randall to William Wirt, February 10, 1828, Wirt Papers; Phillips and Glunt, *Florida Plantation Records*, 128–30; Canter Brown Jr., *Ossian Bingley Hart*, 126.

11. Schafer, "Freedom Was as Close," 157–84; Pine Hill Plantation Papers, 79; Canter Brown Jr., "Race Relations in Territorial Florida," 304; Coles, "'Fields of Glory,'" 300.

12. Rucker, "Blackwater and Yellow Pine," 2:597; *PG*, August 15, 1835, October 14, 1837; Polk, "Pensacola Commerce and Industry," 62–63; Starobin, *Industrial Slavery*, 25–26; Phillips and Glunt, *Florida Plantation Records*, 98; *AS-FN*, 98; Rogers and Clark, *Croom Family*, 121–22; Canter Brown Jr., "'Hopes I Cherished,'" 1–36; Rivers, "Baptist Minister James Page," 43–54.

13. *AS-FN*, 95–96.

14. Ibid.; Rivers, "Baptist Minister James Page," 43–54.

15. Blakey, Lainhart, and Stephens, *Rose Cottage Chronicles*, 67.

16. *AS-FN*, 96, 213, 243, 330; *SAR*, October 21, 1934.

17. Deborah Gray White, "Female Slaves," 101–2; Hine, Hine, and Harrold, *Odyssey*, 133–34.

18. Phillips and Glunt, *Florida Plantation Records*, 62–63, 90–91, 123–24, 160–61; Blakey, Lainhart, and Stephens, *Rose Cottage Chronicles*, 123.

19. *AS-FN*, 242, 257. By will, some slaveholders gave away children of slave women before the children were conceived. See Jesse Handley will, September 4, 1844, Book A, 8–11, Alachua County will records; James H. McArvers will, March 13, 1842, Book A, 150–52, Gadsden County will records; John Lipscomb will, August 27, 1856, Jeremiah D. Reid will, April 17, 1856, Book B, 88–95, Nancy DeLaughter will, June 29, 1864, Book C, 32–41, 89–91, Madison County will records.

20. *TF&J*, March 10, 21, 1860; Amon DeLaughter journal, May 4, 1860, 112; Denham, *Rogue's Paradise*, 136; Deborah Gray White, "Female Slaves," 102–5.

21. Muse, "Negro History," 2; Canter Brown Jr., *African Americans on the Tampa Bay Frontier*, 25–26.

22. Thomas Williams to Moddie Williams, August 22–29, 1857, Thomas Williams Papers; Brown, *Florida's Peace River Frontier*, 140; *AS-FN*, 95.

23. *Seventh Census of the United States*, 1850, 400; Wyatt- Brown, *Honor and Violence*, 105.

24. Williamson, *New People*, 2, 15; Schafer, "Neither Freemen nor Slaves," 599; Hill, "George J. F. Clarke," 197–253; Canter Brown Jr., "Race Relations in Territorial Florida," 290–91; Johnson and Roark, *No Chariot Let Down; Black Masters*.

25. Schafer, "Neither Freemen nor Slaves," 599; Hill, "George J. F. Clarke," 197–253; *SAFH*, March 25, 1829; *James F. Clarke v. Francis J. Avice*, case file no. 103, box 129, St. Johns County superior court records; Jane L. Landers, "Black Society in Spanish St. Augustine," 126–27; *SAFH*, May 12, 1830; May, "Zephaniah Kingsley," 145–59; Canter Brown Jr., "Race Relations in Territorial Florida," 291–92; *Ossian Bingley Hart*, 88, 119, 122, 127; *George W. Clarke v. State of Florida*, January 12, 1846, file no. 58, box 98, St. Johns County circuit court records; Hill, "George J. F. Clarke," 197–253; *TP* 24:800–802.

26. Simpson, Ellen Simpson Collection, "Tales Our Mother Told," 35, 39, 45; Morton, "Recollections of the Morton Family," 1; *Pensacola News-Journal*, May 14, 1972; Nix, "John Hunt," 6; Joseph Forsyth will, Forsyth day book, and Forsyth ledger book in Forsyth Family Papers; Jackson Morton biographical materials in Jackson Morton Papers.

27. Hanna, *Prince in Their Midst*, 229; Canter Brown Jr., "'Hopes I Cherished,'" 2–3; Amon DeLaughter journal, December 25, 1855. This phrase could not be misinterpreted to mean a runaway slave because DeLaughter clearly noted when bond servants absconded by using the term *runaway* or by noting that he gave the fugitive a good "chase." Moreover, it is highly unlikely that he would join a patrol party on Christmas night in Alabama.

28. Mohammad, "Slave's Life in Marion," 39–40; *AS-FN*, 167.

29. Stone, "Profile of Lloyd Davis"; *Wauchula Herald-Advocate*, January 10, 1991; Canter Brown Jr., *Florida's Peace River Frontier*, 102–3, 113, 319, 337; Westergard and Van Landingham, *Parker and Blount in Florida*, 83–89, 160–63.

30. Stone, "Profile of Lloyd Davis"; Canter Brown Jr., *Fort Meade*, 53, 77, 130.

31. May, "Zephaniah Kingsley," 145–59; Schafer, *Anna Kingsley*; Phelts, *American Beach*, 15; Zephaniah Kingsley will, file no. 1202, Duval County probate records; Glover, "Zephaniah Kingsley."

32. Isaiah D. Hart will, September 27, 1861, file no. 900-D, Duval County probate records; Canter Brown Jr., *Ossian Bingley Hart*, 119.

33. Grismer, *Tampa*, 162; Brady, *Things Remembered*, 10, 24.

34. Isaiah D. Hart will, September 27, 1861, file no. 900-D, Francis Richard II will, March 6, 1826, file no. 1756-D, Zephaniah Kingsley will, September 25, 1843, file no. 1203-D, John Brown will, October 14, 1835, file no. 79-D, Duval County probate records; Canter Brown Jr., *Ossian Bingley Hart*, 119–21; Phelts, *American Beach*, 25; Schafer, *Anna Kingsley*; George J. F. Clarke will, August 28, 1834, St. Johns County will records; Hill, "George J. F. Clarke," 197–235; *JN*, March 5, 1847; Schafer, "Neither Freemen nor Slaves," 593–95.

35. Phillips and Glunt, *Florida Plantation Records*, 60; Abbey, "El Destino and Chemonie Plantations," 3–46; Julia Floyd Smith, *Slavery and Plantation Growth*, 60.

36. Mohammad, "Slave's Life in Marion," 38; Denham, *Rogue's Paradise*, 133–34; Flanigan, "Criminal Procedure," 537–64; "Criminal Law."

37. Jacob Bryan died intestate, but see other items in his probate papers, February 28, 1848, file no. 99-D, Duval County probate records; *JN*, December 10, 1847, June 3, September 23, 1848; Mohammad, "Slave's Life in Marion," 38.

38. Amon DeLaughter journal, 13, 89; Berlin, "Slaves' Changing World," 52–56; Joyner, "World of the Plantation Slaves," 81–83; *Down by the Riverside*, 131, 139–40; Deborah Gray White, *Ar'n't I a Woman?*, 27–61; *TP* 26:916.

39. Thomas Frederick Davis, "Pioneer Florida," 221; McGaughy, "Squaw Kissing War," 180; Blakey, Lainhart, and Stephens, *Rose Cottage Chronicles*, 81; *AS-FN*, 330; Groene, *Ante-Bellum Tallahassee*, 149.

40. Escambia County superior court minutes, Book 1, 326; grand jury presentment, November 15, 1849, Gadsden County grand jury records; *TF*, June 5, 1832.

41. Phillips and Glunt, *Florida Plantation Records*, 60; Abbey, "El Destino and Chemonie Plantations," 3–46; Daniel H. Wiggins diary, entry of February 2, 1842; Coles, "Florida Diaries," 488–90; *PG*, April 19, 1851; Rucker, "Blackwater and Yellow Pine," 2:592.

42. Escambia County superior court minutes, Book 1, 326; Denham,

Rogue's Paradise, 117; Dodd, "Horse Racing," 20–25; Gadsden County deed records, Book A, 329; Rivers, "Slavery and the Political Economy," 9.

43. *AS-FN*, 97, 244; Groene, *Ante-Bellum Tallahassee*, 149; Julia Floyd Smith, *Slavery and Plantation Growth*, 94; Housewright, *Music and Dance in Florida*, 273.

9. SOCIAL INTERACTION AMONG BLACKS

1. Blassingame, *Slave Community*, 105–6, 147–48; Rawick, *Sundown to Sunup*, 14–29, 77–94; Genovese, *Roll, Jordan, Roll*, 209–84; Owens, *This Species of Property*, 136–213; Escott, *Slavery Remembered*, 36–70; Webber, *Deep like the Rivers*; Stampp, *Peculiar Institution*; Elkins, *Slavery*.

2. William C. Johnson, "Trickster on Trial," 52–71; Randolph B. Campbell, *Empire for Slavery*, 174–76; Julia Floyd Smith, *Slavery and Plantation Growth*, 30, 94, 210; Eppes, *Negro of the Old South*, 7–20; Blassingame, *Slave Community*, 105–9; Genovese, *Roll, Jordan, Roll*, 443–584; Rawick, *Sundown to Sunup*, 77–93; Owens, *This Species of Property*, 164–81; Joyner, *Down by the Riverside*, 130–40; "World of the Plantation Slaves," 81–86; Deborah Gray White, "Female Slaves," 118–19.

3. U.S. Decennial Censuses, 1840, 1850, and 1860 Florida censuses; *Seventh Census of the United States*, 1850, 396–97; *Population of the United States in 1860*, 50–51; *Quincy Sentinel*, September 18, 1840.

4. *SAEFH*, January 25, 1825; *Tallahassee Florida Intelligencer*, October 6, 1826; *JC*, August 6, 1835.

5. Hall, "African Religious Retentions," 45; *TF*, November 1, 1845; *TFP*, November 17, 1860.

6. Rivers, "Troublesome Property," 113; Phillips and Glunt, *Florida Plantation Records*, 563, 566; *TFS*, June 3, 1855.

7. See, e.g., Jesse Potts will, August 4, 1829, Book C, 245–46, Gadsden County will records; *SAEFH*, March 1, June 14, 1823; *SAFH&SD*, October 18, 1839, May 8, 1840, August 20, 1844; *Tallahassee Florida Advocate*, December 8, 1829, May 26, 1838; *TF*, May 11, 1833, August 8, 1834, June 15, 1839, May 27, 1841; *TFS*, April 21, 1846; *Palatka Whig Banner*, July 28, 1846; *JFN*, May 15, 1846, October 12, 14, 28, November 4, 1854, May 19, 1855; *SAN*, October 18, 1839, June 19, 1840; *TFW*, May 5, 1838; *PG*, August 17, 1822, October 14, 1828; *JEFA*, September 1, 1840; Amon DeLaughter journal, 10, 78; Joyner, *Down by the Riverside*, 217–22; Phillips and Glunt, *Florida Plantation Records*, 561, 567; Cody, "No 'Absalom,'" 563–96; "Naming, Kinship, and Estate Dispersal," 192–211.

8. *Fernandina Florida Mirror*, September 16, November 25, 1882; *AS-FN*, 336. Maurma, a slave of John and Eliza Partridge of Jefferson County, was brought to South Carolina on a slave ship from Africa. Maurma spent the rest of her life from the 1830s to her death in either 1857 or 1858 on the Partridge's

Middle Florida plantation and may have passed stories of Africa down to her family and loved ones. See Rivers, "Troublesome Property," 118.

9. *Fernandina Florida Mirror,* September 16, November 25, 1882; *AS-FN,* 355.

10. *AS-FN,* 93–94.

11. *Tallahassee Weekly Floridian,* May 22, 1877; Charles S. Long, *A.M.E. Church in Florida,* 75.

12. McDonogh, *Florida Negro,* 71–80; *AS-FN,* 3–9, 107–24.

13. Housewright, *Music and Dance in Florida,* 254.

14. de Castlenau, "Comte de Castlenau," 316; Housewright, *Music and Dance in Florida,* 250, 255.

15. Margaret Murray May diary, 78.

16. de Castlenau, "Comte de Castlenau," 243.

17. Kingsley, *Treatise,* 14; Laura Randall to Mr. and Mrs. Wirt, November 2, 1827, Wirt Papers.

18. *AS-FN,* 244; Kingsley, *Treatise,* 14; Blakey, Lainhart, and Stephens, *Rose Cottage Chronicles,* 298.

19. O. T. Hammond to Harvey Hubbard, November 10, 1838, O. T. Hammond Postal Cards; Shane White and Graham White, *Stylin,* 75–84.

20. Daniel H. Wiggins diary, entry of July 7, 1841; Manley and Brown, *Supreme Court of Florida,* 56–57.

21. Housewright, *Music and Dance in Florida,* 248–50; Hammond to Hubbard, November 10, 1838; Margaret Watkins Gibbs memory diary, October 13, 1936, Gibbs Family File, SAHSRL; *AS-FN,* 97; Lewis, "Bartow, West Bartow," 55–58; Murat, *United States of North America,* 98.

22. Laura Randall to mother, September 17, 1828, Wirt Papers; *PG,* October 28, 1848; Kingsley, *Treatise,* 14; *AS-FN,* 97; Wilson, "Association of Movement and Music," 189–99; Thompson, "Aesthetic of the Cool," 200–212.

23. *AS-FN,* 34, 358; Deborah Gray White, "Female Slaves," 118–19.

24. *TFP,* October 13, 1855, January 16, 1858; *TF,* May 11, 1833; *SAEFH,* March 1, 1823; *TFW,* April 28, 1838.

25. *SAEFH,* March 1, 1823; *St. Augustine Florida Gazette,* September 15, 1821.

26. *TFS,* November 4, 1845; *TF,* May 11, 1833, January 1, 1842; *SAN,* June 19, 1840; *JEFA,* October 12, 1839; *SAEFH,* April 17, 1824; *TFP,* August 15, 1855, April 2, 1856.

27. *TF,* January 1, 1832; *JFR,* February 12, July 23, 1856; Shane White and Graham White, *Stylin,* 41–62.

28. *SAEFH,* March 1, 1823; *SAFH&SD,* August 20, 1844; *TF,* November 1, 1845.

29. *AS-FN,* 36; Rivers, "Baptist Minister James Page," 43–54; "Troublesome Property," 104–27.

30. *AS-FN,* 3; Blakey, Lainhart, and Stephens, *Rose Cottage Chronicles,* 24; Rivers, "Baptist Minister James Page," 43–54; "Troublesome Property," 104–27.

31. *AS-FN,* 35, 178; Stephen Harvell interview, 4, box 7, folder 3, Florida Negro Papers.

32. *TF,* October 26, 1837; Canter Brown Jr., "Race Relations in Territorial Florida," 294; Denham, *Rogue's Paradise,* 120–40.

33. Daniel H. Wiggins diary, entry of February 2, 1842; Moseley, "Diary," 21, 45; *TF,* October 25, 1837.

34. Moseley, "Diary," 21; *JEFA,* April 21, 1840; *PG,* April 19, 1851; Eppes, *Negro of the Old South,* 41–44.

35. Amon DeLaughter journal, 14, 18–19, 60; Phillips and Glunt, *Florida Plantation Records,* 63; Deborah Gray White, "Female Slaves," 102.

36. *TF,* October 25, December 6, 1834; Laura Lancaster to Thomas M. Vincent, June 10, 1857, Vincent Family Papers; *TFP,* June 13, 20, 1857; Canter Brown Jr., *Ossian Bingley Hart,* 109; Jefferson County superior court minutes, Book 1, 120, 130; *TFS,* November 22, 1853; *TF&J,* November 26, 1853, October 22, 1859; Leon County circuit court minutes, Book 5, 580, 590, Book 6, 295; *State v. Ned, a Slave* (1853), in Florida Comptroller Vouchers— Criminal Prosecutions, FSA; proclamation of Gov. James Broome, May 15, 1854, Book of Record (Proclamations), Book 1, no. 238, 227–28, RG 156, Series 13, FSA; Amon DeLaughter journal, 48.

37. Hall, "African Religious Retentions," 63; *JFR,* June 3, 1851; Nigh, "Under Grave Conditions," 159–85.

10. INTERACTION BETWEEN BLACKS AND INDIANS

1. Colburn and Landers, eds., *African American Heritage,* 1–18, 128.

2. Covington, *Seminoles of Florida,* 3–27. Onetime slave H. B. Holloway recalled being told as a little boy that "Indians [were run] out of Georgia into Florida." *SN,* vol. 8, pt. 3, p. 287.

3. Mulroy, *Freedom on the Border,* 8; Colburn and Landers, *African American Heritage,* 1; Covington, *Seminoles of Florida,* 3–27; Porter, *Black Seminoles,* 3–7.

4. Jane L. Landers, "Black Society in Spanish St. Augustine," 14–15.

5. Patrick, *Florida Fiasco*; Canter Brown Jr., "Sarrazota," 5–19; *African Americans on the Tampa Bay Frontier,* 9–20; *Florida's Peace River Frontier,* 5–9.

6. James Leitch Wright Jr., "First Seminole War," 565–69; Covington, "Negro Fort," 80; Hawes, "Cannonball"; Canter Brown Jr., "Sarrazota," 5–19.

7. Thomas Frederick Davis, "MacGregor's Invasion," 66–67; Coker and Watson, *Indian Traders,* 320. Concerning the First Seminole War, see Peters, *Florida Wars,* 17–59; "'Defenses of the Floridas,'" 248; Grismer, *Tampa,* 49–50;

Covington, "Negro Fort," 79–91, Giddings, *Exiles of Florida*, 46–56; Mahon, *Second Seminole War*, 18–28; Canter Brown Jr., *Florida's Peace River Frontier*, 22–27; "Sarrazota," 13–16.

8. Canter Brown Jr., "Sarrazota," 5, 12–17.

9. Giddings, *Exiles of Florida*, 97; Canter Brown Jr., "Race Relations in Territorial Florida," 288–89, 300–301; "Florida Crisis," 420–22; Rivers and Brown, "Indispensable Man," 1–23; Mulroy, *Freedom on the Border*, 1.

10. Giddings, *Exiles of Florida*, 97; Canter Brown Jr., "Race Relations in Territorial Florida," 288–89, 300–301; "Florida Crisis," 420–22; Rivers and Brown, "Indispensable Man," 1–23; Mulroy, *Freedom on the Border*, 1; Price, *Maroon Societies*, 1–30.

11. Klos, "Seminole Removal Debate," 129–33; Porter, *Negro on the American Frontier*, 302–303; "Relations between Negroes and Indians," 321–67; Wiley Thompson to secretary of war, April 27, 1835, *ASPMA* 6:534. See also Porter, "Florida Slaves and Free Negroes," 390–421; "Negro Guides and Interpreters," 174–82; and "Negroes and the Seminole War," 427–50.

12. John Lee Williams, *Territory of Florida*, 239–40; Simmons, *Notices of East Florida*, 76; Wiley Thompson to Lewis Cass, April 27, 1835, Office of Indian Affairs, Letters Received, M-234, roll 806; Myer M. Cohen, *Notices of East Florida and the Campaigns*, 78.

13. John Lee Williams, *Territory of Florida*, 214; Mulroy, *Freedom on the Border*, 17, 35–60; Porter, *Black Seminoles*, 111–23; "Florida Slaves and Free Negroes," 390; "Relations between Negroes and Indians," 326; "Negroes and the Seminole War," 428.

14. Glunt, "Plantation and Frontier Records," 267; Thompson to Cass, April 27, 1835, Office of Indian Affairs, Letters Received, M-234, roll 806.

15. Porter, "Negroes and the Seminole War," 441.

16. *TP* 23:991, 24:669; *ASPMA* 6:470–71, 533–34, 7:427; Porter, "Negroes and the Seminole War," 428.

17. Simmons, *Notices of East Florida*, 76; Thompson to Cass, April 27, 1835, Office of Indian Affairs, Letters Received, M-234, roll 806; John Lee Williams, *Territory of Florida*, 240.

18. Canter Brown Jr., "Sarrazota," 5–19; John Lee Williams, *Territory of Florida*, 240; Porter, "Relations between Negroes and Indians," 325; Bell, *Letter*, 4.

19. Canter Brown Jr., *Florida's Peace River Frontier*, 13–14, 26–27, 35–36, 39–40; *African Americans on the Tampa Bay Frontier*, 13, 16–18.

20. Douglas, *Autobiography*, 120–23; Porter, "Negro Abraham," 17–18; *Jacksonville Weekly News-Herald*, April 12, 1888; *Jacksonville Florida Times-Union*, October 30, 1892, January 8, 1895; *Niles' Weekly Register*, January 30, 1836, 365–70.

21. Genovese, *Roll, Jordan, Roll*, 197–98, 475–81; Simmons, *Notices of East*

Florida, 44; Laurence Foster, "Negro-Indian Relationships," 51–57; Helms, "Black Carib Domestic Organization," 82–83; Kobben, "Unity and Disunity," 19, 241, 346–47, 354; William J. Sloan to John C. Casey, June 16, 1853, John C. Casey Papers.

22. Peter H. Wood, *Black Majority,* 183; Dillard, *Black English,* 123–35; Joyner, *Down by the Riverside,* 217–22; Blockson, "Sea Change," 744; Inscoe, "Carolina Slave Names," 527–54; Philip D. Morgan, *Slave Counterpoint,* 451–558.

23. Sprague, *Florida War,* 300; Simmons, *Notices of East Florida,* 44–45, 50, 76; Boyd, "Horatio S. Dexter," 84; Porter, "Negro Abraham," 10; W. W. Smith, *Sketch of the Seminole War,* 21–22.

24. Richard K. Call journal, 365.

25. Porter, "Thlonoto-sassa," 116; "Seminole Flight," 113–33; Rivers and Brown, "Indispensable Man," 2; *SN,* vol. 3, pt. 1, p. 9; *AS-FN,* 27–31, 178–83.

26. Rivers and Brown, "Indispensable Man," 2; Porter, "Relations between Negroes and Indians," 327–41; "Negroes and the Seminole War," 441; *ASPMA* 6:454, 458, 464; Morse, *Report,* 149–50, 310, 311; John Lee Williams, *Territory of Florida,* 214; Cohen, *Notices of East Florida,* 238; Brevard, *History of Florida,* 1:278–79; Potter, *War in Florida,* 15–16.

27. Porter, "Relations between Negroes and Indians," 287–367; "Florida Slaves and Free Negroes," 390–421; "Negro Guides and Interpreters," 174–82; "Negroes and the Seminole War," 427–50; *Black Seminoles.*

28. Peters, *Florida Wars,* 56; Mahon, *Second Seminole War,* 29.

29. On race relations during the territorial and statehood periods, see Canter Brown Jr., "Race Relations in Territorial Florida," 287–307; Rivers, "Troublesome Property," 104–27.

30. *SAEFH,* April 11, 1826; January 21, 1837; Richard K. Call journal, 184–85; Porter, *Black Seminoles,* 64–68; *Army and Navy Chronicle,* October 1837, 269–70; *SAFH,* July 2, 1836; *Jacksonville East Florida Advocate,* October 12, 1839.

31. Giddings, *Exiles of Florida,* 75–80; Canter Brown Jr., *Tampa before the Civil War,* 28–29.

32. *SAEFH,* October 16, 1824; *TF,* June 8, 1839.

33. The principal works on the Second Seminole War are Mahon, *Second Seminole War,* and Peters, *Florida Wars.*

34. Porter, *Black Seminoles,* 33; Mahon, *Second Seminole War,* 129; Porter, "John Caesar"; Glunt, "Plantation and Frontier Records," 268; Rivers and Brown, "Indispensable Man," 3–5; Canter Brown Jr., *Florida's Peace River Frontier,* 39–43.

35. Porter, "Negro Abraham," 2–11; Canter Brown Jr., "Florida Crisis," 428–32; McCall, *Letters from the Frontiers,* 160.

36. *New-Yorker,* April 1, 1837.

37. Canter Brown Jr., "Florida Crisis," 437–38; "Race Relations in Territo-

rial Florida," 303–5; *Florida's Peace River Frontier,* 40–43; *New York Morning Courier and New York Enquirer,* May 4, 1836.

38. Canter Brown Jr., "Florida Crisis," 440–42; *Florida's Peace River Frontier,* 41–43; Laumer, *Dade's Last Command,* 179, 205–206; Porter, *Black Seminoles,* 39–46.

39. Richard K. Call journal, 365; *ASPMA* 7:827–32.

40. Mahon, *Second Seminole War,* 196–99.

41. Peters, *Florida War,* 139–43; Thomas Jesup to J. R. Poinsett, June 7, 1837, Office of Indian Affairs, Letters Received, M-234, roll 290, NA.

42. *ASPMA* 7:827–32; Thomas Sidney Jesup to J. M. Hernandez, January 21, 1837, box 14, Thomas Jesup Papers; Covington, *Seminoles of Florida,* 72–95.

43. Mahon, *Second Seminole War,* 200–204; Peters, *Florida Wars,* 142–43; Rivers and Brown, "Indispensable Man," 8–9; Giddings, *Exiles of Florida,* 156–57.

44. Peters, *Florida Wars,* 143; Mahon, *Second Seminole War,* 143–45, 204; Rivers and Brown, "Indispensable Man," 9; Giddings, *Exiles of Florida,* 156; Canter Brown Jr., "Persifor F. Smith," 407; *Florida's Peace River Frontier,* 43–46; Porter, "Negroes and the Seminole War," 436.

45. Porter, "Florida Slaves and Free Negroes," 409–11; "Negroes and the Seminole War," 440–41; Jesup to Poinsett, June 6, 1838, Thomas S. Jesup Papers; Mahon, *Second Seminole War,* 235–36; Jesup to William L. Marcy, April 3, July 1, 1848, Office of Indian Affairs, Special Files, M-574, roll 13.

46. Rivers and Brown, "Indispensable Man," 13; Covington, *Seminoles of Florida,* 72–95; McReynolds, *Seminoles,* 240; Porter, "Negroes and the Seminole War," 447; Mulroy, *Freedom on the Border,* 32.

47. Rivers and Brown, "Indispensable Man," 13–17; Porter, "Negroes and the Seminole War," 449; entries of January 4–February 19, 1841, Ethan Allen Hitchcock diaries; Ethan Allen Hitchcock to W. W. S. Bliss, March 11, 1841, Ethan Allen Hitchcock Papers; Sprague, *Florida War,* 300; William W. Hoxton to Eliza L. Hoxton, August 26, 1841, Randolph Family Papers.

48. Ethan Allen Hitchcock to John Bell, February 28, 1841, Ethan Allen Hitchcock Papers.

49. *Tampa Sunday Tribune,* January 2, 1955; Rivers and Brown, "Indispensable Man," 1–23; *Jacksonville Weekly News-Herald,* April 12, 1888.

50. Canter Brown Jr., "Race Relations in Territorial Florida," 301–6; Laura Randall to Mr. and Mrs. Wirt, November 2, 1827, Laura Randall to mother, November 3, 1827, Laura Randall to mother, December 29, 1827, Thomas Randall to William Wirt, December 3, 1827, Wirt Papers.

51. Canter Brown Jr., "Race Relations in Territorial Florida," 301–6; Louis Goldsborough to William Wirt, February 1834, Louis Goldsborough to Elizabeth W. Goldsborough, August 28, 1836, Louis Goldsborough to Catherine, November 19, 1839, Louis Goldsborough Papers.

52. Covington, *Seminoles of Florida*, 128–44; Klos, "Seminole Removal Debate," 129–56.

53. F. M. Durrance to Jesse Carter, June 14, 1856, Francis M. Durrance Papers; *Tampa Sunland Tribune*, June 23, 1877; Tillis, "Indian Attack," 180–81; *Tampa Sunday Tribune*, September 26, 1948; Canter Brown Jr., *Fort Meade*, 25–29; *Florida's Peace River Frontier*, 112–15.

54. William J. Sloan to John C. Casey, June 27, November 2, 1853, William H. French to John C. Casey, November 19, 1853, John C. Casey Papers.

55. *TFP*, March 12, 1859. As for slave smuggling at Fort Myers, see chapter 3.

11. SLAVE RESISTANCE

1. Du Bois, *Black Reconstruction*, 12. For a recent study of slaves as rebels on the various plantations and farms throughout the South, see Franklin and Schweninger, *Runaway Slaves*.

2. Jesse Potts will, August 4, 1829, Book A, 93–97, Gadsden County will records; Pine Hill Plantation Papers, 62–70; *JN*, December 10, 1847, June 3, July 29, September 23, 1848; Parish, *Slavery*, 69–73; Blassingame, *Slave Community*, 284–322; Rawick, "Social Analysis of Slavery," 19–20, 34–35; Stampp, "Rebels and Sambos," 367–92; Elkins, *Slavery*, 81–139; Lane, *Debate over Slavery*; Genovese, "Rebelliousness and Docility," 293–314; Wyatt-Brown, "Mask of Obedience."

3. *AS-FN*, 348.

4. Campbell, *Empire for Slavery*, 178; Mormino, "Florida Slave Narratives," 399–419; Rivers, "Troublesome Property," 118.

5. Parish, *Slavery*, 72–73; Stampp, *Peculiar Institution*, 86–140; U.S. Decennial Censuses, 1830 and 1840 Florida censuses, Jackson, Gadsden, Leon, Jefferson, Madison, and Hamilton Counties (population schedules); U.S. Decennial Censuses, 1850 and 1860 Florida censuses, Jackson, Gadsden, Leon, Jefferson, Madison, and Hamilton Counties (slave schedules).

6. Deborah Gray White, "Female Slaves," 110; Berlin, "Slaves' Changing World," 4; see Genovese, *From Revolution to Rebellion*; Ellen McCormick to mother, September 9, 1842, Wirt Papers.

7. Phillips and Glunt, *Florida Plantation Records*, 150.

8. Blakey, Lainhart, and Stephens, *Rose Cottage Chronicles*, 61, 77.

9. Louis Goldsborough to William Wirt, n.d., 1834, Louis Goldsborough to Mrs. Wirt, June 28, 1835, Louis Goldsborough Papers; Ellen McCormick to Catharine W. Randall, March 16, 1843, Wirt Papers.

10. Pine Hill Plantation Papers, 64; *AS-FN*, 253; Phillips and Glunt, *Florida Plantation Records*, 110; Hine, Hine, and Harrold, *Odyssey*, 129–30.

11. *AS-FN*, 356; Laura Randall to mother, December 15, 1827, and to Elizabeth Wirt, February 9, July 11, 1828, Ellen McCormick to Catharine Wirt, October 1, 1843, and to Laura Randall, October 12, 1842, Wirt Papers.

12. Phillips and Glunt, *Florida Plantation Records*, 80; Stampp, *Peculiar Institution*, 103–4; Joyner, "World of the Plantation Slaves," 91–92; Deborah Gray White, "Female Slaves," 111–12; *Ar'n't I a Woman?*, 79–84; Berlin, "Slaves' Changing World," 55.

13. Deborah Gray White, "Female Slaves," 110–11; Phillips and Glunt, *Florida Plantation Records*, 71–72, 88–91, 154–55; Joyner, "World of the Plantation Slaves," 90–91; Abbey, "El Destino and Chemonie Plantations," 80; Eppes, *Negro of the Old South*, 116–17.

14. Phillips and Glunt, *Florida Plantation Records*, 71–72, 88–91, 154–55; Charles W. Bannerman diaries, entries of October 9, 1847, July 30, 1852.

15. Phillips and Glunt, *Florida Plantation Records*, 71–72, 88–91, 154–55; Alexander Randall to Elizabeth Wirt, September 11, 1842, Thomas Randall to William Wirt, April 13, October 14, 1828, Elizabeth Wirt to Laura Randall, October 12, 1837, Louis Goldsborough to William Wirt, February 1, 1834, Ellen McCormick to Elizabeth Wirt, April 15, 1842, Louisa A. Wirt to Elizabeth Wirt, July 14, 1844, Ellen Voss to Catharine Wirt, September 4, 1839, Wirt Papers. For a detailed account of bond servants who were ill, see Charles W. Bannerman diaries, entries of October 1, 1846, September 11, 23, October 9, 1847.

16. Parish, *Slavery*, 70: Blassingame, *Slave Community*, 195; Kingsley B. Gibbs journal, entry of October 4, 1841, 11. Although a practice contrary to law, some slaveholders allowed their bond servants to trade goods. See Florida, *Laws of Territorial Florida* (1822), 182–83, (1827), 147–50.

17. Phillips and Glunt, *Florida Plantation Records*, 80, 174; Pine Hill Plantation Papers, 71; Amon DeLaughter journal, entries of February 16, 1855, February 19, 1857, 16, 60; Joshua Hoyet Frier journal, 35–36; Eppes, *Negro of the Old South*, 89–90; SAFH, February 3, 1830.

18. *Pensacola Floridian*, March 23, 1822; JFN, July 7, December 22, 1855, October 10, 1857; PG, October 14, 1828; TSF, May 21, 1840; *Quincy Sentinel*, November 14, 1843; SAFH, June 7, 1832; TF, May 31, 1839; JFN, October 13, 1855; Canter Brown Jr., "'Hopes I Cherished,'" 2; Joyner, "World of the Plantation Slaves," 92.

19. TFP, November 15, 1856; TF&J, November 8, 1856; Julia Floyd Smith, *Slavery and Plantation Growth*, 105–6; Wetherington, "*Florida Peninsular*'s View of Slavery," 46–71.

20. *Laws of Territorial Florida* (1824), 289–92; TFP, March 17, 24, May 5, 26, 1860; Denham, *Rogue's Paradise*, 136; Amon DeLaughter journal, entry of May 4, 1860, 113.

21. *Ocala Florida Home Companion*, quoted in TFP, February 25, 1860; *Fernandina East Floridian*, March 3, 8, 1860; Hammond, *Medical Profession*, 329–30; Denham, *Rogue's Paradise*, 139, 199–200.

22. Laura Randall to father, June 30, 1832, Wirt Papers; Shofner, *Jefferson County*, 136.

23. Parish, *Slavery*, 71; Joyner, "World of the Plantation Slaves," 96; Blassingame, *Slave Community*, 215–16; *Laws of Territorial Florida* (1824), 289–92, (1836), 13–15. On slave revolt see, e.g., Aptheker, *American Negro Slave Revolts*; Lofton, *Denmark Vesey's Revolt*; Oates, *Fires of Jubilee*; and Ros, *Night of Fire*.

24. Canter Brown Jr., "Race Relations in Florida," 300–307; *Ossian Bingley Hart*, 38–40, 83, 90, 114, 125, 173–74.

25. Du Bois, *Black Reconstruction*, 13; Philip D. Morgan, *Slave Counterpoint*, 450; Blassingame, *Slave Community*, 211–14; Joyner, "World of the Plantation Slaves," 94.

26. *TF*, January 18, 1834; *SAEFH*, October 16, 1824; Canter Brown Jr., "Race Relations in Territorial Florida," 296; Eppes, *Negro in the Old South*, 116–17. On running away see also *TF*, June 1, 1833, September 10, 1836, March 9, 1839; *Tallahassee Florida Intelligencer*, September 29, October 6, November 24, 1826; *PG*, May 23, 1840; *SAFH*, August 4, 1838; *Apalachicolian*, December 26, 1840.

27. Donorena Harris, "Abolitionist Sentiment," 99–127; *TF&A*, September 1, 1829; John Gamble diary, April 1836–November 12, 1838; Pine Hill Plantation Papers, 64; Rivers, "Troublesome Property," 117.

28. *TF&A*, November 1, 1828, October 6, 1829, September 7, 1830; *TF*, February 9, 1839; Franklin and Schweninger, *Runaway Slaves*, 49–67.

29. *TF*, October 24, 1831, March 7, August 22, October 17, 1835, January 6, 1836, August 26, November 1, 1837, January 1, April 4, April 7, September 14, October 20, 1838, January 10, April 20, 1839, January 10, 1846; *PG*, August 17, 1822; March 10, 1838, May 31, August 2, 1839, January 15, 1840, November 1, 1845, December 6, 1845; *JFR*, April 2, July, 23, November 5, 1856, February 18, 1857; *JC*, June 25, 1835, February 14, 1836; *JN*, December 19, 1845; *JFN*, March 19, 1847, October 30, 1852, October 13, 1855; *Tallahassee Florida Intelligencer*, October 6, November 24, 1826; *SAFH*, February 3, 1830, April 5, May 17, August 9, 1832; *SAEFH*, March 1, 1823; *St. Augustine Florida Gazette*, September 15, 1821; *Lake City Columbian*, March 15, 1865; *TFW*, April 28, May 5, 1838; *TFS*, January 28, February 18, March 4, June 3, 1842, November 4, 1845, March 31, April 21, August 18, 1846, September 14, 1847, June 3, 1855; *TSF*, May 21, 1840; *SAFH&SD*, May 8, 1840; *St. Augustine Ancient City*, March 13, 1852; *Quincy Sentinel*, September 18, 1840, January 1, 1841, May 9, June 27, November 14, 1843; *TF&A*, July 20, 1830; *TF&J*, October 27, 1849, April 12, May 10, 1851, June 13, July 31, 1852, November 20, 1858.

30. *PG*, May 20, 1837; *TF&J*, February 20, 1858; *Palatka Whig Banner*, July 1, July 28, 1846; *JFR*, October 3, 1850, November 2, 1856; *JC* April 16, 1835, *JN*, August 7, 1850, January 4, 1851; *JEFA*, September 1, 1840; *SAFH*, March 25, 1829, May 12, 1830, March 29, June 7, 1832, April 1, 1835; *SAEFH*, March 1, 1823.

31. *JN*, March 19, 1847; *TF*, May 11, 1833, September 23, 1837, May 26, 1838,

April 6, June 1, 1839, March 6, 1847; *TFW*, May 5, October 6, 1838; *TSF*, May 21, 1840; *TFS*, October 15, 1841; *TF&J*, January 29, 1853.

32. Pine Hill Plantation Papers, 64; Moseley, "Dairy," 23; Phillips and Glunt, *Florida Plantation Records*, 156–57.

33. *SAEFH*, January 25, 1825; *JN*, March 19, 1847; *JC*, June 25, August 6, August 27, 1835; *Palatka Whig Banner* July 28, 1846; *SAFH*, May 7, 1834, July 29, 1835; *Fernandina Weekly East Floridian*, August 30, 1860; *Apalachicola Commercial Advertiser*, March 11, 1855; *TF*, March 6, 1847.

34. *TF&J*, April 12, June 12, 1851, July 31, 1852; *JC*, August 9, 1835; *JN*, January 4, 1851, January 1, 1853.

35. *ASPMA* 6:453; Laura Goldsborough to William Wirt, February, 1834, Thomas Randall to Wirt, October 12, 1827, Randall to Mrs. Wirt, December 29, 1827, Wirt Papers; Louis Goldsborough to Catharine Goldsborough, November 2, 1827, Goldsborough Papers; *TP* 22:763.

36. *TF*, September 9, 1848; *TF&J*, May 20, 1854; *TFS*, May 5, 1839; Paisley, *Red Hills of Florida*, 178.

37. Canter Brown Jr., "Sarrazota," 14–17; *Nassau Royal Gazette and Literary Register*, March 20, 1822; *TF&J*, February 20, 1858; Julia Floyd Smith, *Slavery and Plantation Growth*, 105–6. For more information on early black flight from Florida to the Bahamas, see David E. Wood, *Guide to Selected Sources*; Porter, "Seminole Negroes in the Bahamas"; Goggin, "Seminole Negroes of Andros Island"; Kersey, "Seminole Negroes of Andros Island Revisited"; Blackett, *Building an Antislavery Wall*, 137.

38. *JFR*, September 22, 1851, February 21, 1856; *SAEFH*, April 17, 1824; *TF*, October 17, 1835; *SAFH*, February 10, 1830, June 16, 1838; *TSF*, May 21, 1840; *Apalachicola Gazette*, February 2, 1839; *TF&J*, May 10, 1851.

39. *JC*, September 3, 1835; Paisley, *Red Hills of Florida*, 175–76. For an interesting account of abolitionists aiding runaways, see Blackett, *Beating against the Barriers*, 87–137.

40. Denham, *Rogue's Paradise*, 187; Order Book A, 137, Jefferson County superior court minutes; Minute Book 4, 247, Leon County superior court minutes; Julia Floyd Smith, *Slavery and Plantation Growth*, 110; *TF&J*, February 20, 1858; *TF*, January 6, 1836, September 2, 1848.

41. Walker, *Trial and Imprisonment*, 32–73; *AS-FN*, 336–39; *SAFH&SD*, December 17, 1844; *JFN*, May 19, 1855; Denham, *Rogue's Paradise*, 97. Sources remain rather silent, as would be expected, on the participation of women, prominent or otherwise, in the antislavery or abolitionist movement in Florida. One recent work, though, explores the role played in the state by women with abolitionist backgrounds in the North such as Chloe Merrick. See John T. Foster Jr. and Sarah Whitmer Foster, *Beechers, Stowes, and Yankee Strangers*. For an interesting discussion of women in the abolitionist movement generally, see Jeffrey, *Ordinary Women in the Abolitionist Movement*, 96–133.

42. *PG*, May 20, 1837; *JFR*, November 14, 1850; *TF*, February 28, 1835; *JFN*, October 12, 1854; Canter Brown Jr., "Race Relations in Territorial Florida," 287–307.

43. Denham, *Rogue's Paradise*, 126; *TF&J*, April 16, 1853.

44. *AS-FN*, 244, 338; Amon DeLaughter journal, entries of October 23, 25, 1856, September 1, November 5, 1859, 51, 103–4.

45. Pine Hill Plantation Papers, 81; Eppes, *Negro of the Old South*, 116–17; *JFN*, March 12, 1853; Joyner, "World of the Plantation Slaves," 91.

46. Ellen McCormick to Catharine Wirt Randall, January 15, 1843, Wirt Papers; Phillips and Glunt, *Florida Plantation Records*, 95–96.

12. SLAVERY AND THE CIVIL WAR

1. The principal works on the Civil War in Florida are William Watson Davis, *Civil War and Reconstruction*; Johns, *Florida during the Civil War*; Nulty, *Confederate Florida*; Coles, "'A Fight,'"; "'Fields of Glory'"; Canter Brown Jr., "Civil War."

2. William Watson Davis, *Civil War and Reconstruction*, 1–318; Canter Brown Jr., "Civil War," 231–46; *War of the Rebellion* (hereafter *ORA*), ser. 1, vol. 6, 402–4.

3. Schafer, "Freedom Was as Close," 158; *Population of the United States in 1860; Compiled from the Original Returns of the Eighth Census*, 53; Coles, "'Fields of Glory,'" 54–63.

4. Canter Brown Jr., *Fort Meade*, 43–48.

5. Canter Brown Jr., *Genealogical Records*, 62–63.

6. Maria Louisa Daegenhardt reminiscences, n.p.; *New York Herald*, September 10, 1864; Coles, "'Fields of Glory,'" 294.

7. Schellings, "On Blockade Duty," 63–65; *American Missionary*, April 1865, 79, September 1865, 209.

8. Schafer, "Freedom Was as Close," 157–71; Charles S. Long, *A.M.E. Church in Florida*, 75; Canter Brown Jr., *Florida's Black Public Officials*, 105–6.

9. Schafer, "Freedom Was as Close"; Coles, "'They Fought like Devils.'" See also Buker, *Blockaders, Refugees, and Contrabands*, 42–58; Martin and Schafer, *Jacksonville's Ordeal by Fire*, 141; Higginson, *Army Life*, 35, 49, 76–77, 84, 91, 97–98, 114, 126–28; *ORA*, ser. 1, vol. 14, 341, ser. 3, vol. 2, 42–43; Cox, *Lincoln and Black Freedom*, 7, 14–15; Nulty, *Confederate Florida*; Boggess, *Veteran of Four Wars*, 69; John Wilder to mother, May 22, 1864, Wilder-Loomis Family Papers; Thomas Benton Ellis Sr. diary, 9; Department of War, United States Colored Troops General Descriptive Books, RG 94, NA; George W. Smith, "Carpetbag Imperialism in Florida," 263–67; John W. Appleton Journal, February 5, 1864, John W. Appleton Papers.

10. Coles, "'They Fought like Devils,'" 37; "'Fields of Glory,'" 155–85; *Battle*

of Olustee; Crowninshield, *History of the First Regiment,* 263; Martin and Schafer, *Jacksonville's Ordeal by Fire,* 141; Canter Brown Jr., "Civil War," 241; Nulty, *Confederate Florida,* 124–69; Boyd, "Federal Campaign of 1864," 21; Blatzell, "Battle of Olustee," 201; Thomas Frederick Davis, *History of Jacksonville,* 134; Johns, *Florida during the Civil War,* 190; Wilson, *Black Phalanx,* 269. Slaves from Florida areas other than the northeastern corner of the state also took up arms against the Confederacy. Tampa's Aaron Bryant, for example, joined the Second (USCI) and saw action in the region. Canter Brown Jr., *African Americans on the Tampa Bay Frontier,* 39; *Florida's Peace River Frontier,* 181. Some of Florida's future public officials were slaves who fought for the Union. See Canter Brown Jr., *Florida's Black Public Officials.*

11. Coles, "'They Fought like Devils,'" 38–39; Lawrence Jackson, "As I Saw," transcript in Lawrence Jackson Papers; William Penniman reminiscences; "Letters from Confederate Soldiers," 481; *Voice from Rebel Prisons,* 4; *Jacksonville Florida Union,* March 11, 1865; Fennell, "Blacks in Jacksonville," 77–100.

12. Valentine Chamberlain to (unidentified), October 10, 1862, PKY; Schafer, "Freedom Was as Close," 158; *ORA,* ser. 1, vol. 35, pt. 2, 53; Rucker, "Blackwater and Yellow Pine," 2:700.

13. *Official Records of the Union and Confederate Navies* (hereafter *ORN*) ser. 1, vol. 16, 580, 689, vol. 17, 269; Buker, *Blockaders, Refugees, and Contrabands,* 42–43; Coles, "Unpretending Service," 44–45.

14. *AS-FN,* 35; Sarah Brown Bryant interview, 4, box 7, folder 3, Florida Negro Papers; Buker, *Blockaders, Refugees, and Contrabands,* 46; *Dade City Banner,* April 4, 1924; Canter Brown Jr., *African Americans on the Tampa Bay Frontier,* 40. On the subject of Confederate salt making generally, see Robert A. Taylor, *Rebel Storehouse.*

15. *ORN,* ser. 1, vol. 16, 689, vol. 17, 737–39, 744; Quarles, *Negro in the Civil War,* 200–202; quarantine regulations, March 15, 1864, in Letters Received, Department and District of Key West, 1861–1865, RG 393, NA; Smart, *Medical and Surgical History,* 675–83; *Philadelphia Inquirer,* September 26, 1862; William H. Foster, "'This Place Is Safe,'" 181; John Wilder to Richard Wilder, July 25, 1864, Loomis-Wilder Family Papers; Dyer, *Compendium,* 3:1723; Ames Williams, "Stronghold of the Straits," 19, 21; *AS-FN,* 179–80; Higginson, *Army Life,* 237. For a discussion of the uncharitable treatment of some slaves by Union troops in Louisiana, see Ripley, *Slaves and Freedmen,* 115–18.

16. Hattie Reed to D. Bryant, March 22, 1863, and O. Stephens to D. Bryant, April 2, 1863, Bryant-Stephens Family Papers; Schafer, "Freedom Was as Close," 168–73; VanLandingham, "'My National Troubles,'" 63–66; Schwartz, *Woman Doctor's Civil War,* 61.

17. J. St. C. Morton to W. H. French, April 22, 1861, L. G. Arnold to W. H. French, April 22, 1861, E. D. Townsend to D. P. Woodbury, December 22, 1863, Department of War, Department and District of Key West, Letters Received,

1861–1868, RG 393, NA; Department of War, Department and District of Key West, Work Returns, 1859–1861, 1861–1865, and Payroll Vouchers, Accounts Current, and Abstracts of Disbursement, Records of the Office of the Chief of Army Engineers, RG 77, NA; Josiah Shinn, "Fort Jefferson and Its Commander, 1861–62," in Lewis G. Schmidt Collection; William H. Foster, "'This Place Is Safe,'" 89–111, 148, 188–90; *Key West New Era*, August 16, 1862; Manucy, "Gibraltar," 308–9; *Philadelphia Inquirer*, August 15, 1861; "View of Key West" in *Harper's Weekly*, April 19, 1862, 34; Harrison B. Herrick diary; Ames Williams, "Stronghold of the Straits," 14. United States military officials allowed many Florida Unionist slaveholders to keep their slaves until the war officially ended in April and May 1865. See, for example, Browne, *Key West*, 9–98; John Wilder to Mrs. M. W. F. Wilder, August 14, 1864, Wilder-Loomis Papers.

18. Rice, "Negro Religion," 5–6; AS-FN, 215: *Fernandina Peninsula*, August 13, 1863; Holder, "At The Dry Tortugas," 87–89; Revels, "Grander in Her Daughters," 268–69 277; Winston Stephens to Octavia Stephens, July 24, 1862, Bryant-Stephens Family Papers; S. Fairbanks to G. Fairbanks, August 27, 1862, George R. Fairbanks Papers; David Flemming pension file, 273.637, Veterans Administration, Pension files, RG 15, NA; *St. Augustine Examiner*, May 1, 1862; Graham, "Home Front," 34–35; Nichols, *Perry's Saints*, 180; Elias A. Bryan diary, 56–57, in Lewis Schmidt Collection; Graham, *Awakening of St. Augustine*, 122.

19. Johns, *Florida during the Civil War*, 309–10; Confederate War Department, Bureau of Conscription, Circular No. 36, December 1, 1864, ORA, ser. 4, vol. 3, 933–34.

20. Prouty, "War Comes to Tampa Bay," 51; McDuffee, *Lures of Manatee*, 146.

21. Drake, *Florida Legislature*, 37–38; Canter Brown Jr., *Florida's Black Public Officials*, 79, 141; Charles S. Long, *A.M.E. Church in Florida*, 55–56.

22. AS-FN, 60; William Bryant to Davis Bryant, October 30, 1861, Bryant-Stephens Family Papers.

23. ORA, ser. 1, vol. 14, 732, 955.

24. AS-FN, 35, 331; ORN, ser. 1, vol. 17, 562–63; Pleasants W. White to James McKay Sr., October 2, 1863, box 2, Pleasants W. White Papers; Robert A. Taylor, *Rebel Storehouse*, 106; Solomon and Erhart, "Race and Civil War," 325, 333; Canter Brown Jr., "Tampa's James McKay," 420; *Fort Meade*, 44–48; Sarah Brown Bryant interview, box 7, folder 3, Florida Negro Papers; *Dade City Banner*, April 4, 1924. On the Confederacy's trade with local cattlemen in peninsular Florida, see Akerman, *Florida Cowman*, 84–97, and Canter Brown Jr., *Florida's Peace River Frontier*, 146–75.

25. Melvin Tibbetts to Christiana V. Tibbetts, June 28, 1863, Melvin Tibbetts Letters; ORN, ser. 1, vol. 20, 618, vol. 35, 53; McPherson, *Ordeal by Fire*, 266–

67; Rucker, "Blackwater and Yellow Pine," 2:699–701.

26. Margaret Watkins Gibbs memory diary; Dillon, "Civil War in South Florida," 243–329; Solomon, "Southern Extremities," 129–52.

27. Etheldred Philips to James J. Philips, December 25, 1862, James J. Philips Papers; Buker, *Blockaders, Refugees, and Contrabands*, 44–50; McDuffee, *Lures of Manatee*, 150–52.

28. Coles, "'They Fought like Devils,'" 40; Rucker, "Blackwater and Yellow Pine," 2:700; Boyd, "Battle of Marianna," 225–42; Farley, *Florida's Alamo*. The Third, Seventh, and Thirty-fifth United States Colored Troops (USCT) took part also in the June 1864 capture of Camp Milton, and the Thirty-fourth, Thirty-fifth, and 102d USCT were involved in the Florida Railroad raid of August 1864. *ORA*, ser. 1, vol. 25, pt. 1, 393–98, 400–403, 427–40, 443–45.

29. Stampp, *Peculiar Institution*, 30; Edwin L. Williams Jr., "Negro Slavery in Florida," Pt. 1, 93–102; "Negro Slavery in Florida," Pt. 2, 187–90; Joshua Hoyet Frier journal, 13; Revels, "Grander in Her Daughters," 275; *AS-FN*, 98; McDonogh, *Florida Negro*, 61; Mrs. L. Thompson, "Reminiscences of the War," in vol. 1, United Daughters of the Confederacy Scrapbooks; Brian E. Michaels, *River Flows North*, 99; Schwartz, *Woman Doctor's Civil War*, 77, 82; *St. Augustine Evening Record*, February 14, 1930.

30. *AS-FN*, 178.

31. Ibid., 331; Helen M. Edwards memoirs; Paisley, *Red Hills of Florida*, 169.

32. Hawes, "One-Time Slave"; Sarah Brown Bryant interview, box 7, folder 3, Florida Negro Papers; Canter Brown Jr., *African Americans on the Tampa Bay Frontier*, 40.

33. Stephen Harvell interview, 3, box 7, folder 3, Florida Negro Papers; *AS-FN*, 80–81, 245, 351; Lykes, *Gift of Heritage*, 8–9; Paisley, *Red Hills of Florida*, 201; Ingle, "Soldiering with the Second Florida Regiment," 336–37; Joyner, *Down by the Riverside*, 225.

34. William S. Murphy will, July 13, 1863, John Finlayson will, February 23, 1865, Book B, 130–31, 155–58, Jefferson County will records; Leon County deed records, Book D, 575, Book E, 550; David Williams will, April 6, 1863, and Jesse Mims will, January 22, 1866, Reel 1, 266–69, 270–71, Escambia County will records; William Ham will, November 9, 1864, and A. J. Hewlitt will, January 21, 1865, Book B, 58–60, 61–63, Alachua County will records; Ben Hopkins will, February 21, 1862, Book B, 159, 419–21, Putnam County will records. For a sampling of other probate records of slaveholders who willed bond servants to their heirs and loved ones from 1861 to 1865, see Gabriel Priest will, September 3, 1861, Books B, G, and H, 73, 82, 129, 770, Putnam County will records; Richard J. Mays will, March 25, 1864, and Nancy DeLaughter will, June 28, 1864, Book 2, 85–87, 89–92, Madison County will records; George T. Ward will, January 8, 1863, Book A, 37–39, William Bailey will, July 16, 1862, Book B, 160, Leon County will records; Cornelius Beasely will, December 2, 1865, I. T.

Webb will, July 6, 1862, B. Bird will, December 30, 1863, and William Budd will, June 27, 1862, Book B, 94, 125, 135–36, 162–65, Gadsden County will records; I. D. Hart will, September 27, 1861, file no. 900-D, Duval County probate records; Edward Bradford to Dear Sir, January 26, 1863, box 515, file 3, Special Collections, FSU.

35. Paisley, *Red Hills of Florida*, 203; Sarah Green will, August 30, 1860, August 17, 1864, Book B., 110, 150, Jefferson County will records; Thomas H. Triplett will, August 30, 1863, Robert D. Sturges will, August 26, 1861, Book B, 116, 127–28, Gadsden County will records. A manager of the William Kilcrease estate hired slaves out from January 1, 1865, until the year's end. He also sold a slave woman and her child on January 10, 1865. William Kilcrease will, May 26, 1860, Book C, 164–71, Gadsden County will records; William Kilcrease file, Gadsden County probate records. The estate of I. D. Hart, who had been a Unionist and Jacksonville founder, rented out several of his slaves from October 1, 1863, to January 1, 1865, to the Union army. See I. D. Hart probate papers, file no. 900-D, Duval County probate papers.

36. *SAR*, October 21, 1934; Revels, "Grander in Her Daughters," 275; Kealing, *African Methodism in Texas*, 199–202; *Tampa Morning Tribune*, March 3, 1896, January 5, 1901; *Jacksonville Florida Times-Union*, February 27, 1896; *A.M.E. Church in Florida*, 110–13. The administrator of Jonathan Robinson's estate sold Stephen, aged 38, for $4,550 and Abraham, aged 25, for $3,100 on February 6, 1865. Jonathan Robinson file, Gadsden County probate papers.

37. *AS-FN*, 351–59; William Kilcrease probate file, Gadsden County probate papers; B. F. Whitner deed, December 31, 1864, Book L, 362, Leon County deed records; Rivers, "Political Economy of Gadsden County," 17–18; Kealing, *African Methodism in Texas*, 201.

38. Canter Brown Jr., "Civil War," 232; Solomon and Erhart, "Race and Civil War," 320–41; *Philadelphia Inquirer*, March 20, 1862; *St. Augustine Examiner*, May 1, 1862; Graham, "Home Front," 26–34; East, "St. Augustine during the Civil War," 82; Browne, *Key West* 92–95; Parks, *General Edmund Kirby Smith*, 329; Phelts, *American Beach*, 15; Blakey, Lainhart, and Stephens, *Rose Cottage Chronicles*, 130, 160–61, 164–65, 182–83; S. Fairbanks to G. Fairbanks, April 21, 29, 1862, George R. Fairbanks Papers; Reed, "Diary"; *St. Augustine Evening Record*, February 14, 1930; McDuffee, *Lures of Manatee*, 126; Canter Brown Jr., *Florida's Peace River Frontier*, 146; Joyner, *Down by the Riverside*, 225–42. Odet Philippe, another prominent citizen and slaveholder, moved into the interior with his bond servants to what is now Pasco County shortly after the Civil War started. DeFoor, *Odet Philippe*, 3.

39. Canter Brown Jr., *Florida's Peace River Frontier*, 137, 146; *African Americans on the Tampa Bay Frontier*, 37; VanLandingham, "'To Faithfully Discharge My Duty,'" 7.

40. Lucas, "Colonel George Washington Scott," 130–35, 141; Paisley, "How

to Escape the Yankees," 53–61; *Red Hills of Florida*, 207; Bennard Overton diary, entry of April 13, 1862; *Savannah Morning News*, October 21, 1874; Canter Brown Jr., *African Americans on the Tampa Bay Frontier*, 37; Etheldred Philips to James J. Philips, December 25, 1862, October 12, December 8, 1863, James J. Philips Papers; Buker, *Blockaders, Refugees, and Contrabands*, 49–51; Collier, *Collier Family*, 24–25; Overman, "After 111 Years," 16; *Albany (NY) Patriot*, March 14, 1861; Mohr, *Threshold of Freedom*, 99–119; Rucker, "Arcadia and Bagdad," 163.

41. *SN*, vol. 11, p. 210; Johns, *Florida during the Civil War*.

42. Etheldred Philips to James J. Philips, December 25, 1862, October 12, December 8, 1863, James J. Philips Papers; Buker, *Blockaders, Refugees, and Contrabands*, 50.

43. Eppes, *Through Some Eventful Years*, 163; *Negro of the Old South*, 109–11; Johns, *Florida during the Civil War*, 307–8; Revels, "Grander in Her Daughters," 261–82; *TFS*, May 6, 1862.

44. Faust, *Mothers of Invention*, 53; Blakey, Lainhart, and Stephens, *Rose Cottage Chronicles*, 75–76, 90–91; Cleveland, "Florida Women," 40–41; *AS-FN*, 181.

45. Hopley, *Life in the South*, 2:279–85; Dovell, *Florida*, 1:503; Deborah Gray White, *Ar'nt I a Woman?*, 56. On the similar situation then developing in southwest Georgia, see David Williams's excellent studies *Rich Man's War* and "'Us Is Gonna Be Free.'" M. N. Fletcher to Dear Son, April 29, 1865, Zabud Fletcher Family Papers, M90-15, FSA.

46. *Laws of Florida* (1861), 38–43; Amon DeLaughter journal, 9, 22, 61, 63, 75, 79, 97–115; *TFS*, May 6, 1862; Rivers, "Madison County," 241; *AS-FN*, 247.

47. McDuffee, *Lures of Manatee*, 132; Winston Stephens to Octavia Stephens, December 12, 1861, Bryant-Stephens Family Papers. Rumors of slave plots and insurrections circulated through Middle Florida. See, for example, Amon DeLaughter journal, passim; Schafer, "Freedom Was as Close," 158; Granade, "Slave Unrest in Florida," 27; Washington M. Ives Journal, November 21, 1860, Washington M. Ives Papers, FSA.

48. Charles S. Long, *A.M.E. Church in Florida*, 55–56, 195; Canter Brown Jr., "'Hopes I Cherished,'" 3–4; *Genealogical Records*, 62–63; *Florida's Black Public Officials*, 79, 109–10, 114, 117, 125–26; Rivers, "Baptist Minister James Page," 47–48; McKinney and McKinney, *History of the Black Baptists*, 23–25, 30–32, 41–42; Housewright, *Music and Dance in Florida*, 331–36; Higginson, *Army Life*, 197–98, 222. See also Seth Rogers, *Letters*.

49. Shippe, *Bishop Whipple's Southern Diary*, 33.

50. *AS-FN*, 214, 245–46, 254, 359–60; Higginson, *Army Life*, 23.

51. *AS-FN*, 214, 245–46, 254, 359–60; Higginson, *Army Life*, 23; Canter Brown Jr., "Civil War," 244–45.

52. *AS-FN*, 246, 331, 351; *SAR*, October 21, 1934; *Jacksonville Florida Union*,

May 27, 1865; Ellen Call Long, *Florida Breezes*, 381; Revels, "Grander in Her Daughters," 267; Coles, "'Terrible and Sad Result,'" 158–60.

53. *AS-FN*, 165–66; *TFP*, July 26, 1866.

54. *AS-FN*, 360.

55. Menard, *Lays in Summer Lands*, 17.

13. CONCLUSION

1. Menard, *Lays in Summer Lands*, 26–27.

BIBLIOGRAPHY

MANUSCRIPTS AND COLLECTIONS

Appleton, John W. Papers. Xerographic copy in the collection of the author.
Bannerman, Charles W. Diaries. FSA.
Bigelow, Robert J. Papers. PKY.
Biographical files. SAHSRL.
Bradford, Thomas A. Papers. Strozier Library, FSU.
Bryant-Stephens Family. Papers. PKY.
Call, Richard K. Journal. FSA.
Casey, John C. Papers. Thomas Gilcrease Institute, Tulsa, Okla.
Chamberlain, Valentine. Letter. PKY.
Daegenhardt, Maria Louisa. Reminiscences. Historical Museum of Southern Florida, Miami.
Davidson, John M. W. Physician's Journal, 1843. Strozier Library, FSU.
DeLaughter, Amon. Journal. Transcript in the collection of Elizabeth Sims, Madison County, Fla.
Durrance, Francis M. Papers. Transcripts at Polk County Historical and Genealogical Library, Bartow, Fla.
Edwards, Helen M. Memoirs. Strozier Library, FSU.
Ellis, Thomas Benton, Sr. Diary. PKY.
Eppes, Susan Bradford. Pine Hill Plantation Papers. Strozier Library, FSU.
Fairbanks, George R. Papers. Strozier Library, FSU.
Fletcher, Zabud. Family Papers. FSA.

Florida Negro Papers. University of South Florida Library Special Collections.
Forsyth Family. Papers. John C. Pace Library, UWF.
Frier, Joshua Hoyet. Journal. FSA.
Gamble, John. Diary. Jefferson County Historical Society, Monticello, Fla.
Gibbs, Kingsley B. Journal. Strozier Library, FSU.
Gibbs, Margaret Watkins. Memory diary. Gibbs Family file. SAHSRL.
Goldsborough, Louis. Papers. LC.
Hammond, O. T. Postal Cards. FSA.
Herrick, Harrison B. Diary. Oswego County Historical Society, Oswego, N.Y.
Hitchcock, Ethan Allen. Diaries. Thomas Gilcrease Museum, Tulsa, Okla.
Hitchcock, Ethan Allen. Papers. LC.
Holland, Griffin W. Papers. Strozier Library, FSU.
Hollingsworth, John. Diary. Strozier Library, FSU.
Howard, Oliver O. Papers. Bowdoin College Library, Brunswick, Maine.
Hurston, Zora Neale. "The Negro in Florida, 1528–1940." Photocopy of ms.
    Jacksonville University Library, Jacksonville, Florida.
Ives, Washington M. Papers. FSA.
Jackson, Lawrence. Papers. PKY.
Jesup, Thomas S. Papers. LC.
May, Margaret Murray. Diary. Strozier Library, FSU.
Morton, Jackson. Papers. John C. Pace Library, UWF.
Moseley, William D. Diary and Other Papers. Strozier Library, FSU.
Overton, Bennard, Rev. Diary. Southern Historical Collection, University of
    North Carolina, Chapel Hill.
Penniman, William. Reminiscences. Southern Historical Collection, University of North Carolina, Chapel Hill.
Philips, James J. Papers. Southern Historical Collection, University of North
    Carolina, Chapel Hill.
Pigeon Creek Baptist Church. Minutes. SLF.
Pine Hill Plantation. Papers. Strozier Library, FSU.
Randolph Family Papers. Virginia Historical Society, Richmond.
Rare Slave Papers. Florida A&M University Research Center and Museum,
    FAMU.
Scarborough, Rabun. Letters. Strozier Library, FSU.
Schmidt, Lewis G. Collection. FSA.
Simpson, Ellen. Collection. John C. Pace Library, UWF.
Snodgrass, Dena E. Collection. PKY.
Solana, O. John, and Harriet Alvarez. Marriage Licence, June 15, 1839. St.
    Augustine Historical Society, St. Augustine.
Spanish Land Grants (Unconfirmed Grants). Microfilmed case files. John
    Germany Public Library Special Collections Department, Tampa, Fla.
Stetson, John B. Collection. PKY.

Tibbetts, Melvin. Letters. John C. Pace Library, UWF.

United Daughters of the Confederacy, Florida. Scrapbooks. SLF.

Vincent Family. Papers. Louisiana State University Library Special Collections, Baton Rouge.

White, David L. Diary. PKY.

White, Pleasants W. Papers. Florida Historical Society, Melbourne, Fla.

Wiggins, David H. Diaries. FSA.

Wilder-Loomis Family. Papers. Yale University Library, New Haven, Conn.

Williams, Thomas. Papers. Burton Historical Collection, Detroit Public Library, Detroit, Mich.

Wirt, William. Papers. Maryland Historical Society, Baltimore, Md.

PUBLIC RECORDS

Agriculture of the United States in 1860, Compiled from the Original Returns of the Eighth Census. Washington, D.C.: Government Printing Office, 1864.

"Address to the Legislative Council of Florida on the Subject of Its Colored Population [c. 1829]." Typescript at Florida Park Service Archives, Tallahassee.

Alachua County. Deed records.

———. Inventories and appraisements.

———. Probate records.

———. Will records.

American State Papers: Indian Affairs. 2 vols. Washington, D.C.: Gales and Seaton, 1832–34.

American State Papers: Military Affairs. 7 Vols. Washington, D.C.: Gales and Seaton, 1832–60.

Bell, John H. Letter from John H. Bell, Acting Agent for the Indians in Florida to the Honorable John Floyd, of the House of Representatives of the U.S. Relative to Indian Settlements in Florida. Washington, D.C.: Gales and Seaton, 1822.

Carter, Clarence E., comp. Territorial Papers of the United States. Vols. 22–26, Florida Territory. Washington, D.C.: Government Printing Office, 1956–62.

Clay County. Probate and will records.

Compendium of the Enumeration of the Inhabitants and Statistics of the United States, Sixth Census, 1840, Agriculture. Washington, D.C.: Rives and Blair, 1841.

Compendium of the Seventh Census, 1850, Agriculture. Washington, D.C.: Government Printing Office, 1854.

Department of War. Department and District of Key West. Letters Received, 1861–68. RG 393, NA.

———. Records of the Office of the Chief of Army Engineers. RG 77, NA.

———. Records of the Union Soldiers Who Served during the Civil War. RG 94. Microcopy No. M-858, NA.

———. United States Colored Troops General Descriptive Books. RG 94, NA.

Duval, John P. *Compilation of the Public Acts of the Legislative Council of the Territory of Florida Passed Prior to 1840*. Tallahassee: Samuel S. Sibley, 1839.

Duval County. Deed records.

———. Inventories and appraisements.

———. Probate records.

———. Will records.

Eighth Census of the United States, 1860, Manufacture. Washington, D.C.: Government Printing Office, 1865.

Escambia County. Civil case files.

———. Criminal case files.

———. Deed records.

———. Inventories and appraisements.

———. Probate records.

———. Superior court minutes.

———. Will records.

Federal Writers' Project. *Negro History in Florida*. Jacksonville: Work Projects Administration, 1936.

Fifth Census or Enumeration of the Inhabitants of the United States as Corrected at the Department of State, 1830. Washington, D.C.: Duff Green, 1832.

Florida. Comptroller. Vouchers—Criminal Prosecutions. RG 350, series 565, FSA.

———. *Florida Reports*, 1853.

———. Governor. Books of Record (Proclamations). RG 156, series 13, FSA.

———. *Laws of Florida*, 1845–65.

———. *Laws of Territorial Florida*, 1822–45.

———. Records of the Department of State. RG 156, series 13. FSA.

———. Territorial auditor. Vouchers. RG 352, series 584, FSA.

Florida Direct Tax Commission. Records. RG 59, NA.

Gadsden County. Deed records.

———. Grand jury records.

———. Inventories and appraisements.

———. Probate records.

———. Tax books.

———. Will records.

Hamilton County. Deed records.

———. Inventories and appraisements.

———. Probate records.

———. Tax books.

———. Will records.

Hillsborough County. Probate records.

———. Will records.

Historical Statistics of the United States, Colonial Times to 1957. Washington, D.C.: Government Printing Office, 1960.

Jackson County. Deed records.

———. Inventories and appraisements.

———. Probate records.

———. Tax books.

———. Will records.

Jacksonville. *Ordinances of the Town of Jacksonville of 1859.* Jacksonville: C. Drew Book and Job Printing Office, 1859.

Jefferson County. Accounts current of executors, administrators, and guardians.

———. Board of commissioners minutes.

———. Superior court minutes.

———. Circuit court minutes.

———. Deed records.

———. Inventories, appraisements, and accounts.

———. Petitions for dower and sale of real estate.

———. Probate records.

———. Tax books.

———. Will records and letters testamentary.

Lafayette County. Tax books.

Leon County. Book of sales of personal estates.

———. Circuit court minutes.

———. Deed records.

———. Inventory and appraisements.

———. Marriage records.

———. Probate records.

———. Records of civil actions.

———. Superior court minutes.

———. Tax books.

———. Will records.

Liberty County. Tax books.

Madison County. Annual returns records.

———. Deed records.

———. Probate records.

———. Tax books.

———. Will records and letters testamentary.

Manufactures of the United States in 1860; Compiled from the Original Returns of the Eighth Census, under the Direction of the Secretary of the Interior. Washington, D.C.: Government Printing Office, 1865.

Office of Indian Affairs. Letters Received, Florida Superintendency of Emigration, 1824–38. Microcopy No. M-234, roll 290.

———. Letters Received, Seminole Agency, 1824–76 (1846–55). RG 75, NA. Microcopy No. M-234, roll 806.

———. Special Files, 1807–1904. Microcopy No. M-574, roll 13.

Official Records of the Union and Confederate Navies in the War of the Rebellion. 30 vols. Washington, D.C.: Government Printing Office, 1894–1922.

Orange County. Minutes of the circuit court.

Polk County. Marriage records.

Population of the United States in 1860; Compiled from the Original Returns of the Eighth Census. Washington, D.C.: Government Printing Office: 1864.

Putnam County. Book of sales of personal estates.

———. Case files.

———. Circuit court minutes.

———. Deed records.

———. Probate records.

———. Will records.

———. Inventory and appraisements.

St. Johns County. Circuit court records. At SAHSRL.

———. Deed records.

———. Marriage records. At SAHSRL.

———. Superior court records. At SAHSRL.

———. Will and probate records. At SAHSRL.

Seventh Census of the United States, 1850. Washington, D.C.: Government Printing Office, 1853–55.

Sixth Census of the United States, 1840, Manufacture. Washington, D.C.: Rives and Blair, 1841.

Sixth Census or Enumeration of the Inhabitants of the United States, 1840. Washington, D.C.: Rives and Blair, 1841.

Statistics of the United States (Including Mortality, Property, etc.) in 1860; Compiled from the Original Returns and Being the Final Exhibit of the Eighth Census. Washington, D.C.: Government Printing Office, 1864.

Thompson, Leslie A. *A Manual or Digest of the Statute Law of the State of Florida.* Boston: C. C. Little and J. Brown, 1847.

United States Congress Serial Set. Washington, D.C.

U.S. Decennial Censuses, 1830–70. Manuscript returns. Available on microfilm at FSA and SLF.

Veterans Administration. Pension files. RG 15, NA.

War of the Rebellion: A Compilation of the Official Records of the Union and

Confederate Armies. 128 vols. Washington, D.C.: Government Printing Office, 1880–1901.

NEWSPAPERS AND PERIODICALS

Albany (N.Y.) Patriot, 1861.
The American Missionary, 1865.
Army and Navy Chronicle, 1837.
Apalachicola Commercial Advertiser, 1849, 1855.
Apalachicola Gazette, 1839.
Apalachicolian, 1840.
Bartow Courier-Informant, 1895–96.
Boston Daily Journal, 1862.
Brooksville Hernando Today, 1999.
The California Illustrated, 1892.
Dade City Banner, 1924.
De Bow's Review, 1858, 1860.
Fernandina East Floridian, 1860.
Fernandina Florida Mirror, 1882.
Fernandina Peninsula, 1863.
Fernandina Weekly East Floridian, 1860.
Georgetown (S.C.) Winyah Observer, 1851–52.
Harper's Weekly, 1860, 1862.
Jacksonville Courier, 1835, 1851.
Jacksonville East Florida Advocate, 1839–40.
Jacksonville Florida News, 1846–57.
Jacksonville Florida Republican, 1850–56.
Jacksonville Florida Times-Union, 1883, 1892, 1895–96.
Jacksonville Florida Union, 1865.
Jacksonville News, 1845–58.
Jacksonville St. Johns Mirror, 1861.
Jacksonville Standard, 1859–60.
Jacksonville Weekly News-Herald, 1888.
Key West New Era, 1862.
Key West Register and Commercial Advertiser, 1829.
Lake City Columbian, 1865.
Magnolia Advertiser, 1829.
Nassau Royal Gazette and Literary Register, 1822.
New York Globe, 1883.
New York Herald, 1864.
New York Morning Courier and New York Enquirer, 1836.
New York Times, 1862.

New York New-Yorker, 1837.

Niles' Weekly Register, 1836.

Palatka Whig Banner, 1846.

Pensacola Gazette, 1822, 1828–30, 1834–35, 1837–40, 1844–46, 1848, 1851, 1853, 1854, 1857.

Pensacola Floridian, 1822.

Pensacola News-Journal, 1972.

Philadelphia Inquirer, 1861–62.

Philadelphia National Gazette and Literary Register, 1821.

Quincy Sentinel, 1840–43.

St. Augustine Ancient City, 1852–53.

St. Augustine East Florida Herald, 1823–37.

St. Augustine Evening Record, 1930.

St. Augustine Examiner, 1862.

St. Augustine Florida Gazette, 1821.

St. Augustine Florida Herald, 1824–37.

St. Augustine Florida Herald and Southern Democrat, 1839–41, 1844.

St. Augustine News, 1839–42.

St. Augustine Record, 1934, 1987.

Savannah Daily Georgian, 1853.

Savannah Evening Journal, 1854.

Savannah Morning News, 1857, 1874.

The Southern Cultivator, 1854, 1856–58.

Tallahassee Florida Advocate, 1828–29, 1838.

Tallahassee Florida Intelligencer, 1826.

Tallahassee Florida Sentinel, 1839–47, 1850–62.

Tallahassee Florida Watchman, 1838.

Tallahassee Floridian, 1832–48, 1851, 1858.

Tallahassee Floridian and Advocate, 1828–32.

Tallahassee Floridian and Journal, 1849–60.

Tallahassee Southern Journal, 1846.

Tallahassee Star of Florida, 1840–43.

Tallahassee Weekly Floridian, 1877.

Tampa Daily Times, 1923–24.

Tampa Florida Peninsular, 1855–66.

Tampa Journal, 1888.

Tampa Morning Tribune, 1896, 1901, 1927.

Tampa Sunday Tribune, 1948, 1955, 1988–89.

Tampa Sunland Tribune, 1877.

Wauchula Herald-Advocate, 1991.

Secondary Sources

Abbey, Kathryn T. "Documents Relating to El Destino and Chemonie Plantations, Middle Florida, 1828–1868." Part 1. *Florida Historical Quarterly* 7 (January 1929): 179–213.

———. "Documents Relating to El Destino and Chemonie Plantations, Middle Florida, 1828–1868." Part 2. *Florida Historical Quarterly* 7 (April 1929): 291–329.

———. "Documents Relating to El Destino and Chemonie Plantations, Middle Florida, 1828–1868." Part 3. *Florida Historical Quarterly* 8 (July 1929): 3–46.

———. "Documents Relating to El Destino and Chemonie Plantations, Middle Florida, 1828–1868." Part 4. *Florida Historical Quarterly* 8 (October 1929): 79–111.

Akerman, Joe A., Jr. *Florida Cowman: A History of Florida Cattle Raising.* Kissimmee: Florida Cattlemen's Association, 1976.

Aimes, Hubert H. S. *History of Slavery in Cuba.* New York: Putnam, 1907.

Alexander, J. H. "The Ambush of Captain John William, U.S.M.C.: Failure of the East Florida Invasion: 1812–1813." *Florida Historical Quarterly* 56 (July 1977): 280–96.

Appleyard, Lula Dee Keith. "Plantation Life in Middle Florida, 1821–1845." Master's thesis, Florida State University, 1940.

Aptheker, Herbert. *American Negro Slave Revolts.* New York: Columbia University Press, 1938.

Arnade, Charles W. "Raids, Sieges, and International War." In *The New History of Florida,* edited by Michael Gannon. Gainesville: University Press of Florida, 1996.

Bailey, David Thomas. "A Divided Prism: Two Sources of Black Testimony on Slavery." *Journal of Southern History* 46 (August 1980): 381–404.

Baldwin, Lewis. "Festivity and Celebration in a Black Methodist Tradition, 1813–1981." In *How Sweet the Sound: The Spirit of African American History,* edited by Nancy-Elizabeth Fitch, 391–98. New York: Harcourt Brace and Company, 2000.

Ballagh, James Curtis. *A History of Slavery in Virginia.* Baltimore: Johns Hopkins Press, 1902.

Bancroft, Frederic. *Slave Trading in the Old South.* New York: Frederick Ungar Publishing, 1931.

Baptist, Edward E. "The Migration of Planters to Antebellum Florida: Kinship and Power." *Journal of Southern History* 62 (August 1996): 527–44.

Barr, Ruth B., and Modeste Hargis. "The Voluntary Exile of Free Negroes of Pensacola." *Florida Historical Quarterly* 17 (July 1938): 3–14.

Bassett, John Spencer. *Slavery in the State of North Carolina*. Baltimore: Johns Hopkins Press, 1899.

Bateman, Fred, and Thomas Weiss. *Deplorable Scarcity: The Failure of Industrialization in the Slave Economy*. Chapel Hill: University of North Carolina Press, 1981.

Bates, Thelma, "The Legal Status of the Negro in Florida." *Florida Historical Quarterly* 7 (January 1928): 159–81.

———. "A Preliminary Study of the Legal Status of the Negro in Florida." Master's thesis, Florida State University, 1927.

Bauer, Raymond A., and Alice H. Bauer. "Day to Day Resistance to Slavery." *Journal of Negro History* 27 (October 1942): 388–419.

Bellamy, Donnie D. "Slavery in Microcosm: Onslow County, North Carolina." *Journal of Negro History* 62 (October 1977): 339–50.

Bennett, Charles. *Twelve on the River St. Johns*. Jacksonville: University of North Florida Press, 1989.

Bentley, Altermese Smith. *Georgetown: The History of a Black Neighborhood*. Georgetown: priv. pub., 1989.

Berlin, Ira. *Many Thousands Gone: The First Two Centuries of Slavery in North America*. Cambridge: Belknap/Harvard University Press, 1998.

———. "The Slaves' Changing World." In *A History of the African American People: The History, Traditions and Culture of African Americans*. Detroit: Wayne State University Press, 1997.

———. *Slaves without Masters: The Free Negro in the Antebellum South*. New York: Pantheon, 1974.

Berlin, Ira, and Philip D. Morgan, eds. *Cultivation and Culture: Labor and the Shaping of Slave Life in the Americas*. Charlottesville: University Press of Virginia, 1993.

Berlin, Ira, and Leslie S. Rowland, eds. *Families and Freedom: A Documentary History of African-American Kinship in the Civil War Era*. New York: Free Press, 1997.

Bickel, Karl A. *The Mangrove Coast*. New York: Coward-McCann, 1942.

Blackett, R. J. M. *Beating against the Barriers: Biographical Essays in Nineteenth-Century Afro-American History*. Baton Rouge: Louisiana State University Press, 1986.

———. *Building an Antislavery Wall: Black Americans in the Atlantic Abolitionist Movement, 1830–1860*. Baton Rouge: Louisiana State University Press, 1983.

Blakey, Arch Fredric. *Parade of Memories: A History of Clay County, Florida*. Green Cove Springs: Clay County Bicentennial Steering Committee, 1976.

Blakey, Arch Fredric, Ann Smith Lainhart, and Winston Bryant Stephens Jr., eds. *Rose Cottage Chronicles: Civil War Letters of the Bryant-Stephens Families of North Florida*. Gainesville: University Press of Florida, 1998.

Blassingame, John W. *The Slave Community: Plantation Life in the Antebellum South.* 2d ed. New York: Oxford University Press, 1979.

———. "Using the Testimony of Ex-slaves: Approaches and Problems." *Journal of Southern History* 41 (November 1975): 473–92.

———, ed. *Slave Testimony: Two Centuries of Letters, Speeches, Interviews, and Autobiographies.* Baton Rouge: Louisiana State University Press, 1997.

Blatzell, George F. "The Battle of Olustee." *Florida Historical Quarterly* 9 (April 1931): 199–223.

Bleser, Carol. *The Hammonds of Redcliffe.* New York: Oxford University Press, 1981.

———, ed. *In Joy and in Sorrow: Women, Family, and Marriage in the Victorian South, 1830–1900.* New York: Oxford University Press, 1991.

Blockson, Charles L. "Sea Change in the Islands: 'Nowhere to Lay Down Weary Head.'" *National Geographic* 172 (December 1987): 735–63.

Boggess, Francis C. M. *A Veteran of Four Wars: The Autobiography of F. C. M. Boggess.* Arcadia: Champion Print Shop, 1900.

Boles, John B. *Black Southerners, 1619–1869.* Lexington: University Press of Kentucky, 1983.

———, ed. *Masters and Slaves in the House of the Lord: Race and Religion in the American South, 1740–1870.* Lexington: University Press of Kentucky, 1988.

Bonnett, Vaughn D. "A Connecticut Yankee at Olustee—Letters from the Front." *Florida Historical Quarterly* 27 (January 1949): 237–59.

Boyd, Mark F. "The Battle of Marianna." *Florida Historical Quarterly* 30 (April 1951): 225–42.

———. "The Battle of Natural Bridge." *Florida Historical Quarterly* 29 (October 1950): 96–124.

———. "Events at Prospect Bluff on the Apalachicola River, 1808–1818." *Florida Historical Quarterly* 16 (October 1937): 55–96.

———. "The Federal Campaign of 1864 in East Florida." *Florida Historical Quarterly* 29 (July 1950): 3–37.

———. *The Federal Campaign of 1864 in East Florida.* Tallahassee: Florida Board of Parks and Historic Memorials, 1956.

———. "Horatio S. Dexter and Events Leading to the Treaty of Moultrie Creek with the Seminole Indians." *Florida Anthropologist* 6 (September 1958): 81–92.

———. "The Joint Operations of the Federal Army and Navy Near St. Marks, Florida, March 1865." *Florida Historical Quarterly* 29 (October 1950): 96–124.

———. "The Seminole War, Its Background and Onset." *Florida Historical Quarterly* 30 (July 1951): 3–23.

Brackett, Jeffrey R. *The Negro in Maryland: A Study of the Institution of Slavery.* New York: Negro Universities Press, 1969.

Brady, Rowena Ferrell. *Things Remembered: An Album of Africans in Tampa.* Tampa: University of Tampa Press, 1997.

Breen, T. H., and Stephen Innes. *'Myne Owne Ground': Race and Freedom on Virginia's Eastern Shore, 1640–1676.* New York: Oxford University Press, 1980.

Brevard, Caroline Mays. *A History of Florida from the Treaty of 1763 to Our Own Times.* 2 vols. DeLand: Florida State Historical Society, 1924.

Brooks, Walter H. "The Evolution of the Negro Baptist Church." *Journal of Negro History* 7 (January 1922): 11–22.

Brooks, William E. *History Highlights of Florida Methodism.* Ft. Lauderdale: Tropical Press, 1965.

Brown, Canter, Jr. "African Americans and the Tampa Bay Area to World War I." In *Things Remembered: An Album of African Americans in Tampa*, by Rowena Ferrell Brady. Tampa: University of Tampa Press, 1997.

———. *African Americans on the Tampa Bay Frontier.* Tampa: Tampa Bay History Center, 1997.

———. *Children on the Tampa Bay Frontier.* Tampa: Tampa Bay History Center, 1996.

———. "The Civil War, 1861–1865." In *The New History of Florida*, edited by Michael Gannon. Gainesville: University Press of Florida, 1996.

———. "The East Florida Coffee Land Expedition of 1821: Plantations or a Bonapartist Kingdom of the Indies?" *Tequesta* 51 (1991): 7–28.

———. "The Florida, Atlantic and Gulf Central Railroad, 1851–1868." *Florida Historical Quarterly* 69 (April 1991): 411–29.

———. "The Florida Crisis of 1826–27 and the Second Seminole War." *Florida Historical Quarterly* 73 (April 1995): 419–42.

———. *Florida's Black Public Officials, 1867–1924.* Tuscaloosa: University of Alabama Press, 1998.

———. *Florida's Peace River Frontier.* Orlando: University of Central Florida Press, 1991.

———. *Fort Meade: 1849–1900.* Tuscaloosa: University of Alabama Press, 1995.

———. *Genealogical Records of the African-American Pioneers of Tampa and Hillsborough County.* Tampa: Tampa Bay History Center, 2000.

———. *Ossian Bingley Hart, Florida's Loyalist Reconstruction Governor.* Baton Rouge: Louisiana State University Press, 1997.

———. "Persifor F. Smith, the Louisiana Volunteers, and Florida's Second Seminole War." *Louisiana History* 34 (fall 1993): 407–10.

———. "Race Relations in Territorial Florida, 1821–1845." *Florida Historical Quarterly* 73 (January 1995): 287–307.

———. "The Sarrazota, or Runaway Negro Plantations: Tampa Bay's First Black Community, 1812–1821." *Tampa Bay History* 12 (fall/winter 1990): 5–19.

———. *Tampa before the Civil War.* Tampa: University of Tampa Press, 1999.

———. "Tampa's James McKay and the Frustration of Confederate Cattle-Supply Operations in South Florida." *Florida Historical Quarterly* 70 (April 1992): 409–33.

———. "'Where Are Now the Hopes I Cherished?' The Life and Times of Robert Meacham." *Florida Historical Quarterly* 69 (July 1990): 1–36.

———. *Women on the Tampa Bay Frontier.* Tampa: Tampa Bay History Center, 1997.

———, ed. "'Very Much Attached to Tampa': The Civil War–Era Letters of Catharine Campbell Hart, 1860 and 1865." *Sunland Tribune* 23 (November 1997): 63–69.

Brown, John. *Slave Life in Georgia.* London: Savannah Beehive Press, 1855.

Brown, William G. *The Lower South in American History.* New York: P. Smith, 1930.

Brown, William W. *A Narrative of My Own Life (A Fugitive Slave).* Boston: Anti-Slavery Society, 1847.

———. *The Negro in the American Rebellion: His Heroism and His Fidelity.* Repr. ed. New York: Citadel Press, 1971.

Browne, Jefferson B. *Key West: The Old and the New.* St. Augustine: Record Company Printers, 1912. Repr., Gainesville: University Press of Florida, 1973.

Browning, Edwin B., Sr. "A History of Concord Baptist Church, 1841–1868." Undated typescript in Strozier Library Special Collections, FSU.

Bryant, James C. *Indian Springs: The Story of a Pioneer Church in Leon County, Florida.* Tallahassee: Florida State University, 1971.

Buettinger, Craig. "Masters on Trial: The Enforcement of Laws against Self-Hire by Slaves in Jacksonville and Palatka Florida." *Civil War History* 46 (June 2000): 91–106.

Buker, George E. *Blockaders, Refugees, and Contrabands: Civil War on Florida's Gulf Coast, 1861–1865.* Tuscaloosa: University of Alabama Press, 1993.

———. *Jacksonville: Riverport-Seaport.* Columbia: University of South Carolina Press, 1992.

———. "St. Augustine and the Union Blockade." *El Escribano* 23 (1986): 1–18.

———. *Sun, Sand and Water: A History of the Jacksonville District, U.S. Army Corps of Engineers, 1821–1975.* Washington, D.C.: Government Printing Office, 1981.

Burton, Orville Vernon. *In My Father's House Are Many Mansions: Family and*

Comunity in Edgefield, South Carolina. Chapel Hill: University of North Carolina Press, 1985.

Campbell, Edward D. C., Jr., and Kym S. Rice, eds. *Before Freedom Came: African-American Life in the Antebellum South*. Charlottesville: University Press of Virginia, 1991.

Campbell, Randolph B. *An Empire for Slavery: The Peculiar Institution in Texas, 1821–1865*. Baton Rouge: Louisiana State University Press, 1989.

Cannon, W. B. "Voodoo Death." *American Anthropologist* 44 (April-June 1942): 169–81.

Cash, W. T. "Newport as a Business Center." *Apalachee* (1944): 13–28.

———. "Taylor County History and Civil War Deserters." *Florida Historical Quarterly* 27 (July 1948): 28–58.

Cash, Wilbur J. *The Mind of the South*. New York: Alfred A. Knopf, 1941.

Chaplin, Joyce E. "Tidal Rice Cultivation and the Problem of Slavery in South Carolina and Georgia, 1760–1815." *William and Mary Quarterly* 49 (January 1992): 29–61.

Chatelain, Verne E. *The Defenses of Spanish Florida, 1565–1763*. Washington, D.C.: Carnegie Institution, 1941.

Chatham, Katherine. "Plantation Slavery in Middle Florida." Master's thesis, University of North Carolina, 1938.

Childs, Thomas. "Major Childs, U.S.A.: Extracts from His Correspondence with His Family." *Historical Magazine*, 3d ser., 3 (April 1875): 280–84.

Cleveland, Mary Ann. "Florida Women and the Civil War." In *Florida Decades: A Sesquicentennial History: 1845–1995*, edited by Lewis N. Wynne and James J. Horgan. Saint Leo: Saint Leo College Press, 1995.

Clifton, James M. "Golden Grains of White: Rice Planting on the Lower Cape Fear." *North Carolina Historical Review* 50 (winter 1981): 266–83.

Clowse, Converse D. *Economic Beginnings of Colonial South Carolina, 1670–1730*. Columbia: University of South Carolina Press, 1971.

Coclanis, Peter A. *Shadow of Dream: Economic Life and Death in the South Carolina Low Country: 1670–1920*. New York: Oxford University Press, 1988.

Cody, Cheryll Ann. "Naming, Kinship, and Estate Dispersal: Notes on Slave Family Life on a South Carolina Plantation, 1786–1833." *William and Mary Quarterly* 39 (1982): 191–211.

———. "There Was No 'Absalom' on the Balls Plantations: Slave-Naming Practices in the South Carolina Low Country, 1720–1865." *American Historical Review* 92 (June 1987): 563–96.

Cohen, David W., and Jack P. Greene, eds. *Neither Slave nor Free: The Freedmen of African Descent in the Slave Societies of the New World*. Baltimore: Johns Hopkins University Press, 1972.

Cohen, Myer M. *Notices of East Florida and the Campaigns*. Charleston: Burgess and Honour, 1836.

Coker, William S. "The Financial History of Pensacola's Spanish Presidios, 1698–1763." *Pensacola Historical Society Quarterly* 94 (spring 1979): 1–20.

———. "Pedro de Rivera's Report on the Presidio of Punta de Siguenza, Alias Panzacola, 1744." *Pensacola Historical Society Quarterly* 84 (winter 1975): 1–22.

———. "Pensacola, 1686–1763." In *The New History of Florida,* edited by Michael Gannon. Gainesville: University Press of Florida, 1996.

———. "West Florida (the Spanish Presidios of Pensacola), 1686–1763." In *A Guide to the History of Florida,* edited by Paul S. George, 49–56. New York: Greenwood Press, 1989.

Coker, William S., and Susan R. Parker. "The Second Spanish Period in the Two Floridas." In *The New History of Florida,* edited by Michael Gannon. Gainesville: University Press of Florida, 1996.

Coker, William S., and Thomas D. Watson. *Indian Traders of the Southeastern Spanish Borderlands: Panton, Leslie & Company and John Forbes & Company, 1783–1847.* Pensacola: University of West Florida Press, 1986.

Colburn, David, and Jane Landers, eds. *The African American Heritage of Florida.* Gainesville: University Press of Florida, 1995.

Coleman, J. Winston, Jr. *Slavery Times in Kentucky.* Chapel Hill: University of North Carolina Press, 1940.

Coles, David J. "Ancient City Defenders: The St. Augustine Blues." *El Escribano* 23 (1986): 65–90.

———. *The Battle of Olustee and the Olustee Battlefield Site: A Brief History.* Gainesville: Olustee Battlefield Citizen Support Organization, 1992.

———. "'Far from Fields of Glory': Military Operations in Florida during the Civil War, 1864–1865." Ph.D. diss., Florida State University, 1996.

———. "'A Fight, a Licking, and a Footrace': The 1864 Florida Expedition and the Battle of Olustee." Master's thesis, Florida State University, 1985.

———. "The Florida Diaries of Daniel H. Wiggins, 1836–1841." *Florida Historical Quarterly* 73 (April 1995): 478–97.

———. "Florida's Seed Corn: The History of the West Florida Seminary during the Civil War." *Florida Historical Quarterly* 77 (winter 1999): 293–311.

———. "'A Terrible and Sad Result': The End of the Civil War in Florida, March–June 1865." In *Proceedings of the 90th Annual Meeting of the Florida Historical Society at St. Augustine, May* 1992. Tampa: Florida Historical Society, 1992.

———. "'They Fought like Devils': Black Troops in Florida during the Civil War." In *Florida's Heritage of Diversity: Essays in Honor of Samuel Proctor,* edited by Mark I. Greenberg, William Warren Rogers, and Canter Brown Jr. Tallahassee: Sentry Press, 1997.

———. "Unpretending Service: The *James L. Davis,* the *Tahoma,* and the East

Gulf Blockading Squadron." *Florida Historical Quarterly* 71 (July 1992): 41–62.

Collier, J. R. *History of a Branch of the Collier Family from the Year 1781 to the Present.* N.p., 1945.

Cooke, C. Wythe. *Geology of Florida.* Tallahassee: State of Florida Department of Conservation, 1945.

———. *Scenery of Florida.* Tallahassee: State of Florida Department of Conservation, 1939.

Corbett, Theodore G. "Migration to a Spanish Imperial Frontier in the Seventeenth and Eighteenth Centuries: St. Augustine." *Hispanic American Historical Review* 54 (August 1974): 414–30.

Cornish, Dudley Taylor. *The Sable Arm: Negro Troops in the Union Army, 1861–1865.* New York: Longman, Green, 1956.

———. "The Union Army as a Training School for Blacks." *Journal of Negro History* 37 (October 1952): 368–82.

Corwin, Arthur F. *Spain and the Abolition of Slavery in Cuba, 1817–1886.* Dallas: University of Texas Press, 1967.

Covington, James. W. "The Negro Fort." *Gulf Coast Historical Review* 5 (spring 1990): 79–91.

———. *The Seminoles of Florida.* Gainesville: University Press of Florida, 1993.

Cox, LaWanda. *Lincoln and Black Freedom: A Study in Presidential Leadership.* Columbia: University of South Carolina Press, 1981.

Crary, John Williamson, Sr. *Reminiscences of the Old South, 1834–1866.* Pensacola: Perdido Bay Press, 1984.

Creel, Margaret Washington. "Gullah Attitudes toward Life and Death." In *Africanisms in American Culture,* edited by Joseph E. Holloway. Bloomington: Indiana University Press, 1990.

———. *"A Peculiar People": Slave Religion and Community-Culture among the Gullahs.* New York: New York University Press, 1988.

Crowninshield, Benjamin William. *A History of the First Regiment of Massachusetts Cavalry Volunteers.* New York: Houghton, Mifflin, 1891. Repr., Baltimore: Butternut and Blue, 1995.

Cudwork, Warren Handel. *History of the First Regiment (Massachusetts Infantry), from the 25th of May, 1861, to the 25th of May, 1864.* Boston: Walker, Fuller, 1866.

Cushman, Joseph D., Jr. "The Episcopal Church in Florida, 1892–1921." Ph.D. diss., Florida State University, 1961.

———. *Goodly Heritage: The Episcopal Church in Florida 1821–1982.* Gainesville: University of Florida Press, 1965.

Davis, Charles S. *The Cotton Kingdom in Alabama.* Montgomery: Alabama State Department of Archives and History, 1939.

Davis, David B. *The Problem of Slavery in Western Culture.* Ithaca, N.Y.: Cornell University Press, 1966.

Davis, Jess G. *History of Alachua County, 1844–1969.* Gainesville: Alachua County Historical Commission, 1970.

———. *History of Gainesville, Florida.* Gainesville: n.p., 1966.

Davis, Mary Kemp. *Nat Turner before the Bar of Judgment: Fictional Treatments of the Southampton Slave Insurrection.* Baton Rouge: Louisiana State University Press, 1999.

Davis, Thomas Frederick. *A History of Jacksonville Florida and Vicinity, 1513 to 1924.* Jacksonville: Florida Historical Society, 1925. Repr., Jacksonville: San Marco Bookstore, 1990.

———. "MacGregor's Invasion of Florida, 1817." *Florida Historical Quarterly* 7 (July 1928): 3–69.

———. "Pioneer Florida: The Pad-Gaud at Pensacola, 1830." *Florida Historical Quarterly* 23 (April 1945): 220–26.

Davis, William Graham. "The Florida Legislative Council, 1822–1838." Master's thesis, Florida State University, 1970.

Davis, William Watson. *Civil War and Reconstruction in Florida.* New York: Columbia University Press, 1913.

De Bow, James B. D. *The Industrial Resources of the Southern and Western States.* 3 vols. New Orleans: Office of *De Bow's Review,* 1852–1853.

de Castlenau, Francis. "Comte de Castlenau in Middle Florida 1837–1838, Notes Concerning Two Itineraries from Charleston to Tallahassee." Translated by Arthur R. Seymour. *Florida Historical Quarterly* 26 (April 1948): 300–24.

———. "Essay on Middle Florida, 1837, 1838." Translated by Arthur R. Seymour. *Florida Historical Quarterly* 26 (January 1948): 199–255.

"'The Defenses of the Floridas': A Report of Captain James Gadsden, Aide-de-Camp to General Andrew Jackson." *Florida Historical Quarterly* 15 (April 1937): 242–48.

DeFoor, J. Allison, II. *Odet Philippe: Peninsular Pioneer.* Safety Harbor: Safety Harbor Museum of Regional History, 1997.

Degler, Carl N. *Neither Black nor White: Slavery and Race Relations in Brazil and the United States.* New York: Macmillan, 1971.

Denham, James M. "Cracker Women and Their Families in Nineteenth-Century Florida." In *Florida's Heritage of Diversity: Essays in Honor of Samuel Proctor,* edited by Mark I. Greenberg, William Warren Rogers, and Canter Brown Jr. Tallahassee: Sentry Press, 1997.

———. "The Florida Cracker before the Civil War as Seen through Travelers' Accounts." *Florida Historical Quarterly* 72 (April 1994): 453–68.

———. *"A Rogue's Paradise": Crime and Punishment in Antebellum Florida, 1821–1861.* Tuscaloosa: University of Alabama Press, 1997.

Denham, James M., and Canter Brown Jr. *Cracker Times and Pioneer Lives, The Florida Reminiscences of George Gillett Keen and Sarah Pamela Williams.* Columbia: University of South Carolina Press, 2000.

"A Diary of Joshua Nichols Glenn, St. Augustine in 1823." *Florida Historical Quarterly* 24 (October 1945): 121–61.

Dibble, Ernest F. *Antebellum Pensacola and the Military Presence.* 3 vols. Pensacola: Pensacola News-Journal, 1974.

———. "Slave Rentals to the Military: Pensacola and the Gulf Coast." *Civil War History* 23 (June 1977): 101–13.

Dillard, Joseph L. *Black English: Its History and Usage in the United States.* New York: Random House, 1972.

Dillon, Rodney E. "The Civil War in South Florida." Master's thesis, University of Florida, 1980.

Dodd, Dorothy. *Florida Becomes a State.* Tallahassee: Florida Centennial Commission, 1945.

———. "Horse Racing in Middle Florida, 1830–1860." *Apalachee* 3 (1950): 20–29.

Doherty, Herbert J. "Antebellum Pensacola, 1821–1860." *Florida Historical Quarterly* 37 (January-April 1959): 332–56.

———. *Richard Keith Call, Southern Unionist.* Gainesville: University Press of Florida, 1901.

———. *The Whigs of Florida, 1845–1854.* Gainesville: University Press of Florida, 1959.

Douglas, Thomas. *Autobiography of Thomas Douglas.* New York: 1956.

Dovell, J. F. *Florida: Historic, Dramatic, Contemporary.* 4 vols. New York: Lewis Historical Publishing, 1952.

Drake, J. V. *The Florida Legislature: An Official Directory of State Government.* Jacksonville: Times-Union Book and Job Office, 1883.

Du Bois, William Edward Burghart. *Black Reconstruction: An Essay toward a History of the Part Which Black Folk Played in the Attempt to Reconstruct Democracy in America, 1860–1880.* New York: Harcourt, Brace, 1935.

———. *The Suppression of the Slave Trade to the United States of America, 1638–1870.* Cambridge: Harvard University Press, 1890.

Dunlop, J. G. "William Dunlop's Mission to St. Augustine in 1688." *South Carolina Historical and Genealogical Magazine* 34 (January 1933): 1–30.

Dunn, Marvin. *Black Miami in the Twentieth Century.* Gainesville: University Press of Florida, 1997.

Dusinberre, William. *Them Dark Days: Slavery in the American Rice Swamps.* New York: Oxford University Press, 1996.

Dyer, Frederick H. *A Compendium of the War of Rebellion.* 3 vols. New York: Thomas Yoseloff, 1959.

East, Omega G. "St. Augustine during the Civil War." *Florida Historical Quarterly* 31 (October 1952): 75–91.

Eaton, Clement. *Growth of Southern Civilization.* New York: Harper, 1961.

Elkins, Stanley M. *Slavery, a Problem in American Institutional and Intellectual Life.* Chicago: University of Chicago Press, 1959.

Elliott, Brenda. *Orange County Black Communities Survey, Phase 1—Seminole County: Project Report.* Orlando: Yeilding and Provost, 1990.

Ellis, Mary L., and William W. Rogers. *Favored Land: Tallahassee.* Norfolk/Virginia Beach, Va.: Donning Company, 1988.

Ellsworth, Lucian, and Linda Ellsworth, eds. *Pensacola: The Deep Water City.* Tulsa: Continental Heritage Press, 1982.

Eppes, Susan Bradford. *The Negro of the Old South: A Bit of Period History.* Chicago: Joseph G. Branch Publishing, 1925.

———. *Through Some Eventful Years.* Macon: J. W. Burke Company, 1926.

Escott, Paul D. *Slavery Remembered: A Record of Twentieth-Century Slave Narratives.* Chapel Hill: University of North Carolina Press, 1979.

Fabel, Robin F. A. "British Rule in the Floridas." In *The New History of Florida,* edited by Michael Gannon. Gainesville: University Press of Florida, 1995.

Farley, Charlotte C. *Florida's Alamo: The Battle of Marianna "As 'Twas Said to Me."* N.p., n.d.

Faust, Drew Gilpin. "Culture, Conflict, and Community: The Meaning of Power on an Antebellum Plantation." *Journal of Social History* (fall 1980): 83–97.

———. *James Henry Hammond and the Old South: A Design for Mastery.* Baton Rouge: Louisiana State University Press, 1982.

———. *Mothers of Invention: Women of the Slaveholding South in the American Civil War.* Chapel Hill: University of North Carolina Press, 1996.

———. "Slavery in the American Experience." In *Before Freedom Came,* edited by Edward D. C. Campbell Jr. and Kym S. Rice. Charlottesville: University Press of Virginia, 1991.

Federal Writers' Project. *Slave Narratives: A Folk History of Slavery in the United States, from Interviews with Former Slaves.* 17 vols. St. Clair Shores, Mich.: Scholarly Press, 1976.

Fennell, Frankie H. "Blacks in Jacksonville, 1840–1865." Master's thesis, Florida State University, 1978.

Fields, Barbara Jeanne. *Slavery and Freedom on the Middle Ground: Maryland during the Nineteenth Century.* New Haven: Yale University, 1985.

Fishel, Leslie H., Jr., and Benjamin Quarles, eds. *The Negro American: A Documentary History.* Glenview: Scott, Foresman, 1967.

Fitch, Nancy-Elizabeth. ed. *How Sweet the Sound: The Spirit of African American History.* New York: Harcourt Brace and Company, 2000.

Flanigan, Daniel. "The Criminal Law of Slavery and Freedom, 1800–1868." Ph.D. diss., Rice University, 1973.

———. "Criminal Procedure in Slave Trials in the Antebellum South." *Journal of Southern History* 40 (November 1974): 537–64.

Flanders, Ralph Betts. *Plantation Slavery in Georgia.* Chapel Hill: University of North Carolina Press, 1933.

Fogel, Robert William, and Stanley L. Engerman. *Time on the Cross: The Economics of American Negro Slavery.* 2 vols. Boston: Little, Brown, 1974.

Foner, Laura. "The Free People of Color in Louisiana and St. Domingue: A Comparative Portrait of Two Three-Caste Societies." *Journal of Social History* 3 (summer 1970): 406–30.

Foster, George M. *The Methodist Episcopal Church in Ocala, Florida, 1844–1953.* Ocala: Ocala Star Banner, 1953.

Foster, John T., Jr., and Sarah Whitmer Foster. *Beechers, Stowes, and Yankee Strangers: The Transformation of Florida.* Gainesville: University Press of Florida, 1999.

Foster, Laurence. "Negro-Indian Relationships in the Southeast." Ph.D. diss., University of Pennsylvania, 1935.

Foster, William H. "'This Place Is Safe': Engineer Operations at Fort Zachary Taylor, Florida, 1845–1864." Master's thesis, Florida State University, 1974.

Fox-Genovese, Elizabeth. *Within the Plantation Household: Black and White Women of the Old South.* Chapel Hill: University of North Carolina Press, 1988.

Franklin, John Hope, and Alfred A. Moss Jr. *From Slavery to Freedom: A History of African Americans.* New York: Alfred A. Knopf, 1967.

Franklin, John Hope, and Loren Schweninger. *Runaway Slaves: Rebels on the Plantation, 1790–1860.* New York: Oxford University Press, 1999.

Fredrickson, George M. *The Black Image in the White Mind: The Debate on Afro-American Character and Destiny, 1817–1914.* New York: Harper and Row, 1971.

Galpin, Rosa. "John C. McGehee." *Florida Historical Quarterly* 4 (April 1926): 186–91.

Gannon, Michael. "First European Contacts." In *The New History of Florida,* edited by Michael Gannon. Gainesville: University Press of Florida, 1996.

Gannon, Michael, ed. *The New History of Florida.* Gainesville: University Press of Florida, 1996.

Gavin, Russell. "The Free Negro in Florida before the Civil War." *Florida Historical Quarterly* 46 (July 1967): 9–17.

Genovese, Eugene D. "American Slaves and Their History." In *Red and Black: Marxian Explorations in Southern and Afro-American History,* edited by Eugene Genovese. New York: Pantheon Books, 1971.

———. *A Consuming Fire: The Fall of the Confederacy in the Mind of the White Christian South.* Athens: University of Georgia Press, 1998.

———. *The Political Economy of Slavery: Studies in the Economy and Society of the Slave South.* New York: Pantheon Books, 1961.

———. "Rebelliousness and Docility in the Negro Slave: A Critique of Elkins' Thesis." *Civil War History* 13 (December 1967): 293–314.

———. *From Revolution to Rebellion: Afro-American Slave Revolts in the Making of the Modern World.* Baton Rouge: Louisiana State University Press, 1979.

———. *Roll, Jordan, Roll: The World the Slaves Made.* New York: Pantheon Books, 1974.

———. "The Treatment of Slaves in Different Countries: Problems in the Application of the Comparative Method." In *Slavery in the New World: A Reader in Comparative History,* edited by Laura Foner and Eugene D. Genovese. Englewood Cliffs, N.J.: Prentice-Hall, 1969.

———. *The World the Slaveholders Made.* New York: Vintage Books, 1969.

———. *Yankee Saints and Southern Sinners.* Baton Rouge: Louisiana State University Press, 1985.

———, ed. *The Slave Economies.* 2 vols. New York: Wiley Press, 1973.

Gibson, James R. *European Settlement and Development in North America: Essays on Geographical Change in Honour and Memory of Andrew Hill Clark.* Toronto: University of Toronto Press, 1978.

Giddings, Joshua R. *The Exiles of Florida; or, The Crimes Committed by Our Government against the Maroons, Who Fled from South Carolina and Other Slave States, Seeking Protection under Spanish Laws.* Columbus, Ohio: Follett, Foster, 1858. Repr., Gainesville: University Press of Florida, 1964.

Gilmore, Al-Tony, ed. *Revisiting Blassingame's "The Slave Community": The Scholars Respond.* Westport, Conn.: Greenwood Press, 1978.

Glatthaar, Joseph T. *Forged in Battle: The Civil War Alliance of Black Soldiers and White Officers.* New York: Free Press, 1990.

Glover, Faye L. "Zephaniah Kingsley: Nonconformist, Slave Trader, Patriarch." Master's thesis, Atlanta University, 1970.

Glunt, James David. "Plantation and Frontier Records of East and Middle Florida, 1789–1868." Ph.D. diss., University of Michigan, 1930.

Goggin, John M. "The Seminole Negroes of Andros Island, Bahamas." *Florida Historical Quarterly* 24 (January 1946): 201–6.

Gold, Pleasant D. *History of Duval County, Including Early History of East Florida.* St. Augustine: Record Company, 1928.

Gold, Robert L. "The Settlement of the East Florida Spaniards in Cuba, 1763–1766." *Florida Historical Quarterly* 42 (January 1964): 216–31.

Gosse, Philip Henry. *Letters from Alabama Chiefly Relating to Natural History.* London: Morgan and Chase, 1859.

Graham, Thomas. *The Awakening of St. Augustine, the Anderson Family, and the Oldest City: 1821–1924.* St. Augustine: St. Augustine Historical Society, 1978.

———. "The Home Front: Civil War Times in St. Augustine." *El Escribano* 23 (1986): 19–46.

Granade, Ray. "Slave Unrest in Florida." *Florida Historical Quarterly* 55 (July 1976): 18–36.

Gray, Lewis C. *History of Agriculture in the Southern United States to 1860.* 2 vols. Washington: Carnegie Institution, 1933.

Greenberg, Mark I., William Warren Rogers, and Canter Brown Jr., eds. *Florida's Heritage of Diversity: Essays in Honor of Samuel Proctor.* Tallahassee: Sentry Press, 1997.

Griffin, Richard W. "The Cotton Mill Campaign in Florida, 1828–1863." *Florida Historical Quarterly* 40 (January 1962): 262–74.

Grismer, Karl H. *Tampa: A History of the City of Tampa and the Tampa Bay Region of Florida.* St. Petersburg: St. Petersburg Printing, 1950.

Groene, Bertram. *Ante-Bellum Tallahassee.* Tallahassee: Florida Heritage Foundation, 1971.

Guide to Supplementary Vital Statistics from Church Records in Florida. 3 vols. Jacksonville: Historical Records Survey, 1942.

Gutman, Herbert G. *The Black Family in Slavery and Freedom, 1750–1925.* New York: Pantheon, 1976.

Hall, Robert L. "African Religious Retentions in Florida." In *The African American Heritage of Florida,* edited by David R. Colburn and Jane L. Landers. Gainesville: University Press of Florida, 1995.

———. "African Religious Retentions in Florida." In *Africanisms in American Culture,* edited by Joseph E. Holloway. Bloomington: Indiana University Press, 1990.

———. "Black and White Christians in Florida, 1822–1861." In *Masters and Slaves in the House of the Lord,* edited by John Boles. Lexington: University Press of Kentucky, 1988.

———. "'Do Lord, Remember Me': Religion and Cultural Change among Blacks in Florida, 1565–1906." Ph.D. diss., Florida State University, 1984.

———. "Religious Symbolism of the Iron Pot: The Plausibility of a Congo-Angola Origin." *Western Journal of Black Studies* 13, no. 3 (fall 1989): 125–29.

———. "'Yonder Come Day': Religious Dimensions of the Transition from Slavery to Freedom in Florida." *Florida Historical Quarterly* 65 (April 1987): 411–32.

Hamilton, Mrs. Donald. "Dempsey Dubois Crews 1806–1893." *South Florida Pioneers* 12 (April 1977): 8–11.

Hammond, E. Ashby. *The Medical Profession in Nineteenth Century Florida: A Biographical Register.* Gainesville: George A. Smathers Libraries, 1996.

Hanna, A. J. *A Prince in Their Midst: The Adventurous Life of Achille Murat on the American Frontier.* Norman: University of Oklahoma Press, 1946.

Harper, Roland M. "Antebellum Census Enumerations in Florida." *Florida Historical Quarterly* 6 (July 1927): 42–52.

Harris, Donorena. "Abolitionist Sentiment in Florida, 1821–1860." Master's thesis, Florida State University, 1989.

Harris, Marvin. *Patterns of Race in the Americas.* New York: Walker, 1964.

Hawes, Leland. "Cannonball Exploded Blacks' Rallying Point." *Tampa Sunday Tribune,* March 19, 1989.

———. "One-Time Slave Sheds Light on Life in Tampa." *Tampa Sunday Tribune,* June 5, 1988.

Helms, Mary. "Black Carib Domestic Organization in Historical Perspective: Traditional Origins of Contemporary Patterns." *Ethnology* 20 (January 1981): 77–86.

Hering, Julia F. "Plantation Economy in Leon County, 1830–1890." *Florida Historical Quarterly* 33 (July 1954): 32–47.

Heyrman, Christine Leigh. *Southern Cross: The Beginnings of the Bible Belt.* New York: Alfred A. Knopf, 1997.

Higginson, Thomas Wentworth. *Army Life in a Black Regiment.* Boston: Fields, Osgood, 1870. Repr., Boston: Beacon Press, 1962.

Hill, Louise Biles. "George J. F. Clarke, 1774–1836." *Florida Historical Quarterly* 21 (January 1943): 197–253.

Hilliard, Sam. B. "Antebellum Tidewater Rice Culture in South Carolina and Georgia." In *European Settlement and Development in North America: Essays on Geographical Change in Honour and Memory of Andrew Hill Clark,* edited by James R. Gibson. Toronto: University of Toronto Press, 1978.

Hine, Darlene Clark, Wilma King, and Linda Reed, eds. *"We Specialize in the Wholly Impossible": A Reader in Black Women's History.* Brooklyn: Carlson Publishing, 1995.

Hine, Darlene Clark, William C. Hine, and Stanley Harrold. *The African-American Odyssey.* Upper Saddle River, N.J.: Prentice Hall, 2000.

History and Souvenir of Bethel Baptist Institutional Church, Jacksonville, Florida. Jacksonville: Bethel Baptist Institutional Church, c. 1920s.

Hitchcock, Ethan Allen. *Fifty Years in Camp and Field.* New York: G. P. Putnam's, 1909.

Holder, Emily. "At the Dry Tortugas during the War: A Lady's Journal." *Californian Illustrated* (February 1892): 183.

Holloway, Joseph E., ed. *Africanisms in American Culture.* Bloomington: Indiana University Press, 1990.

Hopley, Catherine Cooper (pseud. Sarah L. Jones). *Life in the South from the Commencement of the War, by a Blockaded English Subject*. London: Chapman and Hall, 1863.

Horton, James Oliver, and Lois Horton. *A History of the African American People: The History, Traditions and Culture of African Americans*. Detroit: Wayne State University Press, 1997.

Housewright, Wiley L. *A History of Music and Dance in Florida, 1565–1865*. Tuscaloosa: University of Alabama Press, 1991.

Hudson, Larry E., Jr. *To Have and to Hold: Slave Work and Family Life in Antebellum South Carolina*. Athens: University of Georgia Press, 1997.

Hughes, Sarah S. "Slaves for Hire: The Allocation of Black Labor in Elizabeth City, Virginia, 1782–1812." *William and Mary Quarterly* 35 (April 1978): 260–86.

Hundley, D. R. *Social Relations in Our Southern States*. New York: H. B. Price, 1860.

Hurston, Zora Neale. "Letters of Zora Neal Hurston on the Mose Settlement and the Negro Colony in Florida." *Journal of Negro History* 12 (October 1927): 664–69.

Ingle, John P., ed. "Soldiering with the Second Florida Regiment." *Florida Historical Quarterly* 59 (January 1981): 335–39.

Inscoe, John C. "Carolina Slave Names: An Index to Acculturation." *Journal of Southern History* 49 (November 1983): 27–54.

Itkin, Stanley L. "Operations of the East Gulf Blockading Squadron in the Blockade of Florida, 1862–1865." Master's thesis, Florida State University, 1962.

Jackson, Jesse J. "The Negro and the Law in Florida, 1821–1921." Master's thesis, Florida State University, 1960.

Jeffrey, Julie Roy. *Ordinary Women in the Antislavery Movement: The Great Silent Army of Abolitionism*. Chapel Hill: University of North Carolina Press, 1998.

Johns, John E. *Florida during the Civil War*. Gainesville: University Press of Florida, 1963.

Johnson, Alonzo, and Paul Jersild, eds. *"Ain't Gonna Lay My 'Ligion Down": African American Religion in the South*. Columbia: University of South Carolina Press, 1996.

Johnson, Michael P., and James L. Roark. *Black Masters: A Free Family of Color in the Old South*. New York: Norton, 1984.

———. *No Chariot Let Down: Charleston's Free People of Color on the Eve of the Civil War*. Chapel Hill: University of North Carolina Press, 1984.

Johnson, William C. "Trickster on Trial: The Morality of the Brer Rabbit Tales." In *"Ain't Gonna Lay My 'Ligion Down": African American Religion in the South,* edited by Alonzo Johnson and Paul Jersild. Columbia: University of South Carolina Press, 1996.

Joiner, Edward Earl. *A History of Florida Baptists.* Jacksonville: Convention Press, 1972.

Jones, Jacqueline. *Labor of Love, Labor of Sorrow: Black Women, Work, and the Family from Slavery to the Present.* New York: Basic Books, 1985.

————. "'My Mother Was Much of a Woman': Black Women, Work, and the Family under Slavery." *Feminist Studies* 8 (summer 1982): 235–67.

Jones, Maxine D., and Kevin M. McCarthy. *African Americans in Florida.* Sarasota: Pineapple Press, 1993.

Jordan, Winthrop D. *White over Black: American Attitudes toward the Negro, 1550–1812.* Baltimore: Penguin, 1968.

————. *The White Man's Burden: Historical Origins of Racism in the United States.* New York: Oxford University Press, 1974.

Joyner, Charles. *Down by the Riverside: A South Carolina Slave Community.* Urbana: University of Illinois Press, 1984.

————. *Remember Me: Slave Life in Coastal Georgia.* Atlanta: Georgia Humanities Council, 1989.

————. "The World of the Plantation Slaves." In *Before Freedom Came,* edited by Edward D. C. Campbell Jr. and Kym S. Rice. Charlottesville: University Press of Virginia, 1991.

Kay, Marvin L. Michael, and Lorin Lee Cary. *Slavery in North Carolina, 1748–1775.* Chapel Hill: University of North Carolina, 1995.

Kealing, H. T. *The History of African Methodism in Texas.* Waco: C. F. Blanks, Printer and Stationer, 1885.

Kersey, Harry A., Jr. "The Seminole Negroes of Andros Island Revisited: Some New Pieces to an Old Puzzle." *Florida Anthropologist* 34 (December 1981): 169–76.

Keuchel, Edward F. *A History of Columbia County, Florida.* Tallahassee: Sentry Press, 1981.

King, Wilma. *Stolen Childhood: Slave Youth in Nineteenth-Century America.* Bloomington: Indiana University Press, 1995.

Kingsley, Zephaniah. *A Treatise on the Patriarchal or Cooperative System of Society as It Exists in Some Governments, and Colonies in America, and in the United States under the Name of Slavery with Its Necessity and Advantages.* Freeport: n.p., 1829.

Kirk, Cooper C. "A History of the Southern Prebyterian Church in Florida, 1821–1891." Ph.D. diss., Florida State University, 1966.

Klein, Herbert. *Slavery in the Americas: Comparative Study of Cuba and Virginia.* Chicago: University of Chicago Press, 1967.

Klingberg, Frank. *The Negro in Colonial South Carolina: A Study in Americanization.* Washington, D.C.: Associated Publishers, 1941.

Klos, George. "Black Seminoles in Territorial Florida." *Southern Historian* 10 (summer 1989): 26–42.

———. "Blacks and the Seminole Removal Debate, 1821–1835." In *The African American Heritage of Florida,* edited by David R. Colburn and Jane L. Landers. Gainesville: University Press of Florida, 1995.

Knight, Franklin. *Slave Society in Cuba during the Nineteenth Century.* Madison: University of Wisconsin Press, 1970.

Kobben, A. J. F. "Unity and Disunity: Cottica Djuka Society as a Kinship System." In *Maroon Societies: Rebel Slave Communites in the Americas,* edited by Richard Price. Baltimore: Johns Hopkins University Press, 1983.

Kolchin, Peter. *American Slavery: 1619–1877.* New York: Whill and Wang, 1993.

———. "Reevaluating the Antebellum Slave Community: A Comparative Perspective." *Journal of American History* 70 (December 1983): 579–601.

Kuethe, Allan, J. "The Status of the Free Pardo in the Disciplined Militia of New Grenada." *Journal of Negro History* 56 (April 1971): 105–17.

Kulikoff, Allan. *Tobacco and Slaves: The Development of Southern Cultures in the Chesapeake, 1680–1800.* Chapel Hill: University of North Carolina Press, 1986.

Landers, Jane L. "Acquisition and Loss on a Spanish Frontier: The Free Black Homesteaders of Florida, 1784–1821." *Slavery and Abolition* 17 (April 1996): 85–101.

———. "African Presence in Early Spanish Colonization of the Caribbean and the Southeastern Borderlands." In *Archaeological and Historical Perspectives on the Spanish Borderlands East.* Vol. 2 of *Columbian Consequences,* edited by David Hurst Thomas. Washington, D.C.: Smithsonian Institution Press, 1990.

———. "Africans in the Land of Ayllon: The Exploration and Settlement of the Southeast." In *Columbus and the Land of Ayllon,* edited by Jeannine Cook. Darien, Ga.: Lower Altamaha Historical Society, 1992.

———. *Black Society in Spanish Florida.* Urbana: University of Illinois Press, 1999.

———. "Black Society in Spanish St. Augustine, 1784–1821." Ph.D. diss., University of Florida, 1988.

———. "Free and Slave." In *The New History of Florida,* edited by Michael Gannon. Gainesville: University Press of Florida, 1996.

———. "Gracia Real de Santa Teresa de Mose: A Free Black Town in Spanish Colonial Florida." *American Historical Review* 95 (February 1990): 9–30.

———. "Slave Resistance on the Southeastern Frontier: Fugitives, Maroons, and Banditti in the Age of Revolutions." *El Escribano* 32 (1995): 12–24.

———. "Spanish Sanctuary: Fugitives in Florida, 1687–1790." *Florida Historical Quarterly* 62 (January 1984): 296–313.

———. "Traditions of African American Freedom and Community in Spanish

Colonial Florida." In *The African American Heritage of Florida*, edited by David R. Colburn and Jane L. Landers. Gainesville: University Press of Florida, 1995.

Landers, Roger Rice. *"The Last Wildcat": The Short Record of T. B. Ellis, Sr.* Brooksville: Genealogical Society of Hernando County, 1998.

———. "Freedmen's Bureau Becomes a Force in Hernando." *Brooksville Hernando Today*, August 4, 1999.

Lane, Ann J., ed. *The Debate over Slavery: Stanley Elkins and His Critics*. Urbana: University of Illinois Press, 1971.

Lantz, Herman R. "Family and Kin as Revealed in the Narratives of Ex-Slaves." *Social Science Quarterly* 60 (March 1980): 667–75.

Laumer, Frank, ed. *Amidst a Storm of Bullets: The Diary of Lt. Henry Prince in Florida, 1836–1842*. Tampa: University of Tampa Press, 1998.

———. *Dade's Last Command*. Gainesville: University Press of Florida, 1995.

Leckie, William H. *The Buffalo Soldiers: A Narrative of the Negro Cavalry in the West*. Norman: University of Oklahoma Press, 1967.

Lerner, Gerda. *Black Women in White America: A Documentary History*. New York: Vintage, 1972.

"Letters from Confederate Soldiers, 1861–1865." Typescript. Atlanta: Georgia Department of Archives and History, n.d.

Levine, Lawrence W. *Black Culture and Black Consciousness: Afro-American Thought from Slavery to Freedom*. New York: Oxford University Press, 1977.

Lewis, Clifton. "Bartow, West Bartow, and the Andy Moore Family: The Joy and Importance of Discovering African-American History." *Sunland Tribune* 24 (1998): 49–59.

Linsin, Christopher E. "Skilled Slave Labor in Florida: 1850–1860." *Florida Historical Quarterly* 75 (fall 1996): 183–96.

Lisenby, Julie Ann. "The Free Negro in Antebellum Florida." Master's thesis, Florida State University, 1967.

Littlefield, Daniel C. *Rice and Slaves: Ethnicity and the Slave Trade in Colonial South Carolina*. Baton Rouge: Louisiana State University Press, 1981.

Littlefield, Daniel F. *Africans and Seminoles: From Removal to Emancipation*. Westport, Conn.: Greenwood Press, 1977.

Livingston, Richard M. "Dempsey Dubois Crews—1806–1892." *South Florida Pioneers* 12 (April 1977): 8–11.

Lofton, John. *Denmark Vesey's Revolt: The Slave Plot That Lit a Fuse to Fort Sumter*. Kent, Ohio: Kent State University Press, 1983.

Lomax, Ruby Terrill. "Negro Baptizings." In *How Sweet the Sound: The Spirit of African American History*, edited by Nancy-Elizabeth Fitch. New York: Harcourt Brace and Company, 2000.

Long, Charles S. *History of the A.M.E. Church in Florida*. Philadelphia: A.M.E. Book Concern, 1937.

Long, Ellen Call. *Florida Breezes; or, Florida, New and Old*. Jacksonville: Ashmead Bros., 1882. Repr., with introduction and index by Margaret Louise Chapman, Gainesville: University Press of Florida, 1962.

Lonn, Ella. *Salt as a Factor in the Confederacy*. New York: Walter Neale, 1933.

Lucas, Marion B. "The Civil War Career of Colonel George Washington Scott." *Florida Historical Quarterly* 58 (October 1979): 129–49.

Lykes, Genevieve Parkhill. *Gift of Heritage*. Tampa: priv. pub., 1969.

Lyon, Eugene. *The Enterprise of Florida: Pedro Menéndez de Avilés and the Spanish Conquest of 1565–1568*. Gainesville: University Press of Florida, 1974.

Mahon, John K. *History of the Second Seminole War, 1835–1842*. Gainesville: University Press of Florida, 1967.

Mahon, John K., and Brent R. Weisman. "Florida's Seminole and Miccosukee Peoples." In *The New History of Florida*, edited by Michael Gannon. Gainesville: University Press of Florida, 1996.

Malone, Ann Patton. *Sweet Chariot: Slave Family and Household Structure in Nineteenth-Century Louisiana*. Chapel Hill: University of North Carolina Press, 1992.

Maloney, Walter C. *A Sketch of the History of Key West, Florida*. Newark, N.J.: Advertiser Printing House, 1876. Repr., Gainesville: University Press of Florida, 1968.

Mandle, Jay R. "The Plantation Economy: An Essay in Definitions." In *The Slave Economies*, edited by Eugene D. Genovese. 2 vols. New York: Wiley Press, 1973.

Manfra, Jo Ann, and Robert R. Dykstra. "Serial Marriage and the Origins of the Black Step-Family: The Rowanty Evidence." *Journal of American History* 72 (June 1985): 18–44.

Manley, Walter W., II, and Canter Brown Jr., eds. *The Supreme Court of Florida and Its Predecessor Courts, 1821–1917*. Gainesville: University Press of Florida, 1997.

Mann, Susan A. "Slavery, Sharecropping, and Sexual Inequality." In *"We Specialize in the Wholly Impossible": A Reader in Black Women's History*, edited by Darlene Clark Hine, Wilma King, and Linda Reed. Brooklyn: Carlson Publishing, 1995.

Manucy, Albert. "The Gibraltar of the Gulf of Mexico." *Florida Historical Quarterly* 21 (April 1943): 303–31.

Marion County History. Ocala: Star-Banner, 1997.

Martin, Richard A. "The *New York Times* Views Civil War Jacksonville." *Florida Historical Quarterly* 53 (April 1975): 409–27.

Martin, Richard A., and Daniel L. Schafer. *Jacksonville's Ordeal by Fire: A Civil War History*. Jacksonville: Florida Publishing Company, 1984.

Martin, Sidney Walker. *Florida during the Territorial Days.* Athens: University of Georgia Press, 1944.

Mathews, Donald G. *Religion in the Old South.* Chicago: University of Chicago Press, 1977.

May, Philip S. "Zephaniah Kingsley: Non-Conformist, 1765–1843." *Florida Historical Quarterly* 23 (January 1945): 145–59.

McAlister, Lyle N. *The "Fuero Militar" in New Spain, 1764–1800.* Gainesville: University Press of Florida, 1957.

McCall, George A. *Letters from the Frontiers.* Philadelphia: J. B. Lippincott, 1868.

McCord, Jean P. "History of the First Hundred Years of the First Presbyterian Church in Tallahassee, Florida." Typescript in collection of Guyte P. McCord, Tallahassee, n.d.

McDonogh, Gary W., ed. *The Florida Negro: A Federal Writers' Project Legacy.* Jackson: University Press of Mississippi, 1993.

McDuffee, Lillie B. *The Lures of Manatee: A True Story of South Florida's Glamorous Past.* Nashville: Marshall and Bruce, 1933.

McGaughy, Felix P., Jr. "The Squaw Kissing War: Bartholomew M. Lynch's Journal of the Second Seminole War, 1826–1839." Master's thesis, Florida State University, 1965.

McIlwain, William E. *The Early Planting of Presbyterianism in West Florida.* Pensacola: Mayes Printing, 1926.

McKee, Larry. "Plantation Food Supply in Nineteenth-Century Tidewater Virginia." Ph.D. diss., University of California at Berkeley, 1988.

McKinney, George Patterson, Sr., and Richard J. McKinney. *History of the Black Baptists of Florida, 1850–1985.* Miami: Florida Memorial College Press, 1987.

McNally, Michael J. *Catholic Parish Life on Florida's West Coast, 1860–1968.* N.p.: Catholic Media Ministries, 1996.

McPherson, James M. *Ordeal by Fire: The Civil War and Reconstruction.* New York: Alfred A. Knopf, 1982.

McReynolds, Edwin C. *The Seminoles.* Norman: University of Oklahoma Press, 1957.

McRory, Mary Oakley, and Edith Clarke Barrows. *History of Jefferson County, Florida.* Monticello: Kiwanis Club, 1935.

Menard, John Willis. *Lays in Summer Lands.* Washington, D.C.: Enterprise Publishing, 1879.

Michaels, Brian E. *The River Flows North: A History of Putnam County, Florida.* Palatka: Putnam County Archives and History Commission, 1986.

Miller, Janice Borton. "The Rebellion in East Florida in 1795." *Florida Historical Quarterly* 57 (October 1978): 173–86.

Miller, Randall M., ed. *"Dear Master": Letters of a Slave Family.* Ithaca, N.Y.: Cornell University Press, 1978. Repr., Athens: University of Georgia Press, 1990.

Milligan, John D. "Slave Rebelliousness and the Florida Maroon." *Prologue* 6 (spring 1974): 5–18.

Mitchell, Carolyn. "Health and the Medical Profession in the South." *Journal of Southern History* 10 (February–November 1944), 424–46.

Mohammad, Laura. "A Slave's Life in Marion." In *Marion County History.* Ocala: Star-Banner, 1997.

Mohlman, Geoffrey. "Bibliography of Resources Concerning the African American Presence in Tampa, 1513–1995." Master's thesis, University of South Florida, 1995.

Mohr, Clarence L. *On the Threshold of Freedom: Masters and Slaves in Civil War Georgia.* Athens: University of Georgia Press, 1986.

Montgomery, William E. *Under Their Own Vine and Fig Tree: The African-American Church in the South, 1865–1900.* Baton Rouge: Louisiana State University Press, 1993.

Mooney, Chase C. *Slavery in Tennessee.* Bloomington: Indiana University Press, 1957.

Mooney, James L., ed. *Dictionary of American Naval Fighting Ships.* 8 vols. Washington, D.C.: Naval History Division, 1959–1981.

Moore, Albert B. *Conscription and Conflict in the Confederacy.* New York: MacMillan, 1924. Repr., New York: Hillary House, 1963.

Morgan, Edmund S. *American Slavery, American Freedom: The Ordeal of Colonial Virginia.* New York: Norton, 1975.

Morgan, Philip D. "The Ownership of Property by Slaves in Mid-Nineteenth Century Low Country." *Journal of Southern History* 49 (August 1983): 399–420.

———. *Slave Counterpoint: Black Culture in the Eighteenth-Century Chesapeake and Lowcountry.* Chapel Hill: University of North Carolina Press, 1998.

———. "Task and Gang Systems: The Organization of Labor on New World Plantations." In *Work and Labor in Early America,* edited by Stephen Innes. Chapel Hill: University of North Carolina Press, 1998.

———. "Work and Culture: The Task System and the World of Lowcountry Blacks, 1700–1800." *William and Mary Quarterly* 39 (October 1982): 563–99.

Morgan, Philip D., and George D. Terry. "Slavery in Microcosm: A Conspiracy Scare in Colonial South Carolina." *Southern Studies* 21 (summer 1982): 121–46.

Mormino, Gary R., ed. "Florida Slave Narratives." *Florida Historical Quarterly* 66 (April 1988): 399–419.

Morse, Jedidiah. *Report to the Secretary of War of the United States on Indian Affairs.* New Haven, Conn.: S. Converse, 1822.

Morton, Henry. "Recollections of the Morton Family." In *Recollections, Volume II.* Milton: Santa Rosa Democratic Executive Committee, 1980.

Mulira, Jessie Gaston. "The Case of Voodoo in New Orleans." In *Africanism in American Culture,* edited by Joseph E. Holloway. Bloomington: Indiana University Press, 1990.

Mullin, Michael. *Africa in America: Slave Acculturation and Resistance in the American South and the British Caribbean, 1736–1831.* Urbana: University of Illinois Press, 1992.

Mulroy, Kevin. *Freedom on the Border: The Seminole Maroons in Florida, the Indian Territory, Coahuila, and Texas.* Lubbock: Texas Tech University Press, 1993.

Murat, Achille. *America and the Americans.* Translated by Henry J. Bradfield. Buffalo, N.Y.: G. H. Derby, 1851.

———. *A Moral and Political Sketch of the United States of North America.* London: Effingham Wilson, 1833.

———. *The United States of North America: With a Note on Negro Slavery.* London: Effingham Wilson, 1833.

Murdoch, Richard K. *The Georgia-Florida Frontier, 1793–1796: Spanish Reaction to French Intrigue and American Designs.* Berkeley: University of California Press, 1951.

Muse, Violet. "Negro History, Tampa, Florida." In *Negro History in Florida.* Jacksonville: Federal Writers' Project of the Work Projects Administration, 1936.

The Negro in Florida's Cities. Jacksonville: Federal Writers' Project of the Work Projects Administration, 1936.

Nelson, Bernard H. "Confederate Slave Impressment Legislation, 1861–1865." *Journal of Negro History* 31 (October 1946): 392–410.

Nichols, James M. *Perry's Saints, or the Fighting Parson's Regime in the War of Rebellion.* Boston: D. Lothrop Press, 1886.

Nigh, Robin Franklin. "Under Grave Conditions: African American Signs of Life and Death in North Florida." *Markers* 14 (1997): 159–89.

Nix, John C. "John Hunt: Antebellum Brickmaker, Lumberman, and Entrepreneur—One of West Florida's Forgotten Economic Giants." Typescript. Pensacola, 1975 (available at Pensacola Historical Museum).

Nulty, William H. *Confederate Florida: The Road to Olustee.* Tuscaloosa: University of Alabama Press, 1990.

Oakes, James. *The Ruling Race: A History of American Slaveholders.* New York: Alfred A. Knopf, 1982.

Oates, Stephen B. *The Fires of Jubilee: Nat Turner's Fierce Rebellion.* New York: Harper and Row, 1975.

130th Anniversary: Pastors and Peoples, 1838–1968. Jacksonville: Pictorial Church Directories of America, 1968.

Ott, Eloise Robinson, and Louis Hickman Chazal. Ocali Country, Kingdom of the Sun: A History of Marion County, Florida. Ocala: Marion Publishers, 1966.

Otto, John Solomon. "Florida's Cattle-Ranching Frontier: Hillsborough County (1860)." Florida Historical Quarterly 63 (July 1984): 71–83.

———. "Florida's Cattle-Ranching Frontier: Manatee and Brevard Counties (1860)." Florida Historical Quarterly 64 (July 1985): 48–61.

———. "Hillsborough County (1850): A Community in the South Florida Flatwoods." Florida Historical Quarterly 62 (October 1983), 180–93.

———. "A New Look at Slave Life." Natural History (January 1979): 8–30.

Overman, C. H. "After 111 Years, Bagdad Reaches the End." Southern Lumber Journal (March 1939): 16, 71; (April 1939): 44–45.

Owen, Harry P. "Apalachicola: The Beginning." Florida Historical Quarterly 48 (July 1969): 1–25.

Owens, Leslie Howard. This Species of Property: Slave Life and Culture in the Old South. New York: Oxford University Press, 1976.

Paisley, Clifton. From Cotton to Quail: An Agricultural Chronicle of Leon County. Gainesville: University Press of Florida, 1967.

———. The Red Hills of Florida, 1528–1865. Tuscaloosa: University of Alabama Press, 1989.

———, ed. "How to Escape the Yankees: Major Scott's Letter to His Wife at Tallahassee, March, 1864." Florida Historical Quarterly 50 (July 1971): 53–61.

Palmer, Henry Edward. "Physicians of Early Tallahassee and Vicinity." Apalachee (1944): 29–46.

Parish, Peter J. Slavery: History and Historians. New York: Harper and Row, 1989.

Parker, Rosalind. "The Proctors—Antonio, George, and John." Apalachee (1946): 19–29.

Parker, Susan. "Men without God or King: Rural Settlers of East Florida, 1784–1790." Florida Historical Quarterly 69 (October 1990): 135–55.

Parks, Joseph Howard. General Edmund Kirby Smith, C.S.A. Baton Rouge: Louisiana State University Press, 1954.

Patrick, Rembert W. Aristocrat in Uniform: General Duncan L. Clinch. Gainesville: University Press of Florida, 1963.

———. Florida Fiasco: Rampant Rebels on the Georgia-Florida Frontier, 1810–1815. Athens: University of Georgia Press, 1954.

Pennington, Edgar Lagare. "The Episcopal Church in Florida, 1763–1892." Historical Magazine of the Protestant Episcopal Church 7 (March 1938): 3–17.

Peters, Virginia B. *The Florida Wars.* Hamden: Archon Books, 1979.

Phelts, Marsha Dean. *An American Beach for African Americans.* Gainesville: University Press of Florida, 1997.

Phillips, John E. "The African Heritage of White America." In *Africanism in American Culture,* edited by Joseph E. Holloway. Bloomington: Indiana University Press, 1990.

Phillips, Ulrich B. *American Negro Slavery: A Survey of the Supply, Employment, and Control of Negro Labor as Determined by the Plantation Regime.* New York: D. Appleton, 1918.

Phillips, Ulrich B., and James A. Glunt, eds. *Florida Plantation Records from the Papers of George Noble Jones.* St. Louis: Missouri Historical Society, 1927.

Polk, James K. "Pensacola Commerce and Industry, 1821–1860." Master's thesis, University of West Florida, 1971.

Porter, Kenneth Wiggins. *The Black Seminoles: History of a Freedom-Seeking People.* Revised and edited by Alcione M. Amos and Thomas P. Senter. Gainesville: University Press of Florida, 1996.

———. "The Early Life of Luis Pacheco Nee Fatio." *Negro History Bulletin* 7 (December 1943): 52, 54, 62, 64.

———. "Farewell to John Horse: An Episode of Seminole Negro Folk History." *Phylon* 8 (1947): 265–73.

———. "Florida Slaves and Free Negroes in the Seminole War, 1835–1842." *Journal of Negro History* 28 (April 1943): 390–421.

———. "John Caesar, Seminole Negro Partisan." *Journal of Negro History* 31 (April 1946): 362–84.

———. "Louis Pachecho: The Man and the Myth. *Journal of Negro History* 28 (January 1943): 65–72.

———. "The Negro Abraham." *Florida Historical Quarterly* 25 (July 1946): 1–43.

———. "Negro Guides and Interpreters in the Early Stages of the Seminole War, Dec. 28, 1835–Mar. 6, 1837." *Journal of Negro History* 35 (April 1950): 174–82.

———. *The Negro on the American Frontier.* New York: Arno Press, 1971.

———. "Negroes and the Seminole War, 1835–1842." *Journal of Southern History* 30 (November 1964): 427–50.

———. "Notes on the Seminole Negroes in the Bahamas." *Florida Historical Quarterly* 24 (July 1945): 56–60.

———. "Relations between Negroes and Indians within the Present Limits of the United States." *Journal of Negro History* 27 (January 1932), 287–367.

———. "Seminole Flight from Fort Marion." *Florida Historical Quarterly* 22 (January 1944): 113–33.

————. "Thlonoto-sassa: A Note on an Obscure Seminole Village of the Early 1820s." *Florida Anthropologist* 13 (December 1960): 115–20.

Potter, Woodburne. *The War in Florida*. Baltimore: Lewis and Coleman, 1836.

Price, Richard, ed. *Maroon Societies: Rebel Slave Communities in the Americas*. Baltimore: Johns Hopkins University Press, 1979.

Prouty, Ronald N., ed. "War Comes to Tampa Bay: The Civil War Diary of Robert Watson." *Tampa Bay History* 10 (fall/winter 1988): 38–65.

Provence, S. N. "Historical Sketches of the Churches of the Florida Baptist Association." In *Minutes of the 54th Annual Session, 1896*. Perry: Florida Baptist Association, 1896.

Quarles, Benjamin. *Black Abolitionists*. New York: Oxford University Press, 1969.

————, ed. *Narrative of the Life of Frederick Douglass*. Cambridge: Belknap/Harvard University Press, 1960.

————. *The Negro in the Civil War*. Boston: Little and Brown, 1953.

Raboteau, Albert J. *Slave Religion: The "Invisible Institution" in the Antebellum South*. New York: Oxford University Press, 1978.

Rawick, George P. *The American Slave: A Composite Autobiography*. 41 vols. Westport, Conn.: Greenwood Press, 1972–79.

————. *From Sundown to Sunup: The Making of the Black Community*. Westport, Conn.: Greenwood Press, 1972.

————. "Some Notes on a Social Analysis of Slavery: A Critique and Assessment of the Slave Community." In *Revisiting Blassingame's "The Slave Community": The Scholars Respond*, edited by Al-Tony Gilmore. Westport, Conn.: Greenwood Press, 1978.

Reddick, L. D. "The Negro Policy of the United States Army, 1775–1945." *Journal of Negro History* 34 (January 1949): 9–29.

Reed, A. M. "Diary of A. M. Reed, 1848–99." Jacksonville: WPA Historical Records Survey, n.d.

Reiger, John Franklin. "Florida after Secession: Abandonment by the Confederacy and Its Consequences." *Florida Historical Quarterly* 50 (October 1971): 128–42.

Reitz, Elizabeth, Tyson Gibbs, and Ted. A. Rathbun. "Archaeological Subsistence on Coastal Plantations." In *The Archaeology of Slavery and Plantation Life*, edited by Theresa A. Singleton. Orlando: Academic Press, 1985.

Revels, Tracy J. "Grander in Her Daughters: Florida's Women during the Civil War." *Florida Historical Quarterly* 77 (winter 1999): 261–82.

Rhodes, Barbara. *At First: The Presbyterian Church in Tallahassee, Florida, 1828–1938*. Tallahassee: First Presbyterian Church, 1994.

Rice, Lawrence D. *The Negro in Texas, 1874–1900*. Baton Rouge: Louisiana State University Press, 1971.

Rice, Wilson W. "Negro Religion, Bethel Baptist Institutional Church." Typescript. Jacksonville: Federal Writers' Project of the Work Projects Administration, 1936.

Richardson, Barbara Ann. "A History of Blacks in Jacksonville, Florida, 1860–1896: A Socio-Economic and Political Study." D.A. diss., Carnegie-Mellon University, 1975.

Richardson, Martin. "Pensacola, Florida." In *Negro History in Florida*, edited by the Federal Writers' Project. Jacksonville: Work Projects Administration, 1936.

Ripley, C. Peter. *Slaves and Freedmen in Civil War Louisiana*. Baton Rouge: Louisiana State University Press, 1976.

Rivers, Larry E. "Baptist Minister James Page: Alternatives for African American Leadership in Post–Civil War Florida." In *Florida's Heritage of Diversity: Essays in Honor of Samuel Proctor*, edited by Mark I. Greenberg, William Warren Rogers, and Canter Brown Jr. Tallahassee: Sentry Press, 1997.

———. "Dignity and Importance: Slavery in Jefferson County, Florida—1827 to 1860." *Florida Historical Quarterly* 61 (April 1983): 404–30.

———. "Madison County, Florida—1830 to 1860: A Case Study in Land, Labor, and Prosperity." *Journal of Negro History* 78 (fall 1993): 233–44.

———. "Slavery and the Political Economy of Gadsden County, Florida: 1823–1861." *Florida Historical Quarterly* 70 (July 1991): 1–19.

———. "Slavery in Microcosm: Leon County, Florida, 1824 to 1860." *Journal of Negro History* 66 (fall 1981): 235–45.

———. "A Troublesome Property: Master-Slave Relations in Florida, 1821–1865." In *The African American Heritage of Florida*, edited by David R. Colburn and Jane L. Landers. Gainesville: University Press of Florida, 1995.

Rivers, Larry E., and Canter Brown Jr. "African Americans in South Florida: A Home and a Haven for Reconstruction-Era Leaders." *Tequesta* 56 (1996): 5–23.

———. "The Indispensable Man": John Horse and Florida's Second Seminole War. *Journal of the Georgia Association of Historians* 18 (1997): 1–23.

Roark, James, and Michael Johnson. "Strategies of Survival: Free Negro Families and the Problem of Slavery." In *In Joy and in Sorrow*, edited by Carol Bleser. New York: Oxford University Press, 1991.

Rogers, Seth. *Letters of Seth Rogers, 1862–1863*. Boston: J. Wilson and Son, 1910.

Rogers, William W. *Ante-Bellum Thomas County, 1825–1861*. Tallahassee: Florida State University Studies, 1963.

———. *Outposts on the Gulf: Saint George Island and Apalachicola from Early Exploration to World War II*. Pensacola: University of West Florida Press, 1986.

Rogers, William W., and Erica R. Clark. *The Croom Family and Goodwood*

Plantation: Land, Litigation, and Southern Lives. Athens: University of Georgia Press, 1999.

Ros, Martin. *Night of Fire: The Black Napoleon and the Battle for Haiti.* New York: Sarpedon, 1991.

Rosser, John Leonidas. *A History of Florida Baptists.* Nashville: Broadman Press, 1949.

Rucker, Brian R. "Arcadia and Bagdad: Industrial Parks of Antebellum Florida." *Florida Historical Quarterly* 67 (October 1998), 147–65.

————. "Blackwater and Yellow Pine: The Development of Santa Rosa County, 1821–1865." 2 vols. Ph.D. diss., Florida State University, 1990.

Rutherford, Robert E. "Settlers from Connecticut in Spanish Florida: Letters of Ambrose Hull and Stella Hull, 1808–1816. *Florida Historical Quarterly* 30 (April 1952): 324–40.

Savitt, Todd L. *Medicine and Slavery: The Diseases and Health Care of Blacks in Antebellum Virginia.* Urbana: University of Illinois Press, 1978.

Scarborough, William K. *The Overseer: Plantation Management in the Old South.* Baton Rouge: Louisiana State University Press, 1966.

Schafer, Daniel L. *Anna Kingsley.* St. Augustine: St. Augustine Historical Society, 1994.

————. "A Class of People Neither Freemen nor Slaves: From Spanish to American Race Relations in Florida, 1821 to 1861." *Journal of Social History* 26 (spring 1993): 587–610.

————. "Freedom Was as Close as the River: African Americans and the Civil War in Northeast Florida." In *The African American Heritage of Florida,* edited by David R. Colburn and Jane L. Landers. Gainesville: University Press of Florida, 1995.

————. "Plantation Development in British East Florida: A Case Study of the Earl of Egmont." *Florida Historical Quarterly* 62 (October 1984): 172–83.

————. "U.S. Territory and State." In *The New History of Florida,* edited by Michael Gannon. Gainesville: University Press of Florida, 1996.

————. "'Yellow Silk Ferret Tied Round Their Wrists': African Americans in British East Florida, 1763–1784." In *The African American Heritage of Florida,* edited by David R. Colburn and Jane L. Landers. Gainesville: University Press of Florida, 1995.

Schaper, William A. *Sectionalism and Representation in South Carolina.* New York: Da Capo Press, 1968.

Schellings, William J., ed. "On Blockade Duty in Florida Waters: Excerpts from a Union Naval Officer's Diary." *Tequesta* 15 (1955): 55–72.

Schene, Michael G. "Robert and John Grattan Gamble: Middle Florida Entrepreneurs." *Florida Historical Quarterly* 54 (July 1975): 61–73.

Schmidt, Lewis G. *The Civil War in Florida: A Military History.* 4 vols. Allentown, Penn.: priv. pub., 1989–1992.

Schwartz, Gerald, ed. *A Woman Doctor's Civil War: Esther Hill Hawk's Diary.* Columbia: University of South Carolina Press, 1984.

Scott, Rebecca, J. *Slave Emancipation in Cuba: The Transition to Free Labor,* 1860–1890. Princeton, N.J.: Princeton University Press, 1985.

Sellers, James Benson. *Slavery in Alabama.* Tuscaloosa: University of Alabama Press, 1950.

Sernett, Milton C. *Black Religion and American Evangelicalism: White Protestants, Plantation Missions, and the Flowering of Negro Christianity,* 1787–1865. Metuchen, N.J.: Scarecrow and American Theological Library Association, 1975.

Shannon, Fred A. "The Federal Government and the Negro Soldier, 1861–1865." *Journal of Negro History* 11 (October 1926): 563–83.

Shippee, Lester B., ed. *Bishop Whipple's Southern Diary,* 1843–1844. Minneapolis: University of Minnesota Press, 1937. Repr., New York: Da Capo Press, 1968.

Shofner, Jerrell H. *Jackson County, Florida: A History.* Marianna: Jackson County Heritage Association, 1985.

———. *History of Jefferson County.* Tallahassee: Sentry Press, 1976.

Shofner, Jerrell H., and William Warren Rogers. "Confederate Railroad Construction: The Live Oak to Lawton Connector." *Florida Historical Quarterly* 43 (January 1965): 217–28.

———. "Sea Island Cotton in Ante-Bellum Florida." *Florida Historical Quarterly* 40 (April 1962): 373–80.

Siebert, Wilbur H. "The Departure of the Spaniards and Other Groups from East Florida, 1763–1764." *Florida Historical Quarterly* 19 (October 1940): 145–54.

Silverstone, Paul. *Warships of the Civil War Navies.* Annapolis, Md.: Naval Institute Press, 1989.

Simmons, William H. *Notices of East Florida, with an Account of the Seminole Nation of Indians.* Charleston, S.C.: A. E. Miller, 1822. Repr., Gainesville: University Press of Florida, 1973.

Singleton, Theresa A. "The Archaeology of Slave Life." In *Before Freedom Came,* edited by Edward D. C. Campbell Jr. and Kym S. Rice. Charlottesville: University Press of Virginia, 1991.

Smart, Charles. *The Medical and Surgical History of the War of the Rebellion.* Washington, D.C.: Government Printing Office, 1888.

Smith, D. D. *History of John (Virginia) Smith and His Descendants in Connection with the Tobacco Industry in Gadsden County, Florida and Decatur County, Georgia.* Quincy, Fla.: n.p., n.d.

Smith, George W. "Carpetbag Imperialism in Florida, 1862–68." *Florida Historical Quarterly* 27 (October 1948): 263–67.

Smith, John David. *Black Voices from Reconstruction: 1865–1877*. Gainesville: University Press of Florida, 1997.

Smith, Julia Floyd. "Cotton and the Factorage System in Ante-Bellum Florida." *Florida Historical Quarterly* 49 (July 1970): 36–48.

———. "The Plantation Belt in Middle Florida, 1850–1860." Ph.D. diss., Florida State University, 1964.

———. *Slavery and Plantation Growth in Antebellum Florida, 1821–1860*. Gainesville: University Press of Florida, 1973.

Smith, Raymond T. "The Nuclear Family in Afro-American Kinship." *Journal of Comparative Family Studies* 1 (autumn 1970): 57–70.

Smith, W. W. *Sketch of the Seminole War and Sketches during a Campaign*. Charleston, S.C.: Dan J. Dowling, 1836.

Solomon, Irvin D. "Southern Extremities: The Significance of Fort Myers in the Civil War." *Florida Historical Quarterly* 72 (October 1993): 129–52.

Solomon, Irvin D., and Grace Erhart. "Race and Civil War in South Florida." *Florida Historical Quarterly* 77 (winter 1999): 320–41.

Southall, E. P. "Negroes in Florida Prior to the Civil War." *Journal of Negro History* 19 (January 1934): 77–86.

Sprague, John T. *Origin, Progress, and Conclusion of the Florida War*. New York: Appleton, 1848.

Stampp, Kenneth M. *The Peculiar Institution: Slavery in the Ante-Bellum South*. New York: Alfred A. Knopf, 1956. Repr., New York: Vintage Books, 1964.

———. "Rebels and Sambos: The Search for the Negro Personality in Slavery." *Journal of Southern History* 37 (August 1971): 367–92.

Stanaback, Richard J. *A History of Hernando County, 1840–1976*. Brooksville, Fla.: Action '76 Steering Committee, 1976.

Stanley, Amy Dru. *From Bondage to Contract: Wage Labor, Marriage, and the Market in the Age of Slave Emancipation*. Cambridge, U.K.: Cambridge University Press, 1998.

Stanley, J. Randall. *History of Gadsden County*. Quincy: Gadsden County Historical Commission, 1948. Repr., Tallahassee: L'Avant Studios, 1985.

———. *History of Jackson County*. Marianna: Jackson County Historical Society, 1950.

Starobin, Robert S. *Industrial Slavery in the Old South*. New York: Oxford University Press, 1970.

Staudenraus, P., Jr., ed. "A War Correspondent's View of St. Augustine and Fernandina, 1863." *Florida Historical Quarterly* 41 (July 1962): 60–65.

Steckel, Richard H. "Slave Marriage and the Family." *Journal of Family History* 5 (winter 1980): 406–21.

———. "Slave Mortality: An Analysis of Evidence from Plantation Records." *Social Science History* 3 (October 1979): 86–114.

Stephens, Jean B. "Zephaniah Kingsley and the Recaptured Africans." *El Escribano* 15 (1978): 71–76.

Sterling, Dorothy, ed. *We Are Your Sisters: Black Women in the Nineteenth Century.* New York: Norton, 1984.

Stevenson, Brenda E. "Distress and Discord in Virginia Slave Families, 1830–1860." In *In Joy and in Sorrow*, edited by Carol Bleser. New York: Oxford University Press, 1991.

———. *Life in Black and White: Family and Community in the Slave South.* New York: Oxford University Press, 1996.

Steward, Austin. *Twenty-Two Years a Slave, and Forty Years a Freeman.* Rochester, N.Y.: W. Alling, 1857.

Stone, Spessard. *John and William, Sons of Robert Hendry.* Bradenton, Fla.: Genie Press, 1989.

———. "Profile of Lloyd Davis." *Sunland Tribune* 17 (November 1991): 25–26.

Stowell, Daniel W. ed. *Balancing Evils Judiciously: The Proslavery Writings of Zephaniah Kingsley.* Gainesville: University Press of Florida, 2000.

Sydnor, Charles Sackett. *Slavery in Mississippi.* New York: D. Appleton Century Company, 1933. Repr., Gloucester: Peter Smith, 1965.

Tannenbaum, Frank. *Slave and Citizen.* New York: Alfred A. Knopf, 1946. Repr., New York: Beacon Press, 1992.

Taylor, Joe Gray. *Negro Slavery in Louisiana.* Baton Rouge: Louisiana Historical Association, 1963.

Taylor, Orville W. *Negro Slavery in Arkansas.* Durham, N.C.: Duke University Press, 1958.

Taylor, Robert A. "Cow Cavalry: Munnerlyn's Battalion in Florida, 1864–1865." *Florida Historical Quarterly* 65 (October 1986): 196–214.

———. "Rebel Beef: Florida Cattle and the Confederate Army, 1862–1864." *Florida Historical Quarterly* 67 (July 1988): 15–31.

———. *Rebel Storehouse: Florida in the Confederate Economy.* Tuscaloosa: University of Alabama Press, 1995.

Taylor, Rosser Howard. *Slaveholding in North Carolina: An Economic View.* Chapel Hill: University of North Carolina Press, 1926.

TePaske, John J. "The Fugitive Slave: Intercolonial Rivalry and Spanish Slavery Policy, 1687–1764." In *Eighteenth-Century Florida and Its Borderland*, edited by Samuel Proctor. Gainesville: University Press of Florida, 1975.

———. *The Governorship of Spanish Florida, 1760–1763.* Durham, N.C.: Duke University Press, 1964.

Thomas, David Hurst, ed. *Columbian Consequences.* 3 vols. Washington, D.C.: Smithsonian Institution Press, 1989–1991.

Thomas, David Y. "The Free Negro in Florida before 1865." *South Atlantic Quarterly* 10 (October 1911): 335–345.

Thompson, Arthur W., ed. "A Massachusetts Traveler on the Florida Frontier." *Florida Historical Quarterly* 38 (October 1959): 129–41.

Thompson, Robert Farris. "An Aesthetic of the Cool: West African Dance." In *How Sweet the Sound: The Spirit of African American History,* edited by Nancy-Elizabeth Fitch. New York: Harcourt Brace and Company, 2000.

Thrift, Charles T., Jr. *The Trail of the Florida Circuit Rider.* Lakeland: Florida Southern College Press, 1944.

Tillis, James Dallas. "An Indian Attack of 1856 on the Home of Willoughby Tillis." *Florida Historical Quarterly* 8 (April 1930): 179–87.

Trexler, Harrison Anthony. *Slavery in Missouri, 1804–1865.* Baltimore: Johns Hopkins University Press, 1914.

Turner, Maxine. *Navy Gray: A Story of the Confederate Navy on the Chattahoochee and Apalachicola Rivers.* Tuscaloosa: University of Alabama Press, 1988.

Van Deburg, William L. *The Slave Drivers: Black Agricultural Labor Supervisors in the Antebellum South.* Westport, Conn.: Greenwood Press, 1979.

Van Doren, Mark, ed. *The Travels of William Bartram.* New York: Dover, 1928.

VanLandingham, Kyle S. *Florida Cousins: The Descendants of William H. Willingham.* Okeechobee, Fla.: priv. pub., 1967.

———, ed. "'My National Troubles': The Civil War Papers of William McCollough." *Sunland Tribune* 20 (November 1994): 59–86.

———. "'To Faithfully Discharge My Duty': The Life and Career of Perry Green Wall." *Sunland Tribune* 23 (November 1997): 3–12.

Vlach, John Michael. "Afro-American Domestic Artifacts in Eighteenth-Century Virginia." *Material Culture* 19 (spring 1987): 3–24.

———. *By the Work of Their Hands: Studies in Afro-American Folklife.* Ann Arbor: University of Michigan Research Press, 1990.

———. "Plantation Landscapes of the Antebellum South." In *Before Freedom Came,* edited by Edward D. C. Campbell Jr. and Kym S. Rice. Charlottesville: University Press of Virginia, 1991.

A Voice from Rebel Prisons: Giving an Account of Some of the Horrors of Stockades at Andersonville, Milan, and Other Prisons, by a Returned Prisoner of War. Boston: G. C. Rand and Avery, 1865.

Wade, Richard C. *Slavery in the Cities: The South, 1820–1860.* New York: Oxford University Press, 1964.

Walker, Jonathan. *Trial and Imprisonment of Jonathan Walker at Pensacola, Florida, for Aiding Slaves to Escape from Bondage.* Boston: Anti-Slavery Office, 1845. Repr., Gainesville: University Press of Florida, 1974.

Walls, William J. *The African Methodist Episcopal Church: Reality of the Black Church.* Charlotte, N.C.: A.M.E. Zion Publishing House, 1974.

Walsh, Lorena S. "Slave Life, Slave Society, and Tobacco Production in the Tidewater Chesapeake, 1620–1820." In *Cultivation and Culture: Labor and the Shaping of Slave Life in the Americas,* edited by Ira Berlin and Philip D. Morgan. Charlottesville: University Press of Virginia, 1993.

Warner, Joe G. *Biscuits and 'Taters: A History of Cattle Ranching in Manatee County.* St. Petersburg, Fla.: Great Outdoors Publishing, 1989.

Warner, Lee H. *Free Men in an Age of Servitude: Three Generations of a Black Family.* Lexington: University Press of Kentucky, 1992.

Webber, Thomas L. *Deep like the Rivers: Education in the Slave Quarter Community, 1831–1865.* New York: Norton, 1978.

Westergard, Virginia W., and Kyle S. Van Landingham. *Parker and Blount in Florida.* Okeechobee, Fla.: priv. pub., 1983.

Wetherington, R. Wade. "The *Florida Peninsular*'s View of Slavery, 1855–1861." *Tampa Bay History* (fall/winter 1990): 46–71.

White, Deborah Gray. *Ar'n't I a Woman? Female Slaves in the Plantation South.* New York: Norton, 1985.

———. "Female Slaves in the Plantation South." In *Before Freedom Came,* edited by Edward D. C. Campbell Jr. and Kym S. Rice. Charlottesville: University Press of Virginia, 1991.

White, Shane, and Graham White. *Stylin: African American Expressive Culture from Its Beginnings to the Zoot Suit.* Ithaca, N.Y.: Cornell University Press, 1998.

Williams, Ames. "Stronghold of the Straits: A Short History of Fort Zachary Taylor." *Tequesta* 14 (1954): 3–25.

Williams, David. *Rich Man's War: Class, Caste, and Confederate Defeat in the Lower Chattahoochee Valley.* Athens: University of Georgia Press, 1998.

———. "'Us Is Gonna Be Free': Civil War Slave Resistance in Southwest Georgia." *Journal of the Georgia Association of Historians* 19 (1998): 1–14.

Williams, Edwin L., Jr. "Negro Slavery in Florida." Pt. 1. *Florida Historical Quarterly* 28 (October 1949): 93–110.

———. "Negro Slavery in Florida." Pt. 2. *Florida Historical Quarterly* 28 (January 1950): 182–204.

Williams, George W. *A History of Negro Troops in the War of the Rebellion, 1861–1865.* New York: Harper and Brothers, 1888.

Williams, John Lee. *The Territory of Florida: or Sketches of the Topography, Civil and Natural History of the Country, the Climate, and the Indian Tribes from the First Discovery to the Present Time.* New York: A. T. Goodrich, 1837. Repr., Gainesville: University Press of Florida, 1962.

Williamson, Joel. *New People: Miscegenation and Mulattoes in the United States.* New York: Free Press, 1980. Repr., New York: New York University Press, 1984.

Willoughby, Lynn. "Apalachicola Aweigh: Shipping and Seamen at Florida's Premier Cotton Port." *Florida Historical Quarterly* 69 (October 1990): 178–94.

————. *Fair to Middlin': The Antebellum Cotton Trade of the Apalachicola/ Chattahoochee River Valley.* Tuscaloosa: University of Alabama Press, 1993.

Wilms, Douglas C. "The Development of Rice Culture in Eighteenth Century Georgia." *Southeastern Geographer* 12 (May 1972): 45–57.

Wilson, Joseph T. *The Black Phalanx: A History of the Negro Soldiers of the United States in the Wars of 1775–1812, 1861–'65* Hartford, Conn.: American Publishing, 1980.

Wilson, Olly W. "The Association of Movement and Music as a Manifestation of a Black Conceptual Approach to Music Making." In *How Sweet the Sound: The Spirit of African American History,* edited by Nancy-Elizabeth Fitch. New York: Harcourt Brace and Company, 2000.

Womack, Miles Kenan, Jr. *Gadsden: A Florida County in Word and Picture.* Quincy: n.p., 1976.

Wood, Betty. *Slavery in Colonial Georgia, 1730–1775.* Athens: University of Georgia Press, 1984.

Wood, David E. *A Guide to Selected Sources for the History of the Seminole Settlements at Red Bays, Andros, 1817–1980.* Nassau: Bahamas Department of Archives, 1980.

Wood, Peter H. *Black Majority: Negroes in Colonial South Carolina from 1670 through the Stono Rebellion.* New York: Alfred A. Knopf, 1974. Repr., New York: Norton, 1975.

————. "The Changing Population of the Eighteenth-Century South: An Overview, by Race and Subregion, from 1565–1790." In *Powhatan's Mantle,* edited by Peter H. Wood, Gregory A. Waselkov, and M. Thomas Hatley. Lincoln: University of Nebraska Press, 1989.

Wood, Peter H., Gregory A. Waselkov, and M. Thomas Hatley, eds. *Powhatan's Mantle: Indians in the Colonial Southeast.* Lincoln: University of Nebraska Press, 1989.

Woodward, C. Vann. "History from Slave Sources." *American Historical Review.* 79 (April 1974): 470–81.

Woolridge, Nancy Bullock. "Slave Preacher—Portrait of a Leader." *Journal of Negro Education* 14 (winter 1945): 28–37.

Wright, I. A. "Dispatches of a Spanish Official Bearing on the Free Settlement of Gracia Real de Santa Teresa de Mose, Florida." *Journal of Negro History* 9 (April 1924): 144–93.

Wright, James Leitch, Jr. "Blacks in British East Florida. *Florida Historical Quarterly* 54 (April 1976): 425–42.

————. *Creeks and Seminoles.* Lincoln: University of Nebraska Press, 1986.

————. *Florida during the American Revolution.* Gainesville: University Press of Florida, 1975.

————. "A Note on the First Seminole War as Seen by the Indians, Negroes, and Their British Advisers." *Journal of Southern History* 34 (November 1968): 565–75.

———. *The Only Land They Knew: The Tragic Story of the American Indians in the Old South.* New York: Macmillan, 1981.

Wright, Richard R. "Negro Companions of the Spanish Explorers." *American Anthropologist* 4 (1902): 217–28.

Wyatt-Brown, Bertram. *Honor and Violence in the Old South.* New York: Oxford University Press, 1986.

———. "The Mask of Obedience: Male Slave Psychology in the Old South." *American Historical Review* 93 (December 1988): 1228–52.

Wynne, Lewis N., and James J. Horgan, eds. *Florida Decades: A Sesquicentennial History: 1845 to 1995.* St. Leo, Fla.: St. Leo College Press, 1995.

Yetman, Norman R. "The Background of the Slave Narrative Collection." *American Quarterly* 19 (fall 1967): 534–53.

Young, Jeffrey Robert. *Domesticating Slavery: The Master Class in Georgia and South Carolina, 1670–1837.* Chapel Hill: University of North Carolina Press, 1999.

Zelnick, Melvin. "Fertility of the American Negro in 1830–1850." *Population Studies* 20 (1966): 77–83.

INDEX

References to illustrations are in boldface.

Larry E. Rivers is professor of history at Florida Agricultural and Mechanical University. He is the author of more than twenty articles in refereed scholarly journals, including the *Florida Historical Quarterly* and the *Journal of Negro History*. Rivers's work has earned the Association for the Study of African American Life and History's Carter G. Woodson Award and the Florida Historical Society's Arthur W. Thompson Prize.